BUILDING COMMUNICATION THEORIES:
A Socio/Cultural Approach

BUILDING
COMMUNICATION
THEORIES:
A Socio/Cultural Approach

Edited by

FRED L. CASMIR
Pepperdine University

LEA LAWRENCE ERLBAUM ASSOCIATES, PUBLISHERS
1994 Hillsdale, New Jersey   Hove, UK

Lawrence Erlbaum Associates, Inc., Publishers
365 Broadway
Hillsdale, New Jersey, 07642

Library of Congress Cataloging-in-Publication Data

Building communication theories : a socio/cultural approach / edited
   by Fred L. Casmir.
       p.   cm.
   Includes bibliographical references and indexes.
   ISBN-0-8058-1516-3
   1. Communication—Philosophy.   2. Communication—Methodology.
I. Casmir, Fred L., 1928–   .
P90.B8174 1994
302.2′01—dc20   94-9129
                                                            CIP

Books published by Lawrence Erlbaum Associates are printed on acid-free
paper, and their bindings are chosen for strength and durability.

Printed in the United States of America
10 9 8 7 6 5 4 3 2 1

*To my wife, Mina, with gratitude
for the opportunity to do the important
things in life "zusammen."*

Contents

Preface

Concern with various matters related to humans as they communicate has led to an increase in both research and theorizing during the second half of the 20th Century. As a matter of fact, so many scholars and so many disciplines have become involved in this process that it is virtually impossible for any one of us to fully know, understand, and appreciate all that has been accomplished so far.

By bringing together a group of men and women who are not only highly recognized for a variety of professional achievements, but who also bring a deep concern for human beings and their struggles to this collection of essays, I feel that my own limitations as an individual scholar have been overcome. At the same time, in spite of the diverse insights of the various authors, this volume has a clear focus and is based on important assumptions.

It is very difficult to avoid confusion and duplication when we try to organize or describe the field of human communication studies. In the pages that follow *no* attempt was made to completely survey extant communication theories or to provide a comprehensive overview. Nor is this volume meant to address in great detail serious scholarly criticisms that have resulted from inadequate research methods or insufficiently developed theoretical foundations. What the reader will find are some insights into how the process of human sense-making has evolved in academic fields, which are commonly identified as communication, and speech communication or speech, within specific sociocultural settings. Thus you will notice that the authors endeavor to demonstrate the interdependence of all human efforts as we strive to understand our environment and all of our interactions. A strong emphasis on *process*, as we deal with humans engaged in communication and theorizing, should also be apparent. That approach is noticeable when I use the less elegant expression *humans communicating* rather than *human communication* to remind all of us of the vital focal point for our studies. When the term *human communication* is used in this volume, it frequently relates to the academic field rather than the process.

All of us, including scholars, researchers, philosophers, and students need to remain aware that we are products of the sociocultural settings in which our understanding and our theories emerge. For only a few of us will it become possible to revolutionize human understanding. For most it will only be possible to make a small contribution to a slow, painstaking, long-term process, which at times even reverses course and once more embraces earlier insights.

I would like to thank my colleagues who have allowed me to work with them in this challenging and exciting endeavor. A special acknowledgment goes to Professor Stewart Hudson of Pepperdine University who developed and conceived the appendix material entitled "The Romatic or Idealistic Versus the Realistic or Empirical Frames of Reference." My thanks also goes to Linda Santucci, one of my graduate assistants, who made valuable contributions to the time-consuming editing process. A special thanks also goes to Scott Welch, my student assistant, who helped coordinate work with the authors while I was on leave.

Fred L. Casmir

Part I

Theorizing: The Process of Sense-Making

Profusion, not economy, may after all be Reality's key-note
—James (1981, p. 191)

The focus of the book you are about to read is on one important aspect of human sense-making—theory building. It does not represent an attempt to survey all, or even most, existing theories related to humans who communicate. Nor do the authors suggest that one common approach to the development of theory, or an all-encompassing paradigm would be beneficial.

What we *are* striving to make clear is that theories do not develop in some sort of social, intellectual, or cultural vacuum. They are necessarily the results or products of specific times, insights, and mind sets. Theories dealing with the *process* of communication, or communicating, are tied to sociocultural value systems and historic factors which influence individuals in ways often inadequately understood by those who use them.

The process-orientation of this book inevitably leads to an emphasis on the perceptions of human beings. Thus the focus shifts from the subject or area we call "communication" to the *act of communicating*. Of course, a large number of human activities can be included under that heading. Over time, a variety of concepts and explanatory systems have helped to make sense of what we observed. Some earlier attempts to evolve satisfactory explanations were inadequate, but out of them more useful theories emerged. Occasionally, such efforts result in truly revolutionary changes. Quantum physics, with its impact in both the physical sciences and other human endeavors, is one example. Though it is centuries old, Greek logic and its continuing impact on Western thought, is another.

In the pages that follow, we consider the *roots* of theory building—the broader intellectual and cultural assumptions that lead to observable results. Of course, it would be impossible to cover every explanatory system in one volume. However, we hope to establish some foundational principles that are readily applicable as you encounter both new and old theories. Our attempt is to help you become more than a *user* of theories. The single most important principle is our understanding of what a particular theorist brings to his or her effort. That requires us to deal with assumptions held by any given theorist about

the *nature* of human beings,
the *nature* of the environment or universe,
the *nature* of some absolute (its presence or absence).

The sociocultural orientations of the contributing authors in this volume, of course, also play a role in their approaches to theory building. We are all products of Western or Northern cultures. However, that fact alone does not invalidate our perspectives, nor does it automatically make those originating in another culture more valid.

Our focus also stresses the need to understand the scientific process; what it is and how it is applied in a variety of settings to suit a variety of needs. We do not attempt to define, defend, or suggest that there is *one* entity in the world that can be invariably identified as science. Nor do we assume that *one* set of methods, *one* set of tools, or *one* area of human inquiry is superior to all others. Rather, we attempt to understand, if not celebrate, human diversity.

We are also keenly aware of the fact that we live at a time when concern with how we gain knowledge and how we secure evidence to explain what we observe, is widespread. Feelings of imbalance and insecurity pervade our world. As a result, many people who are not scholars or scientists feel a need to learn more about science, and how we should use it in our contemporary world. A recent article from the *Los Angeles Times* illustrates that point.

How do scientists know when they have collected enough evidence to feel comfortable with their conclusions?

The word *proof* practically never appears in scientific literature because most scientists do not think it is appropriate beyond the narrow confines of the pure world of mathematics. At best, in many areas of great public concern, scientists can only offer odds and probabilities, not proof.

"The way that science works is that you have a social process," said James Woodward, philosopher of science at Caltech. "You have people who reach at least initially different judgments about the merits of theories, they argue and produce new evidence, and finally sometimes things get sorted out and you move toward consensus."

"There's no oracle" on the mountain top ready to proclaim the arrival of truth, he added.

"There is a lot of judgment involved," said Peter Gallson, who teaches physics and philosophy at Stanford University.

"But judgment is not necessarily something arbitrary," he said. "Judgment is something you learn over the years." (Dye, May 21, 1990)

From our perspective today, or the way the universe looked to human beings at any given time in history, *various* explanatory perspectives are possible or even plausible, though some may sound strange indeed. We do not want to reach hasty and possibly negative conclusions about the views of others, or about views held in different times. The concepts presented in an essay recently published in the *Chronicle of Higher Education* may help us to develop a more fitting humility about all human sensemaking.

We find ourselves in a bewildering world. We want to make sense of what we see around us and to ask: What is the nature of the universe? What is our place in it and where did it and we come from? Why is it the way it is?

To try and answer these questions we adopt some "world picture." Just as an infinite tower of tortoises supporting the flat earth is such a picture, so is the theory of superstrings. Both are theories of the universe, though the latter is much more mathematical and precise than the former. Both theories lack observational evidence: No one has ever seen a giant tortoise with the earth on its back, but then, no one has seen a superstring either. However, the tortoise theory fails to be good scientific theory because it predicts that people would be able to fall off the edge of the world. This has not been found to agree with experience, unless that turns out to be the explanation for the people who were supposed to have disappeared into the Bermuda Triangle! (Hawking, May, 1989, B2)

In effect, we are not intimating here that any single approach to human inquiry is under all circumstances or *inherently* more adequate or acceptable than another. The paradigms of physics and the physical sciences, for instance, in many ways, served us well. But it has become evident that these models are tools designed for clearly specified circumstances, related to the lawful aspects of a physical, objective universe. At the same time, these models present us with very significant problems when we deal with the perception, actions, insights, and additional aspects of human behavior. Cherniak (1986), for example, warns us about the application of decidable logics making use of effective procedures to the study of human logic, because of their inadequacies.

How large a belief set could an ideal computer check for consistency in this way? Suppose that each line of the truth table for the conjunction of all these beliefs could be checked in the time a light ray takes to traverse the diameter of a proton, an appropriate "supercycle" time, and suppose that the computer was permitted to run for twenty billion years, the estimated time from the "big-bang" dawn of the universe to the present. A belief system containing only 138 logically independent propositions would overwhelm the time resources of this supermachine. Given the difficulties of individuating beliefs, it is not easy to estimate the number of atomic propositions in a typical human belief system, but 138 seems much too low. This argument clearly shows that however people reason, it is not by instantiating a computational device that uses any known effective procedure for deciding propositional logic. If people are "logical" in some way analogous to formal logic, it cannot be because they use any of the proof procedures dear to logicians.

There was a time when we hoped that disagreements between humanists and scientists could be resolved through the application of some generally acceptable logic. Failing that, we hoped that, just maybe, the disagreements would finally "go away." Maybe those who held opposing views would recognize the error of their ways. The problem is, of course, deeper and more significant, at least if you consider the *roots* of the conflicting issues and ensuing debates. More recently, we began to explore the possibility that simplistic dichotomous thinking is really inadequate in attempts to resolve either conflicts between scholars, or the significant problems faced by human beings in today's world.

Some time ago, natural scientists, long accustomed to working with logics requiring dichotomous thinking, concluded that, sometimes the answers to perplexing problems with the category systems they had developed required not "either-or," but a "both," solution. That represented a MAJOR shift in the logic systems we had been accustomed to using. In our own field of scholarly work we have become less interested in *fitting* our theories into some existing, more simplistic logic systems or to relate them to some final, absolute truth. Instead, the *usefulness* of theories, methods or approaches related to our understanding of human behavior has become more important. Our field has become richer for the experience, though we are not yet satisfied with our achievements.

Meanwhile a number of positive side-effects resulted from our change in emphasis. One effect is that in many cases acrimonious debates of the past have been replaced by explorations, thoughtful discussions, and conflict resolution based on a better understanding of our varied undergirding assumptions. Another example is an increasing emphasis on an "ought-we" rather than a "can-we" orientation. In other words, we have increased our awareness of the need for consideration of axiological, moral or ethical issues which result from our efforts. As we strive to construct theories to explain how and why human beings communicate, a growing concern with the roles mechanical or electronic devices *should* play in our lives, is only one specific instance of such axiological issues.

Many of us see an emphasis on values, in relationship to both human actions and the scientific process, as one of the most important concerns of our time. No scholars are more suitably prepared to contribute to our understanding of these contemporary challenges than those found in the discipline of human communication studies—a tradition which spans centuries of human efforts to make sense of humans and their interactions in our world.

REFERENCES

Cherniak, C. (1986). *Minimal rationality.* Cambridge, MA: Bradford Books/MIT Press.

Dye, L. (1990, May 21). Since proof is elusive, science seeks best odds. *Los Angeles Times,* Science/Medicine.

Hawking, S. W. (1989, May 4). A unified theory of the universe would be the ultimate triumph of human reason. *The Chronicle of Higher Education,* B2.

James, W. (1981). *The principles of psychology.* Cambridge, MA: Harvard University Press.

Chapter 1

The Role of Theory
and Theory Building

Fred L. Casmir
Pepperdine University

> *Measured objectively, what a man can wrest from Truth by passionate*
> *striving is utterly infinitesimal. But the striving frees us from the bonds of*
> *the self and makes us comrades of those who are the best and the greatest.*
> —Einstein (1979, p. 24)

FOUNDATIONAL CONCEPTS

Results, conclusions, summaries, the "bottom-line," all these terms relate to concepts that play a significant role in our society. However, they can also be representative of thought processes that are based on shortcuts, oversimplifications, and intellectual laziness. The product rather than the process becomes important in such thinking. Unfortunately, it can be extremely difficult to reason from results or conclusions back to the roots or beginnings of an intellectual process. All of us can thus become dependent upon incomplete interpretations and second-hand analyses or summaries, without becoming partners in the actual development of an intellectual effort or without coming face-to-face with the ideas that the originator of such work considered fundamental to its development.

Theory building is one significant area of human endeavor which frequently suffers from our unwillingness or inability to consider its step-by-step development. In other words, we are often more concerned with the noun-aspect of the word building, the result, the product, than its vital verb-aspect, the process which results in the final product. Both the building blocks and those who use them for their own purposes must be clearly identified if we are to understand the results. This volume is an attempt to deal with the building process of theories and with its component parts, taking into consideration ontological, epistemological, and axiological foundations which determine the eventual form of a theory.

Such foundations emerge out of the sociocultural and historical setting in which scholars work.

What is required is the shifting of the reader's interpretation level. The theories discussed in the chapters to follow do not represent a survey of the field of communication, or one of its subareas. Rather they are illustrations of processes which are based on significant presuppositions and expectations at a given time in history. As you come in contact with other theories, you should be able to apply to them as well the issues or categories developed in this book. The emphasis in this chapter and in those to follow is on the tools used by a theoretician and the use of available intellectual raw materials in a given environment. The beginning point for our considerations thus must be the human being and the sociocultural setting in which such a human being works, not some vague, shrouded-in-mystery foundations which have long since been forgotten. A less critical, less informed approach becomes dangerous, especially if it is assumed that somehow the scientific process or methodology inevitably leads to significant conclusions, even if we do not understand the original data fed into that process, or the assumptions on which it was based.

When I watched, for the first time, the PBS series "The Day the Universe Changed," and later read the accompanying book by James Burke (1985), I was intrigued by a paragraph summarizing the major idea behind the provocative title.

> All communities in all places at all times manifest their own view of reality in what they do. The entire culture reflects the contemporary model of reality. We are what we know. And when the body of knowledge changes, so do we. Each change brings with it new attitudes and institutions created by new knowledge . . . Just as speech needs grammar to make sense of strings of words, so consensual forms are used by a community to give meaning to social interaction. (p. 11)

This book addresses the two fundamental areas of concern mentioned by Burke. First of all, its authors assume that theories, any theories, including those built in the area we call human communication studies, must be understood within their own sociocultural setting. Second, it deals in this first chapter, and more indirectly in subsequent chapters, with the role of the "grammar" applied by all good theoreticians in their work, as they try to make sense of strings of data.

The process of constructing or building theories is intricately connected with human beings, and those human beings, in turn, are intricately interconnected with their cultures and societies. That is the central point made in the pages to come. The fact that we focus on communication provides one important opportunity to focus our efforts. However, the process of theory building and its foundations are the same, or highly similar, for all such efforts in all areas of human intellectual work. Communication studies are not independent efforts; they are part of the total human search for knowledge and understanding.

What has often been spoken of as a kind of weakness in areas like speech and communication, can be conceived of as a strength if one takes the cultural foundations of the scientific process seriously. We have, for many years, borrowed heavily from such academic fields as psychology, sociology, and linguistics, among others. That should have helped us to stay connected with the total human intellectual effort. Unfortunately, in an academic world where "unique" contributions are so highly valued, we have often attempted to denigrate this interdependence. Most communication theories, as is made clear in the chapters to follow, rest on broad intellectual, philosophical, and theoretical foundations which, in turn, are shared by many academic disciplines and areas.

Earlier this century, a group of psychologists, mostly Germans, appropriated the word "Gestalt" (figure or configuration) to summarize their concerns with the interrelationship of a "figure" and its surrounding environment or field. I go a step further in that application, as I develop this chapter. Because our emphasis in this volume is on the process of building theories, I will think of a theoretician's work as "Gestaltung," or the actual process of configuration, not merely the observable results. To do that, we have to lay certain foundations that are common in all theory building, staying aware of the fact that communication studies focus on some special areas of interest, which in turn leads to concerns with specific subjects and issues.

This first chapter is intended to remind you of some of the tools we need to master BOTH in theory building and the critical evaluation of extant theories. The latter is something which, hopefully, will happen even as you read the balance of chapters. Although your focus and mine is on communication, very similar philosophical and methodological concerns are shared by many scholars in all the humanities and social sciences, as you will see throughout this volume.

As each author takes you into his or her own thought processes and illustrates the foundations for the theories discussed, shift your thinking from "product" to "process." The purpose of this volume will be more readily achieved.

THE ROLE OF THEORY

We are constantly challenged to provide explanations in an environment which presents us with a multitude of stimuli—impressions, opportunities, and difficulties. Merely to observe what exists around and within us does not meet the needs of human beings for understanding their experiences. Explanations, or complete explanatory systems represent the human effort to organize these experiences in order to make sense out of them. That is a vital effort if we want to deal effectively with similar experiences in the future.

For our purposes, let us think of theorizing as any attempt by human beings to relate multiple data, facts, or observations, based on some logic because of a need and/or past experience, in order to produce better understanding.

Four important factors are considered here which relate to the construction of theories.

1. Sense-Making
2. Communication
3. Inquiry/Knowledge
4. The Relationship of Theory to our Pragmatically Oriented Society

Sense-Making

There appears to be both a need and an innate ability in humans to take various components of their universe and arrange them in meaningful, useful, or attractive patterns. Art and music are two special instances where forms, sounds, and colors have been arranged or composed in such a way as to provide us with means for interpreting or simply enjoying our world. However, as the arts illustrate very well, while a composition may be meaningful or important to one individual, others may not appreciate it at all. Thus, we should consider Fisher's (1978) admonition that it is wiser for us to question a theory's usefulness, than it is to debate its truthfulness.

There is a profoundly human process involved in theory construction and evaluation, because "the formation of a theory is not just the discovery of a hidden fact, the theory is a way of looking at the fact, of organizing and representing . . . A theory must somehow fit God's world, but in an important sense it creates a world of its own" (Kaplan, 1964, p. 309). Fisher (1985) and Berger and Luckman (1967) drew similar conclusions when they insisted that humans *create* rather than discover reality. Berlo (1960) wrote of a set of tools which we create by organizing our perceptions which are, as Fisher (1978) indicated, "useful" in our analyses and descriptions. Of course, as the example of artistic expressions suggests, there are differences in perception, differences in their organization, and certainly differences in interpretation because of cultural, subcultural, and individual predispositions. More on that subject later.

The debate over how we make sense of phenomena is probably as old as the ability of human beings to communicate. Almost instinctively we can all relate to the search for meaning and the feeling of security its determination produces. It is not just the balance or consistency theorists like Festinger (1957) or Newcomb (1961) who are aware of the phenomenon. All of us have and will continue to experience the stress of uncertainty, and when our attempts at sense-making fail, imbalance results.

Throughout history, human beings have developed various theoretical constructs which represent their attempts to overcome uncertainty and sense of imbalance. To understand that process better is the ultimate purpose of this volume. It is designed to make sense of the sense-making process we call "theorizing." Such an effort is important because as Barnlund (1979) notes, one of the few universals applying to all human beings is the continual process of making sense.

Communication

One vital factor about theorizing has been merely alluded to, not yet discussed in detail. Sense-making can be a profoundly individual experience, but the nature of human cultures and societies makes interaction and the sharing of insights a central factor. We need to remember that "according to the theory of reasoned action, a person's intention is a function of two basic determinants, one personal in nature and the other reflecting social influence" (Ajzen & Fishbein, 1980, p. 6). In other words, while theorizing may often begin with an individual's needs or observations, in many instances these are also shared with or even imposed on others. Four central issues thus emerge:

1. Theory building is closely associated with individual insights and goals.
2. Theory building is a socially mediated process.
3. Communication is central to the social process of theorizing, resulting in attempts to inform and, at times, to persuade others.
4. Science and the scientific processes of inquiry, as well as standardized reporting of our findings, represent significant human accomplishments in their effort to take theories beyond an individual's experience.

Inquiry and Knowledge

Our concern with sense-making, organization, patterning, and providing structure to what otherwise would be chaotic has taken many forms. At times that has led to serious disagreements concerning the BEST means of explanation. James (1948) shared a pragmatist's point-of-view clearly founded on his belief in an experiential base in perception for all human behavior when he wrote "traditional theories of knowledge are too speculative because they ignore the origins of knowledge in the life world" (p. 36). His approach put him at odds with those holding to the received view discussed later, a view which gave rise to many theories in the natural sciences.

On one hand, "science has impressively proved itself to be a powerful way of dealing with certain aspects of our experience" (Weaver, 1962, p. 101). Galileo, for instance, sought to reduce all explanations of reality to a physical base, developing an atomistic point-of-view of the universe. He accepted a paradigm based on matter in motion (Lakoff & Johnson, 1980, p. 14). Descartes exerted great influence with concepts related to his fascination with mechanical toys and automata. As a result, he developed the view that the material world could best be understood in terms of mechanical interaction and the movement of particles originally set in motion by God (Ortony, 1979, p. 37).

Yet, increasingly we have been forced to acknowledge that the traditional approaches used in the natural sciences, especially physics, are not all-sufficient. That is true because the sciences achieve what are at best only comprehensive and accurate systems of description, not explanations (Nagel, 1979, p. 26). Therefore, we have recently begun to acknowledge the role of individual human beings in "doing" science. As Bronowski (1977) noted, "in reality, science is always an arrangement of the facts; and our preference for one arrangement rather than another is a continued attempt to find the truth behind the appearance of nature" (p. 199). Kuhn (1970) discussed a similar notion that communities, including scientific ones, choose preferred models of communication. It may help our search if we remember that Weizsacker (1980) tries to temper our belief in the human ability to discover vital knowledge by citing Nietzsche's conviction that truth is "an adequately well adapted error" (p. 272).

To make sense and to share that process, we thus need disciplined approaches which are systematic and which order our experiences in ways to make them both accessible and testable. In other words, a sense making process which defines our experiences is also making it an easier subject for communication and evaluation.

Theory in Our Practical Society

Human needs differ. At various times, and in different places, our cultures prepare us to provide different responses because "its members are convinced that this is the only correct view of the universe" (LeShan & Margenau, 1982, p. XIII). It is, therefore, important to those of us in the field of communication how *well* we "do" science, not which approach we favor. Prominence should be given to the most fruitful application of tools or methods. Tools are designed for specific jobs. To apply them otherwise is destructive both to the tools and the objects to which they are applied. Hammering screws into a wall is a poor use of both screws and hammers, and it tends to produce unsightly walls as well.

Our search for meaning and understanding must become focused, because the methods we use require planning and demand meaningful outcomes. We move from asking questions to observation to the construction of answers in orderly fashion. Thus the process is reportable and replicable, if required (Littlejohn, 1989, pp. 6 ff.). Whether the method chosen is quantitative or qualitative, whether a field study or laboratory experiment, it only becomes significant when we evaluate the tool in relationship to a task. All fruitful approaches share a common evaluative process that requires the careful and meaningful application of the scientific process to the subject matter. Over the decades, debates concerning the basic value of one approach over another may indeed have satisfied our needs for status, power or self-assertion. However, their contributions to human knowledge and understanding have been questionable, at best.

We should consider the impact cultural expectations have on the role of theory in our own society. North Americans, and others who share our concerns with practicality, pragmatism, and a physical reality almost automatically react negatively to the term, *theory*. That reaction is so pervasive that frequently students forced to confront theory courses, have difficulty staying open to any potential value the subject matter might have for them.

It may help a little to note that all of us theorize—that we all try to make sense of what we do or experience rather than merely describe the process. We often try to answer important "why" questions in addition to those which deal with "what" and "how." The very reason we enroll in a college, consider a specific job offer, choose a marriage, or even a favorite food, commonly represents much more than an impulsive choice of the moment. Frequently, we attempt to construct a valid theory to undergird our decision, or perhaps we use one preformulated, though existing at a low level of awareness.

The fact that we increasingly demand scholars share detailed information concerning the choice and use of their methodologies is an important step in that direction. It may logically follow that we should also require scholars to identify expectations they bring to their work. Perelman (1963) for instance, concentrated part of his work on the fact that any theoretical enterprise has both a "political" and a "rhetorical" dimension. It was his concern that the rhetorical aspects of academic knowledge should be made more explicit in our political settings. That is especially important since all of us in theory development bring at least three important assumptions to our efforts:

1. Assumptions about the nature of human beings.
2. Assumptions about the nature of our environment.
3. Assumptions about the possible existence or nature of something ultimate.

Since our assumptions will, to a large extent, determine the development of any theory, they should be made explicit.

As we try to make sense of our world, as we attempt to communicate what we have learned, and after completing a rigorous scientific process of inquiry, a final step often has to be taken. We may need to convince others that what we have found "really makes a difference" or really "works." As a partner in the culture or society which nurtures the scientist, she or he may decide that such an explanation is very necessary.

THE RELATIONSHIP OF THEORY TO REALITY

Underlying our discussion is the concept that human beings are concerned with gaining knowledge. This knowledge may well provide necessary balance and stability through the process of sense-making, which includes theorizing. Of course, the assumptions we bring to that process greatly influence what we will learn and how we will use that knowledge. As we attempt to create a sense of balance, it may be difficult to accept or even perceive, factors which contradict our expectations.

Bubner (1988) makes that point when he writes ". . . to acquire knowledge always presupposes that some knowledge is already given which can never be obtained from the knowledge acquired" (p. 100). Just how we use knowledge depends on processes of thought and belief which result in our considering, weighing and favoring certain propositions (Margolis, 1973; Burke, 1931, 1945).

At this point we should address an important assumption which has undergirded much scientific work in the past, namely that the objectivity of both scientific observers, and the ensuing process of sense-making, can be realistically expected.

The Role of Perception and the Nature of Social Knowledge

Ever since fundamental disagreements about the nature of human beings and human knowledge were first developed in Greek thought by Aristotle, Plato, and others (see Appendix A for a summary of these concepts), how we know what we know has been a major source of contention. On one hand there are individuals like Veatch (1974), who stress that "the things of the world are what they are in themselves and independently of our attitudes towards them or our opinions of them" (p. 75). Contrast this with Scheffler's (1982) view "that our categorizations and expectations guide by orienting us selectively towards the future; they set us, in particular, to perceive in certain ways and not others" (p. 44), and important differences become evident.

First of all let us consider the orientation labeled "objectivistic." It hinges on our accepting the idea that there is a material universe out there, impinging on our senses in such a way that if we apply appropriate methodologies and use appropriate tools we will all discover the *same* physical reality. This approach has made extensive use of mathematical models and statistics, applying a mechanistic or machine-model to the study of both the universe and human beings. According to this view, scholars simply report observed facts as they are. Important conclusions are drawn from those facts while attempting to identify consistent, lawful behavior or reactions. Such an approach can also be described as deterministic. Determinism is based on the view that antecedents causally determine consequences, because a causal structure is thought to be present in an objective world, including the social environment. It is well represented by what Fisher (1978) describes as the "received view." In the received view, human beings are perceived as performing almost mechanical functions of observation, evaluation and reporting. Because of the predominance of this approach in the natural sciences it has often been called the "scientific" method, with the unfortunate result that others had best copy its methodologies or risk being considered less scientific or nonscientific in their work. This deterministic, objectivistic worldview has been strongly influenced by Greek thought, especially Aristotelian logic, and by the empiricists of Britain and the United States, and scholars active during the Enlightenment.

An unfortunate dichotomy was created when the so-called scientific, objective approach was simplistically contrasted with the humanistic, subjective point of view. Humanists, for example social scientists like Piaget (1971), assert that "the essential starting point here is that no form of knowledge, not even perceptual knowledge, constitutes a simple copy of the reality, because it always includes a process of assimilation to previous structure" (p. 4). Nietzsche (1957) wrote some time ago that all philosophers had pretended to discover insights through cold, pure, divinely untroubled dialectic, while failing to acknowledge their preconceived notions or heartfelt desires—but he questioned the adequacy of such a view.

Popper (1981) has been among those who attempted to overcome the negative effects of the either-or approach of scientific versus humanistic theorizing. He has pointed out that creativity illustrates well how three worlds interact, the physical and those of human law and creation. Thus Popper (1982) describes Beethoven as one who was free to choose his own path, but one who was also restrained by the paths previously selected by others, as well as the restrictions of the world being discovered (p. 129).

My students have found the metaphor of a microscope useful in this regard. Whenever we focus on some physical object or some aspect of it, we must put other things out of focus. I say "must," because our human biological ability does not make it possible to see *everything* at once. Burke (1965) points up this challenge when he discusses perspective, and Perelman (1982) does so as well in his concern with "presence." This human limitation does not mean that other things either disappear or do not exist. They are merely ignored for the moment. The specific focus of the observer results in seeing a particular relationship. An inherent weakness in all human research and theorizing thus becomes apparent: we may often inadvertently ignore what is important or truly related to what we are observing; we may not even become aware of its existence. Rigorous application of the scientific method can assist in overcoming the weakness of human perception. However, since all methods and instruments are developed by human beings in the first place, we must take into account built-in assumptions and weaknesses. This is especially important if "theory is a map" (McCombs & Becker, 1979, p. ix). As Kurt Lewin is reported to have said, there is nothing as practical as a good theory. The emphasis here is on the word *good*. A theory will only predict and explain as well as the initial mapping process allows it to do.

That mapping process certainly should evolve from adequate observation and reporting, but the individual interpretation of findings also plays a part. The very concept of theorizing often includes more than a summary statement about relationships or even about causes-and-effects, such as we are able to provide when we deal with natural laws such as water boiling at a specific temperature and air pressure. It may also result in the creative use individuals make of fundamental insights. For example, building a machine run by steam is directly related to boiling water—but only by way of the application a creative thinker makes of the natural law.

One thing seems clear, reality can be interpreted in a variety of ways. We may define it as something to be discovered, something "out there." Under those circumstances reality becomes something existing outside of human beings, an approach well suited to determinists or objectivists. On the other hand, we may take the opposite point-of-view, namely that reality is dependent on human interaction with and interpretation of it. In both cases the choice depends on the assumptions and presuppositions we *bring* to any discussion of the subject.

Since this conflict has engaged many of our best thinkers, it has generated a variety of suggested solutions to the apparent dilemma. Wittgenstein (1958) wrote, "I am convinced that some kind of reality does exist, either with or without us, but only as a substratum to our perceptions, themselves more or less accurate approximations which, with effort and talented inventions of new metaphors we can come to know somewhat better than we presently do" (p. 178). Wittgenstein's (1958) solution is tentative and distinguished by its propensity to include human interaction in the process of reality determination. As we continue to grapple with "reality," it is important to remember Kaplan's (1964) admonition that even if our purpose is to unify and systematize, that goal is never completely achieved.

In weighing human and methodological limitations, various conclusions can be drawn, but each of them is founded on our need for order, stability, and balance. It is simply easier for us to deal with uniformity than with diversity or complexity. Alderman (1977) spoke of that basic longing for universal oneness as the "experience of uniformity in apparent diversity" (p. 85). To the extent that we think human beings are able to find final, ultimate answers or solutions we may be disturbed or sanguine, encouraged or discouraged by the limitations of our perceptual, descriptive, and explanatory capabilities.

As we seek to understand the cultural and historic heritage of our Western and Northern world, Shibles (1972), reminds us that "Plato was among the first to intellectualize the predicament of human beings as prisoners of their thoughts and actions" (p. 46). However, regardless of the ruminations of such an illustrious philosopher, no absolute value system exists which predetermines our response to Plato's perception of the human condition. Regardless of our final conclusion, we should remember that "in all cases of perception, from the most basic to the most sophisticated, the meaning of the experience is recognized by the observer according to a horizon of expectation within which the experience will be expected to fall" (Burke, 1985, p. 309). Heisenberg (1979) also indicated the perceptual limits we face when he wrote that "in every act of perception we select one of the infinite number of possibilities and thus we also limit the number of possibilities for the future" (p. 28).

A few years ago a T-shirt with the inscription "what you see is what you get" was very popular on our campus. It prompted me to muse about the very issues previously addressed. The Platonic side of me made me wonder if the T-shirt wearers wished to remind us of the influence perception has on human reality. My Aristotelian side made me want to find out if indeed I would "get" the T-shirt if I asked for it. Fisher (1978) tried to resolve our theoretically based disagreements by pointing out that any two (or more) observational and interpretative processes are simply different. Thus, they should not be compared on the basis of which is better or more accurate. I would add that in our contemporary world complexity and multiplicity require the application of all available means for gaining knowledge and understanding, even as Brown (1987) indicated, "The attempt to observe the world requires that we draw on the widest body of accepted knowledge in the design of our observation procedures" (p. 205).

The Role of Order and Structure

At this point in our discussion you might infer I favor simply "letting the chips fall where they may," or some sort of intellectual anarchy. This concern must be addressed.

My first priority is to avoid encouraging anyone to subscribe to what I call the "fit-damn-you" syndrome. As with other concepts, the Greeks were also aware of this problem. You may recall the story of the giant, Procrustes, who invited travelers into his home. At night he would put the short ones on a long bed and stretch them until they fit, and the long ones on a short bed, chopping off whatever was hanging over. Thus: "fit-damn-you!" I am not sure that we can totally avoid our tendency to force things to fit preconceived notions, but I do believe that intellectual honesty demands that we at least attempt to identify the Procrustean "beds" we carry with us as we try to mold the world into the shape we find most comfortable.

Logic and Truth

For us in the United States, because of our specific intellectual heritage, a number of important considerations influence the process leading to better understanding of our assumptions. As mentioned earlier, our intellectual heritage rests heavily on Greek logic. That heritage is so strong that many insist that if something is *logical*, then it is also *true*.

Logic systems are based on internal consistency and redundancy. As a result, the original design of any logic systems makes findings based on the use of its symbols and rules totally predictable. Mathematics is a good example. Any eventually "discovered," any *determinable* relationship, is already built into the system. Mathematics as a logic system cannot seek "outside" itself for proof, for example, look to anything not already within the system. Seeking validation outside the system could prove destructive.

Thus the age-old question teachers pose to pupils, "How much is 2 + 2?" can only produce an *accurate* answer, one that makes use of the components and rules of the system, not a "true statement." The answer "4" is inherent in the boundaries of the system, and no other answer is, therefore, acceptable. Mathematics can only deal with accuracy or the failure to be accurate: Looking for truth requires stepping outside the circle of self-fulfilling prophecies of mathematics. It requires appeal to some absolute, to some ultimate value system or something beyond the mere internal relationships of a logic system.

Herein lies the difficulty in resolving disagreements based on values. Solomon's famous judgment resolving the quarrel between two women who both claimed to be the mother of a child, is a case in point. He suggested that the child should be cut in two, each mother to receive one half. Mathematically and even logically this is a sound solution. From a standpoint of truth or value, however, the *real* mother had to reject Solomon's solution because of her love for her child.

One of the biggest problems we face in the human search for knowledge and understanding resulted from the structural demands of our inherited formal logic systems. The so-called "law of the excluded middle" played havoc with our scientific observations for centuries. The now famous debate in physics as to whether light "IS" waves or particles is but one case in point. It took many decades and some very heated confrontations to finally produce a breakthrough based on a need produced by scientific observations. The answer was, of course, that light really "IS" not neither waves or particles. Rather, light "is" what humans see and need it to be; waves, particles, or other (Pelletier, 1978). The magnitude of that change in human thought is difficult to assess, but it represents a true paradigm shift, and a revolution in traditional thinking as described by Kuhn (1970). Let me hasten to add that I do not see such a shift or "revolution" as something totally new, completely replacing a previously existing entity, with little connection to the original paradigm. The growth of human knowledge, understanding and interpretation, from my perspective, is rather like an attempt to keep a conversation going—it is incremental.

Knowledge based either on logic or on truth should not be seen as dichotomous. While the standards for their evaluation may differ to the extent that they are based on the total human search for balance and for making sense, they remain part of the human explanatory system. If our knowledge and understanding truly approach "reality," concerns with both logic and truth will eventually come to address the same subject matter. If both systems prove adequate to such a task, conclusions could well be the same.

As we arrange various events in useful patterns, we must, of necessity, use earlier insights and linguistic structures or paradigms as a point of reference. Concepts like change, revolution, or paradigm-shift require a common departure point, heavily influenced by whatever already existed. Nevertheless, with recent changes in the natural sciences, dichotomous choices no longer remain the *only* possibilities for acceptable resolution of our disagreements, even in that arena of human efforts.

The Environment of Knowledge and Understanding

At this point in my discussion it becomes important to identify a concept which plays a significant role in this book! It is the assumption that communication studies do not exist in an intellectual, historic, cultural, or social vacuum. If there is one field of human inquiry which has drawn concepts and knowledge from a variety of areas, it is Communication. The impact of quantum physics, for instance, has not only influenced the natural sciences. It also has become part of a more general paradigm shift in communication studies requiring anyone adhering to the principles guiding quantum physics, to abandon the traditional concept of an existing, observable order for that of an order imposed by humans on chaos. Rather than seeking to merely *discover* the existing order in the universe, quantum physicists have instead acknowledged the impact of the observer on the observed. For instance, there is evidence that subatomic matter actually changes during the process of being observed. Moreover, the conclusion drawn from the Second Law of Thermodynamics was that matter never disappears, but rather it returns to a state of *disorganization* or chaos (Whitten, Gailey, & Davis, 1987). From the perspective of a physicist, Jaki (1978) concludes with the startling insight of Diedrot that "the turbulence of all that is, is governed by the order of law; but that turbulence is a law of disorder" (p. 362). Gleick (1987) provides us with an extensive discussion of the significant changes the new physics and its *underlying assumptions* mean to traditional concepts of order.

It is not my intention to describe the total impact of quantum physics. Suffice it to say that recent changes in the field of physics have had an impact far beyond the disciplines of natural science. Time concepts—of considerable interest to students of communication—are being rethought (Hawking, 1988). As Rifkin (1987) points out, there lies a challenge in the idea that "every level of biological reality, from organs to molecules, is woven from the same temporal patterns that give order to the material universe" (p. 44). Focus on this temporal reality is only one of many new research vistas beckoning for communication scholars. The order and stability of the old deterministic paradigm made it seem the most desirable approach.

However, new paradigms require new thinking, as well as new approaches, new methodologies, and new symbol systems. Popper (1983) indicated that "scientific theories are not only instruments, but genuine descriptive statements. They are genuine conjectures about the world" (p. 110). What is significant is an altered perception of scientists as active, creative participants in the scientific process. LeShan and Margenau (1982), for instance, point out we can never even know what a simple compound like water *is*, without human consciousness.

As we strive to bring order to our observations, and gain significant knowledge and understanding, LeShan and Margenau (1982) would remind us that Einstein's claim that the greatest miracle of the universe is its comprehensibility, needs a caveat. "The reason it is comprehensible is that we can only know it as it is construed by human beings and our own words are comprehensible to us" (LeShan & Margenau, 1982, p. 22). Words and symbols thus are important because they influence the study of human attempts to make sense of our environment.

The Role of Language and Epistemology

I do not wish to suggest that language represents a kind of prison for us, one which totally determines our ability to express ideas and severely limits what we can think or know. Thus I do not subscribe to the claims of some linguists that language may be exerting absolute control over our thinking processes (see Sapir, 1921; Whorf, 1965). It is generally conceded that human beings did not start out using language; they had to *invent* it. Deterministic linguistic theories, however, imply that if there were originally no words or language in existence humans could not have thought of anything in their environment. As a result, humans could not have been aware of a need for language either. I personally believe that the development and use of language results from the creative ability of human beings, an ability which precedes language use or language development. However, once language symbols have been developed, we need to respond to their existence. The structurationists suggest a similar process for social systems (see Giddens, 1979, 1983). Their paradigm combines human ability to create systems with our response to their existence. At the same time, the model does not require us to identify such reactions as simplistic responses to existing stimuli.

Moving beyond my basic premise, several issues require our consideration. Using the verb form "is" can be very troublesome for theorists. For instance, whenever we ask "what IS communication?" we create our own conceptual trap. When I say "is," it suggests that there is some sort of physical object to be discovered. The use of "is" allows us to borrow aspects of the deterministic models which the natural sciences have developed. As a result we can make it appear as if all we have to do is develop the right instruments for observation, the right paradigms to describe the phenomenon, and we will be able to deal effectively with what we called the process of "communication." Such thinking, which ignored the fact that the term *communication* did not stand for an object, but a human construct for which no one physical object could be determined, created a plethora of definitions that seemed to lead nowhere (see Dance, 1970).

As I have previously indicated, there seems more value in observing, describing, and categorizing acts of communicating in all their various forms. A process orientation is an integral part of this approach. All we can really observe and categorize at this point are the actions and interactions of human beings as they use verbal and nonverbal symbols to make sense of their world. This is occurring as individuals and members of a society explore, search, and share—thus providing the "subject matter" for scholarly efforts.

This serves to remind us that facts do not speak for themselves. Rather, human beings speak about "facts," which they have identified by using a variety of logic and truth systems. Even scientists do not simply present numbers or data in the hope that colleagues will draw the same conclusions as the original observer— they explain their findings.

Labels and definitions play an important role in any communication process, including theorizing. In spite of the outcry of the 1960s and 1970s, do not "fold, spindle, or mutilate" human beings. Any system of inquiry requires some form of categorization and labeling, as well as an explanation of how and why we used these particular approaches. Communicating requires common terms, common language, and a logical explanation for why we came up with the idea in the first place.

Can we hope to develop some perfect system acceptable to everyone? The prospect of coming up with a single set of concepts is not likely. Human beings are not only merely concerned with categories as "filing" devices. Rather, people recognize that such devices evolve out of basic assumptions, and the shared values and perceptions of human beings. Commonly such assumptions are related to specific perception of the environment and something ultimate which may not be clearly stated or identified. As Schefflen (1974) reminds us, the epistemology which we employ to deal with human communication makes "a great difference in the kinds of answers and meanings we deduce" (p. 44).

A colleague of mine was fond of pointing out that we are all either "lumpers or splitters." That may not have been the most elegant way to contrast holism and reductionism. Still, it helps us to remember that *both* are methods that have their values—and their problems. Taking a frog apart makes it possible to learn much about its component parts, but it does little to help us understand the frog as a living, functioning entity. Looking at a total system, on the other hand, allows us to draw some of those conclusions. At the same time the very complexity of a system may make it virtually impossible to study all its parts at once. Scholars thus find themselves moving back and forth between manageable parts and the entire system. In all cases, our use of language will depend on our assumptions as well as our resulting observational systems.

One point I want to make here concerns the use of language, categories, and epistemology. Sometimes we have difficulty distinguishing between theory and philosophy. Rather than tackling the subject myself, I requested a knowledgeable colleague to provide us with his explanation of the difference. Walter Fisher replied:

> Constructs—like dissonance theory, social convergence theory, attribution theory, the rhetorical situation, and constructivism—are theories. They are not like Aristotle's, Campbell's, Burke's, or Perelman's formulations which are philosophies. Theories are partial explanations; philosophies purport to be full ones, grounded on clearly marked presuppositions: ontological, epistemological, axiological, etc. Quite simply, philosophies are deeper and have wider parameters. They go beyond explanation of particular behaviors or experiences. For example, my construction of the logic of good reasons (in the 1979 QJS article) was theoretical; my formulation of human communication as narration is a philosophical statement. The logic of good reasons construct now forms one component in this philosophy.
>
> There is another important distinction that is often overlooked in teaching rhetorical theory . . . the distinction between philosophy/theory and pedagogy (which may have important philosophical or theoretical implications), such as can be found in the works of Hugh Blair and Richard Whately and James A. Winans. (Fisher, January 16, 1990)

To sum up the epistemological foundation for the study of communication, recall the tool metaphor I used earlier. Remember, various systems are designed to do different things. As we develop communication theories, it is important to bear in mind Hempel's (1949) observation, that the subject matter of physics deals with such concepts as mass, wave length, field intensity, etc. Causal explanations and mathematical manipulations may be well suited to such studies. On the other hand, psychology, for example, studies mental notions which are *toto genre* different from those of the natural sciences. Ellenson (1982) illustrated this difference by reminding us that "environment is where you live; experience is what happens to you in your total surroundings" (p. 14). For those of us concerned with theory building related to communicating, an active, participatory view of human beings holds important promises and challenges. The language and the epistemology we employ should reflect those emphases.

Relating Reality and Theory

The challenge is profound. Theorists may be tempted to *compromise* by providing a makeshift explanation that makes use of the old categories in a new framework. The result would most likely resemble one of Dr. Seuss' animals rather than any meaningful representation of what we can observe in our environment. It reminds me of the discussion President Lincoln is said to have had with Mr. Kennedy, his secretary, while their train stopped in a meadow. Seeing some cows, Lincoln asked Mr. Kennedy to determine how many legs those cows had. Kennedy, of course, indicated they had four. After some discussion, Lincoln asked "How many legs would a cow have if its tail is counted as a leg?" Kennedy balked at that idea, but Lincoln insisted that for the sake of discussion, the tail should be counted as a leg. So, Kennedy accepted the tail as a fifth leg. Lincoln replied: "No, Mr. Kennedy! I don't care what one assumes for the sake of discussion. The cow still has four legs and one tail." Communication theorists need to develop theories using symbols and category systems which fit contemporary insights; but we also need methods and categories which allow us to test what we observe. For the sake of discussion we should neither assume the automatic validity of old assumptions nor of arbitrary new ones.

Let us return to the challenges of identifying theorists' preconceptions of human beings, their environment or universe, and their relationships to some absolute. It is vital that we first address issues which underlie our perceptions. Some of the more important concepts deal with how we see human beings, as active or reactive, as independent or interdependent, as mostly individualistic or as social beings. Do we see the environment as simplex or complex, as static or as changing, and do we perceive these changes as unidirectional or multidirectional? Do we believe in God, some god, some ultimate value system, or not?

Answers to such questions will, in large measure, predispose us to particular perceptions. These preconceptions are similar to the control knobs on a microscope; they tend to determine on what we will or will not focus. It should not be forgotten that as we change our assumptions, as we learn or improve our knowledge and understanding, our focus may be readjusted while we retain our initial observations. If we kept careful records, we might even choose to reexamine our original methodologies and conclusions for purposes of comparison.

Before I discuss concepts which may help us better understand the development and evaluation of theories, let me summarize my central points. Wood (1983) helps us remember ". . . the tendency of the human understanding to presuppose more order and regularities in nature than actually exists" (p. 99). Our need to impose order and consistency can easily pose problems as we theorize about human communication. Gadamer (1988) identifies an important approach which communication theorists should keep in mind, "[The hermeneutical rule that] we must understand the whole from the individual and the individual from the whole . . . thus the movement of understanding always runs from the whole to part and back to whole" (p. 68). To the extent that future theories of communication can adequately deal with both part and whole, our understanding of humans can be improved. In no case should we overlook, however, that we are not merely in the business of identifying and describing. The best theories will be responsive to Toulmin's (1961) challenge to contemporary scientists. "For most of us nowadays the task of understanding Nature is a wider one. Prediction is all very well; but we must make sense of what we predict. . . . That being so, we can never make less than a three-fold demand of science: its explanatory techniques must be not only (in Copernicus' words) 'consistent with the numerical records'; they must also be acceptable—for the time being, at any rate—as 'absolute' and 'pleasing to the mind' " (p. 115). For communication scholars whose roots are in humanistic studies, this comes as no surprise.

THEORY AND COMMUNICATION

For communication scholars theory building requires careful consideration of the subject matter we study. For some time we have stressed the concept of "process." That emphasis suggests that we are not studying some physically identifiable *object* called communication; rather we are focusing on the process of *communicating*. The following example helps to make my point. Some see value in studying structures, institutions, organizations or the general framework within which human interactions take place. But, it seems to me that our contribution as communication scholars should be found in the area of "organizing" or the process of how communication creates an organization. (See Weick, 1969, for a similar emphasis.)

Lanigan (1982) is among those who have proposed alternative approaches to our study of humans communicating. The eidetic, empirical methods he advocates date back to Aristotle's and Plato's concerns. Significantly, the critical descriptive approach he favors centers on the relationships of person and world as well as perception and expression. This holistic view tries to sidestep the traps of dualism or arbitrary separation of cognition and behavior. How to avoid unwarranted, though seemingly practical simplistic empiricistic approaches, concerns many scholars. James (1948), for example, warned that "a simple conception is an equivalent for the world only so far as the world is simple" (p. 8). Instead, he believed that the world in effect is a "mightily complex affair" (p. 8).

Earlier attempts to discover a SINGLE theory of communication to explain communicative behavior in law-like, consistent, predictable fashion, were concessions to the cause-effect emphasis model of the old physics. It was easy to ignore discrepancies, even when we noticed them again and again. Earlier theories of persuasion, for instance, stressed a stimulus-response, cause-effect relationship between speaker and audience, although actual experience indicated far more complex interactions. The motto became "fit-damn-you," in altogether too many circumstances. After all, the *lack of fit* between theory and actual observation would have required a major revision in our thinking.

Change did come, albeit after considerable controversy. Our growth may seem painful and circuitous to some, but such is often the route we must take to develop human knowledge. Even in the physical sciences, as research is conducted, and doors close—knowledge actually expands. Scholars are thus led to the development of new theories, which in turn bring scientists closer to the best possible answer for the moment. Kaplan (1964), though using a discovery-and-reductionist model, provided us with important insights when he wrote, ". . . as our knowledge of a particular subject-matter changes; as our conception becomes more fitting, we learn more and more; the better our concepts, the better the theory we can formulate with them, and in turn, the better the next improved theory" (p. 54).

The relationship of theory to research grows clearer. We may be tempted to approach the two on the basis of traditional dichotomized thinking, but in reality each sustains the other. A symbiotic relationship exists which makes theories more adequate as better research findings emerge. Theory, in turn, provides the opportunity for testing and further research.

Probably one of the reasons why some stress the need for a communication metatheory is explained by Morgan (1980) when he points out that such a paradigm may include "different schools of thought, which are often different ways of approaching and studying a shared reality or world view which are based upon the acceptance and use of different kinds of metaphor as a foundation for inquiry" (p. 607). Such an approach may have been based on the hope that it would help avoid those confrontations which are based on our insistence that one paradigm, one metaphor, one methodology is not only more useful in a given situation, but inherently better.

THEORY BUILDING

The title of this section stresses an important point. Theories are human constructs. They are formulated on the basis of many factors discussed earlier. Theories are pervasive because we need to make sense of those things we encounter in our environment. Theories are thus closely related to the perspectives we bring to them. Cherwitz and Hikins' (1986) realist position points to an extreme and probably impossible perspective-of-all-perspectives. ". . . a thorough understanding of a particular phenomenon can occur only when all relevant perspectives have been discovered, evaluated, and juxtaposed to form a comprehensive view of the object of inquiry and all the characters or aspects it exhibits within the context of particulars in which it stands. It is only through an active seeking out of perspectives that goal can be approached" (p. 157). However, these authors help us to understand that the work of a theorist is not just some kind of glorified "guess-work." Stringent demands made of those who seek understanding should cause us to disabuse ourselves of that notion.

At the same time, Woelfel and Fink (1980) remind us that no theories are ever complete, "regardless of the range of phenomena to which they are meant to apply" (p. 5). Of course, that is something theories have in common with all human knowledge and understanding. Reardon (1981) provides a more tenable position than that advocated by Cherwitz and Hikins (1986) when he points out that a good theory must specify the scope conditions—only then can it provide us with "some way of explaining some portion of reality" (p. 62).

If we consider all these challenges, it is no wonder that some see theory construction as a high risk venture. "Since theoreticians are advancing conceptions of how a slice of physical or social reality works, they run the risk of being wrong" (Berger, 1977, pp. 14–15). The word "wrong" in this context, almost seems to brand such theories as "unscientific."

Much of our work consists of chipping away at a mountain of data, until what is left finally provides us with meaningful information. This process of elimination reminds me of the story about the young boy who locked himself up in his room with a large block of marble. His parents heard him busily working, and when he finally emerged, there stood in his room the statue of an elephant. When his parents asked him in amazement how he had accomplished that feat, he replied, "I simply chipped away everything that did not look like an elephant." Such sculpting can, therefore, be compared to the concept developed in Information Theory, which identifies information as what is "left over" after all the uncertainty has been removed.

Our decision-making process in theory building must include consideration of the generality or specificity of any theory. Pierce (1980) notes that "the ideas and assumption of a theory determine the generality of the theory, that is to how wide a range of phenomena the theory applies" (p. 4). His conclusion is that the most general theory is the best and most powerful because it explains the greatest range of phenomena. We should not overlook the fact, however, that theories can be like elephant guns. That is, as long as the guns are turned on the large animal for which they were intended, they may do their job. On the other hand, big guns turned on small mice result in overkill. Here again, remember the tool metaphor. Tools, including theories, should fit the task. Nothing about the tool is automatically good or bad. Meehan's (1969) simple definition of theory makes my point, "I would myself define a theory as an instrument able to produce useful explanations" (p. 53).

It should be evident by now that there is then a rhetorical, or persuasive, as well as a metaphorical aspect to theory building. Many centuries ago Aristotle gave us a scheme based on Greek perceptions, for the development and evaluation of the "available means of persuasion." More recently Catt (1988) summarized pragmatists' conclusions that metaphor selection leads to a scientist's description of communication and to the selection of distinctive paths of research, in keeping with that *significant metaphor*. Once theories are developed, one of their primary functions is to help us decide "what to observe and how to observe it" (Littlejohn, 1985, p. 14). Next, we consider what other factors, besides focused observation, are vital to theory building.

Origins of Theory

From our earlier discussions we conclude that theory building results from a general concern with knowledge and understanding which most human beings share. That concern relates to all our sense-making activities, which are, in turn related to our desire to experience feelings of balance and exert control over our environment. Knowledge and understanding are important factors in this process. To assure as much valuable and meaningful knowledge as possible, a specific set of rules has been developed. These rules facilitate a systematic process of observation-based inquiry, one that leads to specifiable conclusions. Such a process is scientific if it is rigorously targeted, planned and carried out according to a generally accepted and specified set of standards developed by a scientific community.

The basic process is one designed to result in the determination of relationships among observed objects, people, events, actions, or entities. Theory building goes beyond describing component parts; it attempts to make the relationships or interrelationships of such parts meaningful. As a result, good theories serve explanatory functions which make possible future efforts. They are heuristic.

Theories are sometimes defined as guesses—but significantly as "educated" guesses. Theories are not merely based on vague impressions nor are they accidental by-products of life. Theories tend to result when their creators have *prepared* themselves to discover something in the environment which triggers the process of theory construction. Only if that preparation is available can theory building become a focused effort.

Foundational Issues

The preceding pages have demonstrated that underlying all theoretical constructions are responses to major issues sometimes clearly identified by the theoretician. At other times, we can only guess at the author's assumptions.

One important area is that of ONTOLOGY. The nature of being falls under this heading. How we conceptualize an area of study like communication, or the humans we study, and their relationship to the environment makes an important difference in how we approach any subject for purposes of study and theorizing.

A second issue is EPISTEMOLOGY. Epistemology refers to the study of how we know what we know, dealing both with the *nature* of knowledge and *how* knowledge is gained. My concern with epistemological issues is evident in earlier segments of this chapter. Theoreticians frequently return to epistemological issues, especially in humanistic studies, when they seek to better understand how, when, and why humans communicate.

AXIOLOGICAL aspects should be mentioned as well. Here the concern is with values. The question of whether or not theory can, or should be value-free illustrates the basic nature of such issues. Deetz (1990) is only one of many writers denouncing the study of individual actions as if they existed in a linguistic and social (I would add cultural) vacuum. To Deetz, "systems and structures have important ethical implications that cannot be assessed from looking at individual behaviors and attitudes" (Deetz, 1990, p. 229). Concerns with *interactional mutuality*, as we attempt to persuade or convince others, would result from an axiological emphasis. For Deetz and others like him, ethical concerns thus should be a part of axiological considerations.

All those instances where I discussed the influence of the process of observation on that which is being observed can have a significant axiological dimension. Such debates are today often fueled by "critical" theorists. Disagreements may, for instance, center around the question whether or not social scientists should also be change agents. Axiological issues can thus greatly influence the entire process of theorizing, how it is envisioned and what its most desirable results should be. An "ought" perspective may in some cases replace more deterministic "can" approaches.

WHAT MAKES A GOOD THEORY?

Six criteria are commonly employed to test a theory (see Littlejohn, 1985):

    Appropriateness
    Validity
    Scope
    Heuristic Value
    Parsimony
    Consistent World View

Appropriateness

This term often refers to the epistemological assumptions of a theory. But we could also add axiological and teleological concerns; the latter incorporating concerns with some ultimate end or purpose. We need to be certain that a given theory is developed and used to deal with a specific set of circumstances under study. The selection of the right tool for the task at hand, is vital. That requires consideration of not only the general or specific nature of a theory, but also whether or not it was designed to explain the class of phenomena under investigation. To some it may be unimportant to consider the assumptions or presuppositions of a given theorist. But, as I have emphasized, if a theorist evolved a careful and logical structure, its conceptual foundations cannot be disregarded. When I use another theorist's work, therefore, I must make certain that I apply it as intended. Bending or reshaping it to fit my own needs, and then blaming the originator for inadequate results is never justified.

Validity

Closely related to the concept of appropriateness is the requirement that a good theory must explain what it sets out to explain. Validity represents a claim that a theory truly made sense of a phenomenon in such a manner as to be acceptable on the basis of appropriate scientific or other standards. For example, does a theory fit a given situation or does it produce something which is valuable? Anderson (1987) has addressed the question of validity in detail.

Scope

How general or specific a theory is can be of great importance. But the example of the elephant gun should remind us that dealing with a specific, limited situation may not require a broadly applicable general theory. By the same token, specific theories cannot automatically be assumed to generate widely generalizable understanding. In both cases the requirements and constraints of scope are ignored. Such an oversight makes it unlikely that a theory can adequately serve the purpose for which it was intended. Of course, in all cases we must assume the theorist has specified a theory's limitations. Otherwise, a researcher may be justified in pinpointing original inadequacies involved in the construction of a theory.

Heuristic Value

A good theory opens doors! Whenever a theory stimulates further thought or new *developments* and insights, it fulfills one of the most important roles good theory can play. Even a theory eventually proven wrong or requiring modification can still provide this heuristic stimulus. Subsequent efforts to check the appropriateness of a given theory, as well as possible extensions of the initial effort do, of course, depend on careful, detailed reporting by the author.

Parsimony

At times, my students have concluded that the criteria leading to the development of a good theory mentioned here need to be very complex and stated in such fashion that only the best educated among us can fully understand them. Parsimony indicates that of two possible explanations the most appropriate is the simplest, most direct—without sacrificing the other criteria of a good theory.

Consistent World View

Littlejohn (1989) discusses two World Views in detail. The first of these is based on an empiricist, rational foundation and assumes a knowable, physical reality. This is the view we associate with the natural sciences, one which results in the received view mentioned earlier. It concerns the discovery of invariable laws, and employs highly analytical approaches often based on mechanistic and reductionist paradigms.

The second World View is social, constructivist in nature. People are perceived as active participants in both the observation and creation of their realities. It is process-oriented, and thus, concerned with the roles of human perception and interpretation. Its final aim is not the discovery of natural laws, but rather, of consistencies and redundancies in human behavior which are not identified as simple cause-effect or stimulus-response relationships. Instead they are dealt with as richly complex phenomena requiring our understanding.

The most important aspect of these two World Views is the fact that both are the result of long term developments, in part dating back to the concepts and disagreements developed by Plato and Aristotle, as outlined in Appendix A. Since these are logical constructs, designed on the basis of relatively consistent assumptions about human beings, their environment and some ultimate factor or its absence, it is vital not to attempt to make either World View do the work of the other. This means we cannot utilize the methods and presuppositions of World View I to explain a phenomenon ill-suited to its assumptions, or vice versa. The debate continues over the appropriate use of certain logic systems like mathematics and statistics. The issue is whether or not methods first developed by those who designed the component parts of World View I, are applicable to the more humanistically oriented concerns of World View II.

WHAT MAKES A GOOD THEORIST?

Interestingly enough, most books dealing with theory never consider the role of the theorist. It is almost as if their authors assume that methods or rules can be separated from those who employ them. This is especially disturbing to those who subscribe to a view which identifies humans as active, creative participants, rather than reactive receivers of outside stimuli. I specify several factors that I consider to be vital to adequate theory building.

Curiosity. I am sure there are some theorists who construct a paradigm strictly as a challenge or mechanical task. In most cases those who devote a major portion of their lives to theory construction are individuals who truly seek for answers. Most theorists look at some person, object, or event in relationship to others and ask "why?", expecting to find some meaningful answer.

General Knowledge. The best theorists I have met have an astounding breadth of knowledge. They are seldom interested in only one or a few types of human experience. Frequently, their theories resulted from their ability to see relationships where others could not. For those studying humans communicating, history, religion, psychology, sociology, and archeology provide valuable insights, as do literature and the arts. As a matter of fact, some of our most interesting and valuable insights have evolved out of the work of individuals who discovered new ways of making connections between previously unrelated fields of study or who changed earlier perceptions of order and structure.

Specific Knowledge. It is easy to be misunderstood when developing categories to describe a good theorist. I hasten to add that in addition to the general framework of knowledge which assists a theoretician by soundly grounding concepts in the total human experience, *detailed* knowledge of one or more areas is also vital. The focus of a theory must be based on depth of understanding. Knowing as much as possible about present and past efforts related to a specific area on which a theoretician focuses, helps to avoid unnecessary duplications, tangents or the misinterpretation of observations.

Relational Thinking. I have observed that individuals who concentrate on details or components may have problems seeing them in relationship to each other. As I pointed out, good theories depend on those who can see relationships, especially where others have not. That ability can be critical when it comes to employing both a theorist's general and specific knowledge.

Clear Thinking. Building a good theory is a heady enterprise. Theory building is stimulating, and sometimes the emotional aspects of the process are counterproductive. Thus theoreticians must be able to discipline their thinking. This should include a willingness to submit new ideas to the scrutiny of others, and suspend further efforts until a certain intellectual "distance" is attained. A background in logic and philosophy can provide valuable insights in such scholarly work.

Ability to Organize. Theory building frequently requires the collection of large amounts of data. Only an individual trained to collect and prepare readily accessible information can hope to complete such a challenging task. Much organization is mechanical, a process that requires the disciplined collection and arrangement of data in accordance with some system both the theorist and potential audience considers useful.

Ability to Communicate Insights. If we concede that one reason we develop theories is to communicate our observations, it follows that good theorists must also be good communicators. While a certain amount of jargon is inevitable, a theory is useful only if others can understand it. Clarity, precision, and simplicity in wording are most helpful to those less familiar with the subject matter than the theorist.

Ability to Be Flexible. This category also may cause misunderstandings. Therefore, I hasten to point out that by flexibility I do not mean prematurely abandoning theory building. Nor does flexibility imply disregarding the rules of inquiry demanding specific methods of verification. However, the best theoreticians know when they have reached a dead end or when their abilities are not commensurate with the task. Good theorists do not necessarily stop their work but redirect it—or they make sure that they gain added insights before continuing it. Stubbornness can yield results, but more often than not it only hampers our efforts.

Ability to Suspend Judgment. Because there is great satisfaction connected with a job well done, because of the recognition of our peers, and sometimes because of the professional situation in which we work, there exists a temptation to reach conclusions or report findings before we are truly ready. The results can be devastating. In addition, many of us prove or discover exactly what we first set out to find, ignoring things contrary to our preconceptions. If we are to construct good theories, conclusions must result from a carefully completed task. What has been said earlier about a theorist's ability to think clearly, relates to this discussion as well.

Ability to Listen and Accept Criticism. No one ENJOYS criticism. However, the purpose of listening to criticism is not personal enjoyment, but improvement of one's work. Listening while suspending judgment, encouraging input by knowledgeable critics, and the ability to separate the wheat from the chaff are crucial to the construction of theory. Not all criticism is justified or truly intended to benefit the receiver. Even when criticism is not constructive, it can still be turned into a positive experience—but that may be a more difficult task for the theorist. Still, anyone who helps me accomplish my goals, however inadvertently, is important when I develop a theory.

I am not certain just how many people I know can truly meet *all* of these criteria. Most of us fail some of these tests at least some of the time. By the same token, ideals allow us to aim higher and to critically evaluate our own performance—even if we fail to achieve all of them. Whether or not we can claim excellence in all the areas I have mentioned, all of them can assist us in building theories—especially if they are mixed with a goodly amount of humility.

CATEGORIZING THEORIES

There is a relationship between the development of categories and theorizing. Both are sense-making procedures, attempts to relate and order. For both, usefulness rather than truthfulness is the primary goal. Questioning what a *correct* category "is," creates the same dilemma I have discussed in relationship to theories. Behind such a question is the notion that there is only one correct way to categorize, and that a category is some sort of physical object or entity which has specific properties waiting to be discovered. I would argue that categories are human constructs whose usefulness is best determined by how well they help us accomplish a task.

Bochner (1985) based his categories on the belief that different perspectives are primarily the result of differences in the vocabulary used. His scheme includes:

1. Epicureanism (aim: prediction and control).
2. Hermeneutics (aim: interpretation and understanding).
3. Critical theory (aim: criticism and social change).

All three of these perspective categories share certain features, including the necessity to deal with change.

Another category system has been mentioned previously. It is the broadest and most general, because it identifies theories as being LIMITED, GENERAL or SPECIFIC. General theories could include General Systems Theory (von Bertalanffy, 1968). A more narrowly focused, specific theory would be van Dijk's (1980) propositional approach to utterances. Obviously, this simple system for categorizing theories dealing with humans communicating, discriminates poorly.

A third example of past systems is the one which used various sub-areas commonly included in the academic disciplines of speech, speech communication or communication. INTRAPERSONAL, INTERPERSONAL, SMALL GROUP, ORGANIZATIONAL, MASS, INTERCULTURAL/INTERNATIONAL COMMUNICATION were the most frequent categories. As our knowledge and sophistication increased it became evident that many areas did not really produce their "own" theories. There were instances when it was very difficult to distinguish between the theories based on these categories. For instance, levels of aggregation or the numbers of individuals involved were considered vital distinctions when contrasting mass and interpersonal communication. Realistically, however, the phenomena with which we are concerned cut across these levels, frequently making *specific* theories dealing with so-called mass, group, or organizational communication superfluous (see also, Gumpert & Cathcart, 1986; Reardon & Rogers, 1988). By itself, the number of people involved in a given communication situation may or may not significantly impact the process. Certainly if we are to make such distinctions meaningful, they require much more validation. Often we use insights from one area like interpersonal communication to illuminate the study of another, like intercultural interactions. So-called mass communication includes very strong interpersonal elements best studied by also considering interpersonal communication theories. What I am trying to illustrate is that sometimes existing structures and professional demands, beyond what we hope to achieve as scholars, exert a strong influence on our categories and our work. What we have in such cases is yet another instance of the "fit-damn-you" syndrome.

Few of us could foresee the phenomenal growth of interest in human communication. Now we face a situation where so many theories have been constructed, that there is no easy way to categorize all of them. Littlejohn (1989) recently developed a system more responsive to current needs. His effort is representative of the fact that we are part of a growing, developing, changing field. Littlejohn's (1989) classificatory system includes the following types of theories:

- INTERPRETIVE/CRITICAL (examples cited: Merleau-Ponty, 1974; Pryor, 1981).
- COGNITIVE/BEHAVIORAL (examples cited: Greene, 1984; Skinner, 1957). The former area includes some of the most recent work relating to human communication theories, including a large number of European, most notably German and French theorists. The behavioral area incorporates both older work dating back to the first half of the 20th century and very recent insights based on a better physiological understanding of our cognitive processes.
- INTERACTIONIST/DRAMATIST (examples cited: Goffman, 1974; Mead, 1934).
- CULTURAL/SOCIAL REALITY (examples cited: Pearce & Cronen, 1980; Harre & Secord, 1972; Wittgenstein, 1953). The social reality category includes extensive work done from a rules perspective in an attempt to provide an alternative to the law-perspective of the natural sciences. The second part of Littlejohn's book also includes:
- SYSTEM THEORY and STRUCTURAL THEORIES OF SIGN AND MEANING (examples cited: Eco, 1976; Derrida, 1976; Ekman & Friesen, 1969). This category incorporates nonverbal theories.

All theories in the second segment are discussed under the umbrella term "GENERAL THEORIES." The third segment of the book covers CONTEXTUAL THEORIES, like INTERPERSONAL, GROUP, ORGANIZATIONAL and MASS COMMUNICATION.

To the reader of Littlejohn's book it becomes readily apparent that despite all the categories used, they are still inadequate to address the network of interactive subject matters which make up studies of humans communicating. Indeed, several theories were cross-listed and repeatedly referenced in several segments of the book. Both theory building and category construction, obviously, are important in bringing order and understanding to our human search for knowledge. When trying to superimpose just one concept of order on existing or observable entities, we face a daunting, complex task. When it comes to communicating such a system to others, the challenge is doubled.

Fisher (1978) stressed a concept which helps us avoid the negative aspects of dichotomizing or insisting on one approach as being superior. His careful delineation of PERSPECTIVES on human communication assisted our understanding of the roots and results of any given approach, in any attempt to overcome the difficulties we encounter in the face of numerous, complex category systems. In addition, Fisher was interested in avoiding the confrontations that result when we insist that one approach is BETTER than any other. This volume is an attempt to take further steps in those directions.

ISSUES AND QUESTIONS

A number of foundational issues related to the building and evaluation of theories have been discussed. As you go on, questions should arise as you critically look at the theories used for illustrative purposes, and the approaches taken by the chapters' authors. Hopefully, the following suggestions will get you started, though they are certainly not intended to indicate all of the possibilities for class discussions or your private evaluations. As you consider these questions remember that whenever the term "theorist" is used, it is intended to include also the authors of this volume.

To what extent have the theoreticians discussed in this volume clearly indicated their assumptions and presuppositions? Have they shown an understanding of the roles of their contemporary sociocultural environment, historically related events and their own human limitations in the process of building their theories? What specific ontological, epistemological and axiological assumptions can you identify which helped predetermine the approach taken by each theorist—and possibly even the outcome of his or her work? To what extent have the theorists discussed in this volume done more than describe, but have also succeeded in explaining, a phenomenon? What factors can you identify in communication theories which make more than a very limited contribution to the human search for knowledge and understanding? What would you consider to be "unique" contributions made by communication scholars? What "difference" do you believe the theories discussed here make to the overall future of human existence on our planet?

Obviously, some of the questions I posed are more easily answered than others. Some require a concern with values and philosophical issues which we do not commonly address in theory courses. But if one accepts the role of culture and society as a central part of all academic, scientific, philosophical, intellectual work than we need to dig deeper as we search for *why* as well as *how* and *what* answers.

Maybe some issues raised by the authors of this book will help you in dealing with specific challenges you face in the area of Communication. As I have stressed earlier, tools ought to be fashioned to fit specific tasks, and communication scholars have indeed indicated many specific opportunities for important theory building efforts. Olson clearly identifies the epistemological "mish-mash" in which Communication finds itself. Yet he sees us moving towards paradigm development. Here lies the greatest challenge we face as scholars. Ultimately, our field cannot claim a significant role in theory building until people come to the fore who have begun "to think about thinking in different ways." To help all of us think the "unthinkable" is undoubtedly the one challenge in theory building which will result in those consequences that Burke indicated by the title of his television series and book, "The Day the Universe Changed." What Olson is thinking of is, of course, a significant change from fact-gathering to real theorizing.

Anderson and Goodall are more specific in their concerns for altering the course of the future. They base their reactions on the belief that human experience is relevant to the practices of human sciences. In effect, their concern is not only with results but with the interwoven aspects of the human discovery process, which include those who participate in the process as well as methodologies. We cannot expect, at this point, that the issues they raise can be easily resolved. However, if we are willing to face the challenge and use the tools made available, doors will open or close that may determine much of the future direction of building theories related to humans communicating.

The list of very specific problems we face is as long as the list of subject matters on which scholars in the field are currently focusing. They include, but certainly are not limited to gender related issues, interpersonal interactions in dyads and intimate relationships, multiculturalism and intercultural relations, the role of culture in organizations and institutions, and the role of mass media in the lives of individuals. Fortner repeats the message you will find throughout this book, namely that there is no single map to understanding mediated, or any other communication. His conclusion encourages us to think less of the "unified" approach or the "one-theory" resolution to our imagined or real problems advocated by some. In effect, it appears unlikely that we will even agree to common assumptions about the issues which vex or challenge us. Ultimately then, our need is to decide whether the complexities we must deal with are bane or boon. The authors of the following chapters move us along that road as they apply the tools and concepts that are outlined here.

CONCLUSIONS

This chapter is intended to help you think about the process of theorizing, and to assist you in developing some basic insights into your own search for better understanding. I often ask my students at the beginning of a course on communication theory to touch the tips of their noses. They are usually confused, until I explain that if their nose is flat at the end, it is because they have been trained to act like seals. That is, they have caught so many balls tossed by their trainers that they have become well adapted to their demands. Seals do not ask *why* questions, they only need to know *how* routines.

We now face the reality that machines can perform routine tasks more quickly and more accurately than humans. Of what, then, should the human effort consist? Understanding basic principles, and relationships; attempting to answer *why*, as well as *how*, and *what* questions; and providing "ought we to do it" in addition to "can we do it" perspectives, are increasingly becoming our greatest challenges. This is especially true if we believe in the necessity for ethical or moral judgments. Part of that process needs to include perception of the larger framework, the total environment in which human knowledge and understanding develop. Another crucial aspect is our attempt to understand more about how we know what we know. The domains of ontology, epistemology, and axiology *all* constitute integral parts of our search. Science may be "value free," but scientists are not. "Doing" science cannot be value free because humans are engaged in scientific efforts. Nor should that be the case, as our recent experiences with atomic weapons and ecological devastation amply demonstrate.

How can theory building assist us in our efforts? Because this volume is intended for students, it seems only fitting to have one of my own students provide a list of factors summarizing her conclusions about theory building.

Theories:

- organize and summarize knowledge
- establish patterns or relationships
- help us focus on important variables
- help decide what to investigate
- help us to decide how to observe, clarify what is observed
- help us to predict effects and outcomes of research and
- help us understand the complexity of our world (Achcar, 1989).

This is a meaningful and impressive list. How well theories can do "their" job depends on those who construct them, what presuppositions they bring to their tasks, and how adequately they have prepared themselves to do their work. Since we are students of human communication processes, it should be stressed that fruitful theory building also depends on informed, well-prepared, engaged readers and listeners. Facilitating an understanding of the many aspects of building communication theories is the central purpose of this book.

As we strive to develop more meaningful, more applicable and more fruitful theories it is becoming increasingly evident that we need to challenge some of the basic assumptions which represented the very roots of our work in the past. Exactly what do we mean when we speak of communication as a process? That is an especially important question when one considers that more often than not we have attempted to *infer* process on the basis of results or observed outcomes.

In much of our past work we have not adequately considered the implications of the prefix co- in the word *co*mmunication. There can be little doubt that our theories are significantly impacted when we do *not* assume that meaning is a given, a kind of objective reality which simply exists in any given culture or society, and which can be used by communicators to achieve predetermined results.

Thinking of communicating as a process which leads us to *create* meaning, together, in some form of a dialogical interaction, changes many things. To play with words, I would indicate that the attempt to simply use an existing or assumed logic creates vastly different relations between human beings when we communicate, from those which result when we replace that assumption with a *dia*-logic—an interactive process to create mutually acceptable and useful meaning.

Similarly, what a difference it makes when we question the basic concepts we often have inherited or borrowed uncritically from the natural sciences. For example, for a communication scholar it may be quite beneficial to ask whether or not such concepts as control and prediction are really meaningful, useful or fruitful in building theories for the processes we study. Terms like *control* and *prediction* have an aura of dominance or domination about them, which have little or nothing to do with mutually created meaning. They indicate a feeling of certainty, related to manipulative devices or techniques, which challenge us to carefully consider the ethical or moral issues related to them. Such words, and the assumptions to which they relate, may encourage human beings in general and students of human communication in particular, to think of those who are skilled in their use as authorities not to be questioned or rejected.

As we consider the sociocultural foundations of theory-building in this book, we are asking you to question whether or not we should strive to merely justify belief in the supposedly expert ability of some human beings to exert a predictable influence over others, possibly even against their listener's or receiver's will. If one remembers the mischief such underlying assumptions have caused during many centuries of human history, it behooves us to reconsider what the purpose of our scholarly efforts *should* be, not merely what it can be.

REFERENCES

Achcar, N. (1989). *Graduate class assignment.* Pepperdine University.

Alderman, H. (1977). *Nietzsche's gift.* Columbus, OH: Ohio University Press.

Anderson, A. (1987). *Communication research: Issues and methods.* New York: McGraw-Hill.

Ajzen, I., & Fishbein, M. (1980). *Understanding attitudes and predicting behavior.* Englewood Cliffs, NJ: Prentice-Hall.

Barnlund, D. C. (1979). Communication: The context of change. In C. D. Mortenson (Ed.), *Basic readings in communication theory* (pp. 6–26). New York: Harper and Row.

Berger, C. R. (1977). The covering law perspective as a theoretical basis for the study of human communication. *Communication Quarterly, 25,* 7–18.

Berger, P., & Luckmann, T. (1967). *The social construction of reality.* Garden City, NY: Anchor.

Berlo, D. K. (1960). *The process of communication: An introduction to theory and practice.* New York: Holt, Rinehart and Winston.

Bertalanffy, von, L. (1968). *General systems theory: Foundations, development, applications.* New York: Braziller.

Bochner, A. (1985). Perspectives on inquiry: Representation, conversation and reflection. In M. Knapp & G. Miller (Eds.), *Handbook of interpersonal communication* (pp. 27–58). Newbury Park, CA: Sage.

Bronowski, J. (1977). *A sense of future: Essays in natural philosophy.* Cambridge, MA: The MIT Press.

Brown, H. I. (1987). *Observation and objectivity.* New York: Oxford University Press.

Bubner, R. (1988). *Essays in hermeneutics and critical theory.* New York: Columbia University Press.

Burke, J. (1985). *The day the universe changed.* Boston, MA: Little, Brown.

Burke, K. (1931). *Counter statement.* New York: Harcourt, Brace.

Burke, K. (1945). *A grammar of motives.* Englewood Cliffs, NJ: Prentice-Hall.

Burke, K. (1965). *Permanence and change: An anatomy of purpose.* Indianapolis, IN: Bobbs-Merrill Educational Publishing.

Catt, I. (1988). Im namen des pragmatismus oder philosophische reflexion ist keine untugend [In the name of pragmatism, or philosophical reflection is no vice] Kann man Kommunikation Lehren? *Sprache und Sprechen.* Frankfurt, Germany: Scriptor Press.

Cherwitz, R. A., & Hikins, J. W. (1986). *Communication and knowledge: An investigation of rhetorical epistemology.* Columbia: University of South Carolina Press.

Dance, F. E. X. (1970). The "concept" of communication. *Journal of Communication, 20,* 201–210.

Deetz, S. (1990). Reclaiming the subject matter as a guide to mutual understanding: Effectiveness and ethics in interpersonal interaction. *Communication Quarterly, 38,* 226–243.

Derrida, J. (1976). *Of Grammatology.* G. C. Spivak (Trans.). Baltimore, MD: Johns Hopkins Press.

Eco, U. (1976). *A theory of semiotics.* Bloomington: Indiana University Press.

Einstein, A. (1979). *Albert Einstein: The human side, new glimpses from his archives.* Selected and edited by H. Dukas & B. Hoffman. Princeton, NJ: Princeton University Press.

Ekman, P., & Friesen, W. (1969). The repertoire of nonverbal behavior: categories, origins, usage, and coding. *Semiotica, 1*(1), 49–98.

Ellenson, A. (1982). *Human relations.* Englewood Cliffs, NJ: Prentice-Hall.

Festinger, E. (1957). *A theory of cognitive dissonance.* Stanford, CA: Stanford University Press.

Fisher, B. A. (1978). *Perspectives on human communication.* New York: Macmillan.

Fisher, W. (1985). The narrative paradigm: An elaboration. *Communication Monographs, 52*(4), 347–365.

Fisher, W. (January 16, 1990). Personal communication.

Gadamer, H. G. (1988). On the circle of understanding. In E. K. Specht & W. Stegmuller (Eds.), *Hermeneutics versus Science?* (pp. 68–78). Notre Dame, IN: University of Notre Dame Press.

Gleick, J. (1987). *Chaos.* New York: Penguin Books.

Giddens, A. (1979). *Central problems in social theory: Action, structure and contradiction in social analysis.* Berkeley: University of California Press.

Giddens, A. (1983). *Profiles and critiques in social theory.* Berkeley: University of California Press.

Goffman, E. (1974). *Frame analysis: An essay on the organization of experience.* Cambridge, MA: Harvard University Press.

Greene, J. O. (1984). A cognitive approach to human communication: An action assembly theory. *Communication Monographs, 51,* 289–306.

Gumpert, G., & Cathcart, R. (1986). *Inter/Media.* New York: Oxford University Press.

Harre, R., & Secord, P. (1972). *The explanation of social behavior.* Cambridge, MA: Harvard University Press.

Hawking, S. W. (1988). *A brief history of time: From the big bang to black holes.* New York: Bantam.

Heisenberg, W. (1979). *Philosophical problems of quantum physics.* Woodbridge, CT: Ox Bow Press.

Hempel, C. G. (1949). The logical analysis of psychology. In H. Feigle & W. Sellars (Eds.), *Readings in philosophical analysis* (pp. 373–384). New York: Appleton-Century-Crofts.

Jaki, S. L. (1978). *The road of science and the ways of God.* Chicago, IL: University of Chicago Press.

James, W. (1948). The Sentiment of rationality. In *Essays in pragmatism* (pp. 3–36). New York: Hafner.

Kaplan, A. (1964). *The conduct of inquiry: Methodology for behavioral science.* San Francisco, CA: Chandler.

Kuhn, T. S. (1970). *The structure of scientific revolutions.* Chicago, IL: University of Chicago Press.

Lakoff, G., & Johnson, M. (1980). *Metaphors we live by.* Chicago, IL: University of Chicago Press.

Lanigan, R. (1982). Semiotic phenomenology: A theory of human communication praxis. *Journal of Applied Communication Research, 10,* 62–73.

LeShan, L., & Margenau, H. (1982). *Einstein's space and Van Gogh's sky: physical reality and beyond.* New York: Macmillan.

Littlejohn, S. W. (1985). *Theories of human communication* (2nd ed.). Belmont, CA: Wadsworth Publishing Company.

Littlejohn, S. W. (1989). *Theories of human communication* (3rd ed.). Belmont, CA: Wadsworth Publishing Company.

Margolis, J. (1973). *Knowledge and existence.* New York: Oxford University Press.

McCombs, M. E., & Becker, L. B. (1979). *Using mass communication theory.* Englewood Cliffs, NJ: Prentice-Hall.

Mead, G. H. (1934). *Mind, self, and society.* Chicago, IL: Chicago University Press.

Meehan, M. J. (1969). *Value judgment and social science: Structures and processes.* Homewood, IL: Dorsey Press.

Merleau-Ponty, M. (1974). *The phenomenology of perception* (C. Smith, Trans.). London, England: Routledge & Kegan.

Morgan, G. (1980). Paradigms, metaphors and puzzle solving in organizational theory. *Administrative Science Quarterly, 25,* 605–621.

Nagel, E. (1979). *The structure of science.* Indianapolis, IN: Hackett Publishing Company.

Newcomb, T. (1961). *The acquaintance process.* New York: Holt, Rinehart & Winston.

Nietzsche, F. (1957). Beyond good and evil. In J. W. Robbins, *Answer to Ayn Rand* (p. 3). Washington, DC: Mt. Vernon Publishing Company.

Ortony, A. (1979). *Metaphor and thought.* Cambridge, MA: Cambridge University Press.

Pearce, W. B., & Cronen, V. (1980). *Communication action and meaning.* New York: Praeger Publishers.

Pelletier, K. R. (1978). *Toward a science of consciousness.* New York: Delacorte Press.

Perelman, C. (1963). *The idea of justice and the problem of argument.* New York: Humanities Press.

Perelman, C. (1988). *The realm of rhetoric.* Notre Dame, IN: University of Notre Dame Press.

Piaget, J. (1971). *Biology and knowledge.* Chicago, IL: University of Chicago Press.

Pierce, J. R. (1980). *An introduction to information theory: Symbols, signals, and noise.* New York: Dover.

Popper, K. (1981). Science, pseudo-science, and falsifiability. In R. D. Tweney, M. E. Doherty, & C. R. Mynatt (Eds.), *On scientific thinking* (pp. 92–99). New York: Columbia University Press.

Popper, K. R. (1982). *The open universe, an argument for indeterminism.* Totowa, NJ: Rowman and Littlefield.

Popper, K. R. (1983). *Realism and the aim of science.* Totowa, NJ: Rowman and Littlefield.

Pryor, R. (1981). On the method of critical theory and its implications for a critical theory of communication. In S. Deetz (Ed.), *Phenomenology in rhetoric and communication* (pp. 25–35). Washington, DC: Center for Advanced Research in Phenomenology & University Press of America.

Reardon, K. K. (1981). *Persuasion: Theory and context.* Newbury Park, CA: Sage Publications.

Reardon, K. K., & Rogers, E. M. (1988). Interpersonal versus mass media communication: A false dichotomy. *Human Communication Research, 15*(2), 284–303.

Rifkin, J. (1987). *Time wars: The primary conflict in human history.* New York: Simon and Schuster.

Sapir, E. (1921). *Language: An introduction to the study of speech.* New York: Harcourt, Brace & World.

Schefflen, A. E. (1974). *How behavior means.* Garden City, NY: Doubleday.

Scheffler, S. (1982). *The rejection of consequentialism.* Oxford: Clarendon Press.

Shibles, W. A. (1972). *Metaphor-addresses, essays, lectures.* Madison, WI: Language Press.

Skinner, B. F. (1957). *Verbal behavior.* New York: Appleton-Century-Crofts.

Toulmin, S. (1961). *Foresight and understanding.* New York: Harper & Row.

van Dijk, T. A. (1980). *Macrostructures: An interdisciplinary study of global structures in discourse, interaction, and cognition.* Hillsdale, NJ: Lawrence Erlbaum Associates.

Veatch, H. (1974). *Aristotle.* Bloomington, IN: Indiana University Press.

Weaver, W. (1962). Science and people. In P. C. S. Obler & H. A. Estrin (Eds.), *The new scientist* (pp. 95–111). Garden City, NY: Doubleday.

Weick, K. (1969). *The social psychology of organizing*. Reading, MA: Addison Wesley.

Weizsacker, C. (1980). *The unity of nature*. New York: Farrar, Straus, Giroux.

Whitten, K. W., Gailey, K. D., & Davis, R. E. (1987). *General chemistry* (3rd ed.). Philadelphia, PA: Saunders College Publishing.

Whorf, B. (1965). *Language, thought and reality*. New York: Wiley.

Wittgenstein, L. (1953). *Philosophical investigations*. Oxford, England: Basil Blackwell.

Wittgenstein, L. (1958). *Philosophical investigations*. Oxford, England: Basil Blackwell.

Woelfel, J., & Fink, E. L. (1980). *The measurement of communication processes*. Orlando, FL: Academic Press.

Wood, N. (1983). *The politics of Locke's philosophy: A social study of "an essay concerning human understanding."* Berkeley, CA: University of California Press.

APPENDIX: THE ROMANTIC OR IDEALISTIC VERSUS THE REALISTIC OR EMPIRICAL FRAMES OF REFERENCE

Stewart Hudson
Pepperdine University

> *Every man is born either a Platonist or an Aristotelian.*
> —A. W. Schlegel (1867, p. 194)

The starting point for these differing world views is their differing epistemologies—that is, in their opposing theories of knowledge. The Idealists (Platonists) and Empiricists (Aristotelians) are in fundamental disagreement about the origin, nature, methods of obtaining, and limits of human knowledge. They differ in their answers to the age-old questions: What is truth? How do you find and verify it? Innumerable variations and even overlaps between the two categories are historically available. However, a hunger for unity, wholeness, and ultimate meaning in a chaotic universe is the mark of a Platonist, whether in Kant, in Bergson's vitalism, or Husserl's phenomenology, or even in Herbert Spencer's purportedly empirical evolutionary organicism. Pure empiricism, on the other hand, accepts lack of ultimate or transcendental meaning and even may come to rejoice in subjectivity, relativity, and disconnected individualism. The following chart traces the preconceptions of each major worldview in its purer forms. Here are some typical figures in each camp:

Idealistic (Philosophy—Plato, Hegel, Bergson)	*Empirical* (Philosophy—Aristotle, Locke)
Romantic (Literature—Blake, Coleridge, Thoreau)	*Realistic/Naturalistic* (Literature—Zola, Dreiser)
Organic Systems (Communication—Bertalanffy, R. Weaver)	*Behavioral* (Psychology/Communication—Skinner, C. Osgood)

Platonic	*Aristotelian*
1. Means of discovery of truth or an inner essence through an innate "sixth sense," whether called intuition, conscience, the illative sense (Cardinal Newman), phenomenological reductionism, or even common sense.	1. Truth discovered only through the physical "five senses" with the sensory perceiving mechanisms which allow us to experience the physical world. No sixth sense.
2. Where is highest truth located? In inner core of universe or in mind of God, the master planner. The physical universe we see is merely a dim copy of the master plan in its classical version (Plato).	2. In the physical realm only. "...where truth is—in a well." (Byron—Don Juan)
3. Thus, there is ultimate order, meaning, and design in Nature.	3. Nature is characterized by disorder, evil, and anomalous suffering as much as by benevolence and design. If there is a God, we must conclude he is a cross-eyed carpenter (Hume).
4. So, truth is absolute and *a priori*. The ontological argument is valid, as is the argument from first causes. That is, we can see the designer in the design, say some Platonists—though Newman denies.	4. Truth is relative and subjective, depending on the individual and his particular receiving equipment. You can assume very little or take no truths for granted (that is, you can't assume something true *a priori*— except that happiness is the aim of life— Epicurus, Bentham, Mill). (Thus, Bentham's skeptical method.) The classic example of the unreliability of individual perceptions of truth is Sextus Empiricus' bent stick in the running brook (EMPIRICISM).
5. Thus, individual conduct is judged by absolutes, by "givens." Conscience can be trusted.	5. The proper ethical decision must, therefore, be the result of balancing out competing demands or needs. Ethical truth is relative. You must decide each situation on its individual merits. Individual self-interest or happiness as only remaining absolute becomes the basis of modern economics (Adam Smith), behavioral psychology (Skinner) and evolutionary biology (Darwin).

(Continued)

Platonic	Aristotelian
6. There are superior individuals—Carlyle's heroes—who have a unique insight into the higher order and meaning of life beyond the mere external physical. They have a special relationship to external truth through the superiority of their special "sixth sense"—thus Shakespeare, Cromwell, Fredrick the Great, said Carlyle.	6. There is no special sense or relationship to truth. The common experience of mankind, while by no means a safe guide, is closer to the truth. Your heroes are often tyrants. Egalitarian, anti-totalitarian and anti-aristocratic in the main. Truth is available on approximately equal terms to all men.
7. The ultimate order and meaning of life is available more through the heart—through emotions and desires—than through mere intellect and cold scientific analysis. (You can't tell what an eagle is by measuring his eye or the height of his flight—Blake.)	7. The intellect of man is indeed unreliable, and when the judgment is distorted by emotions and desires, you have little chance to judge correctly. The head over the heart. (Thus Bentham's famous belief that pushpin is as good as poetry, and Macaulay's distrust of poetry as something of an archaic exercise.) Furthermore, the more abstract qualities—the primary qualities of Descartes and Galileo—are more reliable than the more concrete, or secondary qualities, which are intertwined with the emotional associations of the senses (colors, etc.). That is, the qualities which are scientifically measurable with the least interdiction of the fallible individual perceiving mechanism are the most reliable. Recently, the primary qualities have all but disappeared in a continuing movement toward subjectivity (relativity and quantum mechanics).
8. The characteristic medium of expression is poetry—thus the Romantic Movement's eminence. Poetry allows free reign to brilliant images and emotions. Poetry's rapturous, intuitive insight into the heart of the universe is necessarily moral since it connects us with eternal truth. Shelley was entirely serious, then, when he called poets the unacknowledged legislators of the world (and M. Arnold conceived of poetry in much the same way).	8. The novel is the characteristic Realistic mode of expression, allowing as it does a close analysis of motivations. The novel characteristically shows how people lie to themselves as their desires and emotions distort reality. So the ironic psychological penetration of Jane Austen and Henry James' preoccupation with showing the extreme difficulty in accurately perceiving the true nature of a situation, a personality, or a relationship. Ian Watt's *The Rise of the Novel* indicates that the novel form could only have risen where the ground was prepared by the fertilization of the empirical philosophy.

(Continued)

Platonic	*Aristotelian*
9. There is, in every Romantic, a rage for order, for unity, for symmetry and balanced wholeness. Romantics are monists—they see all reality as an integral oneness, not a dualism. So they usually have trouble in accounting for evil in this interconnected oneness.	9. Such an inner order beyond the physical is a pipe dream, and the physical realm is a mess. What we have to do is to rationally reorder this chaos with empirical procedures, verification of experience, and scientific experiment.
10. The Idealist sometimes sees the inner balance of the universe mirrored in such symbols of unity, harmony, and balance as the circle, the eye, the pyramid, the swastika, and numbers like $4 (2 \times 2 = 4)$. (Look at your dollar bill.) Thus, Jung's "Romantic" psychology searches for innate universal symbols of harmony.	10. Harmony is indeed aesthetically pleasing, but it is a mere physical thing, not mirroring any inner reality (Addison and Steele).
11. The Platonist or Romantic operates more deductively than inductively. He operates from *a priori*, given truths.	11. Theoretically, the empirical mind operates inductively, starting its examination without presuppositions, superstitions, and traditions. (As Bacon recommended in denouncing the idols of the cave, marketplace, etc.)
12. The Romantic doesn't see human history as necessarily progressive. Indeed, the Romantic longs for former, more orderly times, for a noble savage, for the golden age, or the Middle Ages before corruption and a polluted society (Rousseau, Carlyle). This is because eternal, unchanging truth was available from the first to the innate sense of those who would turn inward, and, indeed, civilization has dulled our natural, spontaneous insight into it (which the child come straight from the eternal abode still remembers, says Plato and Wordsworth in "Intimations of Immortality"). In the twentieth century Margaret Mead believes she finds the noble savage in Samoa, and a nature uncorrupted by technology becomes a goal of mass ecological movements.	12. The Aristotelian mind, in this modern form, believes in steady human progress, built upon the accumulation of physical knowledge, rather than the unique insights of genius. Indeed, as Mill argues, the noble savage never existed. He is always filthy and a born liar. Hobbes had called life of men in nature "solitary, poor, nasty, brutish of those who would turn inward, and short." Even the Greeks of the Periclean Age would appear only morally rudimentary creatures to our age, and the ancient Greek scientists would be infants compared to any current high school science student. Man's mission is to tame, transform, and use nature for mankind's benefit through science.

(Continued)

Platonic	*Aristotelian*
13. The characteristic continental philosophy is Idealism or Romanticism. Kant, Schelling, Hegel, are their great names.	13. The most characteristic Anglo-Saxon philosophy is Empiricism. Our great names are Locke, Hume, Newton. Benjamin Franklin is perhaps the most characteristic American figure.
14. In politics, tended toward oligarchy and collectivism, communism, and aristocracy: Plato's *Republic*, Rousseau's doctrine of general will, Hegel's justification of monarchy and, in a materialistic, monist form, Marx's communism.	14. In politics, tended toward democracy because of distrust of claims of absolute truth by superior individual with special insight into that supposed truth. Belief in compromise and balance of opposing interests of society—minority vs. majority and individual vs. community rights (Locke and J. S. Mill).
15. In the current democratic political context, generally "conservative" and anti-revolutionary, agreeing with Edmund Burke that custom and old prescriptions are necessary to keep society from chaos. There may be equality before law and before God, but not necessarily so in social and biological reality (R. Weaver).	15. In current politics usually "liberal." Teaches absolute tolerance since men shaped almost entirely by social environment, not innate qualities or absolute standards of truth other than man's inalienable right to happiness. Thus often favors rapid change in society and radical egalitarianism.
16. Aspects of the Platonic frame of mind are represented in modern communication theory by Richard Weaver's hierarchical absolutism, in the phenomenologists' modified sixth sense, and in Kenneth Burke's secular systems approach.	16. The symbolic interactionists, existentialists, critical theorists, and deconstructions represent a progressively more subjective and relative view of reality. In deconstructionism even the Self disappears, leaving only the subjective text (symbols), and Foucault denies any objective standard for incarcerating the insane or criminal.

REFERENCES

Schlegel, A. W. (1867). Quoted in G. H. Lewes, *The history of philosophy* (Vol. I, p. 194). London: Longmans, Green.

Part II

Building Theory:
The Role of Assumptions

How our theorizing is impacted by the settings in which we learn and work is an important consideration if the roots of theory building and not merely its branches are to be understood. The intellectual history of the West or North spans many centuries. During that time a plethora of seemingly conflicting assumptions and ideas have vied for students' and scholars' attention and loyalty. I say "seemingly," because it is significant that such conflicts always evolve and are experienced within a specific social and cultural setting which predetermines their foci, limits, and specific rules for working out solutions.

As previously indicated, such conflicts are similar to the ones addressed by Plato and Aristotle many centuries ago, as far as their espistemologial and ontological bases are concerned. Even value, ethical, axiological arguments have changed little; the subject matter may be different, but the rules and the forms of reasoning used have changed very little. A certain humility is required of scholars. We need to both recognize and acknowledge the debt we owe to those who have preceded us. More importantly, unless we are able to fully appreciate the grand sweep of human history as it relates to the search for understanding, what we undertake tends to prove irrelevant to the future development of humankind.

Such concerns undergird the next two chapters. The age old conflict between science and humanism certainly lends itself well to Scott Olson's discussion of the "renewed" alchemism we are experiencing. More than a simple description of a well-known clash between conceptual assumptions, Olson critically examines the implications of that ongoing struggle for theories about humans who communicate. Anderson and Goodall pick up another, closely related thread in this complex tapestry, when they discuss a more specific attempt to address conceptual problems and confrontations through the development of theoretical and research processes based on the social unit, individual action, and actual practices of members in a given lifeworld. At that point we are led to consider the significant roles culture and society play in all that is discussed throughout this book.

There is no attempt made here to comprehensively survey all aspects of these centuries-old conceptual battles. Rather, the emphasis is on how that process evolves, and what we may expect the results to be when we bring different assumptions about human beings, their environments, and some absolute to our sense-making efforts.

Chapter 2

Renewed Alchemy:
Science and Humanism in
Communication Epistemology

Scott R. Olson
Central Connecticut State University

> *In America the purely practical part of science is admirably understood . . .*
> *but hardly anyone in the United States devotes himself to the essentially*
> *theoretical and abstract portion of human knowledge . . . Nothing is more*
> *necessary to the culture of the higher sciences or of the more elevated*
> *departments of science than meditation; and nothing is less suited to*
> *meditation than the structure of democratic society.*
> —Alexis de Tocqueville (1945, p. 43)

> *All understanding is interpretation.*
> —Hans Georg Gadamer (1975, p. 349)

Medieval alchemists used an approach that was both scientific and humanistic
in their quest to turn lead into gold, a process which they believed meant
perfecting or "healing" the lead. On the one hand, they were dealing with the
elements and constituents of nature, but their method was mystical, exegetic, and
interpretive rather than methodical, empirical, and analytical. Their failure led to
the establishment of a more rigorous scientific method, and with it, the genesis
of modern science, but also to a bifurcation of conceptualization of the world,
in a sense, to a new ontology. Renewed interest in atomism during the Renaissance
accelerated the process, so that contemporary theorists find a huge chasm between
the two. In the *fin de siècle* of the 20th Century, however, there are new
alchemists, epistemological alchemists, who seek to reunite the disparate modes
of thought. Their motivation is not to resume a quixotic journey to transform
base metals into precious ones; rather, it is an epistemological journey to trans-

form Communication[1] from a *bricolage* discipline, one cobbled together from this-and-that, into a coherent field of inquiry.

Scientists and humanists seldom see eye-to-eye, and many consider scientific approaches to communication as the more essentially American. Tocqueville professed the fundamentally practical nature of inquiry in the United States in 1835, and his observations still seem apt. Practical approaches are widely praised in American Communication theory (Craig, 1989), and many scientific researchers consider rhetorical research superfluous. Indeed, a founder of the field, Lazarsfeld (1972), stressed the administrative, utilitarian nature of communication research. The humanist Communication tradition certainly has deeper roots in Europe, but its significance in North America is growing. European schools of thought on communication tend to be more interpretive than analytical. The gap between the two schools seems as wide as the Atlantic Ocean. In Communication theory, a distinction between science and humanism has been as much a product of conceptualizations of the researcher as it is a product of any intrinsic properties in the world they observe; cultural differences lead to ontological differences.

This chapter examines the central epistemological issues related to scientific and humanistic theorizing about communication. It discusses the foundational epistemological problems of dichotomizing communication, paradigming communication, intersubjectifying communication, and tracking the evolution of communication theory. It also examines seven Communication theories that exemplify these problems. Whether science, humanism, or a mix of the two best get the gold out of the lead is a product of the ontological assumptions of the alchemist.

EPISTEMOLOGICAL PROBLEMS

Four foundational epistemological problems confront the student comparing theories of Communication science and humanism. The first concerns defining science and humanism, constructing a meaningful dichotomy which distinguishes between the two—what is the difference between them? A second problem concerns the application of meta-epistemological concepts to communication as a means toward understanding its underlying structure, particularly the applicability of the scientific concept of paradigm to a social science or humanist discipline— does Communication have a paradigm? A third epistemological problem evolves out of a potential bridge between science and humanism: Intersubjectivity—is it a way of linking the objective with the subjective? A fourth problem concerns how the student conceptualizes the movement or evolution of epistemological concepts in Communication science and humanism—are they growing together, apart, or in some parallel direction?

---

[1]Communication will be capitalized when referred to as a discipline.

Defining Science and Humanism

Perhaps the most challenging epistemological question concerns the most basic ontological assumptions of the nature of our relationship to the world around us. How do we know about the world and our experience of it? Is consciousness a split between mind and world (Husserl, 1975), or a continuum? Scientism and humanism have historically different and contrasting responses, as Casmir points out in Chapter 1. To divide science from humanism is itself a difficult epistemological trick worthy of an alchemist, and distinctions have been drawn in many ways. The extent to which they are distinct is itself a product of human values and assumptions. There is, in fact, a "dominant dichotomy" between science and humanism that affects most thinking about the field, but also "alternative dichotomies," which look at the differences differently.

Dominant Dichotomy—Science

One product of the 18th Century Enlightenment was the application of scientific inquiry to disciplines not associated with the physical world, resulting in a science of politics, of mind, of society. Psychology and Sociology are behavioral sciences, and it is from them that Communication borrows many of its methods and theories. Medical science has also affected Communication through the speech sciences of pathology and disorder.

Communication science emerged as a separate field of study from pioneering work in the social sciences. Rogers (1989) placed its origins in the political science of Lasswell, the sociology of Lazarsfeld, and the psychology of Lewin and Hovland, but others were also significant. Communication science looks for knowledge by applying a consistent, reproducible process. Commonly, this process is empirical, which is to say it involves converting observation to data, and placing the data in coherent structures (e.g., charts, tables, graphs). Much Communication science looks at external behavior indicators as manifestations of meaning and intention in the way an astronomer would look at the motion of planets. In its most extreme form, Communication science is positivistic, which is to say that it seeks an "exact and objective knowledge of another mind, as though it were an object in the world" (Divver, 1987, p. 68). This approach is central to the "dominant paradigm" to which Hall (1989) and others of the critical school objected and creates an appearance of naturalism which passes for the real thing. Whether such naive positivism is still widely practiced is debatable, contrary to the contentions of Berger (1989) and others.

I call the traditional, historical model of science Newtonian science after Isaac Newton, a pioneer in the use of this scientific method. Newtonian scientific research and analysis has been assessed based on several essential attributes: reproducibility, objectivity, patterns, and empiricism.

Reproducibility.   First, the results of scientific inquiry are supposed to be reproducible. In other words, if one scientist finds that a certain experiment produces a certain result, when another scientist conducts that experiment the results ought to be the same. This is the most essential attribute of the scientific method, because if the second experiment yields different results, the scientists have not actually isolated and understood the phenomenon in question. Ideally, the community of scientists agrees on the design and results of an experiment. This necessitates two types of scientists: research scientists, who design and conduct experiments; and theoretical scientists, who explain what the results of the research mean and predict the results of future experiments. Ordinarily, experiment and observation precede theory, although this is not always true—some of Einstein's theories and predictions, impossible to verify in his time due to technological limitations, are only now being confirmed or refuted.

Objectivity.   A second historical attribute of scientific inquiry is objectivity. Ideally, the phenomenon observed by the scientist is not affected by his or her observation; similarly, the observational faculties (and in theory the judgment) of the scientist is not affected by any subjective factors—his or her consciousness does not affect the results. Krippendorf (1989) said this attribute is based on a view of the world as independent to the act of observation and that observers should not enter the domain they observe. Einstein, for example, never stopped believing in "a world in itself" governed by laws it was his job to discover (Merleau-Ponty, 1964). By assuming that observation can be objective, Newtonian science assumes that the cosmos is observable and consistent and that it is governed by immutable laws which can be deduced and comprehended through that process of observation. Further, this science assumes that the universe has a concrete reality which is distinct from observation—that, in a sense, the universe is there whether we observe it or not, that the unobserved tree makes a sound when it crashes. Because the universe is objectifiable, observation of it and the conclusions which proceed from them are mutual and universal, not subject to culture.

Scientific communication, then, is acultural when perfectly objective. A powerful symbol of how communication is conceptualized by Newtonian scientists is the plaque on the Voyager II spacecraft (Sagan, 1979). The sounds and scientific/mathematical etchings on the disc attached to the side of the craft assume that the "objective" concepts of the natural universe it displays will be comprehensible to its intended extraterrestrial audience, ignoring the manner of representing this information through human signs and symbols. It was assumed by Carl Sagan and the other designers that the sheer objectifiability of the subject matter will overcome its mere signification.[2]

---

[2]Ironically, Captain Kirk and his starship crew discover in *Star Trek: The Motion Picture* that the Voyager information was not so objective as humans had once thought: an alien creature named V'ger (short for "voyager") horribly misinterprets the message as a request to disinfect the Earth of its human "contaminants."

Patterns. A third attribute of Newtonian science is a reliance on patterns rather than aberrations. A familiar credo in medical schools is "when you hear hoof-beats, don't look for zebras"—an admonition reminding the student that the common is more likely than the obscure. As Kuhn (1970) noted, "Normal science . . . often suppresses fundamental novelties because they are necessarily subversive to its basic commitments" (p. 5). Science generalizes.

Empiricism. Empiricism is the most easily identifiable attribute of Communication science. It is empirical because it builds through experience and observation and concentrates on behaviors, since they are the aspect of human existence most easily objectified. According to Bochner (1985), through discovering general relationships between various phenomena, empiricism attempts to explain and predict them. Kuhn stated that normal science has three modes of empirical inquiry: "determination of significant fact, matching of facts with theory, and articulation of theory" (p. 34).

The danger of empiricism according to Giddens (1989) is that it can be mindless, a mere accumulation of incoherent and unrelated data which obfuscates rather than clarifies. Much of the empirical work in Communication remains what Kuhn (1970) called "mere facts, unrelated and unrelatable to the continuing progress of . . . research" (p. 35). And yet empiricism has been the dominant activity of many, even most, Communication scientists. This is further proof of the nascency of Communication theory: As Krippendorf (1989) quoted Einstein, "the more primitive the status of science is the more readily can the scientist live under the illusion that he is a pure empiricist" (p. 78).

Dominant Dichotomy—Humanism

Communication humanism is more difficult to describe in terms of particular methods or conceptualizations; it exists to some extent as a Derridean (1976) erasure of science. Among the prominent Communication theorists who take a humanist position are Burke, Wittgenstein, the phenomenologists, hermeneuticists, and literary theorists. The traditional, historical model of humanism has been assessed based on attributes which contrast with those of science: irreproducibility instead of reproducibility, subjectivity instead of objectivity, evaluation instead of patterns, and interpretation rather than empiricism.

Irreproducibility. Irreproducibility means that the conclusions one humanist scholar derives from his or her analysis will not and should not be the same as those derived by another. This is necessarily so because each text or phenomenon is subject to many possible understandings, whereas in Newtonian natural science there is perceived to be a single, correct meaning. This is not to say that all readings are equal or that there are an infinite number of readings.[3] The concept

---

[3]This argument has been made on occasion, however, particularly by deconstructionists—see discussion by Eco (1976) and Olson (1990).

of "preferred readings" and Hall's (Fiske, 1989) theory of double articulation limit and focus the number of readings without making the results "reproducible." While multiple reading is inevitable in a humanistic approach, it is also desirable. Knowledge is conceptualized not so much as the uncovering of hidden truths (as it often is in science) but as J. S. Mill's (1973) marketplace of ideas played out in a Hegelian framework—new interpretations replace old, the process generating more sophisticated and appropriate levels of understanding.

One reason why Communication humanism is often irreproducible is that there is no accepted, single method of study; many humanist studies seem to have no method whatsoever. Humanist Communication generally effaces method with findings. The methods it does use may be borrowed from philosophy or literary and art criticism traditions.

Subjectivity. It is the scholar's subjectivity, eschewed in the Newtonian scientific method, that humanism prizes. Here, the world is not so much a physical reality unto itself, but a continuity with human consciousness. As Husserl (1975) noted, consciousness (*noesis*) and the world (*noema*) cannot be split; objects are not so much things in themselves but the product of "knowledge and perception" (Rapaport, 1987). Indeed, whatever meaning exists is constituted by the subject (Merleau-Ponty, 1964).

Taken to its philosophical extreme, humanism can be said to assume that phenomena are dependent on observation, and that without it they do not exist (or that it is meaningless to speak of their existence). So whereas Newtonian science considers a universe of laws and axioms whose existence is independent of human existence, of immutable physical properties that were there before we observed them and will continue to be there after, humanism makes humanity the center of the universe, and considers laws and axioms only insofar as they relate to human experience. At its most rudimentary level, humanism proceeds from Descartes' *cogito*; in its more extreme manifestations, it yields the solipsism of Montaigne and Berkeley.

Subjectivism is not necessarily central to the humanist approach to communication. Phenomenology, established by Husserl, while generally humanistic in subject matter and approach, attempted to remove the subjective element through reduction of external forces and concentration on the object itself, one's own consciousness revealing its true nature. Heidegger resisted attempts to objectify the study of humanist subject matter; in his view, it alienates the observer from the observed and removes the possibility for dialogue.

Evaluation. Another attribute of Communication humanism is evaluation, the putting of value into the thing or phenomenon observed. That is to say, Communication humanism, in many of its incarnations, engages in a process of deciding the worth or value of a text, a speech, an action. Communication science would not and could not have this as a goal, at least not overtly. The study of public address is a good example of the evaluative aspect of humanism: Parrish (1954), for example, evaluated public address in terms of its effectiveness; McBurney and Wrage (1953) evaluated in terms of artistic merit. Humanism focuses on what is unique and original in human endeavor and our observation of it, and values the differences in observation created by humanist critics and scholars. If science generalizes, humanism particularizes. A study of the French revolution, a romantic poem, a cubist painting, or television inevitably chooses what is worth discussing and what is not, whether or not it constructs a manifest hierarchy.

Interpretation.   Humanist Communication is inductive rather than deductive: it builds through interpretation and exegesis and concentrates on texts, since they have the potential to yield a multitude of meanings and readings. This contrasts with the approach of dominant Newtonian science, which assumes that there are physical truths awaiting exposition. Schleiermacher (1978), the founder of general hermeneutics, described hermeneutic interpretation as an art which relates discourse to understanding. Ricouer (1976) felt that interpretation was necessary because words are polysemic—they can be understood in many ways (as opposed to physical laws, which presumably have a single legitimate meaning). Gadamer (1975) asserted that to understand is to interpret, arguing in essence that all reading is an act of translation, an approach consistent with Harold Bloom's (1980) concept of *misprision*—a conception wherein all texts are considered to be "misread."

The dominant dichotomy which contrasts the reproducibility, objectivity, patterning, and empiricism of science with the irreproducibility, subjectivity, evaluation, and interpretation of humanism is not the only way to define and divide the two. Dissident and alternative dichotomies see other aspects of research and scholarship as more significant.

Alternative Dichotomies

A shift in epistemological assumptions has moved these "traditional" views of Newtonian science and subjective humanism, blurring them and the dichotomy they imply. Perhaps because Communication is by nature a *bricolage* discipline (Olson, 1989), the assumptions and approaches of scientism and humanism are nowhere more closely examined and debated. Alternatives to the "dominant dichotomy" result, some from variations on the dominant dichotomy, others from a critical perspective, and others seeing no dichotomy at all.

Variations.   In some alternate dichotomies, particular aspects of the dominant dichotomy disappear. Humanism is not necessarily amethodical. Wittgenstein revealed another aspect of humanism, communication as a system in itself. In *Philosophical Investigations*, Wittgenstein (1953) dismantled language and begins to approach it from the bottom up, giving rise to rules theory. Craig (1989) chose to focus not on the methodology of the approach but rather on its effect and regards both Communication science and humanism to be fundamentally practical; he distinguishes between the empiricist, hermeneutic, and critical approaches to practicality. E. D. Hirsch (Divver, 1987), Northrop Frye (1957), and others believed that science could be brought to humanism through specific textual meanings which are objective, determinate, and reproducible. Frye, in fact, elaborated this into a generic theory of literature which has had a profound impact on the study of popular culture.

Critical Dichotomies. The different ways in which the dichotomy is expressed by Communication scholars adds insight into how fundamental it is to their thinking. Habermas (1972) chose to distinguish between technical, practical, and emancipatory aspects of knowledge—the technical, a manifestation of empirical scientific approaches; the practical, a product of historical and rhetorical approaches; the emancipatory, a result of critical approaches.[4] Hall (1989) avoided the scientism/humanism dichotomy by stressing the dichotomy between critical science/humanism and the "dominant" approach of the field, by which he means traditional Newtonian science and individual-centered humanism. He cited "entrenched individualism" as the attribute of the dominant paradigm most resistant to progress in the field and objected to its reduction of matters concerned with signs and meaning to behavioral empiricism.

Hermeneutics distinguishes science from humanism more on the basis of the purpose it serves rather the position of the scholar to the material. Hirsch, in fact, argues that activities traditionally conceived of as humanist, such as literary analysis, should be as objective, determinate, and reproducible as science. This results in a dichotomy between understanding and explanation (Divver, 1987):

> objectivism need objects to study . . . the study of human activities and works involves the study of meaning and requires 'understanding' rather than explanation. The human sciences address themselves to the problem of understanding other people, which requires an approach distinct from the scientific investigation of the physical world. Thus, the hermeneutic theory of understanding need not situate itself within the epistemological and methodological contexts of either rationalist or positivist method. (p. 61)

A different dichotomy is drawn when one considers the teleological dichotomy within science and humanism: science distinguishes between fact and nonfact, between "truth" and "falsehood," whereas humanism distinguishes between fact and fiction, an act of interpretation which distinguishes literal truths from figurative truths.

---

[4]Critical theory in a sense straddles science and humanism. It makes use of methods from both and is perhaps best distinguished from them by its oppositional stance to "dominant" ways of knowledge.

No Dichotomy. Another alternative approach is to argue that there is no dichotomy at all—that one of these approaches subsumes the other, or that they are two manifestations of the same thing. For example, rhetoric absorbs and encompasses science according to Reiss (1982), who argued logic and reason are syntactical and semiotic. Therefore, the objectification of the natural world by scientists is only a form of discourse, subject to rhetorical criticism. This conception argues that whatever distinctions appear in our understanding of the world are extrinsic to it; that intrinsic distinctions do not exist. The possibility of merging the two, of a unified theory of communication, has become more attractive recently, although it remains elusive.

Marginal Theories. Some Communication theories defy all the dichotomies of science and humanism. Functionalism as described by Thomas (1989) uses Comte's biological and social scientific parameters to examine culture as a functioning whole, applying both scientific and humanistic approaches to an (ordinarily) humanistic topic. The structuralism of Levi-Strauss (1967) and other cultural anthropologists also attempted to systematize the study of culture; Todorov's (1975) study of literary genres was one such attempt to bring method and reproducibility to that most humanist of pursuits, literary criticism. Semiotics, which began as a method of speech science by Saussure (1960), as developed by Eco (1976) attempted to further systematize the understanding of culture at the level of signs using a fairly rigorous and scientific method.[5] Whether or not Marxist approaches exist on the margin between science and humanism is debatable. Marx and Engels certainly considered their approach to be scientific, but in contemporary practice Marxist analysis is more likely to be humanistic in both scope and technique. The critical approach exists on the margin between science and humanism because it aims for the rigor and reproducibility of science while avoiding the presuppositionlessness and ahistoricism (Hall, 1989) of traditional Newtonian scientism.

Clearly, then, there are many ways to define and conceptualize science and humanism—many methods with which to draw a distinction between them. This debate is centered within a larger debate about the nature of the Communication discipline itself, a debate which questions whether traditional scientific methods are appropriate to the study of complex human behavior and how mature the field is. The discussion is fueled by various uses of the term *paradigm*.

Paradigm?

The extent to which the scientific model can be applied to social science is an important epistemological question. Giddens (1989) described three shortcomings to the scientification of social inquiry. First, the social sciences have based their

---

[5]Hall (1989) does not regard semiotics as "scientific" in the ordinary, positivistic sense of the word, however, because it is open to considering historical and methodological issues in its analysis.

models on a misreading of natural science—science is by nature hermeneutic, Giddens argues, a matter the social sciences have failed to recognize. Second, social science proceeds from a causal misconception of human agency; Giddens proposes it integrate "practical consciousness." Third, the social sciences are based on a presumption that just as there are laws of nature, there must be laws of social life.

There are two levels of epistemological problematics in the field of Communication. Before its approaches can be meaningfully contrasted, its legitimacy as a coherent discipline needs to be considered. Clearly, if Communication is not a discipline per se, then no dichotomic schism can exist. The plurality of Communication approaches affects its scholarly entitlement in one of three ways: either Communication is not a discipline; or it is an "interdisciplinary discipline"; or it is a single discipline with competing schools. Hall and Robinson (Robinson, 1989) argued that it is interdisciplinary but a single field, an "interdiscipline," cobbled together by scholars using sociological, psychological, speech-scientific, philosophical, anthropological, and linguistic approaches. Rosengren (1989) argued it is a field populated by four schools: radical humanism, radical structuralism, interpretive sociology, and functionalist sociology. It is efficacious to assume that Communication is legitimately entitled, potentially coherent, and proceed to examine why it finds itself in a quandary of competing approaches.

The inquiry into the scientific or humanist basis of knowledge manifests itself in Communication epistemology as a debate into the centrality of human utterance to human knowledge. The two approaches to knowledge have very different views. The traditional scientific view is as a logical, positivist, and objectifiable interaction, a tool, between persons with goals and objectives. Communication is viewed, consequently, as a window through which a material reality can be perceived. The traditional humanist view sees communication as a form of artistic expression, a unique utterance of illusive meaning ultimately accessible only through exegesis. Communication is seen as a constitutor of reality rather than merely a window on it—our knowledge of the world proceeds from perception, which itself proceeds from linguistic cognition. Although not always specifically articulated or even conceptualized by the practitioner, traditional science essentially views communication as an attempt to describe material reality; traditional humanism views material reality as a product of communication.

Hall's (1989) critique of the "scientism" of the dominant paradigm provides a useful exemplar of the epistemological schism in the field. He described its three principle failings as: (1) an inability to recognize its own presuppositions (indeed, a tendency to see itself as "presuppositionless"); (2) an inability to recognize the social and historical basis of its premises; and (3) an assumption that its models are the end product of human development. Whether this is an appropriate use of the term *paradigm* and an accurate reading of Kuhn (1970), who originated this use of the term, is debatable.

Kuhn's philosophy of science has come to dominate epistemological discussion in the Communication field. He conceptualized knowledge in a

Hegelian fashion as a succession of world views, of paradigms, each sufficient for a time in explaining the nature of the world, but each experiencing a crisis when its model no longer fits empirical data and observation. The old paradigm is rejected in favor of a new world view. During the dominance of any one paradigm, research takes on a confirming role; during paradigm shifts, research shoots off in many directions at once. Even though the concept of paradigm was originally intended as a descriptor of science, in Communication it has if anything been more readily adopted by humanist scholars.

Using a strict interpretation of Kuhn's work disallows its application to Communication. Kuhn (1970) described the early years of physical optics, when each researcher seemed to recreate the field with each new work. At this stage in the evolution of a field, there exists "no standard set of methods or of phenomena that every [researcher feels] forced to employ and explain" (p. 13). A paradigm is the product of scrutiny and criticism between competing ideas. Kuhn goes on to doubt whether any social science has evolved beyond this stage, and even whether they will be able to do so. Communication, as one of the youngest social sciences, lacks the consensus necessary for paradigm. Can Communication, then, be said to be preparadigmatic (Rosengren, 1989)?[6]

Knowledge in a preparadigmatic state has several attributes according to Kuhn. One, the gathering of facts (empiricism) is the primary activity of researchers, an activity which seems nearly random most of the time. Only as the field matures will the value of this data be assessable. Two, the empiricism will tend to observe that which is "at-hand," already available, giving it a commonplace, common sensical quality—the empiricist does not have time or skill to be selective at this stage. Three, this phase is "marked by frequent and deep debates over legitimate methods, problems, and standards of solution, though these serve rather to define schools than to produce agreement" (p. 48). This description is well suited to Communication, which must be considered preparadigmatic.

If Communication doesn't have a paradigm, what does it have? Rosengren (1989) said it has four competing schools, a dominant functionalist sociological school (systems theory, social action theory, interactionism), and dissident radical humanist (critical theory, existentialism), radical structuralist (Marxism), and interpretive sociological (phenomenology, hermeneutics) schools. Giddens (1989) borrowed the concept of *traditions* from Gadamer to describe the current state of the field, a term that recognizes its tentative nature. These terms seem more satisfying because they are consistent with Kuhn, whose system should be retained as a useful predictor of future directions in the field.

Whether Communication is made up of traditions, schools, or a preparadigm, there is a third epistemological issue it must address. It, too, emanates from an

---

[6]Ironically, the fact that this discussion is published in a book is further evidence that Communication is preparadigmatic: Kuhn argues that it is only prior to paradigm that information in a scientific field is distributed via books. In the midst of a paradigm, books are effaced by journals.

ontological problem: The study of Communication has humanity as its subject, but how can we know each other enough to infer meaning in each other's behavior? This raises epistemological problems of turning subject to object—can we study and agree upon phenomena when at a basic level communication is personal and subjective? Some (e.g., Derrida) would argue that we can't, or at least that we can't be sure that we can. Others simply do not regard this as an epistemological problem, content to objectify the behavior around them. Many in the field have resolved this problem through the concept of intersubjectivity.

Intersubjectivity

The dominant dichotomy between science and humanism uses objectivity/subjectivity as a core measure. Because Communication deals with the design and exchange of signs and symbols, this measure becomes fundamental: The sign or symbol has an objective reality, yet its significance is subjective for both sender and receiver. This causes some self-evident epistemological problems, and depending on whether one chooses to study the sign or the act of signification, Communication seems *either* a science *or* a humanity. This problem is partially resolved through the concept of "intersubjectivity."

The concept of intersubjectivity presupposes that for a truth to be valid, it must be derived solely from common human experience. The sociological context of a communication is seen to be as important as the psychological in the formulation of meaning. Although significant in the philosophies of Kant and Hegel (Rosengren, 1989), and Kierkegaard, who saw human existence as the relation of subjective beings to each other, the role of intersubjectivity in communication is particularly articulated by Heidegger, who used it as a basis for his hermeneutics, as the measure of what has been communicated (Desilet, 1991). In fact, phenomenology relies on a notion of intersubjectivity as a precognitive state, a similarity between communicants more important than their dissimilarities. This intersubjectivity can be understood in objective terms—the common human experience validates it as a truth. Heidegger resisted the notion of objectification, however, because it reduces dialogue and alienates the observer from the thing objectified, and argued that subjectivity is a creation of a conceptualization of the world, not an innate predisposition (Divver, 1987). Nevertheless, intersubjectivity is the link between the objectivism of science and the subjectivism of humanism; as Dilthey noted, the "lived experience" of intersubjectivity is the bridge between humanism and positivism (Divver, 1987). Hirsch went so far with his positivism as to conceptualize the human mind as an object which can be known exactly and objectively (Divver, 1987).

For Heidegger (1959), communication is the source of intersubjectivity, because language is in a sense prior to being:

words and language are not wrappings in which things are packed for the commerce of those who write and speak. It is in words that things first come into being and are. (p. 13)

Merleau-Ponty (1964) further elaborated the essential nature of communication to perception by arguing that,

there is not thought and language; upon examination each of the two orders splits in two and puts out a branch into the other. There is sensible speech, which is called thought, and abortive speech, which is called language. (p. 18)

Foucault (1970) took this further, asserting that language prefigures and creates a person rather than vice versa; the individual is a product of "knowledge formations" mapped out by society (Rapaport, 1987). Language, then, is the best window we have on the subjective, but language itself is to some extent objectifiable. This allows for intersubjectivity.

There are problems with the concept of intersubjectivity, of course. Krippendorf (1989) noted that finding an overlap in cognitive representations between communicators is problematic. Husserl spoke of "intentional consciousness," a difficult way to account for the sharing of consciousness alleged to take place during communication (Divver, 1987). Merleau-Ponty (1964) demonstrated that the lesson learned from Saussure is that signs do not mean anything in and of themselves, that meaning comes into being only through the relationships between signs. Those relationships are not always so fixed; Schleiermacher (1978) in fact said that the first grasp of meaning is usually a misunderstanding. In fact, as Hirsch argued, language affects subjectivity and subjectivity affects language (Divver, 1987). Derrida (1973) further argued that intersubjectivity may not create shared meaning because the *différance* between written and spoken language is paradoxical and unavoidable. Without the certainty of intersubjectivity, communication is for Derrida possibly improbable and probably impossible.

Discussions of the subjective, objective, or intersubjective conceptualizations of the nature of knowledge reveal the interplay between scientific, humanistic, and hybrid modes of thought. The twentieth century has seen a great deal of flux, conflict, and confrontation between these various positions. How each conceptualization has evolved and the direction in which it is headed becomes an important issue, and theorists have taken many positions on the state of their evolution.

Conceptual Evolution

There are several perspectives in the field on epistemological change and the dichotomy between science and humanism. Is the practice of science changing? Is the practice of humanism changing? If so, in what ways? Are they coming together or growing apart? Different trends can be drawn from the evidence. The

different positions on these trends can be loosely grouped based on their focus
and conclusions and will be articulated here as the static, perspectival, critical,
convergent, divergent and metaparadigmatic positions.

Static Position

The first and perhaps least sophisticated of these is the static position, which
does not perceive a trend in the theory or practice of either science or humanism.
Not strictly speaking a theoretical position, this may in fact be the predominant
position among most Communication scholars. Practitioners of static science or
humanism practice it the way they learned and accept with little reservation the
science and humanism articulated by the dominant dichotomy. Often, they are
leery of work done by their antithesis: Static Communication scientists find
humanistic work dubious and speculative; static Communication humanists find
scientific work banal and incomprehensible.

A survey of the pervasiveness of this position would be itself an interesting
study. Berger (1989) felt it is virtually hegemonic in its dominance because,

> there seems to be little evidence of revolutionary change in the metatheoretical
> assumptions or research practices of those who publish in mainstream outlets . . .
> The promoters of metatheoretical debates seem to assume that changes in research
> conceptualization and practice flow from alterations in more abstract assumptions,
> a kind of top-down process . . . Another model for change is quite different. Under
> this model, changes arise because researchers realize that the questions they are
> pursuing are producing dead ends, are uninteresting, or are not answerable using
> current methodological tools. (p. 131)

For Berger, the majority of Communication researchers have not yet perceived
that they have hit dead ends. Presumably, over time, the static position will
disappear as more and more Communication scientists and humanists engage in
a process of epistemological self-questioning.

Perspectival Position

The perspectival position examines different schools of thought separately,
rather than from the essentialist perspective demonstrated in the convergent,
divergent, critical, and meta-paradigmatic positions discussed below. The
evolution of science and humanism are treated differently, their different
perspectives considered to be more-or-less irreconcilable. The Communication
discipline itself has huge differences in methods and approach. The subareas of
mass, interpersonal, and organizational Communication can scarcely talk to each
other (Berger, 1989), and scientific and humanistic approaches intersect all three.

An avunculate is an either/or division of some concept, like light/dark or
up/down. According to this perspectival position, the science avunculate of
fact/non-fact is moving in a different direction from the humanist avunculate of

fact/fiction. The traditional approach of science is to distinguish between that which is a fact and that which is not. It is a "fact," for example, that the universe is expanding; it is not a fact that the moon is made of green cheese. The gathering of empirical facts such as these is the first stage of any science according to Kuhn (1970). Natural sciences move beyond this phase fairly quickly once acceptable parameters of observation become refined. At that point, when theory building becomes important, science no longer distinguishes a fact from a nonfact; rather, it distinguishes fact from fiction. A nonfact and fiction are not the same thing: a nonfact is not *true*, whereas fiction can indeed be true. Fiction is not bound by facts. It is where imagination meets theory. It is not necessarily then or ever born out by facts, but it can be. Indeed, science-fiction is fiction about science filled with many fantastic and marvelous ideas (Todorov, 1975). These ideas have actually guided the way we look for facts, determined the kind of facts we choose to perceive, and (although it is fiction) serves to guide future scientific development.[7]

The humanist fact/fiction avunculate is moving in an entirely different direction. In fact, it is moving away from an avunculate. Traditionally, humanists were interested in the distinctions between fact and fiction which now interests science; for example, historians interested in historiography struggle with drawing lines between historical actuality and the narrative "fiction" necessary to convey that actuality.[8] Historical humanism tried to find the truth in facts while weeding out the fictions; literary humanism explored the distinction between mimesis and diegesis. Now, according to historian Gordon Wood (1991), "the blurring of fact and fiction is part of the intellectual climate of our postmodern time—dominated as it is by winds of epistemological skepticism and Nietzschean denials of the possibility of objectivity that are sweeping through every humanistic discipline, sometimes with cyclonic ferocity" (p. 12). Thus, humanism abandons the sense of objective truth and settles for narrative approximations of it. Fact is not distinguished from fiction. There is no avunculate, only different modes of discourse.

The perspectival position doubts that any convergence of science and humanism is possible. Because science and humanism are moving in different directions, the possibility for dialogue is strained. Bochner (1985) for one urged that Communication should abandon the search for agreement on methods and approaches. Therein lies a danger in the perspectival approach: A fatalism that condemns scholars operating in different schools of thought to close themselves off from the work of other schools. Whether or not they can agree on methods

---

[7]Space travel and television are examples of things conceptualized by this form of literature which later came to be. The expression of human hopes and aspirations cannot help but guide subsequent development.

[8]Schama (1991) has developed an interesting experiment into the difficulties of telling history. He mixes internal monologue and point-of-view in his account of historical events, raising important questions about the crafting of history.

and approaches, scholars must work toward that ideal, presuming that coherence will one day be possible.

Critical Position

The critical position shares with the perspectival approach the assumption that science and humanism are evolving, but uses a Hegelian model to account for the change. The dialectic allows for the possibility that antiquated theses will be replaced by more useful and descriptive ones. Therefore, critical scholars speak of a "dominant" paradigm or tradition and a dissident or oppositional paradigm which is replacing it. The dominant paradigm more-or-less corresponds to the dominant dichotomy of science/humanism described above: objectivity, reproducibility, patterns and empiricism in science and subjectivity, irreproducibility, evaluation and interpretation in a distinct and separate humanism. The positivism, empiricism, and individualism of the dominant paradigm are what the dissident paradigm particularly seeks to displace.

The dissident paradigm which critical theory sees overtaking the dominant one is in some ways a blending of scientific and humanist traditions, but is best embodied in the dissident paradigm's attention to power relationships. Further, the dissident paradigm strives to incorporate a self-consciousness about its own methods and assumptions into its approaches, something Hall (1989) and others saw as absent from the dominant paradigm, which regards itself as presuppositionless. A further focus of the critical position is to regard meaning as "a practice, not a thing" (p. 47), replacing the Newtonian conception of the pursuit of knowledge as a treasure hunt with a solution as its end point, with a model of it as a game, with no fixed ending and no single answer.

There is a tendency in some of the critical literature to see the Hegelian dialectic as a kind of historical determinism which is inevitable and predictable, although many have noticed with surprise the persistence of the dominant paradigm (e.g., Berger, 1989). Further, too close a subscription to the dialectic ignores the plethora of competing dissident approaches (e.g., Frankfurt school, structuralism, postmodernism, deconstruction and grammatology, cultural studies) which hardly act as a coherent antithesis. Evolution is not so directional as it is often assumed to be; natural selection tends to suit ideas to contexts and environments without regard for "progress" in history.

Convergent Position

The convergent position looks at the evolution of concepts in science and humanism as two roads coming closer together. Ordinarily, this takes the form of science becoming more humanistic and humanism becoming more scientific— the human is put closer to the center in the practice of science and moved out of the center in the practice of humanism. Humanism is seen to be getting more objective, methodical, and reproducible, while science is getting more humanistic through acknowledging the impact of culture and subjectivity on "objective" truth.[9] Presumably this means that the methods of both are becoming more similar; the optimist might hope for a complete convergence some day. Whether the two can ever significantly overlap their approaches and conclusions hinges on the ability of scientists and humanists to agree about the world using "intersubjective" truth.

Robinson (1989) provided a useful overview of the evolution of Communication science toward more humanistic assumptions. She shows that prior to the 1960s, Communication science maintained its objective, empiricist basis. The publication of Kuhn's treatise in 1962 sent philosophical shock waves through the scholarly community. The objective presumption of scientific research came under increasing scrutiny and disrepute; consensus shattered. "Normal science" could not see phenomena which did not fit its world view (Kuhn, 1970), and yet such phenomena existed; as little by little they came into view, the hegemonic authority of traditional modes of thought gave way. Robinson argues that, in particular, three attributes of Newtonian scientism were discredited: its deductive method was shown to proceed from rhetorical assumptions rather than natural law; its treatment of human subjects as behavioral outcomes rather than causal agents was questioned; and its functionalism was shown to be based on inappropriate and inapplicable scientific models. Giddens (1989) agreed, asserting that social science is based on a false assumption about the nature of natural science, which is in fact interpretive, and that by reducing human agency to social causation, traditional social science ignores the "practical consciousness" that guides the actions of men and women. Bateson (1984), for example, noted that survey data are as much constructed as collected. This implies something other than mere objectivity, in a sense a literary function to the activity of a scientist.

Paradox has led to a further "humanization" of the sciences. Many Communication scholars, although by no means all empiricists, have been moved to believe that the observation of an event affects its outcome. This is known as the Heisenberg Principle. Quantum physics and observations of the behavior of light under different testing tools necessitated an acceptance of this principle early in the 20th Century, but the social sciences have been slow to recognize its significance. Further illogic in science results from the nature of logical systems themselves—their own self-referentiality and inconsistency. Just as the Gödel theorem in mathematics shows how any mathematical system necessarily creates situations which it cannot logically explain, so too do scientific systems create margins which cannot be accounted for or included (see Hofstadter, 1979). Language is subject to similar illogics as noted in Russell's Theory of Logical

---

[9]This is still a somewhat isolated phenomenon, but the possibilities for and incidents of dialogue between the two epistemologies is increasing. At the same time, strictly Newtonian science and subjectivist humanism continues.

Types (Krippendorf, 1989). In spite of these developments in the natural sciences, perhaps most of the Communication scholars interested in humanizing science are not practicing Communication scientists.

The convergent position would argue that just as science is humanizing, the humanities are becoming more scientific. One step in this direction was the abandonment of authorial intention as an interpretive tool in the study of texts. Ricouer (1976), Eco (1976), Frye (1957), Fiske and Hartley (1978), Todorov (1975), Iser (1980), Derrida (1976), and other humanists abandoned the author completely and deal exclusively with meanings that can be found self-contained within a text, a gesture that goes a long way toward reproducibility and objectification. Heidegger went so far as to advocate an antihumanist humanism, one with "Man" (sic) decentered as its subject (Rapaport, 1987).

The convergent position shares with the critical position an enthusiasm for a progressive reading of contemporary history. It also shares with critical theory the frustration that little has changed for many practitioners of dominant science and humanism. It can be argued that theory, particularly in Communication, is scurrying in so many directions at once that mapping trends is premature.

Divergent Position

The divergent position looks at the evolution of science and humanism as two roads moving apart. In some ways, this is similar to the perspectival position, except that looking at the two epistemologies as a divergence implies a recognition of the assumptions and approaches of both; the perspectival position tends to deal with just one or the other and to see no intellectual link between the two. Craig (1989), who saw the field of Communication as essentially unified through its history as a practical discipline, noted the historical discontinuity which separates Communication science from rhetoric. This gap, which he contended was of fairly recent origin in this field, is one which ought to be bridged.

Meta-Paradigmatic Position

A final position on the evolution of science and humanism in Communication can be called meta-paradigmatic, a position which supersedes the others by considering them in a broader context. This position looks at the status of a science or humanity based on Kuhn's (1970) three stages of inquiry: "determination of significant fact, matching of facts with theory, and articulation of theory" (p. 34). Epistemologies themselves go through these phases of growth and development on their way to maturity, whereupon they are superseded by other systems with a greater ability to reconcile observation with theory and prediction.

The first of these phases, the fact-gathering stage, occurs in the preparadigmatic state of knowledge. This is where "mere facts" (Kuhn, 1970) and "mindless empiricism" (C. Wright Mills, quoted in Giddens, 1989) accumulate, where many dichotomies exist, and where there may be little or no coherence to what is observed and reported. This is the preparadigmatic state in which much of the work in Communication is situated. Eventually, some of this data will prove useful in theory-building; other data will prove useless. During the preparadigmatic phase, it is impossible to tell which of these any set of data will become.

The second phase involves coalescing some of the data into a meaningful picture of some phenomenon, a picture that will lead to forming a theory. While Krippendorf (1989) felt it is drastic "to exclude a great many phenomena . . . from scientific penetration, just to preserve the foundations of the existing paradigm" (p. 72), it is a necessary consequence of paradigm evolution. The theory which results is then tested against selected data for verisimilitude. Many Communication science theories have reached this verification level, although while some theories have been validated and others not, they have not yet formed into a paradigm. Even humanist theories have reached the level of testability, such as reader-response (see Eco, 1979 for example) and reception theories (see Jauss, 1982 and Iser, 1980 for example), although methodical tests of them have been scarce.

The third phase occurs when the theory, now dominant, is further articulated and substantiated through research. Communication has not yet reached this phase in either science or humanism: no single paradigm dominates. Whether or not Communication can ever reach such a phase depends on the extent of the applicability of Kuhn's model to the social sciences. In any case, the third phase would eventually be followed by a fourth phase, in which new or suppressed data is shown to be irreconcilable with the dominant model. The discipline begins a fact-gathering phase again and the cycle repeats itself.

These six positions on the evolution of science and humanism generate six very different images of the maturity of and prospects for the field. Together with implicit assumptions about the dichotomous nature of science and humanism, the applicability of the paradigm concept to Communication, and the significance of subjectivity, objectivity, and intersubjectivity to a particular theory, they form an epistemological matrix with which to analyze particular theories of Communication. To show how these issues intersect, it is useful to examine specific exemplar theories which embody these epistemological problems.

EXEMPLAR THEORIES

In order to demonstrate the interplay between science and humanism in Communication epistemology, it is useful to examine exemplar theories to see how they are situated. Some of these, particularly in the humanist tradition, are more like "philosophies" than "theories" (as discussed in Chapter 1)—this is to some extent necessitated by the nature of humanism, which does not always produce testable hypotheses. In order to provide some continuity and focus, the theories selected all concern the role of television in our lives. These have been chosen not necessarily because they are the exemplars of television theorizing, but because they exemplify aspects of science or humanism discussed above in their assumptions and methods. All are concerned with the role of the message conveyed by television, but they come up with very different conclusions. The theories are McLuhan's "medium is the message," Stephenson's Play Theory of mass communication, Eco's semiotics, Hall's "oppositional decoding," Fiske and Hartley's "reading television," Baudrillard's "hyperreality," and Kubey and Csikszentmihalyi's television negentropy.

McLuhan's "Medium is the Message"

The centrality of media to human experience has been debated for some time. Most considerations of the role of media in society examine the messages carried by the media. In fact, Lasswell's (1948) model for the study of communication, "who said what to whom in which channel, and with what effect?", the driving force behind decades of Communication research, emphasizes the sender, receiver, and the content of the message. Innis (Czitrom, 1982) considered media from a different perspective: that of its role in driving the forces behind the history of civilization itself. For Innis, the nature of the technology of communication determined whether a civilization would develop in a spatial or temporal dimension. Because the physical essence of the media technology is given so much significance, this school of thought is often called "technological determinism."

H. Marshall McLuhan, a student of Innis, further developed theories describing media's power to affect human development. McLuhan takes the argument much further than Innis, though, as he considers the role of media in shaping human cognition. Whether his ideas form a theory is debatable; McLuhan's writings are composed of many interlocking theories so complete it forms its own philosophy. They are also frequently so esoteric as to be difficult to access and assess.

McLuhan (1962) began by examining the role of the written word in history. Civilization has thus far gone through five stages: (1) tribal, nonlinear, oral society; (2) pictographic and hieroglyphic writing; (3) development of the alphabet; (4) medieval scholarship; and (5) the Gutenberg galaxy, created by the printing press. This last phase allowed information to become repeatable: a mass-produced commodity. This in turn led to profound changes in the nature of society. The printing press, according to McLuhan, spawned specialization, compartmentalization, markets, nationalism, individualism, and isolation, all due to the mass distribution and portability of the book. Media technology, in other words, changes the nature of civilization.

This media technology is so profound for McLuhan that it supersedes whatever content the medium is trying to convey in its overt message. The medium is *itself* the message for McLuhan (1964): Its "personal and social consequences" (p. 7) are a product of the technology, not what is programmed on it. For example, the message of a television advertisement for cigarettes has more in common with an antismoking television PSA than it does with a cigarette advertisement on radio. This certainly flies in the face of our common sense notion of meaning and messages, but McLuhan's case is persuasive, and in fact forms the basis for many subsequent humanist theories of media, including Baudrillard's (discussed later).

To show how the medium is the message, McLuhan (1964) divided media into two types based on their level of definition, the extent to which they are "filled with data" (p. 22), and the amount of participation this definition generates in the audience. McLuhan labeled "hot" those media which are high definition and consequently low in involvement. He cited the alphabet, books, and movies as examples. The opposite is "cool" media, which are low definition but high involvement, such as hieroglyphs, comic books, and television. It may seem strange to consider television higher in involvement than a book; most readers consider reading a more intense process than television, the watching of which is full of distractions. But McLuhan was describing the amount of cognitive "filling in" which is required; when a medium is low in definition, it is less filled with data; this must be provided instead by the viewer or reader. Like Seurat's pointilism, the observer adds coherence. The message the observer gets from television is "coolness."

Because television is "cool" in the way that hieroglyphs were cool, McLuhan felt it will lead to a sixth stage of civilization. The viewing of television is a communal experience not unlike gathering around a tribal fire. It closes society, makes it more proximate, more oral, less linear, less visual, less compartmentalized, less nationalistic. For McLuhan, this meant that through the television medium, world society is becoming a "global village"—a single postliterate tribe.

> Not only does the visual, specialist, and fragmented Westerner have now to live in closest daily association with all the ancient oral cultures of the earth, but his (sic) own electric technology now begins to translate the visual or eye man back into the tribal and oral patterns with its seamless web of kinship and interdependence. (p. 50)

Individualism becomes as impossible and irrelevant in this interwoven society as it is in a preliterate culture.

McLuhan's effect on the subsequent history of media theory is complex.[10] He has certainly had little effect on Communication science; his approach is too interpretive. Communication humanists borrow some ideas from McLuhan, but

---

[10] While McLuhan's theories have been only partially absorbed by media scholars and virtually ignored by the media themselves, as a person he has proven an irresistibly larger-than-life character for the media. He appears as himself in Woody Allen's *Annie Hall* to rebut a Communication professor who has misunderstood his theories, worked closely with Timothy Leary on the "turn on-tune in-drop out" campaign, and been transmogrified into the powerful but mad academic Brian Oblivion in *Videodrome*.

seldom wholesale. For example, his notion of the fading of individualism finds interesting parallels in Hall and Baudrillard (discussed later), although they would contend that individualism never existed to begin with. Students of global culture do find evidence of McLuhan's predictions, but his theories are not scientifically or humanistically reviewed—they remain the first and only complete system for explaining the nature of media, but as such remain aloof from more mundane scientific and humanistic theories.

Stephenson's "Play Theory"

While McLuhan crafted his elaborate philosophy of media, mainstream Communication scholars followed the traditional "administrative" model of research begun by Lasswell and Lazarsfeld. The result was effects studies and other forms of behavioral research quite different from McLuhan's conjectures. It is this model of Communication which still dominates popular conceptions of the field. Within the tradition, though, there has been considerable debate about methods and conclusions.

One who objected to the mainstream of scientific media research was William Stephenson. Stephenson felt that research was preoccupied with the negative aspects of media—both in terms of the power of its deliberate propagandizing function and the unintended (but nevertheless malicious) behavioral effects it caused. Asserting that the predominant function of the media, enjoyment, had been overlooked in favor of theories of social control and convergent selectivity, he set out to demonstrate scientifically the pleasurable nature of mass media consumption. The result is *The Play Theory of Mass Communication* (Stephenson, 1988), originally published in 1967. The theory is interesting because its hypothesis concerns a subjective function of the television audience, a function normally associated with humanism, but uses an empirical, objectifiable, and reproducible method, a scientific method, to defend it.

Simply stated, the theory argued that the mass communication audience is engaging in a form of play. By play, Stephenson did not necessarily mean a game, but *subjective play*, the complex intrapersonal use of fantasy and imagination. What the player gains from play is self-enhancement. In fact, it was his thesis (Stephenson, 1988) that "the daily withdrawal of people into the mass media in their after hours is a step in the existential direction, that is, a matter of subjectivity which invites freedom where there has been little or none before" (p. 45). Television liberates. For Stephenson, play takes several forms, each served by the mass media: a moment of pretending; an interlude in the day; an exercise in autonomy; an act of seclusion. Because these functions are so primary, the mass media perform an important constructive function in society.

> Mass communication in its play aspects may be the way a society develops its culture—the way it dreams, has its myths, and develops its loyalties; what it does in the way of inculcating work may be quite a different matter. What kind of

culture is it, for example, that thinks only of learning, production, and work? (p. 48)

In the process of producing pleasure, then, the media also create social coherence.

Stephenson attempted to use an objective, scientific methodology (the Q-sort) to account for television play, a process that is not entirely successful, since "play phenomena of a subjective sort do not easily lend themselves to such kinds of statistical distribution . . . this blend of the subjective and objective is still too recalcitrant to the scientific temperament" (Sutton-Smith, 1988, p. xix). The Q-method allows persons to declare their state of mind as they perceive it themselves. This inner experience provides a basis for examining the relationship an individual constructs between pleasure and media, an attempt at intersubjectivity. Stephenson's lengthy discussion of methodology, and also Kubey and Csikszentmihalyi's, discussed below, is further evidence that Communication is preparadigmatic.

Play theory is due for a rediscovery by Communication theorists; Stephenson's discussion of the role of the audience was well ahead of its time, but his effect on the field has not been profound. The idea of television as play is well suited to many postmodern notions of the reader, and his discussion of the pleasure associated with television viewing corresponds to the concept of *jouissance* often used in cultural studies. It also corresponds in some ways to the concepts of a tactical use, a poaching, of television by its viewer found in Certeau (1984), whose work is finding adherents in Fiske and others.

Eco's "Semiotics"

Semiotics, the "science" of signs, began with Saussure's (1960) *Course in General Linguistics*. Saussure studied the relationship between speech and writing. Semiotics is interested in signs and defines a sign as the point where the signifier, the thing which does the representing, and the signified, the thing represented, meet. Sometimes a sign is "natural": the signifier embodies some attributes of the thing it signifies, such as onomatopoeia in spoken language and a hieroglyph in written language. More often, the relationship between the signifier and the signified is "asserted": The connection between the two is arbitrary; the signifier does not embody properties of the signified. The written word "river," for example, is an asserted sign because the five ink scratchings which constitute the signifier share few common properties with the thing they signify.

Semiotics has evolved in two directions since the publication of the *Course*. One approach to semiotics, dominated by French philosopher Roland Barthes, is exclusively humanist in its interpretation of signs; in fact, it is most like literary criticism. In *Mythologies*, Barthes (1972) argued that mythology is a kind of speech determined by discourse rather than the type of story it tells. He proceeded to create a mythology of modern life populated by wrestlers, laundry detergent, the brain of Einstein, and television. The other approach to semiotics is much less literary, and as much like science as it is like humanism. This is the approach adopted by Umberto Eco, who in *A Theory of Semiotics* (1976) and *The Role of the Reader* (1979) attempted to develop an elaborate, reproducible system for the analysis of signs. Eco's semiotics is more a system than a theory, but because it attempts to create patterns out of observed phenomena, it is considered a theory here.

The basis of Eco's semiotics is a system for denoting the relationship that exists between the signifier and signified, their sign-function. Eco asserted that the content of a sign is not the signified itself, but a cultural conception of it; to clarify the distinction, he used symbols to designate the appropriate role each device plays in the formula.

/   (single slash) = the sign itself, the signifier

//   (double slash) = the signified, something "real", for example, an object

<<   (double carrot) = the cultural conception of the signified embedded within the sign; not the same thing as the signified, but a culturally accepted notion of what the signified represents; an intellectual form or absolute image of the thing

In dealing with the sign-function for river, /river/ refers the sign itself, the letters on a page; //river// refers to the actual object; and <<river>> refers to the concept, the visualization of a river, to "riverness." This system allows for fairly specific and reproducible discussions of signs and their relationship to each other and to social responses to them. For example, "river" can lead to a succession of responses and subsequent signs. The sign /river/ can lead to associations of beauty or ugliness:

sign ➡	conception ➡	other sign ➡	other conception ➡	related conception
/river/ ➡	<<river>> ➡	/clear/ ➡	<<clearness>> ➡	<<beauty>>
/river/ ➡	<<river>> ➡	/polluted/ ➡	<<pollution>> ➡	<<ugliness>>

The //river// in question can be either //beautiful// or //ugly//; our responses to /river/ and <<river>> are culturally conditioned. <<Beauty>> and <<ugliness>> are very much culturally conditioned, so the signs /beauty/ and /ugliness/ have a nearly infinite polysemy.

Because each sign contains so many possibilities for association, Eco agreed with Gadamer that understanding is a process of interpretation. Communication cannot be precise because sign-functions cannot be separated from other sign-functions.[11] The analysis of texts becomes problematic when the number of

---

[11]Derrida's conception of *erasure* is an elaboration of this. For Derrida, signs denote both what is there and what is not; in fact, it can only be understood as what it is and is not, since what it is not defines what it is. /River/ therefore denotes both <<riverness>> and <<not riverness>>.

meanings they possess seem infinite, creating "open" texts. To overcome this problem, Eco (1979) considered a "model reader" and a shared code of meaning conceived by the author to guide him or her in the production of the text. Television avoids this problem to some extent by encouraging "closed" texts, by forcing particular responses. Television is nevertheless still susceptible to "aberrant" interpretation. The reader of a text in a sense determines its status:

> the æsthetic dialectics between openness and closedness of texts depends on the basic structure of the process of text interpretation in general . . . the reader finds his (sic) freedom (i) in deciding how to activate one or another of the textual levels and (ii) in choosing which codes to apply. (p. 39)

Eco retained a humanist conception of individual control over texts, if not the notion of an "individual," which is rejected by Hall and other critical theorists who borrow from Eco.

Eco may in fact be the most influential of the theorists mentioned here, because the science of signs he borrows from Saussure is the basis of Hall's, Fiske and Hartley's, and Baudrillard's philosophies, discussed next, as well as many others. The influence of these theories goes far outside the Communication field to affect the studies of linguistics, modern languages, anthropology, sociology, and others.

Hall's "Oppositional Decoding"

Critical theory has occupied a dissident position in communication research for some time. Although some would argue that its prevalence has paradoxically made it the "dominant paradigm" (e.g., Becker, 1989), critical theory needs to be situated oppositionally, since it is composed of many separate methods, approaches, and theories. Perhaps critical theory is more a school than a theory. In any case, critical theory has been interested in media, especially television, as an embodiment of power relationships in capitalist society. The Frankfurt School is generally attributed with the genesis of critical theory; its method of analyzing communication from the perspective of political-economy has had a significant impact on Communication theory.

One exemplary critical theorist is Stuart Hall, founder of the Center for Contemporary Cultural Studies in Birmingham, England. Unlike Hall's critical counterparts in North America (e.g., Schiller, Smythe, Mosco), Hall did not merely apply Marxist theory to media; rather, he expands and illuminates it, merging it with semiotic, literary, and feminist techniques. The Center studied not only media, but ethnography and language as well.

Hall's (1980) theory of "oppositional decoding," reprinted in *Culture, Media, Language* is a good starting point. He began by demonstrating that messages exist within a discursive form and that this form directs both the encoding and decoding of the message. Consequently, mere information cannot be conveyed; it must adopt some discourse for transmission, and consequently convert signified to signifier. How the message is decoded is not easily subjected to behavioral methodologies and positivistic analysis (such as those used by the scientific approaches of uses and gratifications or effects research), but through a careful analysis of discursive signs and the power relationships they manifest. Hall rejected the traditional methods and practices of "dominant" science, using instead elements of humanistic approaches to understand the message. His humanism has no room for individualism, however: The person is regarded as an interplay of social factors such as race, class, and gender.

Hall (1980) borrows extensively from Eco's semiotics when he begins to analyze these signs. One problem posed by televisual signs is that they are *iconic*—they "look like" the thing they represent. Just as a painting by Magritte warns "*ceci n'est pas une pipe*," so is the icon not the thing it signifies. Nevertheless, iconic signs are often seen to be "natural" (i.e., "real") codes because they share properties with their signified: a video of a flower looks something like a flower; the word "flower" does not. This encourages certain decodings. Yet while the denotative level of the code is closed, its connotative level is open to a hierarchical polysemy.

At one end of this polysemy, there is the dominant or preferred interpretation of messages; dominant because they "have the institutional/political/ideological order imprinted in them and have themselves become institutionalized" (p. 134). The dominant meaning is the one the television programmers, and particularly the advertisers, intend and prefer the audience to follow; when they do, they are operating within what Hall called the dominant-hegemonic code. Often, however, members of the audience do not produce this interpretation of what they see, producing consternation and dismay among programmers. These alternative positions take two forms: a negotiated code and an oppositional code. The negotiated code, "acknowledges the legitimacy of the hegemonic definitions to make the grand significations (abstract), while, at a more restricted, situational (situated) level, it makes its own ground rules—it operates with exceptions to the rule" (p. 137). In other words, when an advertising campaign fails, it is because the audience is negotiating a different meaning than the one intended; the desire to buy batteries but confusion over brand is an example of this: the dominant message of advertisers has not gotten through. The oppositional code, on the other hand, occurs when the audience interprets the message in a contrary manner: the decision not to buy batteries because they are environmental hazards, for example. When audiences begin oppositionally interpreting messages, a struggle over discourse has begun and the dominant code loses power.

Hall inverted the normal conception of subjectivity and objectivity in television messages. A common assumption is that the encoded message is itself objective, but conditioned by the subjective interpretation by its audience. Hall felt the opposite is the case: that the effect within members of the audience is objective and systematic because the message prescribes the parameters of interpretation available. The internal processes of an audience member, then, are objective, not subjective. What we think about what we see is externally determined. There is no need for intersubjectivity, only interobjectivity.

Hall's use of critical theory combined elements of both science and humanism. On the one hand, he objectified the site of meaning by denying the existence of the "individual," thus rendering the study of processes ordinarily considered subjective to be objective. Similarly, his method of analysis was fairly rigorous, relying on a reproducible approach to semiotics (Eco-centric rather than Barthes-centric). On the other hand, Hall was primarily interpretive in his analysis and, like most critical theorists, was certainly evaluative. As such, Hall's theory occupies a middle-ground between science and humanism.

Fiske and Hartley's "Reading Television"

Television is seldom considered an aesthetic medium, least of all by scholars. Usually, it is discussed in terms of its intention, channel, technology, or behavioral effects. Discussing television as an art form comparable to literature or sculpture would seem peculiar indeed to Lasswell, Lazarsfeld, Lewin, and Hovland. Such an approach is truly evaluative and interpretive and demonstrates a particularly humanist aspect of inquiry. Examining television for its aesthetic value involves rethinking literary theory.

Media theorists John Fiske and John Hartley (1978) broke with tradition by treating television programs as an art form worthy of critical consideration, developing a literary theory of television texts. This they did to illustrate their hypothesis that the actual process of television watching is unlike the passive, "couch-potato" assumption made by almost all television researchers who precede them. Instead, Fiske and Hartley asserted that television viewing is so active that it should be considered a form of "reading."

Fiske and Hartley used humanist arguments to support their contention, aligning themselves with Barthes, Metz, Wollen, and Hall. They began by demonstrating that Shakespeare's work was accused by critics in his own time of promoting idleness, irreverence, poor work habits, and of pandering to plebian taste—criticisms often leveled at television. Over time, they argued, critics came to see Shakespeare in a different light as new tools were developed for literary analysis. These tools are not necessarily appropriate to the study of television, so television is regarded in much the same way the plays had originally been. The development of new critical tools will, they said, lead to a new status for television. Television has a language, they contend, in the way that Shakespeare does.

The literary value of television derives from its manipulation of signs. Just as the great writers of Western literature provoke aesthetic response through the manipulation and inversion of conventions, television similarly accords freedom of perception to its viewers through playing "fast-and-loose" with the semantic

relationship between signifier and signified, concepts derived from Saussure and
Eco.

> Television is certainly aware of the arbitrariness of many of its codes, and while
> not criticizing them, certainly celebrates them. What we, the audience then *do* with
> the message is another matter . . . What we do suggest is that taking television as
> we find it, we, the audience, are spontaneously and continuously confronted with
> this framework and must negotiate a stance towards it in order to decode and thus
> enjoy the entertainment in which it is embodied. (Fiske & Hartley, 1978, p. 19)

As Stephenson believed, freedom is enhanced, since contrary to the popular
critical notion, television's sophisticated language enables a number of different
readings. As such, it is deserving of critical examination.

Fiske and Hartley (1978) engaged in such an examination in a number of
ways. As a justification for why a literary approach to television texts is necessary,
they demonstrated the inadequacies of content analysis in accounting for individual programs or the act of viewing. They then examine in detail the signs,
codes, and functions of television. Television commercials are cited as sophisticated manipulators of figurative devices like metaphor and metonymy.

One reason why Fiske and Hartley felt the aesthetic study of television is
important is that its codes are analogous to normal codes of perception, a notion
similar to Eco's and Hall's discussion of the correspondence between signifier
and signified in iconic language. This means that television is in a "position of
cultural centrality" and that the boundary dividing television from reality is
indistinct. Television and reality affect each other extensively, further blurring
the distinction, and further necessitating interpretation and evaluation.

Fiske and Hartley use the model of the bard to explain the role that television
plays in society, a medieval model which nicely suits an alchemy metaphor.
Because the interpretation of television codes is determined within culturally
defined parameters more than individual tastes and analysis, "television functions
as a social ritual, overriding individual distinctions, in which our culture engages
in order to communicate with its collective self" (p. 85). The bardic model
describes this function accurately because, as Fiske and Hartley defined it, a bard
mediates language as needed by a culture, is situated at the center of cultural
activity, communicates orally, and perpetuates myths. In contemporary society,
these roles have been taken on by television.

The "reading television" approach has been very influential in media analysis
and popular culture scholarship since its introduction. The term *reading* is now
widely used to refer to active television viewing. These subsequent studies have
branched in two directions: One branch is interested primarily in television
criticism and has become considerably less theoretical, applying conventional
literary analysis techniques to television programming, for example, Marc's
(1984) *Demographic Vistas*; a second branch is interested instead in the response

of television "readers" and is more theoretical, borrowing from reader-response and reception theory, for example, Ang's (1985) *Watching Dallas*.

Baudrillard's "Hyperreality"

In the idealist tradition, the universe within the mind supersedes the external, physical universe. Mass media have historically been analyzed by materialists because media represent the individual being affected by forces external to the singular mind. More subjective approaches have been among the most recent developments in understanding media, and through the reception theory of Jauss and Iser they can be traced to the German Idealism of Fichte and Kant. Reception theory examines how messages are created by the "receiver" rather than the "sender"; in a sense, the receiver *is* the sender. Consequently, it is the universe within the mind that dictates how media are consumed, not the desires of the original sender. At the same time that these subjective approaches examine reception, critical theory takes a materialist position that the desires of the receiver are manipulated by the sender.

French media theorist Jean Baudrillard represents a merging of the idealist and materialist traditions; his philosophy combines semiotics, Marxism, and McLuhan. Baudrillard's materialism is particularly evident in his earlier work, especially *For a Critique of the Political Economy of the Sign* (1981), an attempt to reconcile the Marxist theory of capital with semiotics. *Simulations* (Baudrillard, 1983) and *The Evil Demon of Images* (Baudrillard, 1987) put forward his thesis that postmodern civilization is constituted by hyperreality, a situation in which signifiers no longer refer to "real" signifieds, but rather to other signs. Thus the syntactical function of signs effaces the pragmatic and semantic functions (see Todorov, 1975 for discussion of these functions.)[12] The "evil demon" of modern media is that they do not represent a bridge to material reality but are instead an abyss.

The notion that synthetic images replace natural ones is not new; Boorstin (1978) for example talked about Gresham's law of pseudo-events. For Baudrillard, however, the destructiveness of modern images extends beyond their mere distance from the material world; their malevolence is that in failing to refer to anything except other signs, the image sets in motion "the extermination of its own referent" through "the implosion of meaning in which the message disappears on the horizon of the medium" (1987, p. 23). Television, in particular, creates a black hole which swallows memory, so that signs build up on signs until like a collapsed star everything is sucked in and nothing let out. Because there remains no illusion that they refer to anything but themselves, signs cease to have the magical element that they have when they simulate something.

Black holes suck in heat as well as light, so television culture leaves us with media several degrees below McLuhan's "cool"—for Baudrillard (1987),

---

[12]Baudrillard (1987) would deny that meaning has been lost—for him, there never has been a semantically referential meaning to signs.

television culture is "cold" (pp. 25, 31). Baudrillard resurrected and inverted McLuhan by asserting that neither the content nor the medium is the message: There is no message. For postmodern culture, reality signifies signs, and not vice versa, and life is perceived as a movie, not a movie as life; without verisimilitude, there is no meaning. Ultimately Baudrillard abandoned semiotics because he feels it mistakenly tries to domesticate signs, something he regards as an impossibility because signs have now taken on an independent life of their own.

Baudrillard was clearly humanistic in his approach. There is room in his theory for empirical testing, although how that would be done is a genuine problem in experimental design. His influence in communication theory and research has been growing, although the fatalism of his philosophy leaves little room for elaboration. Effects research continues undaunted.

Kubey and Csikszentmihalyi's "Negentropy"

Some research into the effects of cocaine suggests that as more of the drug is consumed, the brain alters chemically so that the world appears less interesting to the user until more cocaine is consumed. Is there a parallel in the heavy use of other simulated emotions? Media effects studies have examined questions of heavy media consumption before; Baudrillard discusses how it distances us from the signs it signifies. What if, like a narcotic, the time heavy viewers spend with television makes the rest of their life less interesting?

Americans Robert Kubey and Mihaly Csikszentmihalyi, borrowing from effects researchers (and with passing reference to Stephenson), argued in *Television and the Quality of Life* (1990) that persons want their lives to have order (or "negentropy") and need their values to be reaffirmed, that television allows them to give the appearance of such a structure, but that certain vulnerable members of society become overtly dependent on the simple reaffirmations that television offers. This thesis is not a new one, but Kubey and Csikszentmihalyi's methodology and conclusions move out of the "effects studies" category into Kuhn's second-order theory-building.

Much of the data produced by the study seems to substantiate the humanist theories of popular literature and literary formula proposed by Cawelti (1976). There has been very little empirical research to verify reader-response and reception allegations, which is unfortunate because they represent one of the most likely bridges between science and humanism;[13] Kubey and Csikszentmi-

---

[13] This raises another issue in the evolution of communication epistemology: dialogue between scientists and humanists may not be hampered by ontology, but instead by pedagogy: in practice, researchers and theorists will stick to the techniques with which they are the most comfortable. Reader-response and reception theory practitioners tend to be philosophers and literary critics, not epistemologists. Whatever testable assertions their theories generate are likely to go untested because they lack sophistication in data collection. Consequently, reader-response criticism ironically deals only infrequently with actual readers reading.

halyi helped by building supports for such a bridge because they treat reader-response assumptions as testable hypotheses.

Kubey and Csikszentmihalyi were not alone in trying to accumulate data on reader responses. There are many ways to study television viewing, none of them perfect, each distorting the event they study per the Heisenberg principle. Ang (1985) solicited letters from *Dallas* viewers in a rather unscientific, uncontrolled, but nevertheless valuable fashion because it "observed" the viewers in their natural environment; Liebes (1988) assembled an international audience in a living room to view an evening of American television programming. These approaches are a recognition of the post-Kuhnian scientific principle that the act of observing affects observation. Kubey and Csikszentmihalyi used the Experience Sampling Method, in which volunteers are fitted with beepers that go off randomly, after which they record their activity and emotional state. This had the advantage of comparing the subjects' emotional and physical status during TV viewing with other activities but not to particular programming.

Humanist television studies are primarily interested in television content, but content is not Kubey and Csikszentmihalyi's interest. They even suggest it shouldn't be any researcher's interest because emotional responses to television are *prior* to content and, it seems, similar across all the content of television. This is in a sense an empirical validation of McLuhan's notion that television content is effaced by the effects of its medium. Thus, a humanist approach such as Fiske and Hartley's would be considered invalid. Kubey and Csikszentmihalyi's data also contradicted the concept of the active television "reader" in Fiske and Hartley, but this is certainly to some extent an effect of their chosen methodology and assumptions. The more text-intensive approaches of Ang and Liebes demonstrate to the contrary that audiences can be both active and diverse in their readings of television.

Kubey and Csikszentmihalyi's approach, then, did not address the interesting and important issues of how gender, class, religion, education, and ethnic factors create readings of television of varying complexity. By ignoring content, by veering away from the possibility of a humanist approach in favor of a scientific one, they disable themselves from accounting for the extremely close readings some audiences bring to television shows like *Twin Peaks*.[14] Kubey and Csikszentmihalyi's (1990) assertion that "to reach the widest audience possible, much content is purposely made easy to decode" (p. 100) further subverts the possibility of crossing the chasm between science and humanism; their empirical

---

[14]*Twin Peaks* is one of many shows that encourage close readings of the text; *St. Elsewhere* and *The Singing Detective* are other examples. Casual viewing of these programs is difficult if not impossible. Of course, such programs have never been the mainstream of American television programming, and the first two scarcely made it to a second season. The fact that few viewers actively "read" television does not invalidate the "reading television" argument, however, any more than the predominance of pulpy novels on best-seller lists invalidates the notion of a close reading of *Finnegan's Wake*.

data substantiate the assertion en masse, but ignore the multitude of sophisticated television viewing subcultures in the United States and elsewhere. Indeed, a very active reader of *Twin Peaks* might watch *Cheers, General Hospital, The Tonight Show with Jay Leno* and other programs with passivity. The data will smooth over the important times when watchers do become readers; the method as practiced here cannot allow for humanist conclusions.

Comparing Kubey and Csikszentmihalyi to Stephenson shows some of the paradox of "reproducible" science—the data may be reproducible, but that doesn't mean the conclusions will be. Interestingly, Kubey and Csikszentmihalyi's conclusions were diametrically opposed to Stephenson's. Stephenson (1988) felt that "the daily withdrawal of people into the mass media in their after hours is a step in the existential direction, that is, a matter of subjectivity which invites freedom where there has been little or none before" (p. 45). Kubey and Csikszentmihalyi felt instead that television is a form of captivity, robbing its viewers of freedom. Paradoxically, both are right; the difference in their findings results because one study is macroscopic (Kubey and Csikszentmihalyi), the other microscopic.

Humanist textual analysis doesn't end with the dominant reading, but allows for other readings: reasonable and bizarre, affirmative and dissident, actual and theoretical. Yale literary critic Harold Bloom (1980) saw these different readings as the well-spring of creativity. Kubey and Csikszentmihalyi's results are of predominant interest as a snapshot of normative television viewing behavior. At this writing, it is too soon to judge the influence of their work, but the data could prove so useful to reader-response critics that, if the chasm between communication science and humanism ever permits them to find it, it could revolutionize the application and methodology of their work.

Media Meaning

These seven theories provide a cross-section of Communication theory. Each of these theorists attempts to explain the "message" of television, each through a different interplay of reproducibility or irreproducibility, of objectivism or subjectivism, of patterning or evaluation, of empiricism or interpretation. McLuhan's humanist philosophy and historiography led him to conclude that the medium itself is the message; most of his assertions are untestable and therefore irreproducible, primarily suitable for the interpretation and evaluation of the medium. Stephenson's scientific approach to humanistic questions about television use and his assumption of individual motivations and aspirations led him to conclude that play is the message; while his method used empiricism to look for patterns, his analysis drew upon humanistic sources. Eco's semiotics combined the rigorous method and reproducibility of science with the interpretation of humanism to produce a theory situated somewhere between the two; for him, what messages mean is a negotiation between the signs with which they mean and the interpretation the reader of those signs brings to bear upon them.

Hall elaborated on Eco's semiotics by exploring the power relationship implicit in meaning: signs have a dominant interpretation they push upon the viewer, but the viewer may bring to bear oppositional codes to create other meanings; he suggested that the process of decoding is objective, not subjective, and seemed to regard critical theory as a form of science, although its subject matter would ordinarily be considered humanistic; the effect is like science without the objectivity. Fiske and Hartley added aesthetic meaning to the list by suggesting that the decoding of television messages may be very sophisticated; they used tools of literary criticism ordinarily associated with humanism. Baudrillard felt that referential meaning had been lost from signs: that they retain only syntactical meaning; his conception of "hyperreality" is not only untested but untestable because he described a cognitive shift whose dissonance cannot be avoided. Finally, Kubey and Csikszentmihalyi used traditional scientific methods to show that television has a narcotizing effect on its audience; using McLuhan's (1964) "personal and social consequences" (p. 7) as a measure of message, its message removes its audience from social interaction.

The meaning of television, then, is a product of the conceptual assumptions one makes when regarding it. Looking at it with a presumption of objectivity and with an empirical method produces certain kinds of conclusions about it, usually a macroscopic, patterned, and antithetical position; proceeding from a presumption of subjectivity and interpretation leads to other conclusions, usually more microscopic, viewer-specific, and neutral or affirmative. What is television really? The descriptive natures of these theories are as much a result of their conceptualization of television, indeed of their implicit ontological assumption and epistemological approaches, as they are of any intrinsic properties of television itself. The smoke is so thick from all the alchemy that it is hard to tell whether it's gold or lead in the test tube.

SUMMARY

This chapter has examined some of the issues concerning the nature of science and humanism in Communication theory. It began by describing the dominant dichotomy between the two, a dichotomy which contrasts reproducibility with irreproducibility, objectivism with subjectivism, patterning with evaluation, and empiricism with interpretation. It also considered other possible dichotomies. The status of Communication theory in paradigm evolution was considered, as was the role of intersubjectivity in reconciling scientific with humanistic methods. Six positions on the evolution of scientism and humanism in the field were described. Seven theories that exemplify the shifting nature of science and humanism were examined. It was concluded from this examination that the nature of the theory is as much a product of its implicit conceptualizations as it is of the thing the theory seeks to explain.

It is difficult to say with assurance in which evolutionary direction the science and humanism embodied in these exemplars are moving. Eco and Stephenson seemed to be converging science with humanism; Hall took the critical position; McLuhan and Fiske and Hartley were perspectival, seeking to evolve humanistic conceptions alone; the most contemporary of the theorists, Baudrillard and Kubey and Csikszentmihalyi, can be best explained from the static position, implying no movement is taking place at all. Perhaps the meta-paradigmatic position is the only way to account meaningfully for them all: they all are part of a single, incoherent stage in the evolution toward paradigm.

In spite of the epistemological mish-mash that appears to be churning in the core of Communication, the field has been an active participant in the ferment of twentieth century philosophy. It has both had a profound impact upon it from outside the field, and has had a significant impact on other fields of learning as well. More than many disciplines, it has also had an impact on the culture-at-large. A close examination of the history of twentieth century philosophy reveals that Communication played a significant role in shaping conceptualizations of science and humanism.

Philosophers of science and humanism not ordinarily associated with the field have had a profound and sometimes unwitting impact upon it. This chapter has spoken at length about the Kuhn's impact. Philosopher Sandra Harding (1986) has demonstrated a gender basis (and bias) in the theory and practice of the hardest of the hard sciences, having a significant impact on feminist and critical theories of Communication and other dissident approaches. Philosophers of humanism have also had a significant effect, such as the work of Frye and the reception and reader response theorists. Communication has had a significant impact on other fields as well. The "communications school" of European theory was heavily influenced by Communication research, and Eco, Baudrillard, Jauss, and Barthes find themselves drawn to integrating or rebutting its models and approaches.

The impact of Communication science and humanism on the non-academic world has been less mixed. The popular press tends to rely on scientific models and theories of media to the detriment of humanist ones, even when the approaches are scientifically dubious (such as certain analyses of "subliminal messaging" in the media) and even, paradoxically, when these theories and approaches are overtly hostile to the media which report them (such as a television report of a medical study which claimed that television viewing is linked to excessively high cholesterol levels in children; the report predictably inferred a causal link). Another cultural effect of the interplay between Communication science and humanism is the increasing interest in "postmodern" science, for example, cyberpunk and virtual reality. These new reality-models are a nexus between contemporary Communication science and humanist theory.

In spite of the coherence the popular press finds in it, Communication theory seems further from a paradigm now than it has been in the past. But then alchemy is no closer to turning gold to lead. Alchemy was the only way of doing things before more were developed. Science and humanism separated because each could address particular problems of knowledge and knowing that the other could not. The quest for turning lead to gold has been abandoned, not because it is not a desirable outcome, perhaps not even because it didn't work, but because we began to think about thinking in different ways. Alchemists felt that lead could be "healed" into gold; new alchemists hope to "heal" a schism they see in Communication theory, bringing science and humanism together. That would bring about a shift from preparadigm to paradigm, from fact-gathering to real theory. Without the directionless fumbling of alchemists there would be no chemistry. The epistemological mish-mash in which Communication finds itself is leaden, but also another step toward paradigm, toward gold.

REFERENCES

Ang, I. (1985). *Watching Dallas*. New York: Methuen.
Barthes, R. (1972). *Mythologies*. New York: Hill and Wang.
Bateson, N. (1984). *Data construction in social surveys*. London, England: Allen and Unwin.
Baudrillard, J. (1981). *For a critique of the political economy of the sign*. St. Louis, MO: Telos Press.
Baudrillard, J. (1983). *Simulations*. New York: Semiotext(e).
Baudrillard, J. (1987). *The evil demon of images*. Sydney, Australia: Power Institute of Fine Arts.
Becker, S. (1989). Communication studies: Visions of the future. In B. Dervin, L. Grossberg, B. O'Keefe, & E. Wartella (Eds.), *Rethinking communication* (Vol. 1, pp. 125–129). Newbury Park, CA: Sage Publications.
Berger, C. (1989). Back to the future: Paradigm monologues revisited. In B. Dervin, L. Grossberg, B. O'Keefe, & E. Wartella (Eds.), *Rethinking communication* (Vol. 1, pp. 130–134). Newbury Park, CA: Sage Publications.
Bloom, H. (1980). *A map of misreading*. Oxford, England: Oxford University Press.
Bochner, A. P. (1985). Perspectives on inquiry: Representation, conversation, and reflection. In M. Knapp & G. Miller (Eds.), *Handbook of interpersonal communication* (pp. 27–58). Beverly Hills, CA: Sage.
Boorstin, D. (1978). *The image*. New York: Atheneum.
Cawelti, J. (1976). *Adventure, mystery, and romance: Formula stories as art and popular culture*. Chicago, IL: University of Chicago Press.
Certeau, M. de (1984). *The practice of everyday life*. Berkeley, CA: University of California Press.
Craig, R. (1989). Communication as a practical discipline. In B. Dervin, L. Grossberg, B. O'Keefe, & E. Wartella (Eds.), *Rethinking communication* (Vol. 1, pp. 97–124). Newbury Park, CA: Sage Publications.
Czitrom, D. (1982). *Media and the American mind*. Chapel Hill, NC: University of North Carolina Press.
Derrida, J. (1973). *Speech and phenomena* (D. Allison, Trans.). Evanston, IL: Northwestern University Press.
Derrida, J. (1976). *Of grammatology* (G. Spivak, Trans.). Baltimore, MD: Johns Hopkins University Press.
Desilet, G. (1991). Heidegger and Derrida: The conflict between hermeneutics and deconstruction in the context of rhetorical and communication theory. *Quarterly Journal of Speech, 77*, 152–175.

Divver, A. (1987). Tracing hermeneutics. In J. Natoli (Ed.), *Tracing literary theory* (pp. 54–79). Urbana, IL: University of Illinois.

Eco, U. (1976). *A theory of semiotics.* Bloomington, IN: Indiana University Press.

Eco, U. (1979). *The role of the reader.* Bloomington, IN: Indiana University Press.

Fiske, J., & Hartley, J. (1978). *Reading television.* London, England: Methuen.

Fiske, J. (1989). Representations of power: Paradigms and politics. In B. Dervin, L. Grossberg, B. O'Keefe, & E. Wartella (Eds.), *Rethinking communication* (Vol. 1, pp. 169–172). Newbury Park, CA: Sage Publications.

Foucault, M. (1970). *The order of things: An archaeology of the human sciences.* New York: Pantheon.

Frye, N. (1957). *An anatomy of criticism.* Princeton, NJ: Princeton University Press.

Gadamer, H. (1975). *Truth and method.* New York: Crossroads.

Giddens, A. (1989). The orthodox consensus and the emerging synthesis. In B. Dervin, L. Grossberg, B. O'Keefe, & E. Wartella (Eds.), *Rethinking communication* (Vol. 1, pp. 53–65). Newbury Park, CA: Sage Publications.

Habermas, J. (1972). *Knowledge and human interests.* London, England: Heinemann.

Hall, S. (1980). Encoding/decoding. In S. Hall, D. Hobson, A. Lowe, & P. Willis (Eds.), *Culture, media, language* (pp. 128–138). London, England: Hutchinson.

Hall, S. (1989). Ideology and communication theory. In B. Dervin, L. Grossberg, B. O'Keefe, & E. Wartella (Eds.), *Rethinking communication* (Vol. 1, pp. 40–52). Newbury Park, CA: Sage Publications.

Harding, S. (1986). *The science question in feminism.* Ithaca, NY: Cornell University Press.

Heidegger, M. (1959). *An introduction to metaphysics.* New Haven, CT: Yale University Press.

Hofstadter, D. (1979). *Gödel, Escher, Bach: An eternal golden braid.* New York: Basic Books.

Husserl, E. (1975). *The Paris lectures.* The Hague, Netherlands: Martinus Nijhoff.

Iser, W. (1980). *The act of reading: A theory of aesthetic response.* Baltimore, MD: Johns Hopkins University Press.

Jauss, H. (1982). *Toward an aesthetic of reception* (T. Bahti, Trans.). Minneapolis, MN: University of Minnesota Press.

Krippendorf, K. (1989). On the ethics of constructing communication. In B. Dervin, L. Grossberg, B. O'Keefe, & E. Wartella (Eds.), *Rethinking communication* (Vol. 1, pp. 66–96). Newbury Park, CA: Sage Publications.

Kubey, R., & Csikszentmihalyi, M. (1990). *Television and the quality of life: How viewing shapes everyday experience.* Hillsdale, NJ: Lawrence Erlbaum Associates.

Kuhn, T. (1970). *The structure of scientific revolutions.* Chicago, IL: University of Chicago.

Lasswell, H. (1948). The structure and function of communication in society. In L. Bryson (Ed.), *The communicating of ideas* (pp. 37–51). New York: Institute for Religious Studies.

Lazarsfeld, P. (1972). *Qualitative analysis: Historical and critical essays.* Boston, MA: Allyn and Bacon.

Levi-Strauss, C. (1967). *Structural anthropology* (C. Jacobson & B. Schoepf, Trans.). New York: Anchor Books.

Liebes, T. (1988). Cultural differences in the reading of television fictions. *Critical Studies in Mass Communication, 5*(4), 277–292.

Marc, D. (1984). *Demographic vistas: Television in American culture.* Philadelphia, PA: University of Pennsylvania Press.

McBurney, J., & Wrage, E. (1953). *The art of good speech.* Englewood Cliffs, NJ: Prentice-Hall.

McLuhan, H. M. (1962). *The Gutenberg galaxy: The making of typographic man.* Toronto, Canada: University of Toronto.

McLuhan, H. M. (1964). *Understanding media: The extensions of man.* New York: McGraw-Hill Books.

Merleau-Ponty, M. (1964). *Signs.* Evanston, IL: Northwestern University Press.

Mill, J. S. (1973). *The Utilitarians: An introduction to the principles of morals and legislation.* Garden City, NY: Anchor Books.

Olson, S. (1989). Mass communication: A bricolage of paradigms. In S. King (Ed.), *Human communication as a field of study: Selected contemporary views* (pp. 57–86). Albany, NY: State University of New York Press.

Olson, S. (1990, June). *Reading meta-television: A new model for reader-response criticism.* Paper presented at the conference of the International Communication Association, Dublin, Ireland.

Parrish, W. (1954). The study of speeches. In W. Parrish & M. Hochmuth (Eds.), *American speeches.* New York: Longmans, Green.

Rapaport, H. (1987). Phenomenology and contemporary theory. In J. Natoli (Ed.), *Tracing literary theory* (pp. 148–176). Urbana, IL: University of Illinois.

Reiss, D. (1982). *The discourse of modernism.* Ithaca, NY: Cornell University Press.

Ricouer, P. (1976). *Interpretation theory: Discourse and the surplus of meaning.* Fort Worth, TX: Texas University Press.

Robinson, G. (1989). Communication paradigm dialogues: Their place in the history of science debate. In B. Dervin, L. Grossberg, B. O'Keefe, & E. Wartella (Eds.), *Rethinking communication* (Vol. 1, pp. 204–208). Newbury Park, CA: Sage Publications.

Rogers, E. (1989). Communication: A field of isolated islands of thought? In B. Dervin, L. Grossberg, B. O'Keefe, & E. Wartella (Eds.), *Rethinking communication* (Vol. 1, pp. 209–210). Newbury Park, CA: Sage Publications.

Rosengren, K. (1989). Paradigms lost and regained. In B. Dervin, L. Grossberg, B. O'Keefe, & E. Wartella (Eds.), *Rethinking communication* (Vol. 1, pp. 21–39). Newbury Park, CA: Sage Publications.

Sagan, C. (1979). *Murmurs of the earth: The Voyager interstellar record.* New York: Ballantine Books.

Saussure, F. de (1960). *Course in general linguistics.* London, England: Peter Owen.

Schama, S. (1991). *Dead certainties: Unwarranted speculations.* New York, NY: Knopf Publishers.

Schleiermacher, F. (1978). The hermeneutics: Outline of the 1819 lectures. (J. Wojijik & R. Haas, Trans.). *New Literary History, 10*(1), 1–16.

Stephenson, W. (1988). *The play theory of mass communication.* New Brunswick, NJ: Transaction Books.

Sutton-Smith, B. (1988). Introduction to the transaction edition. In W. Stephenson, *The play theory of mass communication* (pp. ix–xx). New Brunswick, NJ: Transaction Books.

Thomas, S. (1989). Functionalism revised and applied to mass communication study. In B. Dervin, L. Grossberg, B. O'Keefe, & E. Wartella (Eds.), *Rethinking communication: Paradigm exemplars* (Vol. 2, pp. 376–396). Newbury Park, CA: Sage Publications.

Tocqueville, A. (1945). *Democracy in America.* New York: Vintage.

Todorov, T. (1975). *The fantastic: A structural approach to a literary genre* (R. Howard, Trans.). Ithaca, NY: Cornell University Press.

Wittgenstein, L. (1953). *Philosophical investigations.* Oxford, England: Basil Blackwell.

Wood, G. (1991). Novel history. *New York Review of Books, 38*(12), 12–16.

Chapter 3

Probing the Body Ethnographic:
From an Anatomy of Inquiry
to a Poetics of Expression

James A. Anderson
University of Utah

H. L. Goodall, Jr.
Clemson University

> *C'est en observant que l'on apprend, mais c'est en participant que l'on comprend.**

Ethnography had its earliest glimmerings in travel literature and reached its adolescence in the service of colonialism. It became a method of inquiry upon the determination that culture and not genetics explained more of the differences among the peoples of the earth. It is the theoretical stance of culture which makes ethnography a justified practice of inquiry (Barrett, 1984; Spiro, 1986; White, 1968).

For our purposes, culture can be defined as a communally held understanding which extends into the world and directs some part of our response to the world. This understanding results from and is maintained by discursive and other practical work. This definition sets the parameters for the ethnographic project: the element of study is the social unit (community, group, family); the object is the commonly held significances of the social unit upon which individual action is based; and the data used in evidence are the practices of the members in their lifeworld (many are probably reading this text in the lifeworld of the American college student).

To put it another way (by attacking it from the other end): culture assumes that the (relevant) actions of individuals are motivated, justified, and thereby

---

*The insight of a graduate student at the University of Montreal. Supplied by Laurence Shute, Editor, *Western Social Science Association Newsletter*.

understood by a worldview held in common by the members of some social unit. To understand that worldview is to understand the human behavior that springs from it. Our understanding of that worldview is developed through the careful study of the signifying routines which define the members as members.

ETHNOGRAPHY AS A BODY OF KNOWLEDGE

To illuminate the argument we are crafting here, let's simplify the language considerably—granting that it won't be as precise. The argument for ethnography is based on the assumption that people *don't* just do things. They do things that are meaningful. Further things are not intrinsically meaningful but are meaningful inside some system of significance. The ethnographer's job then is to find out what people who belong to a system of significance do, to determine how what they do is meaningful inside that system; and ultimately to explain the system itself.

Ethnography privileges a direct experience of the methods and practices of the collective membership. This direct experience is called participant-observation. Participant observation requires the ethnographer to be in the lifeworld of the collective under study (pitch your tent in the village; sign up for a course of study at a college) and in many ways to adopt the lifestyle of the membership (hang around the campfire; start wearing Levis and carrying books on campus). There are many levels of participation and many activities of observing. For example, adopting the rhythms of the collective for resting, working, eating, and the like is one level of participation; becoming competent in one of the workforces is another. Observational activities include being present and taking notes, tracing movement patterns, collecting titles, as well as interviewing informants.[1]

There is always a dynamic tension between participating and observing as centering one's activity on one side generally precludes an adequate job on the other. Ethnographers continually move back and forth between the two poles. Inadequate observation or inadequate participation (and, of course, both) are each a basis for rejecting an ethnographic study.

The material, public contribution of any ethnographic study is quite simply the ethnographic monographic that appears in print. (For some classic examples, see Bateson, 1958; Benedict, 1946; Firth, 1936; Malinowski, 1922; Mead, 1928; or Radcliffe-Brown, 1922/1948. More recent communication examples can be found in Benson, 1981; Carbaugh, 1988; Goodall, 1989b; Pacanowsky, 1988; or Philipsen, 1975.) The knowledge claim is the attributed understanding of the culture under study.

---

[1]There is a large body of literature which discusses ethnographic methodology. A few useful examples are J. Anderson (1987), Ellen (1984), Hammersley and Atkinson (1983), Lofland (1971, 1976), Sanday (1979), and Spradley (1980). The reader is also directed to Gravel and Ridinger (1988) for a recent annotated bibliography.

Written in this expository voice, ethnography seems a sort of straightforward "see it, do it, write it" affair. As a matter of fact, however, every bit of the activity is a site of great controversy. It is this assemblage of controversies that is the actual interest of this chapter. For in the controversies that infiltrate the activities of ethnography are the central arguments which surround communication theory.

THE BODY IN QUESTION: THE ANATOMY
OF ETHNOGRAPHIC INQUIRY

Remarkably we can begin near the beginning by considering the motivating conditions of the ethnographer. Ethnography is a mainline activity of anthropology, but in communication, it is talked about far more often than conducted (J. Anderson, 1987; Hickson, 1983; Philipsen, 1977). Part of this disparity arises from the appropriation of ethnography by scholarly communities in communication who are opposed to the worldview conceptualizations of traditional (1940–1970) social science. Within these arguments ethnography is raised up as the better way to justified claim. The argument in communication is simply part of a much larger argument which has ebbed and flowed in the social sciences from their beginnings (Husserl, 1970; Weber, 1978). The argument has many variations, but at the core of nearly all are the twin questions of: (a) whether humanity lives in a world largely restructured in its own image or in one in which the forces of action are outside human practice and (b) whether the individual is an agent or a site of the motives for behavior.

The Reality of the Body: Determinism and Agency

The first question attempts to determine if we live in a socially created reality which differentially interprets the facts of the physical universe. (Snow is a boon to a skier and a bane to a commuter.) Or if we live in a reality whose physical facts are so powerful that our modifications are trivial. (Medical science seems to advance yet all of us still die.) To put it another way, if it is true that "boys will be boys" then we waste our time trying to persuade them to be otherwise. But if the "boys" which boys will be are the product of social practices then what boys will be will differ from one culture to another.

At the point that we accept the premise that who we are is largely under the control of social practices, we move the primary explanation of the human condition from genetics and physiology to the methods of socialization and enculturation. In this formulation, the location of our science changes, but not its nature. What we have done is to have taken the principles of material determinism (the forces which determine our fate are outside our practices) and reproduced them in those practices in a world of social determinism. The reality of social determinism is one which is by and large structured by human activity, but that activity is on such a grand scale as to be unassailable by the individual and even beyond all but the most wrenching of collective action. In any given culture, it is still true—until the appropriate revolution—that boys will be boys. Most social science is practiced on the foundation of social determinism. Social determinism maintains the appearance of traditional science—a very successful activity in the material area—but moves the activity into an arena (human behavior) of interest to people who call themselves social scientists.

In strict social determinism, the boy goes about the business of being a boy with little choice in the matter. As an individual he is the site of the intersection of social forces more powerful than he. In fact, if we had perfect knowledge of those forces, we would not need the individual in our explanation of his very own action. In this perspective, ethnography serves as a method of discovery by which the determining social forces are revealed.[2] Once we understand the determining forces, we understand that culture and all the behavior it engenders.[3]

The move from material determinism to social determinism is generally used to distinguish the social sciences from the natural ones. It is the "agency answer" to the second question which divides the social sciences per se and propels ethnography to the front of that division. Social determinism most decidedly rejects the principle of individual agency and most of immediate collective agency too. As we shall see, agency is the eroding force that levels the peaks of social determinism for if the boys that boys will be are the result of social practices *under our control*, we[4] can *decide* what boys will be.

Theorizing on agency never reaches that level of individual freedom, of course. Instead agency as it appears in social theory is well surrounded by deterministic boundaries both material and social. Nevertheless, agency (which we can define simply as the ability to choose to do otherwise) means that outcome of deterministic forces is under some local control. That circumstance, no matter how bounded, changes the character of the science we do in three important ways: (a) It constrains the reach of one's conclusions (generalizability over condition); (b) limits their duration (generalizability over time); and (c) forms

---

[2]One can see how quickly this practice of ethnography would become the handmaiden of colonialism. As the more powerful culture seeks to control the less, the promise that the revealed knowledge of the forces which permit the lesser to function will be available only to the more powerful (ethnographies are not printed in native languages or in native discursive forms) is very attractive. It is not by chance that there were no European ethnographies during this period.

[3]There are combinations of material and social determinism—such as structuralism—in which not only do social forces determine the behavior of individuals but those forces are ontologically the same from culture to culture and vary only in their particular cultural expression (Levi-Strauss, 1963). Gender, then, would be seen as a force in all cultures and some sort of boy would have to be created in each. (In that degenerate claim, the sign of sex differences is used to verify the production of gender. As long as one accepts sex differences, there has to be gender.)

[4]How much this "we" means you and I as contrasted with large social collectives is a matter of debate.

an irreducible barrier of uncertainty (expansionism rather than reductionism in claim). Therefore, some boys will be boys, but others not. And, the some boys will not always be boys. In fact, boys (as an operating social distinction) may disappear altogether. (Think of how the concept of "girls" has changed in the past decade or two.) Because these issues have important implications for the understanding of ethnography, we spend some time with each.

In a theoretically determined world, valid relationships discovered with any part of a population should hold true for the whole population. We should be able to extend the conclusions of our analysis beyond the particular conditions in which our respondents were observed. Why? Because the forces that led to the appearance of one behavior over another in the circumstances of our observations are (presumably) the same forces in place in any other set of circumstances where we could observe. Therefore, if boys were boys for us, we would expect boys to be boys elsewhere also.

The presence of agency as a theoretical element, however, means that there is no definitive study of any social collective. Any particular study involves the participation in and observation of local performances which partially represent the determining forces of the material and the social as well as collective and individual agency as the product of the actual social actors (including the ethnographer) involved.[5] This interaction of agency and determining forces means that any set of observations is a unique product of the conditions of observation per se. Knowledge claims arising from those observations may be true, but they are locally true. They cannot be exported to any other set of conditions.

The import of this conclusion is that traditional ethnographies which made encyclopedic claims about the nature of whole cultures (Evans-Pritchard and the Neur or Mead and the Samoans) are simply hyperextended. Evans-Pritchard (1940) studied a village the population of which presented their own practices of being Neur. The presumption of agency would insist that had he studied some other village the description of the Neur would have been different in substantial ways.[6] Agency locates claim in the conditions of analysis.

A Body Restricted by Time

One author of this chapter (J. Anderson, 1987) has been part of a consortium of ethnographers studying media use in family life for nearly 15 years. The evidence over that period is that of change. The family life of the mid 1970s is not the

---

[5]This implication is also true for surveys, experiments and all other methods in the study of social action.

[6]This last phrase "in substantial ways" is, of course, the issue. Nearly every theorist will grant that the particular circumstance affects the conclusions drawn. Determinists consider those differences to be trivial. Social action theorists consider that given the potential for local action, one cannot assume the differences to be trivial. The significance of the difference all agree will appear has to be demonstrated.

family life of the early 1990s. This consortium may some day cease its study. It if does, it will be from fatigue, disinterest, or whatever—not because the group had achieved a grasp on what family life is and will be. Social actors move the realm of their performance faster than analysis can take a fix. Anderson's families of 1985 cannot exist now as they did then. A modern-day Malinowski or Mead cannot determine whether the claims of the originals were true because the cultures which were studied no longer exist. In plain terms, agency means that any claim about social practices is outdated when it is made.

A Body Held in Fundamental Uncertainty

Restricting claim by condition and time creates an irreducible barrier of uncertainty in our knowledge of social practice. Consider Anderson's problem in studying families or Goodall's problem in studying corporate organizations. Neither can know whether knowledge of this family or this organization will be useful in understanding that family or that organization. Each collective of social actors will produce its own understanding of how a collective like that will work. Each collective studied will add that particular understanding to our stock of knowledge about collective behavior. No matter how many we study, we will always be justified in studying one more. The permanent knowledge which we build is one of steady but unpredictable change. There are no constants like gravity or the speed of light. The science of social practices is, therefore, expansionistic whereas the science of physics, for example, is reductionistic. The difference is worth a fuller explanation: Reductionism as a character of science can be understood from the following. The science of human behavior is the explanation of human behavior. Our explanations start with the observation that everyone is different. If that claim is incontrovertably true, then we need one explanation for every individual and each new individual requires a new explanation. If, however, we note that we're not all different; some things about individuals are (mainly) the same across all individuals. In our explanations, we can then split the individual (called atomization) into components of difference and components of similarity. Because our explanations of the components of similarity will hold true for all individuals, we have reduced the total number of explanations needed to understand an individual. As that can be claimed as a goal of science, only the components of similarity become the proper object of study. The practice of claiming extractable similarities as the proper object of scientific study is called reductionism. Grand reductionism is the claim that all knowledge will reduce to the "laws" of physics (or those of communication).

Reductionist explanations must necessarily transcend time and place for them to be useful. The greater the transcendence the greater the utility and the more possible is the goal of grand reductionism. If one's theoretical perspective limits transcendence (as agency does), then understanding difference becomes as important as understanding similarity. (Radical proponents of agency celebrate difference.) An acceptance of difference as of equal importance with similarity means that the scientific explanation of social practices will have common themes drawn from the similarities across circumstances but will also always be expanding to account for the differences. There is (presumably) no limit on the invention potential of agency.[7] In this perspective, each individual or grouping of individuals can be seen as a local (identified in time and place) and partial representative of the infinite variations possible on the themes of material and social determinates.

One can perhaps see how this perspective privileges the ethnographic approach. If claim is located in time and place, ethnography is the analytic method of "being there when." Most proponents of the agency perspective would argue that one has to experience a system of social practices in order to understand it. Ethnography is the method of experience. We can see the movement of ethnography from its traditional home in anthropology to other disciplines (such as communication) as a consequence of the decline of material and social determinism and the rise (or better, the rebirth) of social action theories in scientific and critical inquiry.[8] (No method exists without its empowering theory and no theory remains in contention without a practical means of study.)

ADDRESSING THE BODY: OBJECTIVITY, INTERSUBJECTIVITY, INTERPRETATION

The work we have done with agency and determinism has changed our initial "see it, do it, write it" formulation into a "see it, do it, write it again (and again)" notation. This may seem like a trivial difference, but its impact weakens the traditional structure of valid knowledge claims we call science. The consequence of agency is to forever ban sentences that begin with: "The American family is characterized by" or "Two principles govern all forms of organizations" or "The Balinese cockfight ritual is an expression of." What must be substituted is: "The American families in my study showed" or "In 1991 in the such and such organization, two principles ran through the practices of organizing" or "At the Balinese cockfight I attended."

The central claim of agency is that the object of study is not fixed but reformulates its practices in time and place through choice. Well-conducted, objective observations will, therefore, arrive at significantly different conclusions. (Consider studying an East German family in 1988 and one in 1990.) Because

---

[7]This formulation of expansionism does not deny atomism or the validity of transcendent components of explanation as some formulations do. It argues that those latter explanations by themselves are not enough.

[8]A discussion of social action theories is beyond the purview of this chapter. Suffice to say that agency is central as well as the question of interpretivism we will discuss shortly. For examples, see Anderson and Meyer (1988), Giddens (1976), Sigman (1987).

the object of study (social practices) reformulates itself in unpatterned ways, scientific knowledge of these practices must also reformulate itself to accommodate the change. As long as the rate of change is fairly slow, the knowledge claims arising out of objective analysis can have a duration of value. They have a useful "shelf-life."[9] The community of science can, at least, come to agreement that such was how things were—in that time and place—even if uncertain as to how things are.

The next question that gets raised, however, scatters the field even more. The question asks, "Is the *objective* analysis of social practices possible?" This question introduces us to the perspective of interpretivism. (A good, short review of interpretivism is offered by Kirschner, 1987; see also Rabinow & Sullivan, 1987.)

Interpretivism is contrasted with objectivism. Both are concerned with the manner in which we make sense out of experience. To begin our analysis of these terms, both agree that the individual is a fallible observer. The objectivist believes, however, that the source of individual fallibility is error that can be corrected to at least a human level of perfection through practices of independent verification. These practices are formulated under the principle of intersubjectivity, which holds that if a claim is to be valid it must first be reliable—several observers must independently observe the facts of the claim. This notion of reliability is based on the belief that regardless of culture or linguistic membership, experience is—at its foundation—the same for all of us. For the objectivist, when the facts of the claim are reliable, they are substantively no longer in doubt (although the explanation of the facts—the claim—may be). Objectivism allows us to get to a solid foundation of argument.

Interpretivists argue that intersubjectivity is a political/ideological process and not a foundational insight. The significant facts of inquiry are never primitive or incontrovertible, but are, rather, constructed.[10] For example, the facts of a particular study might be the data from a questionnaire. It is certainly a matter of *fact* that an actual number of respondents selected a given response on the questionnaire form. But that fact is a construction of the form itself. Asking the question in a different way or providing different responses would change the facts that the questionnaire provides. It is, indeed, the job of the person designing the questionnaire to anticipate the facts that will be developed from its administration. That the questionnaire is a product of human effort governed by the conventions of good workmanship of a research community means that the questionnaire is ideologically embedded and politically implicated.

---

[9] We see, for example, decadism as a practice of explanation: the '80s as the decade of self-indulgence and greed; the '90s as a rebirth of social concerns. That we can characterize a decade in its first year is a good example of the social construction of reality in process.

[10] All human practices are filled with constructed facts. That we stop at a stop sign is not materially true but a function of collective agreement. Constructed facts are not the product of individual subjectivity. The individual does not get to decide whether a stop sign means stop. To stop or not is a different question.

To press the example a bit further, we typically ask questions relating to the color of one's skin but not relating to the color of one's eyes. We ask the one question of color but not the other because this society is in part organized around that issue. By asking the question of race (read color) and presenting the findings organized by race, the researcher participates in and helps to maintain the socially constructed racial divisions. Faced with this implied criticism an objectivist researcher might be quick to complain that she or he is merely reporting what's there. The interpretivist's reply would be something like "It's true that society is racially organized, but it is so organized by social practices one of which is social research. It is something that this society does and you are an agent of the practice."

Interpretivism strips the cloak of innocence from the body of social inquiry. Objectivity is not veridical but just another social practice—one of many positions, voices, images which can be adopted to do the work wanted to be done. Objectivity is like patriotism, artistry, and authority of various kinds, which allow us to say and do certain things.[11]

Interpretivism calls all of the practices of ethnography into question. What seemed earlier in this chapter as a straightforward, "see it, do it, write it," now becomes a very self-conscious reflection on the whole process.

Seeing—observation—as the passive experience of a social milieu is based, as is all signification, on the recognition of difference which itself requires some stance inside familiarity. Significant observations gain their significance from their deviation from the ordinary. The "ordinary," however is itself a social performance. The notable observation clearly depends on who is observing. The observer is an agent doing the work of a collective from which she or he comes.

Doing—participation—as a means of gaining access to the underlying understandings by which action makes sense is a political engagement of the membership. Genuine participation is granted by the membership not mimed by the ethnographer (dressing up is not enough). This empowerment, however marginal, invokes the ethnographer as a political actor in the collective. This invocation is precisely the point of participation, of course, but it clearly strikes the stance of neutrality from the scene.

Writing—the ethnographic argument—as the sole material trace of the research is the embodiment of the power relationship between the research community and the collective of study. Though the oft stated end of the ethnographic argument is to present the other, the other is powerless in this presentation (Friedrich, 1988). What gets said, what claims are made, what positions are advanced are all under the control of the research community (for a contrary method, see Savage, 1988).

---

[11]In this way, Dr. Ruth can carry on conversations about sexual behavior which might otherwise be suppressed because they are conducted in the name of objective science. One might suspect their popularity, however.

A DIALOGUE OF ISSUES

As you might suspect, there has been considerable discussion over the issues raised by the rejection of innocence in research (e.g., Brodkey, 1987; Clifford, 1988; Clifford & Marcus, 1986; Simon & Dippo, 1986; Wengle, 1988). Resolution of these issues involves taking some prior stance from which to argue. Your authors (Anderson & Goodall) had a variety of means available to show, at least, some of the issues and the resolutions attempted (one of which would be a pose of critical objectivity). Our concern in the choice was to present the sense of the struggle which exists across the larger research community and to show how members of particular intellectual communities must suppress doubt in order to get on with the business of inquiry. Our choice was to present a dialogue between the two of us over selected topics in ethnography. The dialogue is a set of written exchanges in which we try to establish our own positions on these issues. The reader should seek no final resolution.

Professor Anderson:

Let's start by organizing some of the problematic points in defining the ethnographic project. Let me take 5 which seem to galvanize folks into discussion: the arrangement of human action, the human as site or agent, the accessibility of motive for action, the nature of writing, and the nature of claim.

1. The presupposed arrangement of human action (behavior) has divided the research community into (at least) cognitivist, behaviorist, structuralist, and interpretivist camps. Each one sees human action as organized in different ways. For example, these separate claims have been advanced:

(a) Behavior is best described in causal linkages (represented in behaviorist, cognitivist or structuralist viewpoints).
(b) Human action is best understood in a semiotic web of meaning (interpretivists).
(c) Human action is best described as conjunctures or the local intersection of resources, opportunities and agents (cultural studies).

Given (a), the ethnographic project becomes the discovery of the central unities of the organism and its language (structuralist viewpoint) or those unities as produced by the socialization activities of a society (cognitive perspective) or as produced by conditioning practices (behaviorist). Given (b), the project is the explication of socially held meanings. Given (c), the project is the critical analysis of the political arrangement of resources, opportunities, and agents.

2. As we have discussed, the human individual as site or agent appears to be one of those vital but often unspoken differences among us. Consider:

    (a) The individual as site views the individual as the point where internal and external forces are acted out. Free agency is denied and choice of any sort is suspect as a deficient explanation (behaviorists, cognitivists and structuralists).

    (b) The individual as agent ranges from the position of free agency (not used in science) to the commonly used notion of the individual as a socially bounded agent. The acting agent is an agent of some social membership. Choice is a permitted explanation (interpretivists and cultural studies).

The presence or absence of agency in explanation appears to be one of the more clear dividers.

3. The accessibility of the motive (cause, meaning) for human action has considerable import for the methods of study chosen. We can see the connections in the following:

    (a) The cause for human behavior is made present in linked, observable acts (behaviorist).

    (b) The motive for human behavior is open to careful, direct and indirect observation (cognitivist, structuralist).

    (c) The meaning of human behavior is ambiguously apparent in discursive and other performative practices (many interpretivists).

    (d) The meaning of human behavior is itself a social production (some interpretivists and most cultural studies).

The move here is from the most objective to the most political.

4. The nature of writing:

    (a) For behaviorists, cognitivists and structuralists (in an interesting fracture) ethnographic writing is representational. Writing is innocent (though for structuralists, language is not).

    (b) For interpretivists, writing is not objective but subjective representing a perspective on phenomena in which the writer is implicated. Writing is not innocent but the writer may be.

    (c) For cultural studies, writing is itself a political act which makes use of events for its own purposes and must be contained (or disciplined) in reflexive analysis. Neither writing nor the writer is innocent.

As with agency, writing clearly divides the various approaches.

5. Knowledge claims—the centrality of ethnographic explanation:

(a) For behaviorists, ethnographic explanation is preprobative. True knowledge claims are transcendental, reductive and directed toward control.

(b) For most cognitivists also, ethnography is preprobative.

(c) For structuralists, multiple ethnographies reveal the underlying structural unities of human action (just as multiple measurements reveal the "true" location of a star).

(d) For most interpretivists, central concepts (power, race, gender) are enacted in local performances. Ethnographies document those performances to give a partial and expanding understanding of the concepts.

(e) Cultural studies "poach" (appropriate) ethnographies.

Ethnography is centered in structural anthropology and interpretive social science. It is prescience for behavioralists and cognitivists and another resource of cultural studies. Ethnography is directed at explaining the "other." Its method is narrative which may draw upon observation, informants, presence, and/or participation as its resources. At the center of its performance is the task of writing. Writing permeates the effort in site notes, field notes, interview schedules, transcriptions, episodes, and final arguments. The task is finished when the writing is done.

Professor Goodall:

It is interesting that the 5 problematics with which we begin are problematics of theory rather than fieldwork. For me the 5 problematics serve as signs of an academic impulse that privileges talk (in this case, writing) about theory over actual field research. I begin my part of this discussion this way because I want to underscore the notion that what fieldwork experience teaches is a healthy skepticism about academic categories for what is considered real or true within our discourse communities. For example, the explanatory power of a descriptor such as "human action," or its discrete attendant theoretical adjectives (cognitivist, behaviorist, structuralist, and interpretivist) has very little functional utility when taken into the complex mix of everyday life. To use them in the field is to find only what they tell you to look for, which is to leave out all that does not fit or that lives in the blurring of those discrete categories. With this general caveat in mind, let me address the 5 problematics we have agreed to discuss.

1. The arrangement of human action depends entirely upon the relationship between the researcher and the informant or subject, and is contextualized by the perspective(s) or angle of approach used by the researcher to describe and detail the nature of that relationship. My position on this issue places all theoretical positions within the head and body of the researcher (where they actually reside in real life) and locates all explanations for human action within the resultant

web of meanings attributed to the actions by the collaboration of the researcher and the researched.

This premise underscores the fundamentally dialogic nature of field research but admits (albeit reluctantly) that the final product of that dialogue will be a written outcome (the ethnography) that necessarily privileges the discourse objectives of the researcher over the various discourses and objectives contained within the dialogues. Does this mean that human action is best understood as Jim Anderson's a, b, or c positions? The answer to this riddle (and I prefer the term "riddle" to "question" on this issue) is as independent or dependent a variable as the psyche and senses of the researcher.

2. The human individual as site or agent is best understood in fieldwork as both. As a site, the human individual is the embodiment of cultural inscriptions which beg to be read as meaningful. As an agent, the human individual is always acting purposefully, even if that purpose is culturally determined. The ethnographic project is to discover the meanings human individuals hold for the cultures that contain, maintain, and constrain them; and it is to accomplish this task comparatively by moving between the culture(s) producing the ethnographer and the culture(s) producing the subject of the ethnography. Hence, the human individual (both the ethnographer and the subject) is both site and agent whose meanings and purposes are constructed in dialogue which is, itself, always a comparative act.

3. The accessibility of the motive (cause, meaning) for human action is, as Jim has pointed out, an interesting issue that has considerable import for the methods of study chosen. Given that I agree with his outline of possibilities, let me here expand upon the practical question of when motive gets attributed and how meanings get constructed in ethnographies.

Clifford Geertz (1988) has written a remarkable essay with the intriguing title "Being There, Writing Here." His title captures, for me, the essence of the issue of attributing motive and meanings because it marks time and place as the difference between doing the field research and writing the ethnography. While field work is proceeding *in vivo* as experience, motives and meanings are handled in a self-sustaining manner. This means that while "there" the researcher deals with motive and meanings in ways sufficient to maintain the self and to maintain the practical action which permits the fieldwork to get done.

When the ethnography is being written, *in vivo* as reconstructed experience mingled with reflection and shot through with autobiography and prose decisions, motives and meanings tend to take on new dimensions that were both revealed in the field and concealed by the fact that they were unspoken there. In other words, the fact that one signifying sentence must flow into another in the written ethnography is different from the fact that one experience must flow into (rub against, disturb, mix with) another experience unbounded by the rationality of sentence-constructions in fieldwork. Here we have the difference that matters in questions of motives and meanings, a difference of experience (being there) and signifying that experience (writing here). The two spheres of ethnographic work are never equivalent. Neither are their attributions of motive and meanings.

4. The nature of writing is, for me, what distinguishes the ethnographer from the researcher who has merely been collecting data in the field. One does not go into ethnography to learn about cultures, but to write about them. This means that the learning is done through the writing and not the other way around. This statement comes fully equipped with some heavy-duty implications. To begin with, the choice of "being an ethnographer" is a profound philosophical commitment that very much transcends ordinary concerns about the utility of fieldwork methods or even prose styles. Not everyone is suited for this line of work. Unlike traditional methods of social science, ethnography is neither theory-driven, method-bound, nor formulaic in its research report. Ethnography requires a person who is comfortable living with contingencies, who is good at associating with others from widely diverse backgrounds and interests, and who likes to write. As such, ethnography is more of a calling than a career, and the decision to do it—as well as the ability to do it well—seems to require more of a particular, identifiable, but oddly ineffable attitude toward living and working than belief in method.

The previous paragraph may seem to have overstepped the boundaries of the question of writing, but I don't think so. Writing, after all, is done by a person, and the nature of the person seems inextricably linked to the nature of the writing.

5. Knowledge claims are always contingent for the ethnographer. They are localized, situated, and dependent. This is why the ethnographer's obligation is to report on the process that produced the knowledge claims, and, where possible, to show (rather than tell about) how that knowledge claim was generated, situated, localized, and rendered dependent on the time, place, and circumstances of its discovery.

I agree with Jim's assessment of the ways in which knowledge claims are understood by various theoretical camps. However, I want to emphasize that one way in which knowledge claims generated by interpretive ethnography differs from other forms of social science is with the issue of generalizations.

The task of interpretivists is to write about a culture at a particular moment in time rather than to locate within that culture certain truths that can be articulated across cultures and times. There is a political angle to this position. The need to generalize is a product of Western social science's practice of valuing knowledge claims that help predict and control. This is, essentially, a colonizing attitude that privileges the scientist over the subject and that seeks to homogenize (or at least gloss) cultural differences at the expense of those members of the culture who value the differences (but who don't get to write ethnographies).

This is, in part, what Jim means when he uses the term *innocence*. To the extent that ethnographers participate in the colonizing of cultures implicates them as political coconspirators in the project of Western science, a project that (in my view) devalues the individual human for the sake of the cultural generalization.

Writing the ethnography, then, becomes a political statement. For interpretivists, the writing style, the format, the characterizations of informants, the descriptions of cultural sites, the attributions of meanings and motives, and the tentativeness of conclusions are acts of political consciousness directed against (or at least positioned in opposition to) the dominant forms of Western social science. These are political acts of resistance, and primarily resistance to the idea that generalizations are the point of doing social science research. Embedded with the interpretivist critique is opposition to research and writing that robs individuals of their differences, that robs cultures of their uniqueness, that privileges theory over research, and that distances the observer from the persons and things observed.

Perhaps now you, reader, can see why the choice to become an ethnographer is a profound philosophical (and political) decision. And perhaps now you, reader, can see why the issue of writing style—for the ethnographer—transcends all other conceptual categories. Writing is not merely an act of translation, but an act that purposefully blurs the traditional distinctions between epistemic and ontic parameters. What gets written is not just knowledge of culture, but how that knowing was acquired by a human being implicated in the production of that knowledge (see Goodall, 1989a).

Professor Anderson:

Buddy Goodall's initial statement can be read as an antiintellectual stance (which some ethnographers are wont to take) that romanticizes the validity of the field experience. It is certainly true that concepts that identify different frameworks of scholarly interpretation will hardly serve as pick-up lines around the office manager's coffee pot. But it is also true as Buddy quite rightly points out that the contribution to public knowledge which ethnography makes is contained wholly in the writing and not in the personal experiences of the ethnographer in the field. It is in this writing where the discipline of a perspective makes its appearance in clearly dominating terms. Buddy writes his ethnographies in a particular manner as do we all—his from an interpretivist perspective—not because his fieldwork experiences guide his fingers on the keyboard but because he believes certain principles to be true. Principles held prior to and confirmed by his fieldwork. His ethnographic argument is crafted not only to engage some culture, but also to advance a particular position. It does not advance the cognitivist, behaviorist, or structuralist position, but it could, and it certainly does advance some position.

Ethnographers, as figures in the business of the production of public knowledge, are themselves the production of some scholarly collective whose culture permeates every line they write. Experience and the contract between researcher and researched is not purifying. An event in the lifeworld is an event *to someone* not an event in and of itself. Yes, there are facts—this person rather than that person, this act rather than that—but the story of the event, and there is no other event but the story, is a piece of someone's craftsmanship (Hess, 1989). It is this craftsmanship that is our topic and the conventions and codes that direct it. The only protection the reader has from the seduction of realism in ethnography is to continually make present the alternative directions to which the flock of ethnographic facts might be herded.

The contest is vital because in the courts of inquiry, just as in the courts of law, the story we hold to be true is the one on which we will act. And this is, dear reader, exactly where Professor Goodall ends up in his comments. We are each forced in the writing to act as if something else were true. To act as if human action was of this character rather than that; to act as if motive can be discussed or not; and on through the list. An ethnography is an accomplishment of social action based on extractable premises not a regurgitation of reality.

Finally (on this topic), there is nothing about ethnography that requires a radical positioning against the traditions of Western social science. Indeed most of ethnography is bedded down in snuggled closeness with them. But ethnography with its personal immersion, its denial of a screen of conventionalized methods, and its clear dependence on the researcher as the instrument of its action can be used by particular intellectual communities to motivate the questioning in which we see Buddy engaged at the close of his section.

At the same time it is important to point out that we own the enemy. While the effects of colonizing can obviously be seen in the "traditional" social science argument, the production of the argument is undoubtedly from equally emancipatory motives as interpretive ethnography might be. What we view in Buddy's closing comments is the construction of the "other" through which the self can be revealed. Laying out the character of traditional arguments establishes the ground on which the interpretive figure can be drawn.

The formulation of the other that the self might be known is precisely what all ethnography, traditional or interpretive, is about (Marcus & Fisher, 1986). The other is signified by the recognition of difference (Bachnik, 1987). This difference is the difference that the ethnographer observes, in which she or he participates, about which she or he writes, and which the reader recognizes. We ensure this difference by traipsing off to distant places; it's not by chance that there are few ethnographies of "our own." We may use the knowledge of this difference to extoll our moral superiority or to justify the technological extinction of some culture or to celebrate its differentness (Ramos, 1987).

Finally (for my round), we ought to consider the role of the reader. The ethnographer's work might be done when the writing is finished, but the course of public knowledge has just begun. It is the collective of the reader that determines that course. Most ethnographies are read by other ethnographers (or their students). Ethnography, as all science writing, serves first to reaffirm the community of practitioners. When read by nonmembers, ethnography suffers the fate of someone else's scriptures—certainly picturesque, and, perhaps, a good thought here and there, but not really legitimate. Finding legitimation among readers has been a continuing theme in ethnography leading some to "out-science" their critics and leading others to reclaim the critical in empirical science.

To understand the role of the reader in inquiry is to understand that the demands of practical action motivate knowledge not the other way round. The foundation of ethnography was not pure science but the service of Western religio/political ends. All Western science methods have been so implicated (Anderson, 1988b; Lazarsfeld, 1941). Writing of any sort to move out of its own community must serve the purposes of others. Witness the popularized ethnographies such as Malinowski's *The Sexual Life of Savages* (1929) or Mead's *Sex and Temperament in Three Primitive Societies* (1935) whose very titles reveal their social and political service.

Ethnography as well as all other forms of inquiry, as harmless practices of sequestered academics, goes mostly unread. We let the police tell us the truth of the street gangs; we let Bureau officials tell us the truth of native Americans; we let welfare officers tell us the truth of the homeless. It is probably clear that I feel that ethnographers along with most other scholars have failed to take their proper place in society.

Professor Goodall:

Jim ends on an important note that I also want to address, but to do that, there are two corollary issues he raises in his response that lay the groundwork for that discussion. The first issue is the idea that there is a way to read my position on the problematics as "antiintellectual" due to a "romanticizing" of fieldwork experience; the second issue is the whole notion of readership for ethnographic work.

To see the interpretive position that I advocate as *antiintellectual* and *romantic* is to comment rather directly on what an intellectual and nonromantic position on ethnography would be. It is to suggest, I think, that writing done in the service of theory-building is properly intellectual, and that this less complex, less ambiguous, and less poetic writing, which more easily serves an additive model of traditional social science is not only *nonromantic* but, given the general intellectual goal of theory-building, entirely preferable. To this I respond: tsk, tsk.

Let me elaborate. Embedded within Jim's argument is an assumption about an intellectual discourse community—a readership—that guides how the ideas of intellectual and non-intellectual, romantic and non-romantic get constructed. This intellectual discourse community is comprised of academic specialists and is, if we borrow for a moment Chaim Perelman's (1969) categories for audiences, a highly technical one. Highly technical audiences are, according to Perelman, keenly responsive to the highly specialized languages of science and social sciences; furthermore, they tend to be induced or persuaded to the extent that the work in question addresses—and adheres to—their highly specialized interests.

For me this is not the ideal audience I envision for my interpretive ethnographic work. Nor is it, I argue, the audience envisioned by a whole group of interpretive ethnographers who have made statements to this effect (see, for example, Rose, 1990; Jackson, 1989; Van Maanen, 1988; and especially Davis, 1985, 1988). For us, there is a *higher* audience we seek ideally to address and to gain respect from; that audience (to use Perelman's term) is a *universal* audience. A universal audience draws a wider crowd; it includes all academics as well as other highly specialized language users, but also describes intelligent ordinary citizens who are capable of reading a work for its comment and correspondence to their own lives, their own experiences, insights, sources of judgment and (small "t") truth.

This is an important distinction for two reasons. First, it explores one of the reasons why interpretive writing is more approachable (by which I mean it requires less technical language expertise) than traditional academic writing. Simply put, we seek a broader, public audience that, while including the specialists from our own disciplines and allied areas also respects the judgments of intelligent lay readers. And second, it suggests that the purpose of our writing is not limited to narrow academic/intellectual concerns. As Jim rightly observes, scholars and ethnographers have failed to take their proper place in society because their work stops short of social action. Alive in the interpretive camp are voices who oppose that failure, and who are seeking—through their more universal narratives, language styles, and everyday concerns—ways of encouraging social action through our work. Put a little differently, if cultural critique can be read and understood by a broader public audience, our work can become evidence useful for building the framework for social action.[12]

I have already moved into the second issue I wanted to discuss—readership. But let me use this issue of social action to explore some of the characteristics of the universal audience/reader envisioned by interpretive ethnographic work. First, let me begin by pointing out that what Jim says regarding the lack of ethnographies about the dominant, Western world is historically true but is changing. This is due, in part, to anthropology's self-admitted problem of running out of exotic Others to study due to the advent of technologies and other forms of cultural colonization (McGrane, 1989).

But it is also due to the "discovery" (appropriation?) of field research methods by sociologists, social psychologists, social workers, communication scholars, etc., who turned fieldwork techniques for the cultural construction of the exotic Other

---

[12]Social action is a code phrase which implicates science as a critique and force for change in society. It is founded on the position that science—as with all inquiry—is an agent in the social construction of reality.

toward folks closer to home. This move has had rhetorically significant consequences for the readership of ethnographic studies: The more ethnographers write about families, organizations, groups and communities that a universal public audience can identify with, the more likely two institutional forces will collide.

The first institutional force includes the publishers of (especially) book-length ethnographic studies that seek public sales from their publications;[13] the second institutional force includes the various mass media that colonize academic work for translation as "news" or "features" to their audiences.[14] When these two institutions collide, one result is that ethnographic work that is done "close to home" and that involves members of the media's targeted audience becomes—I hate to put it this way, but I think it is a truthful descriptor—useful. Another outcome is that academic ethnographers who are doing such work and who tune-in to those broadcasts often wonder: "if them, why not me?" And here we implicate the ethnographer capable of writing for a public audience directly in a quest for a more "universal" audience for one's writing.[15]

Finally (for my part of this turn, anyway), let me discuss the very important issue of "who gets to tell the story of culture to the public" raised by Jim in his last response. You will recall that his conclusion was that "we let police tell us the truth of the street gangs; we let the Bureau officials tell us the truth of native Americans; we let welfare officers tell us the truth of the homeless." In sum, our limited readership for ethnographic work also limits the extent to which we, as academics, are involved in social action.

I think what Jim is leaving out of that otherwise accurate depiction of "who gets to tell the story" is the pervasive influence of media. The reason why the police, the Bureau, and the welfare officials' stories are heard is because these individuals are (a) the localized site of authority on issues they are paid to deal with, and (b) because they do not usually speak through highly technical language codes that require a highly specialized audience to understand. In turn, media professionals seek them out as sources of truth because they can understand and validate the information these sources provide.

---

[13]This is also true for non-profit publishers such as university presses. In order to expand the range of what they can publish they also seek works that have sales potential to cover those less public, more esoteric scholarly works that may sell only to university libraries. It is important to note here that many trade publishers also are interested in ethnographic work if it is written for a broader public audience. The most interesting recent case is Wade Davis's *The Serpent and the Rainbow* (1985), which became both a trade market best-seller and was made into a (admittedly rather bad and exploitative) popular movie.

[14]Consider, for example, the extent to which National Public Radio and Public Television makes use of academic writers and academic work. As of this writing this seems to be increasingly true of prime-time commercial network shows as well.

[15]I am, of course, also implicating myself in this statement. I can say that I was very pleased to get a favorable review of *Casing a Promised Land* (Goodall, 1989c) in the LA Times Book Review as well as my spot on National Public Radio discussing the book's implications for high technology cultures. Furthermore, this has been a natural part of my ethnographic quest—to gain a broader public audience for not only my work, but the work of academic professionals generally.

For ethnographers—as well as any other class of academics—to speak authoritatively to the public on issues such as street gangs, native Americans, or the homeless requires the ability of our work to address a universal audience and the cooperation of the media in defining us as authorities capable of speaking to the interests of their viewers, readers, and listeners as constituent members of that universal audience. Clearly this is not as neat nor as easy as that sentence makes it appear to be. Wrapped up in issues of media access are deeply rooted negative sentiments among some academic professionals about "pandering to the masses" as well as issues of human jealousy when a "media star" has an office in your department. There are no answers for these questions because these questions have been around in the communication community at least since the Sophists and have yet to be resolved. In every age what this controversy has produced has been individuals who risk the negative sentiments and colleaguial jealousies as well as those who perpetrate the risk by speaking badly about those individuals and voting against them at tenure and/or promotion time. As Kurt Vonnegut puts it: "So it goes."

I am encouraged, however, by a reading of the history of science that shows us that the model for scholarly acceptance always is located in the physical sciences and then, usually within the next generation, trickles down to the social sciences. I am encouraged by this because the hard sciences have produced a generation of scholars who do address a universal audience and who do not seem to suffer badly among their colleagues for those actions. I am thinking here specifically of Stephen Jay Gould and Lewis Thomas, but there are others. Perhaps this generation of interpretive ethnographers in a wide variety of disciplines will be the proud inheritors of this legacy.

Professor Anderson:

I'm afraid I'm not so sanguine about the effectivity of media and their audiences. Neither are contextualized to motivate action (Kubey, 1990). The proper audiences for science are in the arenas of political activity. I realize that this position is directly contrary to the myth of value free science, but that myth no longer serves us well. It is quite clear that people act on their beliefs and that science must actively acknowledge not only its rightful place but also its rigorous ethical responsibility as an agent in the creation of those beliefs.

There is much more to be said on the issues we have raised to this point, but there is too much ground yet to be covered. In this turn, I would like to break into the category of experience. It would seem that we can better understand the relationship between writing and experiencing and of the relationship between writing and reading in the invocation of experience if we can understand more of the dimensions of experience.

Human experience is based on the ability to differentiate. Without differentiation, there is but a constant flow of energy between the world and the individual.

With the ability to differentiate the individual can use external or internal variations to punctuate the flow of energy into different phenomena. Differentiation is supported by signifying or the signing of difference. Signification frees the individual from the eternal present and creates the past and offers the future. (Some theorists do not separate differentiation from signifying. But there appears to me to be some theoretically useful work that can be done with the separation: Perhaps something about recognizing ineffable changes in the present.) Signification clearly participates in differentiation. The boundaries of the sign participate in the boundaries of the phenomenon and signification as a learned language teaches us a particular punctuation.

What one experiences then (and finally the connection) depends on the differences which are put to work. Understanding the domain of the other depends, therefore, on coming to know the differences which make a difference not for me but for them (Stoller, 1987). To appropriate one of your examples (Goodall, 1990)—and one on which we may disagree—I can "read" a parking lot at any time, but I come to know what the parking lot means in the domain of the other only after considerable socialization. (Whether we disagree depends on the degree of otherness we presume, I suppose. If the parking lot speaks *only* of the cultural concerns of gender, class, ethnicity, and age, then an uninitiated read is appropriate. But if the parking lot also speaks of an organizational culture, then the read is premature.)

For me, ethnography begins with trespassing on the domain of the other. I am attempting to place and move my body through that domain in some growing approximation of the appropriate rules. It is through my body that I experience the climate, the atmospheric quality, space and distance, the textures and sound and light values it presents, its odiferous characteristics, the palate of tastes—the resource of differences. It is through the body that I learn of the kinesthetic requirements of its placement and positioning and of the efficiencies and inefficiencies of movement. The domain of the other writes on my body. At this level I assume that my body responds as any other body responds. It registers heat and cold, light and dark, bitter and sweet, rough and smooth, and so on. I begin to understand the resource of sensory differences that the domain has to offer. (I don't think I'm arguing any primitive authenticity of experience here, but if it's 37 steps down the hallway for me, it's pretty close to that for any adult of my size. On the other hand, I can feel the heat, but within a pretty wide range, I don't know yet if it is hot. Within that range, which changes according to conventional dress and activity, hot is a discursive not a physical state. Of course, I know if I'm hot, but I don't know if it is hot in the domain of the other.)

What is written on the body can be considered the material facts of the site. By this designation, I am recognizing that for such "facts" there is a clear connection to the material resources of reality construction and that relatively little work is needed for their maintenance as facts. I am not saying, on the other hand, however, that such facts are objectively given to an observer. (I cannot walk through the material of which my neighbor's 8 foot wooden fence is made, but its purpose is not to keep me out.) Human action is rarely well understood at the material level.

In fact, we move very quickly from material facts to more socially constructed facts. An example of this move is the move from sex to gender. Difference by sex is a material fact. Difference by gender makes use of the material difference to differentiate a broad range of social action. The facts of gender (women earn less money, have lower rates of promotion, do more housework) are socially constructed facts. The socially constructed fact that women earn less money than men is no less real than the material fact of 37 steps from here to there. The difference is that the circumstances that permit the appearance of the latter are material and those of the former are contained in social practices. To change the fact of 37 steps requires the relocation of either here or there; to change the fact of lower earnings requires changes in the discursive justification of such wage practices not wholesale sex change operations.

It is possible that socially constructed facts with a more direct link to material differences are both more vulnerable to change and impossible to eradicate. They're more vulnerable to change because the obvious link renders the social claims implausible.

The material and social come clearly together in the actors at the site. There is the material individual of James Anderson in the department of communication. But the performing character of Jim is a coproduction that varies considerably depending on the characterizations supported by the collective as well as the casting resources available at the moment of enactment. Further, the role that Jim plays depends on the characterization enacted and the action going down. Coming to know a person means coming to know the range of people possible. (My line of argument here is based on the concept of the dependent rather than the essential self. See Anderson and Meyer, 1988.)

The appearance of who is one of the reasons that presence is such a valuable commodity. For example, to discover that a person "cheats like crazy" on the golf course (behaves in a manner which will support an interpretation of cheating) allows a greater range of discursive performances using that person. But to make that discovery requires a copresence on the golf course. The copresence, of course, creates a reciprocity of vulnerability. (It is, perhaps, this lack of reciprocity *in the writing* which renders the traditional ethnography suspect.) The experience of another, then, is a coproduction which says as much about self (Hodge & Kress, 1988).

What I am pressing is a view of experience which completely implicates the observer. Ethnography begins in the process by which the strange becomes familiar. Done right, it is argued, the resources of familiarity are those which emanate from the domain of the other rather than those imported by the observer. But the "familiarity" is obviously the work of a particular agent whose interpretive performance is all that we, the readers, have. And, further, because the writing is directed toward the domain of self, the ethnographer has to recast the experience of the other into the discursive practices of the self and cannot use the "expert" resources of either. It is clear that representation of the other or even the representation of one's experience of the other is not possible. Ethnography is quite properly the critique of self. It is the critical analysis of one's own based on the stance granted by the domain of the other.

In the writing, the ethnographer attempts to invoke the experience in the reader. The reader for her or his part creates an interpreted text as a local agent of collectives which direct that accomplishment. It is in the readers' role that ethnography's contribution is realized. Appealing to the wrong readership—we both agree—negates the contribution.

Professor Goodall:

We have agreed that authorship and readership are problematic to ethnographic projects. I propose that in this turn we dedicate ourselves to the delicate weave of the interdependent observational, representational, and rhetorical processes that create the authorship/readership relationship.

What I want us to do is to examine the essential issues about the interpenetrations of self, other, and context in ethnographic writing. For me these interpenetrations are informed by a philosophy of radical empiricism (Goodall, 1991; Jackson, 1989).

The Nature and Culture of Reality

One of the essential issues to the radical empiricist philosophy is how constructing rhetorics[16] may be used to display and interpret *multiple copresent ethnographic realities*. To begin this exploration requires an explanatory introduction to the idea of the communicative dimensions of experience, a discursive space that contains the intersections of constructing rhetorics of written texts and the dialogic foundations of multiple copresent ethnographic realities. From this discursive space we can enter an ongoing conversation in literary and cultural studies concerning the need for "a more heterodox view of what constitutes a legitimate research text" (Strine, 1988, p. 499).

Let me begin, then, with my claim: Conducting fieldwork and constructing narratives involve interdependent dialogic and rhetorical processes. By this I mean

---

[16] The term "constructing rhetorics" is intended to serve simultaneously as a sign for the problem of description in ethnographic texts and the postmodernist project to view language and textual construction as an always dialogic process between observer/observed and writer/reader. My use of the blurred grammatical boundary between verb and adjective positionings represented by the term "constructing" is intended to reference William Gass's (1970) commentary about the impossibility of descriptions in literature, only constructions. Hence, the stance taken throughout this essay is that rhetorical inducements act in dialogic ways when texts are viewed as constructing the realities they claim to represent. Obviously, the paradox here is unavoidable and as such forms a necessary part of my conversational strategy.

that both the fieldwork and its narrative begin in mystery and move, using the vehicles of empirical observation, experience, and encounter, through a field of representational possibilities for "meaningful orders of persons and things" (Sahlins, 1976) to some sense of completion or resolution, however contingent or partial.

By applications of intelligence directed at the ever-expanding, ever-evolving texts, the observer/writer creates the dialogic (Bakhtin, 1984, 1986; Bialostosky, 1986) foundations for understandings induced rhetorically by the language of the experiences said to "belong" to the scene (Burke, 1965, 1968). The ongoing narrative—the tale the teller shapes and tells about the experience as she or he moves through it—strives in words and strategies that are not equivalent to the experience to capture, nevertheless, the "story" in and of the critical site (Geertz, 1988; Langellier, 1989).

Let us begin at the outset of this discussion with the premise that the word *reality* as it is normally used in everyday speech to refer to the "empirical," refers in fact to trifurcated sites of meanings bounded by the communicative dimensions of experience. I apologize for both the structuralist implications and the awkward poetic of this term, but it seems less cumbersome than other discursive choices such as the antiquated, yet superiorly melodic "sursumcorda mix" or the only partially inclusive, McKeonesque phrase "perspectival diremption" (McKeon, 1972). For our purposes here I maintain that:

1. The word "reality" simultaneously holds referents that point to or assume the existence of a physical, "natural" world of facts and yet privileges our own selectively perceived and processed phenomenological constructions and interpretations of those facts (see Berger, 1970). This privileged reading may be based on observations and beliefs about how people and things work, how people and things are, or what people and things ought to be. All readings thus constructed are privileged, and all privileged readings have some basis for justification, verification, negation, playfulness, or some artistic combination thereof.

2. The site of our constructions and interpretations of "reality" are created and constituted in symbolic codes that invite participation in their meanings at both digital and analogic levels (Goodall, 1983; Haley, 1976). These meanings at once make all symbolic codes into metaphors, as well as metaphors about metaphors, and at either level (and often both at the same time) invite participation to a reading of *reality* that is necessarily partial and not necessarily true. Language is our attempt to order chaos (however you want to read this juxtaposition, wherever you want to place the emphasis), to make something out of everything and nothing, and to render all things at once immediate and personal as well as distant and abstract (see Olney, 1972).

3. The site that we call reality is a discursive space in the communicative dimensions of experience (van Peursen, 1972). The communicative dimensions

of experience are the dialogic, linguistic, contested spaces in which we make discourse, converse, offer arguments, bargain and negotiate with some "other(s)" to support the metaphors we believe best represent and account for what we have lived through or thought about (see Gunn, 1982). It is within the communicative dimensions of experience that we bring the word reality into the realm of both legalistic argument (Toulmin, 1958) and narrative rationality (Fisher, 1984), choice domains of discourse that suggest rules, rituals, and boundaries that in the act of their speaking appropriate, aggregate and/or negate various senses of "reality" according to some intention or purpose.

I am in accord here with the view that reality, at least in an objective sense, exists and in the fact of its existence constrains what can be said about it (Railsback, 1983), but cannot in any complete sense actually be communicated, or yield objective truth (Goldzwig & Dionisopoulos, 1989). Our words aren't large enough to hold the all of reality, but even if they were the space for their enactment as well as any claims made about it would still be contested. Reality exists, then, both as an objective presence outside of the metaphorical filters of human language and within the imaginative and linguistic realms of the communicative dimensions of experience. It is, however, within the communicative dimensions of experience that narratives about reality exist and do the business of inducing us to listen and to participate in their constructions.

The Communicative Dimensions of Experience

The communicative dimensions of experience are socially construct*ing* as well as socially construct*ed*. This means more than is usually implied by the invocation of the familiar Berger and Luckmann (1967) phrase, because the trifurcated simultaneous plurality of reality put forth here asks us to conceive not of one dominant, consensus site for negotiations of our coconstructions of meaning, but rather invites us to participate in an ongoing multivocal process of various counter-constructions, various sources of metaphorical approach and political resistance to the shifting sites of meanings (see Morgan, 1986; Mumby, 1987; Norton, 1989; Strine, 1989). There is, strictly speaking, no one reality available to the mutually constructed and constructing communicative dimensions of experience (see especially Sampson in Shotter & Gergen, 1989); there are, instead, multiple *copresent* realities.[17]

This trifurcated view of reality has serious implications for the constructing rhetorics we develop to represent the always dialogic nature of fieldwork. John Van Maanen (1988), for example, describes realist, confessional, and impres-

---

[17]I do not claim any of this as novel insight on my part. For generations there have been similar claims made by philosophers, poets, psychoanalysts, literary theorists, scientists, novelists, and mystics who, however they gained access to the consciousness within which was embodied for them this observation, located the site of the problem in the translation of experience to the experience of the translation.

sionist tales as ways of writing narrative that display, in their different stylistic and narrative embodiments, different ways of reading and representing reality. But more importantly, he recognizes that "ethnographies are documents that pose questions at the margins between two cultures," and with Barthes (1972), he sees this act of creation and representation as one of "necessarily decod[ing] one culture while recoding it for another" (p. 4). Hence, there is no "transparent" text any more than there can be a "neutral" language code.

Two important dimensions of ethnography that are frequently left out of the literature on how fieldwork is experienced and translated into a written text (and the effects one has on the other) are the interpenetrations of self and other that carry a variety of psychosocial and linguistic as well as cultural weights. For example, Wengle (1988), in a treatment of the "identity-dystonic" effects induced by "the self-doubts about the meaning of their life and work experienced by . . . anthropologists during their fieldwork" (p. xx) laments that in many well-publicized cases:

> The problem was that no two ethnographers seemed to be able to agree on what their people were really like . . . Although it is reasonable to assume that there are many factors that condition the nature of the differing interpretations of each investigator, surely one that must be considered is the personality of the investigator and its effect on his [sic] interpretation of field data. (pp. xxi–xxii)[18]

If *personality* can be viewed within the contexts of the communicative dimensions of experience described earlier as the outward embodiment of a characteristic style, of a way of experiencing and inscribing the narratives of one's life onto the practice of one's profession, then it is reasonable to assume that personality (as style and narrative) has important epistemological implications. The self—in the experience of fieldwork as well as in its reporting of what was experienced—is a written self, and that writing is done both within an evolving, personalized, dialogic cultural framework as well as with an appreciation of the institutionalized audience for the report. Hence, the written self is never certain. Self-doubt, as well as the awareness of the various mysteries of

---

[18]I can do no better than the author in describing this problem. Here are his words: "John Dollard and Hortense Powdermaker, for example, disagreed in their characterizations of America's Deep South. Margaret Mead and Reo Fortune, similarly, offered different interpretations of Arapesh culture. . . . As disquieting as these disagreements might appear, they pale in significance when compared to the Redfield/Lewis controversy. . . . Briefly, in 1951, Oscar Lewis restudied the Mexican village of Tepoztlan, where Robert Redfield had conducted fieldwork in 1930. Redfield, with his 'folk' leanings, had portrayed a friendly and harmonious peasant village, whereas Lewis, with a darker eye, saw a village beset by turmoil, envy, and hostility. These two accounts differed on nearly every matter; small details, broad interpretations, impressions of world view, all were portrayed differently. The most recent of these controversies is, of course, the currently famous Mead/Freeman debate . . . revolv[ing] around the 'true' nature of Samoan culture, in which life was either idyllic with little storm and stress, or nasty, brutish, and violent, depending on who one happens to believe" (p. xxi).

self, are part of the natural epistemics of textual construction whose presence and struggle within the narrative form an important part of its *ethos*.

As we have discussed, the "Other(s)" in fieldwork is similarly problematic. As a site of cultural inscription, the "Other(s)" has been historically defined as an "exotic" or "alien" species (see McGrane, 1989), someone to be engaged, observed, probed, and ultimately understood as a cultural product as well as the coproducer of said cultural text. The act of defining the "Other(s)" as culturally distinct, exotic, alien, is an interesting rhetorical move that carries with it intriguing strategies for writing ethnography (Neumann, 1989). To maintain that distance requires a delicate balance in the narrative between observer self-doubt that folds into what can only be described as contingent certainty about what one has observed. The result, for a reader, is a gradual dialogic constructing of varying degrees of textual authority, of the author's *ethos*, that depends on reporting stories that display rich textual description and detail (a grammar of knowing, capable of establishing familiarity and commonplaces) set within a broader narrative context of general ontological uncertainty (a rhetoric of mystery, capable of inducing belief).

What gets reported as reality is what lives within the rhetorical body of the writer and gets inscribed upon the narrative body of her or his work. What counts as real is what happens at the observed intersections that form the weave and tensions of experiential and authorial contexts, the emergent and mysterious borders of self, other, and language that are read, dialogically, as the constructed and constructing narrative experiences of the text. Viewed this way, immersion in fieldwork that is informed by this existential and phenomenological grounding is best understood as radical empiricism, "a philosophy of the experience of objects and actions in which the subject itself is a participant" (Edie, 1965, p. 119; Jackson, 1989, p. 3).[19]

---

[19]Radical empiricism is more fully, and excellently, explicated in Michael Jackson (1989). Briefly, this position on the doing of fieldwork and the writing of ethnography assumes a dialectical view of life that "remains skeptical of all efforts to reduce the diversity of experience to timeless categories and determinate theorems, to force life to be at the disposal of ideas" (Jackson, p. 2). Furthermore, this perspective views the character of lived experience as worthy of exploration, and sees in it "both the rage for order and the impulse that drives us to unsettle or confound the fixed order of things" (Jackson, p. 2). Hence, lived experience is always a construction of self and other within contexts, and that construction is never fixed nor static because "we are continually being changed by as well as changing the experience of others" (Jackson, p. 3). This perspective encourages a focus on the interactions of self and subjects, the explication of context and historical specificity, and values the narrative expressions of those encounters over more systematic, orderly, or procedural methods of codifying experience or explaining culture, communication, and behavior. With George Devereaux (1967), radical empiricists celebrate the autobiographical self and biographical Other(s) as part of the experimentation process, and see the exclusion of "the lived experience of the observer from the field of the observed . . . [as] a regrettable disturbance, . . . a stratagem for alleviating anxiety, not a rule of scientific method" (Jackson, p. 4). The senses of understanding that radical empiricism is informed by and hopes to inform may be said to be "to grasp the ways in which ideas and words are wedded to the world in which we live, how they are grounded in the mundane events and the experiences of everyday life" (Jackson, pp. 5–6).

Lived Experience as Mystery

Let us, then, investigate the philosophical nature of a radical empiricism that values participation in lived experiences, recognizes the importance of these borders, and the sense of narrative mystery and uncertainty that informs them. My use of the term *mystery* here is drawn from the dual influences of Gabriel Marcel (1949, 1950, 1987) and Kenneth Burke (1969). For Marcel, mystery is a way of approaching participation in the existential drama and phenomenology of everyday life. Mystery is contrasted with *problem* as an essential difference of Being, a difference that informs how and why humans view their own lives as well as the lives of others, and provides a locus of motives and reasons for behavior, choice, and speech. Mystery encourages us to see ourselves as integrally connected to Others, as coconstructors of a developing narrative of live in which the narratives themselves become intertwined, and with them so too does our sense of Being. "Problem," by contrast, encourages us to divorce our experiences and sense of self from Others, to divide the narratives of "us" from the narratives of "them," and to see in that division of narratives a natural superiority of the "observer-us" to the "objects-them" because our task is not to narratively engage or mingle with "them," but instead to narratively "solve" the "problem" suggested by that original division.

To see the interpenetrations of the texts of life as mysteries is to see in them tensions of self and Other, a drama of narrative structures upon which are constructed larger narratives of Being and within which lie, always, a "question in which what is given cannot be regarded as detached from the self" (Marcel, cited in Gallagher, 1975, p. 32). The purpose of narrative participation and the spell of dramatic tension, for Marcel, are inextricably linked to the process of knowing and of making known, of seeing and living the connectedness, of artistic creation and self-realization. To be able to confront the mysteries of living as mysteries, to enter and to participate in them, is to be involved in that creative process, and to be involved in that process is to realize the interdependence of self and Other(s).

Marcel's philosophical world-view holds particular promise for the practice of ethnography informed by a philosophy of radical empiricism. It provides a way of understanding why ethnographic narratives constructed out of the mysteries of self and Other(s) are distinguishable from ethnographic narratives that view the Other (and the Other's culture) as a problem. It is indeed how the author lives through the experience and writes about it that shapes the knowing and showing evident in the text (see Jackson, 1989, pp. 170–187). Thus, whether that experience is viewed as an existential, phenomenological mystery in which truth "is in the interstices as much as it is in the structure, in fiction as much as in fact" (Jackson, 1989, p. 187) or as a problem to be addressed or corrected through various but specific applications of scientific reasoning in which truth is revealed, constant, and binding, makes a difference, and a very important one.

Kenneth Burke's view of mystery achieves particular import at this juncture. For Burke (1969):

> Mystery arises at that point where different kinds of beings are in communication. In mystery there must be strangeness; but the estranged must also be thought of as in some way capable of communion. . . . The conditions of mystery are set by any pronounced social distinctions, as between nobility and commoners, courtiers and king, leader and people, rich and poor, judge and prisoner at the bar, 'superior race' and underprivileged 'races' or minorities. Thus even the story of relations between the petty clerk and the office manager, however realistically told (emphasis mine), draws upon the wells of mystery for its appeal . . . And all such 'mystery' calls for a corresponding rhetoric. (p. 115)

Burke's argument is not about writing ethnography, but instead addresses how particular doctrines drawn from Marx and Carlyle allow us to give a reading to rhetoric as naturally persuasive and always about revealing and concealing sources of consciousness. It is in respect to how consciousness is arrived at that I think his argument can be appropriated to our discussion of how radical empiricism informs the writing of ethnography.

First, I begin with Burke's observation about mystery being derived from the recognition that there are different classes of beings, and by direct implication there are also different classes of rhetoric inherent to the experiences of being those beings. We are indeed separated by our languages, vocabularies, sensitivities to meaning, and representative cultural codes into different classes of language users/abusers. To appropriate Weber's original phrase for our discussion of the borders of self and other that mark the empirical territories of mystery, we and the persons we study are, in and through the fieldwork experience, thus always suspended in webs of significance that we ourselves have spun. But significance is also a source of difference which can reveal the equipotential for what George Steiner (1973, p. 224) calls "alternity," that makes us, as Jackson (1989, p. 187) says, "subjects and agents of our own existence" and experiences. In the narratives of fieldwork informed by radical empiricism—by immersion and participation in the lived experiences of everyday life—different classes of beings do not share contexts and languages to become like one another, but instead to mark the borders, to preserve our individual and cultural integrities, to keep separate and often unequal realities, to maintain the mystery while constructing the narratives.

Burke's description of the sources for mystery in social relations also focuses on the impossibility of locating one definitive reality text, one overarching or underlying narrative perspective, thus necessitating consideration of alternative constructing rhetorics capable of attaining some (always contingent) correlation between lived experience and textual display. This passage has particular import for the writing of ethnography informed by radical empiricism because within this philosophical framework truth and untruth, reality and alternity, mystery, rhetorics, and narratives are the naturally occurring conditions of the experience of fieldwork.

The purpose of writing ethnography is the exposition and interpretation of those experiences, and "the value of and place of different discursive styles have to be decided by the situation we find ourselves in and the problems we address" (Jackson, 1989, p. 186). To accomplish this task requires, I think, an appreciation first of the nature of the "plural present" that informs the experience of radical empiricism, and second, an investigation of alternative constructing rhetorics capable of writing the plural present onto the body of ethnographic texts.

The Plural Present as Bodies in Dialogue

This is the place within the mystery we are participating in and constructing to introduce the notion of the "plural present" (Paz, 1989). I introduce this term to stand in place of "multiple copresent ethnographic realities" because it is shorter, more poetic, and references two concurrent, interpenetrating conversations that I believe have relevance to our discussion of the doing and writing of fieldwork. The first conversation concerns the need to construct the site of an ethnographic textual reality as a critical and dialogic space within the communicative dimensions of experience, a conversation that locates critical discourse within the broader domains of cultural critique. The second conversation concerns the desire expressed by a variety of scholars to open up the contexts of textual representations of the ethnographic experience, a conversation directed at challenging the rhetorical authority of conventional institutionalized forms of representing and reporting knowledge. In this section I show why these concerns are epistemologically and ontologically connected, and how their connections reveal a new and radically different framework for doing and reporting empirical research.

First, then, let us engage the issue of the plural present. Within the communicative dimensions of experience there must be some recognition of difference between the worlds of experience of self and other(s). This recognition brings with it a naturally occurring, Heideggerian sense of Being-in-the-world grounded in a full and historically particular immersion in the mutually constructed experiences of living. With this recognition also comes an appreciation for the problematic translation of the plural present into the constructing rhetorics of empirical research that reveal intertextual representations.

Mikhail Bakhtin (1986, pp. 60–102) provides a theory of dialogic criticism especially useful for critical scholars interested in a broad range of reports (including, but certainly not limited to ethnographic investigations) of self, other, and context. His theory focuses on the communicative utterance as a processual, critical site that inherently involves at least one speaker (with a field or range of dialogic stances and voices) and at least one listener (also with a field or range of dialogic stances and voices) sharing in an active, historically and specifically situated struggle for meaning. This description of the critical site of an utterance and its focus on the shared quest for meaning parallels, for our purposes, both the dialogic ethnographic encounter of self and other within a context and the rhetorical constructing process of narrative textual immersion characteristic of reader/writer engagement.

Although there are many ways to interpret dialogic theory as a source of critique (see especially Bialostosky, 1989; Fiske, 1986; Morson, 1986; Newcomb, 1984; and Strine, 1988), I focus here on the idea of multiple voices both as a native feature in the power relations of ethnographic reality-constructing projects and as a problem at the borders of creative expression and institutionalized genres of reporting ethnographic work. To do this I am adopting the voice of an advocate, a rhetorical option that encourages the forwarding of an argument capable of gaining warrantable assent to its claims.

Cultural critique should represent the communicative utterance as a critical site of meaning. To accept this claim requires viewing culture "not as an object to be described, neither [as] a unified corpus of symbols and meanings that can be definitively interpreted. Culture is contested, temporal, and emergent . . . thoroughly historicist and self-reflexive" (Clifford, cited in Clifford & Marcus, 1986, p. 19). It also requires opening up the text of culture to intertextual voices, voices that represent not merely the dominant, nor merely the emergent sources of power relations, but also those voices that represent the marginalized interests and passions of individuals and groups not typically heard from in ethnographic accounts. In this sense, as Bernard McGrane phrases it, "Culture is . . . and culture is *relative*" (1988, p. 25; emphasis mine).

Professor Anderson:

The concepts of constructing rhetorics and of the dialogic relations in ethnography are valuable in their introduction at this point in our discussion. Characterizing the narratives of fieldwork and ethnographic claim as the product of constructing rhetorics takes an affirmative stance on the rejection of innocence in scholarly writing. The power of claim in a world of social construction is that it makes sense of the world in language that both describes and persuades (Sangren, 1988; Roth, 1989). Claim is its own agent of truth.

On the other hand, characterizing the essential relationships in ethnography as dialogic underlines the requirement that no single perspective should prevail. Just as a conversation represents the contribution of all who participate so observation and participation and experience and writing coinform one another. If I as an ethnographer tell the tale as *it is*, I do so only by suppressing the multiple realities of any tale to be told. Any claim of inquiry—scientific or critical, nomothetic or hermeneutic—must contain an attempt to manage the appearance of reality. That management is often contested and, in postmodern fact, should always be contested (Tyler, 1987). The rhetorical management of reality is the basis of the cultural critique at which Buddy arrives at the end of his round.

The "so what" of all this is that all scholarly inquiry—including the hardest of science—inevitably involves the ascension of some elements and suppression of others to the benefit of some argument forms and the bane of their competitors. As Foucault (Gutting, 1989) has remarked, "everything is dangerous." A current critique of ethnographic as well as other social science writing has been the traditional suppression of other voices. This is a concern that I suspect we will visit in Buddy's next turn.

Professor Goodall:

Thus far we have examined the dialogic and rhetorical foundations of the plural present. In this discussion we have considered the trifurcated nature of reality, the dialogic inscription of self, other, and context upon the fieldwork experience of the observer and the observer's rhetorical translation of those experiences onto the body of the report, and the plural present nature of ethnographic textual encounters that emphasize the inducements of style and the importance of multi-vocal accounts in the shaping of the report. We need to consider, in the section that follows, the ways in which all of these concerns coalesce into a series of pragmatic problems for institutionalized genres for ethnographic research reports.

To get into this discussion I invoke a problem anthropologists have recognized (but not necessarily dealt with) that seems indigenous to the project of writing the plural present in communication research. The problem, stated simply, is *what gets left out that becomes who gets left out* of the ethnographic research report.

For example, Renato Rosaldo (1989) believes that the voices of Chicanos (and particularly Chicano women poets) are largely absent from North American cultural critiques, and that the "force of passion" inherent to intense emotional experiences for all of us have been similarly marginalized as a source of textual representation and knowing. Perhaps, he suggests, it is the combination of these forces of textual absence and an absence of adequate textual representation that coalesce to produce its effect.

The Body of the Text: A Politics of Composition

The struggle to capture a sense of the plural present and to give voice to a different read of the ritual of composition has direct relevance to the writing of fieldwork. Every text in fieldwork (as every life in experience) has many voices, many styles, and therefore makes available many invitations to participate, to join in the constructing experience, to read and to misread. There can be no one essential or privileged "true text" nor "true style" to govern a reading, which seems to imply rather directly that there should be no one essential institutionalized text.

Charles Bazerman's (1988, pp. 257–274) investigations of the "behaviorist rhetoric" of social science reports provides us with an entry into the cross-disciplinary conversations about institutionalized boundaries and the problem of writing a plural present into research reports. Bazerman's critique asserts that the problem of institutionalized boundaries has implications beyond simple adherence to formats for reporting citations and the do's and don'ts for writing the scholarly article. He observes, first, that the "subject" of a research project has been transformed into an "object," someone or something to be observed and categorized, not engaged nor encountered—a shift of emphasis and wording that privileges the experiences and knowledge of the researcher over that of the subject and essentially separates the two from each other in the contexts endorsed by the writing of the research report.

But the rules for scholarly writing also address the issue of authorship. Bazerman (1988) writes:

> Instead of a reasoner about the mind, the author is a doer of experiments, maker of calculations, and presenter of results. The author does not need to reason through an intellectual or theoretical problem to justify or design an experiment, nor in most cases does he or she need to identify and take positions on arguments in the literature. To produce new results, the author must identify behavior inadequately described and design an experiment to exhibit the behavior in question. With the methodological problem reduced to obtaining uncontaminated results, carefulness rather than good reasoning becomes the main characteristic to be displayed in the methods section. (p. 272)

This model for scientific writing is founded on the principle of "incremental encyclopedism," in which the "function of the article is . . . to add a descriptive statement to an existing body of such statements" (p. 273). While Bazerman's (1988) work specifically addresses the writing of the experimental scholarly article, there are some clear implications for any disciplinary genre of formal academic writing that favors the form over its content. Specifically, there seem to be four ways this "incremental encyclopedism" affects the writing of scholarship, all of which have overt and subtle impact on the writing of the fieldwork experience.

First, it encourages the view that following procedures is more important than immersion in the full evolving processes and interpenetrations of contexts in what is being studied. This is the sort of thinking that values the continuation of linear bureaucratic problem-solving over more innovative, less boxed logics and that sees the following of received procedures as a reasonable (read: less problematic) substitute for original, counter-intuitive, resistant, and/or creative thought.

Second, incremental encyclopedism favors an additive view of scholarship that assumes the cross-disciplinary construction of one grand theory that can be articulated to explain all of human behavior and culture. This project has largely failed in the twentieth century (see Bell, 1982) but the whole perspective is particularly odious if one reads into a grand theory an encouragement of a concurrent dominant research and writing ideology that it inherently seems to sponsor. Furthermore, on more pragmatic grounds, the idea that the multiple and

diverse languages currently being spoken across academic borders, the languages
being used to construct knowing as well as what is capable of being made known
would ever coalesce into one grand theory or explanation is, at best, ironic.

Third, formula science writing has rhetorically shaped acceptable ways of
publishing scholarship. In science and social science writing, this has meant a
general shortening of the length of the article. Not only does brevity encourage
a kind of scholarly minimalism, it also induces a kind of scholarly shorthand in
the form of jargon and acronyms. Furthermore, it disencourages consideration
of competing perspectives within the framework of any single essay (Bazerman,
1988). This leads to a struggle for a dominant research ideology on a particular
subject that asks a reader to accept one reading of reality based on its command
of available journal space. This struggle raises the practical question of how an
alternative textual construction that did not conform to the scholarly epistemic
and ontologic norms be located within this discursive space?

Fourth, the formula narrative encourages us to view authors and dates as
"landmarks" in a linear progression of "findings" (Bazerman, 1988, p. 274). This
tactic does not encourage consideration of alternative arguments or points of
view, nor does it encourage submission of work that will not easily "tie-into"
the existing body of literature. The outsider's voice is marginalized, if not wholly
abandoned. For fieldwork experiences the dominant voice is that of the outsider,
and unless the fieldwork experience can be shown to tie-into some existing
theoretical or methodological argument current in the literature, there is difficulty
in "demonstrating relevance" to communication journals' audiences.

In these four issues we can clearly see the practical action by which the
appearance of reality is managed and the suppression of other voices, of which
Jim spoke, is accomplished. If we are to consider an alternative, we must begin
by examining the standards of its practical action.

The Body of the Text: The Poetics of Composition

Reality is, regardless of the position taken toward what constitutes it, a socially
(and, in this case, professionally) constructed terrain that can exist because there
are formal, more-or-less agreed upon standards for its construction as well as for
determining what reality lives in it. Ben Agger (1989), for example, sees:

> Writing as a social and political relationship both reflecting and constituting the
> ensemble of social relationships describing experience in a highly differentiated
> world. The permeable boundary between text and world requires a double reflection
> at once addressing the preponderant objectivity of the world dominating the
> disempowered subject and, from the other direction, interrogating writing that
> remakes a world infiltrating writing as its bounteous, unavoidable subtext (much
> deeper than mere "subject matter"). Aware of its own literary ground in authorial
> desire, a new version undoes the untrapping discourse of the power of the social
> by approaching the world in a confident way yet beholden to its own motives of

advocacy. This undoing is not the same "topic" simply handled differently but a breathing of motive into the purposely dehumanized text of science as ways of both getting scientism off our backs and showing the possibility of subject-object, text-world, human-human rapprochement, if not their full identity. . . . Criticism designed to break the umbilical link with a discipline threatening to swallow marginal writing . . . models a textual practice (a) refusing intellectual closure, (b) regarding itself as creative self-expression (not only "communication"), and (c) inviting others to address it dialogically as it addresses other versions in self-confidently incomplete prose. (pp. 335–336)

Agger's (1989) agenda is to address the political nature of scientifically-informed and institutionalized standards for writing that claim "a freedom from desire" (p. 372) while imposing ideology and constraining what can be known by disciplining what can be expressed. His critique, then, sets up the dilemma of how to establish critical standards for scholarship that both adheres to the principle of the plural present and yet must somehow fit into the story offered to the wider community of scholars. Considered as a disciplinary and cross-disciplinary exigence, this dilemma can be defined not so much by its *episteme* as by the assumption of its bifurcated "ontic unity" (Castaneda, 1989, p. 204). Put simply, how can a discipline open up its professional space to include stories that do not "look like" much less "fit into" its historical and evolutionary dialogue?

I believe the centerpiece of the formula-driven argument is the assumption that the reality that has been constructed in the social sciences may be a partial rendering of the world, but at least it can be made known in a style that assumes a certain symmetry of values and standards for judging its worth among writers and readers—a standard of ontic unity. Without using those standards, how would "we" know how to evaluate a report?

This is, within the boundaries of the communicative dimensions of experience, the discursive territory of what I am calling here "necessary constraints." This is where the boundaries are drawn that mark the space for what counts as a research report and what counts as something other than a research report, a narrative that is "merely" novel, insightful, clever, or well-written. And, as a result, this is where what counts as reality must be negotiated by standards that must always assume only a partial reading of what is already a partial reading of the truth.

My position is informed by the arguments I have previously advanced about how dialogic and rhetorical fieldwork realities are constructed and what the process of research and writing does to that constructing in the first place. Although it may read as if I am trying to privilege ethnographic depictions of reality over other reports, I must protest that I am, in fact, *not.* The discipline of communication and its literatures need all sorts of reports, from all sorts of reporters. Only in the mix that is characteristic of the experiences of living—both within the dominant research and writing ideology and against the furthermost reaches of its margins as well as in the wide mental and behavioral spaces in between—are we likely to draw individual and collective portraits of the communicative dimensions of experience. Because that is where our discipline lives, as well as where our depictions of reality are negotiated, should that not also be the architectonic principle that informs our understanding of what constitutes a research report?

I think so. But this does not mean that I do not also see the need for articulated standards (however wide they may need to be), a critical framework, for evaluating alternative research reports. We cannot compete in the professional realm of published research if we cannot express and explain the standards we use to evaluate the reports that we, as a discipline, endorse.

Toward that end, we offer the following observations about how to evaluate writing that displays the plural present in ethnographic narratives. We do this not to prescribe what the standards for critique should be so much as to turn the scholarly conversation toward a new and necessary topic, and to issue through this discourse a general invitation to others to participate. Here are our recommendations:

1. Aesthetic and rhetorical standards for determining the quality and value of literary work are a historical part of our critical apparatus, and therefore can and should be applied to works that reveal an epistemic informed by literary traditions. Beauty, as well as truth, should be jointly considered (Goodall, 1989c). The evaluative criteria for the ontic unity of the story should be expanded to include all texts that represent human understanding, and the narrow criterion for ontic unity that would marginalize forms and styles of understanding that do not fit the dominant research and writing ideology should be set aside.

2. Any research report must be carried out within the weave of a context or situation. The descriptive adequacy of that situation must be evaluated as a part of the descriptive adequacy of the research being reported. Standards for descriptive adequacy in ethnographic reports should include consideration of the physical, economic, dramatic, and hierarchical dimensions of the context as well as how the context evolved while the research was conducted (see Goodall, 1990).

3. Any research report must involve an author(s) and subject(s), a self and Other(s), whose behavior in constructing the weave of the context is always problematic and never certain. The tentativeness and relativity of dialogic performances, including the conversations that inform those performances, should be considered a natural part of the research being reported and may be informed by dialogic criticism (see Bialostosky, 1989; Strine, 1988; Strine & Pacanowsky, 1985).

One of the principle features of dialogic criticism as informed by a decidedly Bakhtinian reading, is the privileging of "the novel as the genre that most fully actualizes such relations by artistically organizing the diverse voices of a contemporary world into mutually revealing responsiveness, and he [Bakhtin] would allow 'novelized' criticism and 'novelized' critical theory to work toward the same kind of organization within their own domains of discourse" (Bialostosky, 1989, p. 224). Dialogic criticism is applicable, most directly, to a dialogic text.

4. The author(s)'s personal history and autobiography are necessarily part of the context she or he participates in. Reports of how self-awareness and past personal experiences have informed the reading given to a research situation should be encouraged to be read as a natural part of the data. To use this standard within the territory of critical judgment means, first, to open up the text to include such statements (see Benson, 1981; Goodall, 1989b, and Pacanowsky, 1988 for examples) and, second, to bring to the critical judgment an informed stance about the role of the autobiographical self in the construction of texts that shape self and Other(s) (see Gunn, 1982; Olney, 1972).

5. Subjects for a research report should be considered as biographical subjects, not dehumanized "objects" of study. Attempts to articulate their personhood, who and what they are and have been, should be seen as necessary correlates to the author's autobiographical accounts.

Only in the displayed space of negotiated self-and-other narratives can a full reading of the communicative dimensions of experience be realized. To accomplish this standard requires, I think, accepting the concept of "mystery" as the shaping force of the narrative, or at least to not require every text to fit neatly into writing formulas informed by the concept of "problem." It would also require close textual reading of the negotiations between self and Other(s) for thematic unfoldings of human experiences and the various psychological, sociological, and dramatic critiques inspired by the reading.

The text of conversations, then, would expand its borders from the spatial and critical territories of "data" to include the interpenetrations of self and Other(s) as biographical and autobiographical performing selves (see Moerman, 1988, especially pp. 101–120), as well as "voices" capable of revealing perceptual, directional, and atmospheric qualities (see Bakhtin, 1984; Ihde, 1986, pp. 27–47) that lie before and beyond rule-bound linguistic concerns.

6. The struggle for descriptive and dialogic adequacy is a natural part of contemporary American prose at this end of the twentieth century (C. Anderson, 1987). An author's right to question the adequacy of what he or she has been writing, as well as to provide alternative readings of the context and its meanings, should be seen within the realm of the "thick" descriptions (Geertz, 1988) called for by scholars sensitive to the rhetoric of writing.

This standard would inform critical judgment on at least three discursive fronts. First, it would encourage multiple readings of the "data" provided by constructions of self, Other(s), and context—there would no longer need to be "a" privileged reading of the text. Second, alternative readings could be encouraged to be presences "within" the text, in addition to encouraging responses "outside" of the text by critics and readers. Journal articles, for example, could include the critic's comments that the author was asked to respond to as part of the constructing rhetoric of the "final" and "officially-sanctioned" text. Third, the author's sensitivities to the problems and mysteries of narrative should be seen as part of the framing of the narrative itself, not as an unnecessary detour into esoteric domains that have "little to do" with what is being reported.

7. Narrative style should be assessed by its ability to induce a participative reading of the text, to inform the reader in an insightful and meaningful way, and to encourage the advancement of knowledge through dialogic and rhetorical involvement that both contributes to and resists the dominant ideology of the issue as well as of the constructing of the written texts. As such, a text should be evaluated by its ability to induce a sense of "jamming" (Eisenberg, 1990), of shared participation and activity that does not necessarily require shared cognitive meanings. The text should open up, rather than close off, invitations to join in its performance.

CONCLUSIONS

We began this essay with a brief explication of the history of ethnographic practices. These practices implicated ethnographers and ethnographies in neocolonial activities. Neocolonialism as a naive political practice remained relatively entrenched in scholarship until the mid-1960s; since then both the overt and subtle mechanisms of these neocolonial practices have problematized both the work and the writing of ethnographers.

In the second section of this essay we explored some of those problematics. We detail (admittedly at some length) how ethnographic practices are a major cultural site for implicating and extending theories of human communication and human communication research. In this section we explored a variety of issues relevant to theory construction and research practices, and although there were several points of important departure between us, we agreed at the end of this section that questions of authorship and readership were at the semiotic heart of an intersection of ethnographic fieldwork, ethnographic writing, and the positioning of those practices in a postmodern, postcolonial quest for non-neo-colonialism.

It was at this juncture that we introduced "the plural present" as a way to reduce (never fully replace) the problematics of inherent neocolonialism in ethnography (and, by extension, into other realms of doing and writing research reports). We began this argument by viewing reality as a plural present, existing discursively within the language boundaries that mark the communicative dimensions of experience. Within this realm all representations of what is real are partial, linguistic, dialogically realized and rhetorically formulated. There can be no one privileged reading of reality because there is no one privileged reality text.

Against this theoretical construction we then advanced a series of practical arguments about the problems of reporting the ethnographic experiences of fieldwork informed by radical empiricism in alternative narrative styles of scholarship. We approached the problem this way because one of the major assumptions guiding current research and writing in American social science informs a professionally constructed text for what counts as reality that favors a narrative style that diminishes the personal roles of both the author(s) and subject(s) as well as "the weave of context" (Goodall, 1990) that is epistemically, ontologically, and phenomenologically relevant to the "truth" or "findings" that are ultimately revealed.

Our position in this dilemma is clearly aligned with those who favor opening up journal space for alternative styles of reporting reality (Agger, 1989; Anderson, 1988a; Bazerman, 1988; Benson, 1981; Castaneda, 1989; Goodall, 1989c; Jackson, 1989; Pacanowsky, 1988; Strine, 1988). This position is informed by our belief that human experience is relevant to the practices of the human sciences, and that the shaping force of stories about how the research was conducted, who the researcher and subjects thought they were and what they thought they were doing while the work was being dialogically constructed, are as much a part of the method as they are a part of how findings and truths were arrived at and should be reported. But this is only a statement of what must be considered to be a political as well as a philosophical position, and not an invitation to privilege the reading it encourages.

So, what does the future of ethnography hold for communication theory and research? Or, put differently, what does the future of communication theory and research hold for the doing and writing of ethnography? The answers here are necessarily elusive and interdependent. The only certainty is that the future is where all of us—if we are lucky—will live and work. Our hope is that this chapter, and its arguments for altering the course of that future, are worthy of your serious attention and intellectual consideration.

REFERENCES

Agger, B. (1989). *Socio(onto)logy: A disciplinary reading*. Urbana, IL: University of Illinois Press.
Anderson, C. (1987). *Style as argument*. Carbondale, IL: Southern Illinois University Press.
Anderson, J. A. (1987). *Communication research: Issues and methods*. New York: McGraw-Hill.
Anderson, J. A. (1988a). Editor's introduction. *Communication Yearbook 12*. Newbury Park, CA: Sage.
Anderson, J. A. (1988b, April). *Dressing science in ordinary clothes*. Paper presented at the University of Utah Department of Communication colloquium, Salt Lake City.
Anderson, J. A., & Meyer, T. P. (1988). *Mediated communication: A social action perspective*. Newbury Park, CA: Sage.
Bachnik, J. M. (1987). Native perspectives of distance and anthropological perspectives of culture. *Anthropological Quarterly, 60*, 25–34.

Bakhtin, M. M. (1984). *Problems of Dostoevsky's poetics* (C. Emerson, Ed. and Trans.). Minneapolis, MN: University of Minnesota Press.

Bakhtin, M. M. (1986). *Speech genres and other late essays* (V. W. McGree, Trans.). Austin, TX: University of Texas Press.

Barrett, S. R. (1984). *The rebirth of anthropological theory.* Toronto, Canada: University of Toronto Press.

Barthes, R. (1972). *Mythologies.* London, England: Paladin.

Bateson, G. (1958). *Naven* (2nd ed.). Stanford, CA: Stanford University Press.

Bazerman, C. (1988). *Shaping written knowledge: The genre and activity of the experimental article in science.* Madison, WI: University of Wisconsin Press.

Bell, D. (1982). *The social sciences in the twentieth century.* Cambridge, MA: Harvard University Press.

Benedict, R. (1946). *The chrysanthemum and the sword: Patterns of Japanese culture.* Boston, MA: Houghton Mifflin.

Benson, T. (1981). Another shootout in cowtown. *The Quarterly Journal of Speech, 67,* 347–406.

Berger, P. L. (1970). The problem of multiple realities: Alfred Shutz and Robert Musil. In M. Natanson (Ed.), *Phenomenology and social reality: Essays in memory of Alfred Shutz* (pp. 200–237). The Hague: Martinus Nijhoff.

Berger, P. L., & Luckmann, T. (1967). *The social construction of reality.* Garden City, NY: Anchor.

Bernard, H. R. (1988). *Research methods in cultural anthropology.* Newbury Park, CA: Sage.

Bialostosky, D. H. (1986). Dialogics as an art of discourse in literary criticism. *PMLA, 101,* 788–797.

Bialostosky, D. H. (1989). Dialogic criticism. In D. Atkins & L. Morrow (Eds.), *Contemporary literary theory* (pp. 214–228). Amherst, MA: University of Massachusetts Press.

Brodkey, L. (1987). Writing critical ethnographic narratives. *Anthropology and Education Quarterly, 18,* 67–76.

Burke, K. (1965). *Permanence and change: An anatomy of purpose* (2nd rev. ed.). Indianapolis, IN: Bobbs-Merrill.

Burke, K. (1968). *Counter-statement.* Berkeley, CA: University of California Press.

Burke, K. (1969). *A rhetoric of motives.* Berkeley, CA: University of California Press.

Carbaugh, D. (1988). Cultural terms and tensions in the speech at a television station. *Western Journal of Speech Communication, 52,* 216–237.

Castaneda, H-N. (1989). *Thinking, language, and experience.* Minneapolis, MN: University of Minnesota Press.

Clifford, J. (1983). On ethnographic authority. *Representations, 1,* 118–146.

Clifford, J. (1988). *The predicament of culture.* Cambridge, MA: Harvard University Press.

Clifford, J., & Marcus, G. E. (Eds.). (1986). *Writing culture.* Berkeley, CA: University of California Press.

Davis, W. (1985). *The serpent and the rainbow.* New York: Simon & Schuster.

Davis, W. (1988). *A passage of darkness.* Chapel Hill, NC: University of North Carolina Press.

Devereaux, G. (1967). *From anxiety to method in the behavioral sciences.* The Hague: Mouton.

Edie, J. (1965). Notes on the philosophical anthropology of William James. In J. Edie (Ed.), *An invitation to phenomenology: Studies in the philosophy of experience* (pp. 110–132). Chicago, IL: Quadrangle Books.

Eisenberg, E. M. (1990). Jamming: Transcendence through organizing. *Communication Research, 17,* 139–164.

Ellen, R. F. (Ed.). (1984). *Ethnographic research: A guide to general conduct.* London, England: Academic Press.

Evans-Pritchard, E. E. (1940). *The Neur.* Oxford, England: Clarendon.

Firth, R. (1936). *We, the Tikopia.* London, England: Allen & Unwin Ltd.

Fisher, W. R. (1984). Narration as a human communication paradigm: The case of public moral argument. *Communication Monographs, 51,* 1–22.

Fiske, J. (1986). Television: Polysemy and popularity. *Critical Studies in Mass Communication, 3,* 391–408.

Friedrich, P. (1988). Multiplicity and pluralism in anthropological construction/synthesis. *Anthropological Quarterly, 61,* 103–112.

Gallagher, K. T. (1975). *The philosophy of Gabriel Manel.* New York: Fordham University Press.

Gass, W. H. (1970). *Fiction and the figures of life.* New York: Alfred A. Knopf.

Geertz, C. (1988). *Works and lives: The anthropologist as author.* Stanford, CA: Stanford University Press.

Giddens, A. (1976). *New rules of sociological method: A positive critique of interpretative sociologies.* London, England: Hutchinson.

Goldzwig, S. R., & Dionisopoulos, G. N. (1989). John F. Kennedy's civil rights discourse: The evolution from "principled bystander" to public advocate. *Communication Monographs, 56,* 179–198.

Goodall, H. L. (1983). The nature of analogic discourse. *The Quarterly Journal of Speech, 69,* 171–79.

Goodall, H. L. (1989a). A cultural inquiry concerning the ontological and epistemic status of self, other, and context in communication research. In G. M. Phillips & J. T. Wood (Eds.), *Speech communication: Studies honoring the 75th anniversary of the Speech Communication Association* (pp. 264–292). Carbondale, IL: Southern Illinois University Press.

Goodall, H. L. (1989b). On becoming an organizational detective: The importance of context sensitivity and intuitive logics in communication consulting. *The Southern Communication Journal, 55,* 42–54.

Goodall, H. L. (1989c). *Casing a promised land: The autobiography of an organizational detective as cultural ethnographer.* Carbondale, IL: Southern Illinois University Press.

Goodall, H. L. (1990). Interpretive contexts for decision making: Toward an understanding of the physical, economic, dramatic, and hierarchical interplays of language in groups. In G. M. Phillips & J. T. Wood (Eds.), *Group skills and group outcomes* (pp. 197–224). Norwood, NJ: Ablex.

Goodall, H. L. (1991). *Living in the rock n roll mystery: Reading context, self, and others as clues.* Carbondale, IL: Southern Illinois University Press.

Gravel, P. B., & Ridinger, R. (1988). *Anthropological fieldwork: An annotated bibliography.* New York: Garland.

Gunn, J. V. (1982). *Autobiography: Toward a poetics of experience.* Philadelphia, PA: University of Pennsylvania Press.

Gutting, G. (1989). *Michel Foucault's archaeology of scientific reason.* Cambridge, England: Cambridge University Press.

Haley, J. (1976). *Problem-solving therapy.* New York: Basic Books.

Hammersley, M., & Atkinson, P. (1983). *Ethnography: Principles in practice.* London, England: Tavistock.

Hess, D. J. (1989). Teaching ethnographic writing: A review essay. *Anthropology and Education Quarterly, 20,* 163–177.

Hickson M. III, (1983). Ethnomethodology: The promise of applied communication research? *Southern Speech Communication Journal, 48,* 182–195.

Hodge, R., & Kress, G. (1988). *Social semiotics.* Ithaca, NY: Cornell University Press.

Husserl, E. (1970). *The crisis of European sciences and transcendental phenomenology* (Trans. with introduction by D. Carr). Evanston, IL: Northwestern.

Ihde, D. (1986). *Consequences of phenomenology.* Albany, NY: SUNY University Press.

Jackson, M. (1989). *Paths toward a clearing: Radical empiricism and ethnographic inquiry.* Bloomington: Indiana University Press.

Kirschner, S. R. (1987). "Then what have I to do with thee?": On identity, fieldwork, and ethnographic knowledge. *Cultural Anthropology, 2,* 211–234.

Kubey, R. (1990). Television and the quality of family life. *Communication Quarterly, 38,* 312–324.

Langellier, K. M. (1989). Personal narratives: Perspectives on theory and research. *Text and Performance Quarterly, 9,* 243–276.

Lazersfeld, P. F. (1941). Remarks on administrative and critical research. *Studies in Philosophy and Social Sciences, 9,* 2–16.

Levi-Strauss, C. (1963). *Structural anthropology.* New York: Basic Books.

Lofland, J. (1971). *Analyzing social settings.* Belmont, CA: Wadsworth.

Lofland, J. (1976). *Doing social life.* New York: Wiley.

Malinowski, B. (1922). *Argonauts of the western Pacific.* London, England: G. Routledge and Sons.

Malinowski, B. (1929). *The sexual life of savages.* New York: Halcyon House.

Marcel, G. (1949). *The philosophy of existence* (M. Harari, Trans.). New York: Philosophical Library.

Marcel, G. (1950). *Mystery of being* (Vols. 1 & 2). (R. Hague, Trans.). London, England: Harvill Press.

Marcel, G. (1987). *The participant perspective: A reader* (T. W. Busch, Ed.). Lanham, MD: University Press of America.

Marcus, G. E., & Fisher, M. J. (1986). *Anthropology as cultural critique.* Chicago, IL: The University of Chicago Press.

McGrane, B. (1989). *Beyond anthropology: The story of the other.* New York: Columbia University Press.

McKeon, R. (1972). Communication as an architectonic, productive art. In L. Bitzer & E. Black (Eds.), *The prospect of rhetoric* (pp. 44–63). Englewood Cliffs, NJ: Prentice-Hall.

Mead, M. (1928). *Coming of age in Samoa.* New York: William Morrow.

Mead, M. (1935). *Sex and temperament in three primitive societies.* New York: William Morrow.

Moerman, M. (1988). *Talking culture: Ethnography and conversation analysis.* Philadelphia, PA: University of Pennsylvania Press.

Morgan, G. (1986). *Images of organization.* Newbury Park, CA: Sage.

Morson, G. S. (1986). *Bakhtin: Essays and dialogues on his work.* Chicago, IL: University of Chicago Press.

Mumby, D. K. (1987). The political function of narrative in organizations. *Communication Monographs, 54,* 113–127.

Neumann, M. (1989, May). *The "problem" of evidence in ethnographic research.* Paper presented at the International Communication Association convention, San Francisco.

Newcomb, H. (1984). On dialogic aspects of mass communication. *Critical Studies in Mass Communication, 1,* 34–50.

Norton, C. S. (1989). *Life metaphors.* Carbondale, IL: Southern Illinois University Press.

Olney, J. (1972). *Metaphors of self.* Princeton, NJ: Princeton University Press.

Pacanowsky, M. E. (1988). Slouching towards Chicago. *The Quarterly Journal of Speech, 74,* 453–467.

Paz, O. (1989, October). *Tanner lecture on human values.* The University of Utah, Salt Lake City.

Perelman, C., & Olbrechts-Tyhra, L. (1969). *The new rhetoric.* Notre Dame, IN: Notre Dame University Press.

Peursen, C. A. van. (1972). *Phenomenology and reality.* Pittsburgh, PA: Duquesne University Press.

Philipsen, G. (1975). Speaking "like a man" in Teamsterville: Cultural patterns of role enactment in an urban neighborhood. *The Quarterly Journal of Speech, 61,* 13–22.

Philipsen, G. (1977). Linearity of research design in ethnographic studies of speaking. *Communication Quarterly, 25,* 42–50.

Rabinow, P., & Sullivan, W. M. (Eds.). (1987). *Interpretive social science: A second look.* Berkeley: University of California Press.

Radcliffe-Brown, A. R. (1948). *The Adaman Islanders.* Glencoe, IL: The Free Press.

Railsback, C. C. (1983). Beyond rhetorical relativism: A structural-material model of truth and objective reality. *The Quarterly Journal of Speech, 69,* 351–363.

Ramos, A. R. (1987). Reflecting on the Yanomami: Ethnographic images and the pursuit of the exotic. *Cultural Anthropology, 2,* 284–318.

Rosaldo, R. (1989). *Culture and truth.* Boston, MA: Beacon Press.

Rose, D. (1990). *Living the ethnographic life.* Newbury Park, CA: Sage.

Roth, P. A. (1989). Ethnography without tears. *Current Anthropology, 30,* 555–569.

Sahlins, M. (1976). *Culture and practical reason.* Chicago, IL: University of Chicago Press.

Sanday, P. R. (1979). The ethnographic paradigm(s). *Administrative Science Quarterly, 24,* 527–538.

Sangren, P. S. (1988). Rhetoric and the authority of ethnography: "Postmodernism" and the social reproductions of texts. *Current Anthropology, 29,* 405–435.

Savage, M. (1988). Can ethnography be a neighborly act? *Anthropology and Education Quarterly, 19,* 3–19.

Shotter, J., & Gergen, K. J. (1989). *Texts of identity.* Newbury Park, CA: Sage.

Sigman, S. J. (1987). *A perspective on social communication.* Lexington, MA: Lexington Books.

Simon, R. I., & Dippo, D. (1986). On critical ethnographic work. *Anthropology and Education Quarterly, 17,* 195–202.

Spiro, M. E. (1986). Cultural relativism and the future of anthropology. *Cultural Anthropology, 1,* 259–286.

Spradley, J. P. (1980). *Participant observation.* New York: Holt, Rinehart and Winston.

Steiner, G. (1973). *After Babel.* London, England: Oxford University Press.

Stoller, P. (1987). Son of Rouch: Portrait of a young ethnographer by the Songhay. *Anthropological Quarterly, 60,* 114–123.

Strine, M. S. (1989). The politics of asking women's questions: Voice and value in the poetry of Adrienne Rich. *Text and Performance Quarterly, 9,* 24–41.

Strine, M. S. (1988). Constructing "texts" and making inferences: Some reflections on textual reality in human communication research. In J. A. Anderson (Ed.), *Communication Yearbook 11* (pp. 494–501). Beverly Hills, CA: Sage.

Strine, M. S., & Pacanowsky, M. E. (1985). How to read interpretive accounts of organizational life: Narrative bases of textual authority. *The Southern Speech Communication Journal, 50,* 283–297.

Toulmin, S. (1958). *The uses of argument.* Cambridge, England: Cambridge University Press.

Tyler, S. A. (1987). *The unspeakable: Discourse, dialogue, and rhetoric in the postmodern world.* Madison, WI: The University of Wisconsin Press.

Van Maanen, J. (1988). *Tales of the field: On writing ethnography.* Chicago, IL: University of Chicago Press.

Weber, M. (1978). *Economy and Society: An outline of interpretive sociology* (G. Roth & C. Wittich, Eds.). Berkeley, CA: University of California Press.

Wengle, J. (1988). *Ethnographers in the field: The psychology of research.* Tuscaloosa, AL: The University of Alabama Press.

White, L. A. (1968). On the concept of culture. In R. A. Manners & D. Kaplan (Eds.), *Theory in anthropology: A sourcebook* (pp. 15–20). Chicago, IL: Aldine.

Part III

The Foundations
of Communication:
Human Beings and Language

There are *two* components included in all our efforts to make sense of the processes human beings develop when they communicate: (a) individuals and (b) symbol—or language systems. This seems like an oversimplification after I have belabored the complexity of theory-building which focuses on communication. Indeed, as the next chapter will demonstrate, approaches to "self" and "language" have been as varied and often as confrontational as all other human efforts to expand our knowledge and understanding. It will not take you long to recognize the conceptual trends and sociocultural roots already mentioned, as we endeavor to deal as adequately as possible with the process of theory building.

Wayne Beach discusses what and how we observe, analyze, and provide evidence for the interactional phenomenon. In that effort he focuses on both theory- and research-related issues, which remind us of the interdependence of these two areas in a scholar's world. Close examination of the transcript of a court case included in his chapter serves another important function for readers of this book. If we are to build useful theories related to social interaction and language, we need to provide detailed, meaningful analyses of such interactions. In other words, ultimately the soundness of the structures we endeavor to raise will depend on carefully laid foundations. What emerges as a significant insight is the fact that much yet remains to be done. If we are to move further along the road to understanding the significant, interactive roles played by both individuals and language whenever human beings are communicating, we cannot afford to rest on our laurels.

Chapter 4

Orienting to the Phenomenon*

Wayne A. Beach
San Diego State University

> *You should allow yourself, for some bit of time, to listen for the recurrent simplicities in the organization of conversation. It doesn't matter who's talking . . .*
>
> —Sacks (1974)

> *The assumption that no order of detail in interaction can be dismissed a priori as insignificant has had two major consequences for conversation analytic researchers. The first has been a general retreat from premature theory construction in favour of a more strongly empirical approach to the study of social action . . . an avoidance of the abstract theoretical constructs . . . every effort is made to render empirical analyses answerable to the specific details of research materials and to avoid their idealization . . . the data of interaction will, in all their aspects and unless proven otherwise, exhibit systematic and orderly properties which are meaningful for the participants.*
>
> —Heritage (1984, pp. 242–243)

With the advent of the journal *Communication Theory*, representing what Craig (1991) foresees as the coming of age of an academic field (p. 1), "contributions such as this edited volume are not just timely but indispensable. Opportunities to systematically address elemental features of *communication* and *theory*—their

---

*This chapter has been adapted from, and originally appeared under the same title, in James A. Andersen (Ed.), (1990), *Communication yearbook, 13*, 216–244, Newbury Park, CA: Sage Publications.

relationships, problems, and promises—cannot be underestimated. For researchers, educators, and students alike the ongoing task involves *excavations* of basic roots and taken for granted assumptions emerging from attempts to describe and explain inherently *social*, human behavior. These are problematic exercises; no finalized solutions are proposed nor delivered. Rather, this chapter (and, I assume, others in this volume as well) are designed to "stimulate reflection and productive dialogue on fundamental questions of scope, purpose, and method . . . that speaks to central problems and concerns of communication theory" (Craig, 1991, pp. 1–2).

The specific focus of this chapter rests with *language and social interaction*, and may be summarized as follows: Whenever language and social interaction comprise the locus of communication inquiry, certain basic questions emerge regarding interactants' and researchers' methods for displaying, detecting, and thus orienting to phenomena constituting social order. The following questions are central both to the present essay and to the future course of communication theory and research:

- Have we located a phenomenon yet?

- Would we recognize a phenomenon of interest if we *observed* one communicatively "at work"—as speakers and hearers orient to the occasions in which they are interactionally engaged?

- What evidence could be provided that is available for critical inspection to all researchers interested in the discovery and justification of that phenomenon?

- How would we know that a phenomenon is convincingly and uniquely of one type rather than another?

- To what extent is the object of study a phenomenon-in-the-world and an artifact of the research enterprise?

These are deceptively complex queries, applying equally well to all modes of inquiry focusing upon the organizing features of language and social interaction. With increasing regularity, however, such questions are being raised by researchers attempting to understand rudimentary features of everyday conversation. Throughout Zimmerman's (1988) overview of the "conversation analytic (CA) perspective" in *Communication Yearbook 11*, for example, attention is drawn to how speakers and hearers noticeably achieve interaction in the first instance, that is, by and for themselves (cf. Jefferson, 1973; Schegloff, 1986). Consideration is also given to how researchers go about the business of observing, analyzing, and providing evidence for the existence of an interactional "phenomenon."

Guided by the foregoing questions, issues and recurring problems associated with "orienting to the phenomenon" are examined from five interrelated perspectives. First, an overview is provided of CA's basic commitment to the study of naturally occurring interaction. Consideration is given to the location and recognition of social phenomena, wherein phenomena consist of conversational activities existing (in the first instance) independently of the research enterprise. Second, a reflexive consideration of *coding*, as a set of activities enacted by all interactional researchers, is offered. When coding tasks are viewed as achieved orientations to social order, it becomes possible to render them as problematic. Doing so addresses how the routine nature of coding tasks leads to their typically being overlooked as methodical glosses of phenomena routinely oriented-to by speakers and hearers. Third, readers are invited to examine a transcribed segment of video recorded interaction. This segment is provided so as to demonstrate, empirically though in introductory fashion, how speakers and hearers orient to phenomena that make up a "social occasion." The turn-by-turn analysis of this segment begins to locate how particular phenomena are shaped and fashioned within the environment of a three-party speech exchange system. Such an exercise informs and thereby directs both the analyst and readers in the search for patterns and recurring orientations by participants. Fourth, it is argued that phenomena exist in and through interactional sequences. Invoking macro-concepts "external" to the talk itself (e.g., power, status, identity) serves only to gloss the detailed and achieved character of routine social occasions. Finally, this chapter concludes with an overview of specific methodological and thus theoretical issues implicit within the positions developed above. Particular attention is given to the degree and type of correspondence between researchers' and interactants' methods for displaying and detecting social phenomena.

LOCATING AND RECOGNIZING PHENOMENA

A basic tenet of CA is the recognition that social order, evident within the detailed and contingent activities of societal members, exists *independently* of social scientific inquiry. Irrespective of the possibility of being examined and in some way analytically dissected for purposes of research, everyday interactants simply go about their business performing routine and often mundane tasks. Whether these tasks are occasioned during family dinners, service encounters, corporate meetings, prayer support groups or any other type of interactional involvement, the indisputable fact is that they are ordinarily achieved in the course of daily life in the process of "doing being" (Sacks, 1984b) a friend, a parent, a customer, a boss, a prayer partner, a lawyer, a doctor, and so on. How these tasks get done is a direct function of ways in which persons' identities get worked out turn-by-turn, moment-by-moment, through the methods employed to accomplish the routine character of everyday living. In the eventual course or evolution of a conversational involvement (cf. Goffman, 1981), the practical consequences of interactions (e.g., their outcomes) evidence little more or less than how participants display and detect one another's orientations to the occasion-at-hand. Exactly what gets achieved is undeniably the upshot of how speakers and hearers fashion, shape, and make available to one another their understandings of the local environment of which they are an integral part.

For conversation analysts, the unparalleled goal is to seek understandings of the independent and natural existence of social order. The reliance upon carefully produced transcripts of audio and video recordings, allowing for repeated hearings, viewings, and inspections of "actual and determinate" (Schegloff, 1986) sequences of interaction, reflects a basic commitment to employing research methods fashioned after the phenomenona being examined. Although neither recordings nor transcriptions are conversations in and of themselves (Zimmerman, 1988), they nevertheless preserve and embody the integrity and distinctiveness of many conversational activities. Such activities are drawn from natural settings, examined *on their own merits* as interesting phenomena—for example, openings and closings in telephone conversations (Schegloff, 1968; Schegloff & Sacks, 1973), compliments (Pomerantz, 1978a), teases (Drew, 1987), laughter (Jefferson, 1979, 1985a, 1985b), audience responses to public speaking (Atkinson, 1984a, 1984b, 1985)—and made available to readers (in the form of transcribed instances of interaction) for their critical inspection. Evidence for claims regarding the routine ways in which interactions get done is, within the constraints of publication outlets, offered to the public rather than remaining within the relative privacy of a researcher's workplace. Shared analyses of actual conversational instances (with priority given to repeated listenings of recordings, aided by carefully produced transcriptions) are invited, simply because the detailed nature of ordinary talk is best *seen* by readers in unison with descriptions and explanations of some phenomenon. In short, working *with* recorded and transcribed data (as heard and seen) is qualitatively different than merely writing and/or talking *about* the intricate ways in which participants organize conversation. As Zimmerman (1988) notes,

> as procedures *in use*, they [participants] reflexively fashion and engage the detailed opportunities and constraints of actual circumstances of talk and thus serve as a resource for permitting speakers-hearers to *achieve* that order for one another, and hence, for the analyst. (p. 409; emphasis added)

It becomes obvious that when some phenomenon is purported to exist within interaction, it is much more difficult to show exactly what a given set of methods and/or techniques (or series of "action sequences," see Heritage, 1984, 1985; Pomerantz, 1978a, 1978b, 1984) are *occupied* with. For example, what an utterance is achieving in its placement and construction; how a series of utterances is overlapped or latched together to accomplish particular activity-types; the ways in which coparticipants display and thereby build understanding into interaction vocally and nonvocally; and/or the methods for both creating and repairing routine problems as conversation unfolds. Consequently, there appears to be a growing realization by researchers working with conversational materials of the time and detail required to describe and explain instances and sequences thoroughly. One analytic priority of such research efforts is to produce insightful (and inherently defensible) accounts of the routine tasks of social life. More specifically (as noted previously), the attainment of such a priority entails orienting as best as possible to the same kinds of phenomena produced, in the first instance, by and for interactants as they routinely orient-to, and therein organize, occasions comprised of their participative efforts.

Ironic as it may seem, however, most communication researchers are not trained to look *directly* at interaction itself. Only rarely is interaction examined *on its own merits* as an achievement—as ordinary and collaboratively produced sequences of action, used and relied upon by speakers and hearers to get the work of social life done. Thus, many researchers are retooling to accommodate the detailed organization of naturally occurring talk, while at the same time training students not to dismiss prematurely some phenomenon as insignificant or disorderly (cf. Heritage, 1984, p. 241; Zimmerman, 1988). In this sense seemingly "small," and what may at first appear to be relatively unimportant phenomena (e.g., pauses, overlaps, turn-constructions, laughter, gaze, gesture) turn out to be dense achievements (e.g., Goodwin, 1981). Microinteractional achievements comprise both the organization of "larger" units of social order such as *power, identity, gender,* or *culture* (cf. Beach & Lindstrom, 1992; Boden & Zimmerman, 1991; Drew & Heritage, 1992; Schegloff, 1987) as well as less encompassing yet no less important social encounters such as telephone calls, family picnics, courtroom interrogation and testimony (cf. Atkinson & Drew, 1979), or medical diagnostic interviews (cf. Frankel, 1984, 1990; Heath, 1992; Maynard, 1989a, 1989b, 1991, 1992). Thus, providing convincing accounts of the detailed nature of conversational organization is, in the very least, a formidable task—one in which issues regarding the location and recognition of some "phenomenon" must constantly be examined rather than being discounted as trivial or untimely.

Such issues have been repeatedly and directly addressed within sociology (e.g., see Atkinson & Heritage, 1984; Button, Drew, & Heritage, 1986; Heritage, 1984; Psathas, 1979; Schenkein, 1978; Sudnow, 1972; Zimmerman & West, 1980); they have also been raised by speech communication researchers representing a diverse set of concerns with language, interaction, and features of everyday conversation (e.g., Beach, 1982, 1983, 1989, 1991a, 1991b, 1991c, 1992; Craig & Tracy, 1983; Ellis & Donahue, 1986; Hopper, 1991a, 1991b, 1992b; Nofsinger, 1991; Pomerantz, 1989). Yet it is important to recognize that nearly 2 decades ago Harvey Sacks (see 1984a, pp. 26–27) articulated the need for treating "interactions as products of a machinery," the goal being to "see how finely the details of actual, naturally occurring conversation can be subjected to analysis that will yield the technology of conversation." Similarly, Schegloff's (1986) concerns with the study of conversation have long been rooted in:

what appears to be the primordial site of sociality—direct interactions with others. Wherever else we might locate [the] society—the economy, the polity, the law, the organized systems for the reproduction of the population and the membership of the society, etc.—the organization of persons dealing with one another in interaction is the vehicle through which those institutions get their work done. On these and other grounds, interaction and talk-in-interaction merit recognition as a strategic locus of the social. It is at the elucidation of this fundamental aspect of social life that inquiries such as this are aimed. (p. 112)

TOWARD A REFLEXIVITY OF CODING

All research on interaction is grounded in some form of coding. This claim holds true, minimally, in the following simplistic and somewhat generic sense: *Coding* is a set of activities necessarily transforming the first-order world of doing (and displaying the experience of being involved in) interaction, into various kinds of evidence and claims regarding interaction as a topic of inquiry. The nature and degree of these transformations varies considerably, depending upon questions raised, basic commitments to research methods employed, and what counts as "data" in the process of providing answers to certain questions.

Viewed in this manner, methods may be understood as arguments generating from sequences of events (see Jackson, 1986; Jacobs, 1986) commonly referred to by researchers as observations, measurements, transcriptions, procedures, steps, and the like. These sequences of events may or may not be linear in their evolution. Yet in each and every case, certain categories, labels, and/or classifications must be invoked in order to render some claimed phenomenon as existing, thus providing for the very possibility of the phenomenon to be describable and retrievable for purposes of analysis. Moreover, researchers must somehow compare and contrast instances of observed and/or measured phenomena with one another, so as to identify similarities and differences among the instances being examined. Finally, continued observations and/or measurements require ongoing categorizing—coding or placing of instances in various groups. As types of instances evolve into constructed sets of categories or "groupings," the routine work of coding involves discernment among (and the creation of new) categories for organizing and making sense of social order.

As briefly sketched before, *coding* is not a sequence of activities that one group of researchers does and another does not. Rather, coding is inevitable in the achievement of scientific inquiry; it is how sense is made in and through the discernment and imposition of order on the social world via the location, categorization, and identification of types of instances. Moreover, determining how a corpus of instances constitutes a given phenomenon is also a form or phase of coding, simply because attention is rendered to similarities and differences between instances with respect to criterion attributes of that being observed. The important issue when examining coding, therefore, is not who engages in coding and who does not. Rather, the focus should be upon how coding gets accomplished (e.g., the methods enacted or "schemes" employed) and the ways in which coding—as an inevitable set of abstracting, transforming moves—accounts for the original (first-order) set of interactional achievements. Put simply, the focus should be on how coding re-presents underlying patterns of the social world. Because the enactment of coding routines determines, in an ultimate sense, those empirical findings we subsequently put forth as knowledge claims, there exists a need to reflexively examine our procedures for revealing how the social world gets organized and worked out—by and for the members themselves.

Such reflexivity presupposes a shift from coding as a taken-for-granted resource to a problematic set of achievements in need of critical inspection. It is only through reflexive examinations of research achievements that relationships can be made evident between the social world and researchers' accounts of interaction.

Coding as Achievement

As an achievement, coding may be viewed synonymously with how researchers come to locate phenomena and make sense of interaction by imposing scientific order upon the social world (and its working features). Coding is the general process of translating *raw data* into *symbolic data* (cf. Ford, 1975, pp. 383–395), and coding is constituted by a set of moves through which gathered data are observed and made sense of, that is, *ordered* so as to be used and relied upon in the explanation of patterns constituting some phenomenon. These coding moves constitute the accounting practices of the researcher(s); they reflect the situated production of analysts' practical methods for shaping data into analyzable, reportable, and thus readable forms. Coding accomplishments are frequently unarticulated, and thus taken for granted, as useful resources for understanding how findings and results got produced by the "research machinery" (cf. Ford, 1975; Garfinkel, 1967; Sacks, 1984a).

The intermittent formulation of coding methods, as meaningful data, reflects a heuristic concern for constant refinements of observational techniques. Studying how coding gets done (and even reported as an activity) is not particularly useful as an end in and of itself. Rather, reflexive examination allows for the possibility of questioning underlying presuppositions of empirical outcomes as displayed connections between theory and method. A reflexivity of coding can also reveal gaps and overlaps between conceptual intrigue and empirically justified "reality."

While it is not news to suggest that an essential reflexivity exists between knowledge claims and modes of observation (e.g., Delia & Grossberg, 1977; Fisher, 1978; Kaplan, 1964; Phillipson, 1973; Polanyi, 1962), it is somewhat of a different claim to suggest (as discussed in a subsequent section), that coding methods inevitably function to gloss (and perhaps even misrepresent) the phenomena accounted for in the guise of empirical findings. The key issue, however, is the nature and degree of glossing that occurs, and the implications such glossing holds for understanding how interaction gets organized.

A useful point of departure for understanding coding is Garfinkel's (1967, Chapter 1) classic examination of coding achievements. Throughout daily "commonsense situations of choice" (p. 19), Garfinkel and his associates were curious about how staff members accomplished their daily routines within the UCLA outpatient clinic. In asking the question "By what criteria are its applicants selected for treatment?", they decided to investigate clinic records "Because clinic folders contain records that clinic personnel provide of their own activities . . ." (p. 18). They employed two graduate students to examine 1,582 folders, transfer relevant information to coding sheets, and subsequently ran conventional reliability tests to assess coders' level of agreement. These tests were run because it is typically assumed that level of coder agreement at some point in the research process presumes "agreement on the end results" (p. 20). Their concerns with reliability coefficients, however, went beyond their routine employment as a resource for substantiating agreement of coders. The research focused on not only the actual practices through which "reliability" was obtained, but also how it became possible for coders to "follow coding instructions." Rather than considering coders to be "right or wrong" in their answers (i.e., codes), it was assumed that "whatever they did could be counted correct procedure in *some* coding 'game.' " The question was, what were these "games?" (p. 20).

It was discovered that in the process of attempting to follow coding rules, coders relied more heavily on their practical knowledge of the organizational activities of the clinic to make decisions about clinic folders than they did the *a priori* instructions. Coders engaged in several *ad-hocing* procedures that better allowed them "to grasp the relevance of the instructions to the particular and actual situations they were intended to analyze" (p. 21). In attempting to "fit" and classify the contents of the folders, ad hoc considerations attained priority over the coding rules themselves. Only by "ad hocing" could the coders work with the "a priori" category scheme, suggesting that instructions are essentially incomplete and inherently "indexical" guidelines for research procedures. Garfinkel and his coworkers concluded that ad-hocing procedures were inevitable simply because *that's what happens* when coders rely upon their native competence as part of the research "arrangement."

Coding instructions ought to be read instead as consisting

of a grammar of rhetoric; they furnish a "social science" way of talking so as to persuade consensus and action within the practical circumstances of the clinic's daily organized activities. (p. 24)

Garfinkel's (1967) study of coding practices has much to say about research as a practical, orchestrated achievement. In particular, the relationships of reliability coefficients and validity claims are questioned. It raises as problematic the basic difficulties involved in training coders to follow instructions or rules, and thus casts doubt on exactly what "interrater reliability coefficients" imply when employed as an argument for "getting at the phenomenon." Coders must agree on more complex issues such as: What counts as an instance of the phenomenon being observed?; How might instances be coded into categories that, in varying degrees, are glosses of the detailed work of speakers and hearers?; How should problematic decisions be resolved as ambiguity arises throughout the coding procedure?

Of equal if not greater importance, however, are basic questions regarding the creation of categories imposing artificial order onto interaction. To the extent categories do not emerge from or re-present underlying achievements of interactants, they remain macro-concepts invoked as an explanatory resource for "getting at the phenomenon." Similarly, coding instructions may themselves prove ambiguous in light of categories employed.

An extended example may be useful here. In an examination of coders trained to employ the REL/COM manual and category system as a means of studying "relational control" (see Beach, 1980, 1981), an analysis of training session recordings and coder diaries revealed specific problems in the routine accomplishment of coding. First, problems were frequent in following the "transactional coding rule" whereby each act should be coded as it relates to the previous act. Exactly what counted as an *act* became problematic, as did the coding of acts adjacent to a prior act yet not appearing to be designed as a receipt of a speaker's turn-at-talk. Second, coding "transactionally" was further complicated by the fact that coders were instructed to determine "the definition of the relationships among communicators, that is, how the communicator interprets her or his relationship with other." Here coders had difficulty understanding how they were to impute "interpretations" from transcripts or recordings. Third, exactly what counted as a "unit of analysis" (i.e. "an uninterrupted verbal utterance; an act; independent of length.") was difficult to operationalize: What counted as an "interruption" (compared, for example, to an "overlap")? How carefully were "interruptions" displayed in the transcripts and "hearable" in recordings? What kinds of conclusions should be drawn about "relational control" upon the occurrence of an "interruption"? Fourth, the "moves vs. turns" rule was particularly troublesome, since coders were instructed to assign one of five codes (i.e., dominance, structuring, equivalence, deference, submissiveness) to each and every act. As might be expected, however, coders frequently determined that certain acts contained multiple "control" functions. Thus: Which portion of an act had more impact on the control dimension of an utterance-in-sequence? One utterance studied during a training session included what coders believed to possess six different "functions": an insult, an expression of opinion, a humorous statement, a disagreement, a question, and an "I don't know." Coders were perplexed, yet gradually reached a consensus that, in this and other cases, they would individually attempt to "average" the contents of each utterance and in so doing make a categorical judgment best reflecting the *tone* of the act. Though none of the coders felt satisfied with the outcome, the training manual did not provide a sufficient alternative; they had to improvise.

Although other problems did emerge throughout coding (e.g., questions were raised about working alone and in pairs, determining how often to assess reliability among coders, and the extent to which working with transcripts and recordings was an "equivalent" task), perhaps the most revealing and recurring finding was coders' unanimous agreement that the five categories of relational control did not reflect nor capture the subtleties of conversational control in everyday interaction. This task was described as "fitting a square peg into an undersized round hole," and "taking an axe to a spider web."

In summary, all coding tasks involve routine problems in need of resolution. *How* coding is achieved has much to say about the degree of correspondence between theories and findings. And in a sense, the reflexive stance of not taking coding for granted refines understandings of how research methods abstract and transform the detailed workings of interactants as they orient to phenomena.

Coding and Transcribing

In the prior discussion of how conversation analysts attempt to locate and recognize phenomena, it was noted how the use of transcriptions of naturally occurring interactions, drawn from and employed in unison with audio and video recordings throughout analysis, are carefully produced so as to mirror the unfolding details of conversational activities. Fashioned after the interactions being examined, care is taken to produce an adequate record of events that actually (rather than "presumably," "hypothetically," or "could have") occurred. Arguing for the theoretical relevance of transcriptions, Ochs (1979) notes:

> A pervasive sentiment among those who draw from [speech] performance data is that the data they utilize are more accurate than intuition data: Their data constitute the real world—what *is* as opposed to what *ought* to be. (p. 43)

Although transcriptions are themselves subject to constant refinement and adjudication, so as to more precisely capture and reflect recorded talk-in-text, the key issue is what they are designed to "attend to." Jefferson (1985a) summarizes this point in her examination of laughter by observing:

> transcription is one way we try to "get our hands on" actual occurrences in order to study social order in fine detail. The crucial point is that we are, in whatever ways we go about it, trying to proceed by detailed observation of actual events . . . that the detailed study of small phenomena can be useful and informative, that the results may be orderly, that without "close looking at the world" one might not know such phenomena exist, and that the absence of a range of phenomena from the data base upon which theories about the social world are built can be consequential. (pp. 26–27)

As detailed attention is given to the production of transcripts of naturally occurring interactions, the more readily available phenomena become to the analyst. Whether the analyst is conducting an unmotivated search through a transcript, or seeking multiple instances of particular types of phenomena (e.g., overlaps, pauses, laughter tokens, repairs, presequences, question-answer pairs), analysis is constrained by (a) the quality of the recordings and transcripts available, (b) how phenomena are described as achieved in character, and (c) relationships among descriptions offered and the organization of actual recorded events.

WORKING THROUGH A TRANSCRIBED SEGMENT

It may be useful at this point to examine, in some detail yet quite informally, the following segment of interaction. This examination provides readers with the opportunity to inspect (and thereby gain a sense of) how this extended instance unfolds—the nature of the occasion being organized, participants' orientations to and creation of the task at hand, how phenomena such as identities, power, and status get worked out and are embodied in the talk itself—and thus to ground prior discussions of CA and coding in an actual instance of interaction.

The following segment is drawn from a growing corpus of video recorded courtroom interactions. In a rather unmotivated fashion, my attention was drawn to this segment as it appeared both interesting and deserving of further inquiry. An analysis of this extended segment begins to locate what interactants are "up to" in achieving a courtroom hearing, and is not exhaustive in its location and recognition of a "phenomenon"— at least not in the sense that a large corpus of instances of some phenomenon are displayed and examined for recurring features (see, for example, Beach, 1991c). Rather, as will become apparent, working through this segment evidences the kinds of data and issues routinely addressed in CA research in the process of searching for patterns of social interaction. It also reveals the necessity of constantly cycling back to the transcriptions (and recordings, when available) to check and refine observations made, and ultimately of substantiating any conclusions put forth as empirical claims. (Transcription symbols are described in the appendix of this chapter. Speaker designations are: J = Judge; D = Defendant; PL = Plaintiff Lawyer.)

(1)   ELAC:T5:CU v. ADAMS—121–180

121   J: So the *claim* of exemption: u:::h
122   further proceedings can go *off* calendar
123   subj ect to the receipt (0.8) by: thee: =
                  [   ]
124   D: Sir ((raises hand, leans forward in chair))
125   J: = uh (1.4) > you're still gonna be invo:lved <

126   so it's (.) gonna go to yo u
                                    [   ]
127 PL: > *Ya* (.) your honor um <
128   (0.4) my question: u:h since we have no
129   *an*swer from the *ma*rshall i:s uh whether the
130   (1.4) thousand dollars was uh (0.3) *plus* was
131   being held in the b*a*nk account
132   (0.8)
133 J: I dunn↑o
           [   ]
134 D: It's be-   It's being he:*l*d (I dun no-)
                              [   ]
135 PL: Well wh y don't we
136   rel*ea*se all m*o*nies all over: (0.8) for a thou sand
                              [   ]
                              ((D shakes head))
137   *doll*ars your honor
138   (2.6)
139 J: Re*spo*nse?
140   (0.8)
141 D: I- I feel that it sh*u*dn't.
142   (1.6)
143 D: (eh) be- b- > for the *sim*ple reason that they
144   din't- < (1.8) i- it's very con*fu*sing an (0.3)
145   what ↑ *I* want to know your hon*o*r is (0.8)
146   why wasn't I s:*e*rved with a sup*ee*nee ta (.)
147   ap*pe*ar in *cou*rt that's wha- con*fu*ses me
                                    [   ]
148 J: Not- n*o*t *in*to
149   that.
           [   ]
150 D: Okay aright sir=
151 J: = You'(ve) - =
152 D: = aright =
153 J: =*won* the claim of exemption
                         [   ]
154 D: o k a y okay =

```
155  J:   = you've got the claim of reduced by::. (    )
                                           [          ]
156  D:                                         And
157       I'm will ing to live by-
               [    ]
158  J:        (wey)
159  D:   I'm willing to go by my agreement
                             [                  ]
160  J:                           Please don't interr u(pt)=
161  D:   = Okay (.) well I'm sor ry
                              [   ]
162  J:                           By: uh > several
163       hundred < dollars.
164           (1.2)
165  J:   U(m) (1.2) and u:h (1.0) I need to know why:
166       (0.2) you still need the two installments as
167       long as there's a thou:sand are you =
168  D:   = Because th at(s)
                  [    ]
169  J:               Are  you s  t  a  r  : ving because=
                      [           ]
170  D:                       the only rea-
171  J:   =of the second (.) five hundred that's
172           (0.8)
173  D:   Ye:s (.) your honor I (am)
174           (1.2)
175  J:   (Then the) moneys uh held by the mar:shall are
176       to be: released to thee uh (0.6) defenda:nt?
177       except the five hundred (0.8) to be (.)
178       released (2.6) to the (uh) plaintiff Creditors
179       Underwriters
180       ((Judge continues))
```

Even a preliminary inspection of the foregoing segment reveals evidence that the occasion being organized is some kind of court proceeding. For example, J appears to be addressed as "sir" by D (lines 124, 150), as "your honor" by both PL and D (lines 127, 137, 145, 173), and there are references to "marshall" (line 129), "defendant" (line 176), and "plaintiff" (line 178). The mere use of these address-terms in unison with certain invoked identities, however, does not substantiate how J, D, or PL orient to phenomena emerging within this segment of an informal hearing.

Before turning to an analysis of the interactional environment of this hearing, however, it might be useful to inform readers that this proceeding began the civil 10:00 AM call involving the collection of a debt by Creditor's Unlimited from Mark Adams (names have been changed so as to protect court participants). It was the second of two hearings concerning a proposed settlement (e.g., balance due, installment payment and dates) convened by J to discuss a motion filed by D. This segment is approximately ninety seconds in length, occurring 2 minutes and 30 seconds into a proceeding lasting 6 minutes and 50 seconds.

Closing and Opening

We begin by noticing that J, as turn-occupant, appears to initiate a closing of the "official" business of the motion (i.e., "the c*laim* of exemption:") in lines 121–123. That this turn-at-talk is in fact an attempt to close down the hearing and thus take it "*off* calendar" (line 122) also seems to be recognized by D and PL.

First, D's "Sir" in line 124 is an unsolicited (i.e., self-selected) utterance, inserted in close proximity to a possible turn completion by J (projected by "calender", line 122), yet overlapping with "subj ect"—a "syntactically coherent next utterance component" (Jefferson & Schegloff, 1975, p. 3). D's "Sir" was positioned in such a way as to indicate sufficient and carefully attended recognition that J had reached a "transition place"—the closing down of a motion being only one transition-relevant example. And by not elaborating, D orients to J's continuation in a manner preserving the "one party talks at a time" assumption of conversational turn-taking (cf. Sacks, Schegloff, & Jefferson, 1974).

Second, following J's (lines 125–126) " > you're still gonna be in*vo*:lved < so it's (.) gonna go to yo u," PL achieves overlap onset ("*Ya*", line 127) in a minimal and transitory fashion by starting up within the final sound and thus word produced by J (cf. Jefferson, 1983). PL's overlapped utterance does exhibit an immediate response to J's query, yet it also displays his recognition that J is, for all practical purposes, nearing completion of closing down the motion. In this sense there is more at work here in PL's 127–131. PL's response to J's query appears rushed, as evidenced by the quickened delivery "*Ya* (.) your honor um < " (line 127), as though he is orienting less to J's query than to the opportunity for asking J a question about the "thousand dollars" owed to his client. While more could be said about the manner in which PL constructs his question to J in 128–131, the point remains that as J attempted to take the proceeding "off calendar," PL raised a question meriting possible further consideration by J.

In summary, D's "Sir" is slotted in close proximity to the business being initially closed down by J in lines 121–122. Such proximity provides a first possible opportunity for raising a new and/or related topic or issue by D, or possibly clarifying and/or questioning previously transacted business. There is additional evidence indicating the usage of such a slot, namely, PL's response to J's prior turn and extension with his own question (lines 127–131). In short, it may be at just this point in the hearing that J becomes informed of additional business yet to be taken care of, at least part of which is directly related to the motion at hand (e.g., payments).

Having briefly worked through this initial sequence, certain questions should now appear particularly relevant: What phenomena were J, D, and PL orienting-to in lines 121–131? How were they achieving this orientation, and what consequences might these achievements hold for analysts attempting to understand courtroom interaction? If one reinspects lines 121–131, as follows, it should become increasingly clear that the routine work of courts has something to do with taking care of business (e.g., getting cases in and moving them along).

```
121  J:    So the claim of exemption: u:::h
122         further proceedings can go off calendar
123          subj ect to the receipt (0.8) by: thee:=
             [    ]
124  D:    Sir   ((raises hand, leans forward in chair))
125  J:    = uh (1.4) > you're still gonna be invo:lved <
126         so it's ( . ) gonna go to yo u
                              [   ]
127  PL:                      > Ya ( . ) your honor um <
128         (0.4) my question: 'u:h since we have no answer
129         from the marshall i:s uh whether the (1.4)
130         thousand dollars was uh (0.3) plus was being held
131         in the bank account
```

Yet at the same time, both defendants and lawyers may have agendas they would like to have considered that are (at least for them) also important "business." One problem is: When and how might these agendas be raised and subsequently treated in some fashion by the court (i.e., J)? For example, J did not yield the floor by acknowledging D's "Sir" in line 121, D did not continue without receiving J's deferral, and it was only after J asked PL a question that PL gained access to the floor and subsequently asked his own question.

Though any conclusions to be drawn thus far must emerge from a short segment of interaction, the following observations might be made: (a) As current speaker, J takes extended turns-at-talk and does not yield the floor until his current turn is completed. Constructing and completing extended turns is thus one integral part of "doing being a judge"; (b) Access to the floor is heavily influenced by J's willingness to provide the opportunity for others to speak. Perhaps it is the case that in the ways and to the extent provided by J, the floor may be (and typically is) taken up by co-participants of the hearing. If this is the case, defendants and lawyers must attend closely to the opportunities provided by judges. Whether such opportunities are self-selected recognitions of possible utterance completions (as in D's "Sir"), and/or elaborations/extensions of a response requested by the judge and thus granting floor-access (as with PL's question to J), it is clear that phenomena such as "overlaps" are not random, loosely occasioned utterances within courtroom or other interactional settings. Rather, they are artful techniques displaying precise orientations to the occasion-at-hand.

Initiating the "Complaint"

Exactly what D's "Sir" in line 121 projected, however, cannot be determined until and unless one moves forward to the portion of the segment beginning with line 135:

```
135  PL:                              Well why don't we
136       release all monies all over: (0.8) for a thou  sand=
                                        [              ]
                                       ((D shakes head))
137       =dollars  your honor
138           (2.6)
139  J:   Response?
140           (0.8)
141  D:   I- I feel that it shudn't.
142           (1.6)
143  D:   (eh) be- b- > for the simple reason that they
144       din't- < (1.8) i- it's very confusing an (0.3)
145       what ↑I want to know your honor  is (0.8)
146       why wasn't I s:erved with a supeenee ta (.)
147       appear in court that's wha- confuses me
                                        [          ]
148  J:                                 Not- not into
149       that.
```

Here PL's question to J is subsequently marked by a noticeable pause in line 138, after which J elects not to answer PL's question by opting instead to request D's response (line 139). Following a short pause (line 140), D constructs a multifaceted turn (lines 141–147) in which several different yet related activities are achieved. He begins by disagreeing with PL's prior suggestion and quickly moves onto what may appear to be a partial justification (see Atkinson & Drew, 1979, Chapter 5) for disagreeing—the providing of an account of the position he is constructing. This justification remains incomplete, or so D states in line 144, because "i- it's very con*fus*ing."

However, a closer inspection of the organization of lines 141–144 might yield a competing explanation regarding whether a justification was, in fact, being provided by D—and if not an explanation, it might offer an alternative course of action rationally tied to D's subsequent utterance in lines 145–147. The alternative is to treat lines 141–144 as leading up to what appears to be one type of "complaint" in lines 146–147, "why wasn't I *s:er*ved with a sup*ee*nee ta ap*pea*r in *cou*rt." D produces several false starts and self-repairs ("I- I"; "(eh) be- b-"; i- it's") (cf. Schegloff, Jefferson, & Sacks, 1977), fails to complete "for the *sim*ple reason that they didn't" (lines 143–144) by immediately stating his own confusion, and finally explicitly informs J that all he really wants to know is information regarding why he was not served with a subpoena. Viewed in this light, D used his first direct and granted access to the floor in a manner leading up to the formulation of an apparent "complaint" that did not emerge following his "Sir" in line 124. In so stating his concerns and constructing the turn in this manner, D gives priority to responding directly to PL's suggestion (to "rel*ea*se all the monies over:", line 136) by stating "I- I feel that it sh*ud*n't. (1.6) (eh) be- b-" (line 143).

Such priority given to floor access by D is only one indicator of the importance of using turns as valued opportunities for expressing feelings, setting agendas, and thereby interjecting more "personal" concerns within the handling of "official" business in a routine court hearing. In this instance, the significance of D's 141–147 is rooted in the timing and placement of his turn-at-talk, as well as the artful construction of a turn including (in part) an answer to PL's question, a preface to an account, and a possible complaint.

The phrase *possible complaint* is employed here to call attention to the fact that little has been said about an issue central to the analysis of D's turn: Exactly what makes D's "why wasn't I *s:er*ved with a sup*ee*nee ta ap*pea*r in *cou*rt" (lines 146–147) *hearable* as a "complaint"? To begin answering such a question one might focus upon features of D's constructed turn. At least (but not exclusively) three features of lines 146–147 appear to indicate such a hearing. First, D's "why wasn't" might be heard as one form of accusation attributing possible blame to the failure of the court to act appropriately and on his behalf (as a defendant with legal rights). The "why wasn't" (as one type of negative formulation) can be usefully contrasted with a construction such as "Was I served . . .", for example, in which the latter could have functioned as a simple request for information. Yet another possibility could have been an instance such as "Would you please tell me if there was a problem in serving me with a complaint?", a more polite request leaving open the possibility that the court was not necessarily at fault in serving the defendant. Second, the mode of delivery apparent in lines 146–147 of D's turn begins to suggest that D was troubled by the possibility of not having been served a supoena. The words "*s:er*ved," "sup*ee*nee," "ap*pe*ar," and "*cou*rt?" were delivered with vocal emphasis by D. Note especially his prolongation of the first portion of "*s:er*ved." Finally, attention might be drawn to D's "what ↑ *I* want to know . . .", most importantly the stress on "*I*" as an indicator of D's concern in gaining knowledge about the subpoena process.

Dismissing the Initial "Complaint"

While the constituent features of D's turn construction may well be crucial to understanding the delivery and hearability of a portion of D's lines 141–147 as "offering up a complaint," the work produced by D in 141–147 does not necessarily predetermine and thus guarantee J's receipt and treatment of D's expressed concerns. Of equal if not greater importance in assessing how D's 146–147 might be hearable as a complaint, however, is to examine how J oriented as next speaker to D's prior turn. Though D would likely have preferred that his turn be responded to with positive appraisal by J, such is not the case in lines 148–149. Here J overlaps his turn onto D's prior with the dismissal "Not- n*o*t *in*to that." Two brief observations merit attention here. First, that the overlap occurred in this instance should not be surprising, since it is quite possible that J had ample time to notice how and what D was up to in his 141–147 construction. Whatever else D's turn might have been an instance of, as noted previously, it was more than a direct and detailed response to PL's suggestion in lines 135–137. Second, built into J's rather abrupt response is an assessment that what D was doing was somehow untimely and/or inappropriate (cf. Pomerantz, 1984).

Orienting-to the "Complaint's" Dismissal

Yet something more may be at work here, namely, J informing/reminding D that he has gotten what might be roughly formulated as a "good deal" up to this point in the hearing. To substantiate this observation, once again it is useful to move to subsequent actions taken by J and D in order to achieve an even better grasp of each participant's orientation to the local environment of the sequence. Notice what J added onto his dismissal in the form of an explanation of his position:

```
148  J:                          Not- not  into
149          that.
           [    ]
150  D:     Okay  aright sir=
151  J:     =You'(ve) -=
152  D:     = aright =
```

```
153  J:    =won the claim of exemption
                       [          ]
154  D:                       o k a y    okay=
155  J:    =you've got the claim reduced by::.  (    )
                                      [       ]
156  D:                                        And
157        I'm  will  ing to live by-
                  [    ]
158  J:      (wey)
159  D:   I'm willing to go  by  my  agreement
                             [              ]
160  J:                      Please don't interr u(pt)=
161  D:   = Okay  ( . ) well I'm sor ry
                              [   ]
162  J:                      By: uh > several
163        hundred < dollars.
```

In lines 151, 153, 155, and 162–163 J informs/reminds D that he has won the claim of exemption *and* got the claim reduced by several hundred dollars. Of course J is not required nor judicially mandated to provide such an explanation, but did so nonetheless. Perhaps J oriented to his own dismissal of D's 141–147 as overly abrupt, thus quickly moved to soften its potential impact on D. (Early on in the hearing, prior to segment [1], J acknowledged how D had been ignored and uninformed in this case, and thus had every right to be confused as to the details of the proceedings. In addition, D was without legal counsel, and at times J attempts to "fill in" details as the hearing unfolded.) Both the tonal qualities of J's voice and his request "Please don't interr u(pt)" in line 160 would further indicate an orientation whereby J was attempting to assist D's understandings of court proceedings.

Overlapped with J's dismissal of D's 141–147 and subsequent explanation are several compliant utterances from D (lines 150, 152, 154, 156–157, 159, and 161). D's first "*O*kay aright sir = aright" (lines 150, 152) displays immediate deference to the force of J's dismissal. Yet shortly after the overlapped compliance continues in line 154, D not only overlaps once again but appears a bit overly eager in lines 151–157 and 159 to comply with the unfolding situation (see also his softened compliance and possible apology in line 161). In and through these few turns-at-talk, D displays his recognition of J's attempts to inform/remind him of his already having won the "claim of exemption." Yet there is somewhat of an irony in this recognition, given that this short flurry of activity was itself initiated with D's 141–147—not with an effort to offer any kind of appreciation to J for his understanding and favorable ruling on the motion.

Packed into lines 141–163 there is a rather intricate balance struck between the possibility of complaining and dismissing on one hand, and explaining/ requesting and compliance on the other. It is as though the adjacency of D's complaint and J's dismissal hinge, for the moment at least, on a quick flurry of mutual challenge and even rejection. Yet immediately thereafter, J and D appear to collaborate in supporting one another—even to the point where J accommodates D with a request rather than a command in line 160, followed by D's compliance and possible apology in line 161. In each of these action-types, both J and D orient symmetrically and instantaneously to the other's displayed orientations.

The negotiated character of this interactional segment evidences how it is that such different orientations eventuate in a collaboratively produced structure. It is also an instance of a legally constrained encounter, evident in and through a set of methods allowing each participant the opportunity to achieve preferred outcomes. However, in D's case, opportunity was shown not to be synonymous with the satisfaction of having his concerns addressed—at least up to this point in the hearing.

Back to the Motion

A final comment on this instance drawn from communication in a courtroom. Should the reader have lost track of the original business-at-hand addressed prior to D's multifaceted turn (lines 141–147), namely PL's question suggesting that the entire thousand dollars be released to the creditor, it should become clear in lines 165–180 that the lack of resolution of this issue has not gone unnoticed by J. Here it is apparent that the unspecified reason underlying D's disagreement in line 141 had to do with his needing $500 for living expenses, a realization displayed in J's question (lines 169, 171) and finally confirmed by D in line 173. This possibility might imply that D's priorities rested less with receiving living expenses, than with attaining some kind of restitution regarding his not having been served with a subpoena.

The analysis offered herein is only partial in the sense that the hearing continues with D once again raising concerns about not having been served with a subpoena to appear in court. He does so in a location following an attempted closing down of "business" by J, yet in such a manner and slot that J receipts D's prior turn by taking the time and effort to provide a set of legal responses. Additionally, interesting contrasts emerge within the second handling of D's concerns, and there is much to say about J's eventual dismissal of D from court. Exactly how D takes certain liberties not tolerated by J, however, requires another discussion of achievements—one intended to illustrate how it is that forms of legal interaction exist, in the first instance to participants themselves, as they display and thus orient to the moment-by-moment problems routinely addressed in courts.

OCCASIONING IDENTITIES IN THE TALK

To say that defendants have rights in a hearing is to identify the possibility that a claim may be made or an exception taken about due legal process. How this work gets done offers insight into the interdependence of "official" and "personal" agendas, not to mention the displayed competencies involved in opening, closing, and adapting to numerous courses of action. But to describe the ways in which phenomena such as "complaints" emerge and are oriented-to as court business is achieved, is to explain the local environment within which power and status are occasioned *in* the talk as speakers and hearers employ diverse methods for accomplishing an informal hearing. The articulation and unpacking of these methods allows for the possibility of understanding the turn-by-turn organization of an occasion, and thus the interactional machinery produced by and for the participants themselves. By turning directly to actual instances of interaction as displays of social order, rather than attempting to account for the detailed work of participants by invoking macro-concepts such as power, status, identity, or related forces "external" to the talk itself (e.g., institution, age, gender, ethnicity, socioeconomic position), priority is given to the talk itself.

In short, attention is given to the sequentially relevant features comprising and constituting these more encompassing concepts and theories, and in so doing research inquiries begin from the "bottom up" rather than the "top down." The preceding section of this chapter displays the work of speakers and hearers routinely engaged in interaction as they attend to the moment-by-moment evolution of a conversational involvement, and accordingly such is the research priority of those examining the sequential character of social occasions.

Contrasting Theoretical Alternatives

One alternative is to impose, a priori, a series of macro-concepts and theories "onto" the interaction as a template (comprised of selected categories, terms, and so on) intended to carve out understandings of the detailed workings of speakers and hearers. One result of such an orientation is the recurring difficulty of describing some phenomenon, and attributing to that phenomenon specific features and components, without providing actual instances as evidence of the claims made for other's inspection and consideration. In light of these concerns, it is not uncommon to finish reading an article in which a phenomenon is proposed suggesting interesting and possibly even compelling implications regarding social interaction. Yet questions remain about the extent to which the phenomenon being queried exists within social order "in the first instance" (cf. Schegloff, 1986), as compared to having been given birth as a useful tool (or possibly even an artifact) of the research enterprise. Specifically, readers may query: What would an instance of such a phenomenon look like? From where and under what circumstances did this phenomenon emerge? What is the detailed nature of the phenomenon as it is oriented-to and noticeably worked out by speakers and hearers in normal, everyday settings? These questions are most certainly applicable to an issue such as agenda-setting in courts and/or more casual conversations. The brief data analysis offered in the preceding section only begins to raise issues surrounding the sequential character of phenomena such as complaining and responding to complaints (dismissals being only one possible response-type).

An examination of van Dijk's (1987, 1989) sociocognitive perspective on power and discourse, for example, provides an expansive overview of how people may exercise power over others in interaction across a variety of settings. Attention is also given to specific features and definitions of power. One example is: "If A limits B's cognitive or social action control, A may be said to have power over B" (p. 5). How might we orient to "limits" and "over" as interactional achievements?

Turning to a review of research on courtroom interaction, van Dijk offers summaries of such findings as restrictions on turn-allocation and speech acts, obligations to answer questions when requested (and in specific manners), questions functioning as informative and accusatory, lack of topic control by defendants and witnesses, and how *style* may influence ongoing talk (e.g., powerless styles are noticeable by such features as "the frequent use of intensifiers, hedges, hesitation forms, and questioning intonation" [p. 45]). While these summarized findings may begin to articulate a framework for understanding the constraints on talk in courts, they should not be mistaken for empirical generalizations replacing (or, in many cases, adequately formulating) the detailed orientations displayed by court participants (e.g., see Atkinson & Drew, 1979; Maynard, 1984). A close examination of segment (1), for example, reveals that informal hearings—though equally binding and "official" as an occasion—are comprised of interactions exhibiting less restricted turn-allocations than "formal" examination formats (i.e., direct, cross, redirect, and rebuttal), fewer and different restrictions on answering questions, a more diverse use of questions than either *informative* or *accusatory*, and more active contributions by the judge and defendant in controlling *topic*.

In fact, the latter instance of *topic* provides a pointed example of distinct differences between the "macro" approach taken by van Dijk and the microanalytic examination of talk sequences evidenced in CA research. When examined as an interactional achievement, *topic* remains as an extremely difficult *concept* to get a handle on—to articulate (and provide evidence for) in its organized manifestations and conversational variations (e.g., see Beach, 1991c; Button & Casey, 1984; Maynard, 1980; Maynard & Zimmerman, 1984). As treated by van Dijk, however, topic control (and related components of courtroom interactions, such as *sequencing* and *speech acts*, cf. Beach, 1990) is assumed to be working in particular ways and thereby influencing particular court outcomes, even though such components are in each and every case glossed as interactional achievements.

To describe and explain the complex orientations of court participants, it is at times useful to summarize research findings as a means of formulating the empirical nature of participants' solutions to routine matters and problems. Yet when the argument is offered that power is the key issue in accounting for the precise nature of institutional discourse, questions must be raised about what *counts* as power in particular interactional environments. This is especially the case when, as apparent in van Dijk's overview, researchers' methods for gaining access to interactional phenomena remain unarticulated. Without careful consideration of the manner in which empirical results are generated—or even raising the more basic question of what counts as *data*, and the ways and extent to which such data are made available to readers for their critical inspection—the tendency is to disregard social order in its naturalistic state by invoking macro explanatory concepts offering minimal information about how interaction gets done.

A final example may prove beneficial here. After critiquing the work in Atkinson and Drew's (1979) *Order in Court* for paying little attention "to the social and legal power structures that become manifest in such interactions," van Dijk (1987) provides the following argument:

> It may certainly be granted that we may first need insight into the properties of courtroom talk, before we are able to pinpoint conversational specifics as expressions of power or social structure. On the other hand, it may be argued that many properties of conversational organization in court, such as strategies of face-keeping and impression management, or persuasive defense and directive accusation, as well as of turn allocation and speech act control in the first place, can of course not be understood without a presupposed knowledge of their functions and goals in the courtroom and the legal process. In other words, instead of methodical ignorance of the properties of the social context, we argue for an interplay between conversation analysis and social analysis, in ways that continue and refine the analysis of strategic verbal interaction proposed by scholars such as Goffman. (cited in Goffman, 1967, p. 44)

Several questions might be raised in response to this position: Exactly how might such concepts as "face-work and impression management" or "strategy" influence courtroom contexts if they are not, in the first instance, displayed and oriented-to by speakers and hearers as methodical achievements? Of what practical benefit is locating "properties of the social context" *outside* of the interaction itself? How is it possible to identify "social and legal power structures that become manifest in the interactions," if not by turning initially and directly to sequencing of the talk by and for participants? These and related questions rest on the assumption that even though analysts inevitably trade on their "presupposed knowledge" while examining interactional data (cf. Turner, 1970), so doing does not satisfy the requirements for providing evidence of the claims and positions taken. A simple example may suffice here: If speaker designations were removed from a carefully produced transcript of courtroom interaction, analysts should be able to provide evidence of the *context* in and through the methods employed to achieve orientations to the problems at hand. And if *power* eventually emerged as a relevant category for describing ways in which sequences get organized, it would most certainly be invoked only as a global reference accounting for the constituent features/methods comprising speakers' and hearers' achievements.

METHODOLOGICAL ISSUES AND THEORETICAL CONSEQUENCES

One methodological issue of interest stems from an earlier discussion of the inherent independence of social order: By definition naturally occurring interactions exist apart from being isolated as a topic of research, and irrespective of the possibility of being discovered and dissected for purposes of social science. When research commitments rest with the recovery and reconstruction of the social world, as best as possible "on its own merits," attempts are made to seek evidence for claims regarding *how* interaction is the vehicle for accomplishing the world of everyday life. By gathering and examining in detail transcribed versions of audio and video recordings of everyday talk and providing available evidence of transcribed instances for readers' critical inspection, conversation analysts attempt to minimize the diverse ways in which research orchestrations, as methodical achievements, produce data and findings *only* as a result of the methods employed in the investigation process. This claim is not to say that CA results can be separated from the research practices relied upon to capture interaction. Rather, the point here is that priority is given to speakers' and hearers' displayed methods for organizing everyday settings, as phenomena routinely existing *even if* they were not gathered for subsequent scientific analysis.

Any consideration of the correspondence between a researcher's and an interactant's methods necessarily leads to the question: To what extent do all research orientations inevitably transform, reflect analogies of, and in varying degrees distort the sense and structure of interaction that is produced by and for speakers and hearers? Though this question is considerably easier to raise than to answer, it does draw attention to further issues: If researchers are not looking directly at interactional achievements in natural settings, what counts as data? From what resources is evidence drawn for purposes of substantiating claims? And in what ways might the circumstances and methodical solutions to everyday interactions vary from natural to contrived concepts, settings, and simulations?

There is a responsibility shared by speakers, hearers, and communication researchers alike: To enact methods for displaying and detecting social order. Ingrained within interaction and the researching of interaction are certain basic constraints inherent to the achievement of the task-at-hand, namely, showing how talk unfolds in and through the identification and use of key practices for accomplishing such tasks. The patterns comprising these tasks ultimately reflect both the sense and structure of social order.

As noted, both routine social encounters and research investigations are methodical achievements, understandable as managed attempts to enact certain procedures in the process of structuring and making sense of ordinary talk (and demonstrating the working machinery through which sense gets made). Understanding the complex relationships between collaborative productions of interaction and social scientific formulations of how interaction gets done (an inherently reflexive enterprise) is of central importance to ethnomethodological work in general (e.g., see Garfinkel, 1967; Sacks, 1984a).

Alternative Approaches to Social Phenomena

Having provided a brief glimpse of selected commitments and research practices of CA, it may be useful at this juncture to examine how such commitments differ from alternative empirical and theoretical approaches. Given the focus on stable and locally occasioned (i.e., detailed, contingent, turn-organized, moment-by-moment) features of naturally occurring interactions, Zimmerman (1988) has noted how the general approach of CA seems to reflect:

> a methodological posture seemingly at odds with the procedures generally favored in social science at large . . . [and an] apparent disregard of mainstream topics and methodologies not only in its initiating discipline of sociology, but also of communication. (pp. 2–3)

The priorities and commitments unique to CA reflect an obvious dispreference for certain empirical orientations to social order, especially those whose methods reflect an insensitivity to the natural contingencies of interaction. Concerns rest with research methods that unreasonably alter, and thus distort, the detailed work "*produced* and *oriented to* by participants as orderly and informative, and relied upon as a basis for action" (Zimmerman, 1988, p. 4). Questions are raised regarding the extent to which research methods fail to capture, display, and allow for the possibility of accounting for how speakers and hearers actually create phenomena they collaboratively produce, that is, in and through the "rules, techniques, procedures, methods, maxims . . . that can be used to generate the orderly features we find in the conversations we examine" (Sacks, 1984b, p. 413). Put simply: To what extent (and in what precise ways) are social phenomena artificially constructed and/or lost as a function of researchers' methods for observing interaction?

Though Jefferson's (1985a) concerns rest exclusively with how glossing procedures in conversations get done—as "a formulation which, on its occurrence, is quite adequate, but which turns out to be incomplete, ambiguous, even misleading" (p. 462)—we might herein borrow a few of her observations to formulate the problem of research methods, and theoretical consequences, in yet another way: "Most roughly, a gloss can be a generalization and/or somewhat inaccurate and/or incomplete and/or a masking or covering-up of what really happened" (p. 436). Since no report or "telling about" some event can totally escape glossing in some manner, at least in the sense that it is impossible to break each and every datum and circumstance "down into its bedrock details" (p. 436), the key issue is how glossing occurs and the consequences projected by its occurrence. The implications for understanding research methods, although diverse, hinge on what may appear upon first glance to be a rather straightforward matter: How research reports do justice to the phenomenon under investigation. Determining (as well as possible) what *counts* as "justice," and the implications of how researchers get their work done, is what Garfinkel (1967) has aptly formulated as the "problematic crux of the matter" (p. 10).

As Heritage (1984) observes, researchers' methods tend to promote a "process of idealization":

> The contemporary methodology of conversation analysis has maintained Sacks's pioneering focus on the details of actual interactions and his effort to forestall the process of idealization. Its insistence on the use of data collected from naturally occurring occasions of everyday interaction is paralleled by a corresponding avoidance of a range of other research methodologies as unsatisfactory sources of data . . . These include: (1) the use of interviewing techniques in which the verbal formulations of subjects are treated as an appropriate substitute for the observation of actual behavior; (2) the use of observational methods in which data are recorded through field notes or with pre-coded schedules; (3) the use of native intuitions as a means of inventing examples of interactional behavior; and (4) the use of experimental methodologies involving the direction or manipulation of behavior. These techniques have been avoided because each of them involves processes in which the specific details of naturally situated interactional conduct are irretrievably lost and are replaced by idealizations about how interaction works. (p. 236)

To extend Heritage's argument, when interaction is explicitly treated as data (i.e., a phenomenon in and of itself) it is typically coded into abstract and idealized categories, the results of which produce findings bearing vague and, thus, problematic relationships to the organizing and sequential features of the interaction observed. In this sense, coding schemes are limited in their descriptive and even explanatory potential while functioning to gloss, in an idealistic and/or artificial fashion, the detailed organization of participants' displayed orientations to actual occasions of talk. A key issue here is the overall "goodness of fit" (i.e., the nature and type of correspondence) between members' methods for accomplishing tasks, researchers' categories for "capturing" and re-presenting these methods, and exactly what kinds of explanations alternative analyses can and cannot provide about how interaction gets done (see Jacobs, 1988; Wieder, 1988). Not only are selected concepts/categories (e.g., power) incapable of capturing speakers' and hearers' methods for achieving tasks, but (as noted previously) rarely is coding itself examined as an inherently indexical (i.e., essentially incomplete and thus problematic) set of practical achievements.

CONCLUSION

A central concern of this chapter has been to articulate the need for assessing the ways in which interactants and researchers orient to phenomena. Such an assessment has much to do with priorities and methods in the production and analysis of social order, both "in the first instance" as speakers and hearers organize occasions, as well as in a reconstructed (scientific) sense as attempts are made to explicate those organizing features of everyday (naturally occurring) interaction. In the latter sense, moving directly to the analysis of carefully produced transcriptions generated from audio and video recordings of social occasions, reflects a commitment to locating social order within actual talk sequences.

Though only a single episode of courtroom interaction was offered and examined to evidence the kinds of analytic tools available when working through a sequence of talk (cf. Schegloff, 1987), it should be noted that this appears not to be an isolated instance. These data were drawn from a larger ongoing project, one in which a corpus of video recorded hearings reveals recurring and collaborative orientations by speakers and hearers. Within those moments when judges attempt to close down the business of the court, for example, such closings provide openings for defendants and lawyers to achieve their agendas. Several methods employed to get such moments worked out have been identified and described in earlier portions of this chapter, but the analytic task is to make sense of a growing set of fragments revealing such orientations and, in so doing, locate the phenomena and account for the shape of its organization.

Collections and analyses of numerous fragments of naturally occurring interactions are central to conversation analysis, and becoming increasingly relevant to researchers whose priorities rest with interaction as an achievement. An ongoing task is to locate and recognize other phenomena and justify their empirical nature. Problems requiring resolution involve how to treat empirically the ways in which interactants orient to whatever phenomena emerge during the course of routine talk (cf. Sacks, 1963). The elucidation of these methods reveals how communication is finely organized and fashioned after interactants' orientations to social occasions.

REFERENCES

Atkinson, J. M. (1984a). *Our master's voices: The language and body language of politics.* London, England: Methuen.

Atkinson, J. M. (1984b). Public speaking and audience responses: Some techniques for inviting applause. In J. M. Atkinson & J. Heritage (Eds.), *Structures of social action: Studies in conversation analysis* (pp. 370–409). Cambridge, England: Cambridge University Press.

Atkinson, J. M. (1985). Refusing invited applause: Preliminary observations from a case study of charismatic oratory. In T. van Dijk (Ed.), *Handbook of discourse analysis, Vol. 3: Discourse and dialogue* (pp. 161–181). London, England: Academic Press.

Atkinson, J. M., & Drew, P. (1979). *Order in court: The organization of verbal interaction in judicial settings*. London, England: Methuen.

Atkinson, J. M., & Heritage, J. (Eds.). (1984). *Structures of social action: Studies in conversation analysis*. Cambridge, England: Cambridge University Press.

Beach, W. A. (1980). *Reflexivity and the analysis of conversational coding*. Boston, MA: American Educational Research Association.

Beach, W. A. (1981). *Perspectives on the analysis of conversational sequencing in group systems*. Unpublished doctoral dissertation, University of Utah.

Beach, W. A. (1982). Everyday interaction and its practical accomplishment: Progressive developments in ethnomethodological research. *Quarterly Journal of Speech, 68*, 314–327.

Beach, W. A. (1983). Background understandings and the situated accomplishment of conversational telling-expansions. In B. Craig & K. Tracy (Eds.) , *Conversational coherence: Studies in form and strategy* (pp. 196–221). Newbury Park, CA: Sage.

Beach, W. A. (Ed.). (1989). Sequential organization of conversational activities. Special issue of *Western Journal of Speech Communication, 53*, 85–246.

Beach, W. A. (1990). On (not) observing behavior interactionally. *Western Journal of Speech Communication, 54*, 603–612.

Beach, W. A. (1991a). Avoiding ownership for alleged wrongdoings. *Research on Language and Social Interaction, 24*, 1–36.

Beach, W. A. (1991b). Searching for universal features of conversation. *Research on Language and Social Interaction, 24*, 349–366.

Beach, W. A. (1991c). *"Okay" as projection device for fuller turn: Displaying 'state of readiness' for movements to next-positioned matters*. Unpublished manuscript.

Beach, W. A. (1992). Transitional regularities for 'casual' "okay" usages. *Journal of Pragmatics, 19*, 325–352.

Beach, W. A., & Lindstrom, A. K. (1992). Conversational universals and comparative theory: Turning to acknowledgment tokens-in-interaction. *Communication Theory, 2*, 24–49.

Boden, D., & Zimmerman, D. (1991). *Talk and social structure*. Cambridge, England: Polity Press.

Button, G., & Casey, N. (1984). Generating topic: The use of topic initial elicitors. In J. M. Atkinson & J. Heritage (Eds.), *Structures of social action: Studies in conversation analysis* (pp. 167–190). Cambridge, England: Cambridge University Press.

Button, G., Drew, P., & Heritage, J. (Eds.). (1986). Interaction and language use. Special issue of *Human Studies, 9*, 107–321.

Craig, B., & Tracy, K. (Eds.). (1983). *Conversational coherence: Studies in form and strategy*. Newbury Park, CA: Sage Publications.

Craig, R. T. (1991). Editorial. *Communication Theory, 1*, 1–3.

Delia, J., & Grossberg, L. (1977). Interpretation and evidence. *Western Journal of Speech Communication, 41*, 32–42.

Drew, P. (1987). Po-faced receipts of teases. *Linguistics, 25*, 219–253.

Drew, P., & Heritage, J. (Eds.). (1992). *Talk at work: Interaction in institutional settings*. Cambridge, England: Cambridge University Press.

Ellis, D. G., & Donahue, W. A. (1986). *Contemporary issues in language and discourse processes*. Hillsdale, NJ: Lawrence Erlbaum Associates.

Fisher, B. A. (1978). *Perspectives on human communication*. New York: Macmillan.

Ford, J. (1975). *Paradigms and fairy tales: An introduction to the science of meanings* (Vol. 2). London, England: Routledge & Kegan Paul.

Frankel, R. (1984). From sentence to sequence: Understanding the medical encounter through microinteractional analysis. *Discourse Processes, 7*, 135–170.

Frankel, R. (1990). Talking in interviews: A dispreference for patient initiated questions in patient-physician encounters. In G. Psathas (Ed.), *Interaction competence* (pp. 231–262). New York: Irvington Publishers.

Garfinkel, H. (1967). *Studies in ethnomethodology*. Englewood Cliffs, NJ: Prentice-Hall.

Goffman, E. (1967). *Interaction ritual: Essays on face-to-face behavior.* Garden City, NY: Doubleday.

Goffman, E. (1981). *Forms of talk.* Oxford, England: Basil Blackwell.

Goodwin, C. (1981). *Conversational organization: Interaction between speakers and hearers.* New York: Academic Press.

Heath, C. (1992). The delivery and reception of diagnosis in the general practice consultation. In P. Drew & J. Heritage (Eds.), *Talk at work: Interaction in institutional settings* (pp. 235–267). Cambridge, England: Cambridge University Press.

Heritage, J. (1984). *Garfinkel and ethnomethodology.* London, England: Polity Press.

Heritage, J. (1985). Recent developments in conversation analysis. *Sociolinguistics Newsletter, 15,* 1–18.

Hopper, R. (1991a). Hold the phone. In D. Boden & D. Zimmerman (Eds.), *Talk and social structure* (pp. 217–231). Cambridge, England: Polity Press.

Hopper, R. (Ed.). (1991b). Ethnography and conversation analysis after *Talking culture.* Special section in *Research on Language and Social Interaction, 24.*

Hopper, R. (1992). *Telephone Conversation.* Bloomington: Indiana University Press.

Jackson, S. (1986). Building a case for claims about discourse structure. In D. G. Ellis & W. A. Donahue (Eds.), *Contemporary issues in language and discourse processes* (pp. 129–148). Hillsdale, NJ: Lawrence Erlbaum Associates.

Jacobs, S. (1986). How to make an argument from example in discourse analysis. In D. G. Ellis & W. A. Donahue (Eds.), *Contemporary issues in language and discourse processes* (pp. 149–168). Hillsdale, NJ: Lawrence Erlbaum Associates.

Jacobs, S. (1988). Evidence and inference in conversation analysis. In J. A. Andersen (Ed.), *Communication yearbook, 11,* 433–443. Newbury Park, CA: Sage.

Jefferson, G. (1973). A case of precision timing in ordinary conversation: Overlapped tag-positioned address terms in closing sequences. *Semiotica, 9,* 47–96.

Jefferson G. (1979). A technique for inviting laughter and its subsequent acceptance declination. In G. Psathas (Ed.), *Everyday language: Studies in ethnomethodology* (pp. 79–96). New York: Irvington Press.

Jefferson, G. (1983). Notes on some orderlinesses of overlap onset. Tilburg, Netherderlands: Tilburg Papers in Language and Literature, No. 28.

Jefferson, G. (1985a). The interactional unpackaging of a gloss. *Language in Society, 14,* 435–466.

Jefferson, G. (1985b). An exercise in the transcription and analysis of laughter. In van Dijk (Ed.), *Handbook of discourse analysis, Vol. 3: Discourse and dialogue* (pp. 25–34). London, England: Academic Press.

Jefferson, G., & Schegloff, E. (1975). *Sketch: Some orderly aspects of overlap in natural conversation.* American Anthropological Association. Mimeo.

Kaplan, A. (1964). *The conduct of inquiry.* New York: Thomas Y. Crowell.

Maynard, D. W. (1980). Placement of topic changes in conversation. *Semiotica, 30,* 263–290.

Maynard, D. W. (1984). *Inside plea-bargaining: The language of negotiation.* New York: Plenum Press.

Maynard, D. W. (1989a). Perspective-display sequences in conversation. In W. A. Beach (Ed.), Special issue of *Western Journal of Speech Communication, 53,* 91–113.

Maynard, D. W. (1989b). Notes on the delivery and reception of diagnostic news regarding mental disabilities. In D. T. Helm, W. T. Anderson, A. J. Meehan, & A. W. Rawls (Eds.), *The interactional order: New directions in the study of social order* (pp. 79–106). New York: Irvington.

Maynard, D. W. (1991). On the interactional and institutional bases of asymmetry in clinical discourse. *American Journal of Sociology, 92,* 448–495.

Maynard, D. W. (1992). On clinicians co-implicating recipients' perspective in the delivery of diagnostic news. In P. Drew & J. Heritage (Eds.), *Talk at work: Interaction in institutional settings* (pp. 331–358). Cambridge, England: Cambridge University Press.

Maynard, D. W., Zimmerman, D. H. (1984). Topical talk, ritual, and the social organization of relationships. *Social Psychology Quarterly, 47,* 301–316.

Nofsinger, R. E. (1991). *Everyday conversation*. Newbury Park, CA: Sage.

Ochs, E. (1979). Transcription as theory. In E. Ochs and B. Schieffelin (Eds.). *Developmental pragmatics* (pp. 43–72). New York: Academic Press.

Phillipson, M. (1973). Theory, methodology, and conceptualization. In P. Filmer, M. Phillipson, D. Silverman, & D. Walsh (Eds.), *New directions in sociological theory* (pp. 77–116). London, England: MIT Press.

Polanyi, M. (1962). *Personal knowledge*. Chicago: University of Chicago Press.

Pomerantz, A. M. (1978a). Compliment responses: Notes on the cooperation of multiple constraints. In J. N. Schenkein (Ed.), *Studies in the organization of conversational interaction* (pp. 79–112). New York: Academic Press.

Pomerantz, A. M. (1978b). Attributions of responsibility: Blamings. *Sociology, 12*, 115–121.

Pomerantz, A. M. (1984). Agreeing and disagreeing with assessments: Some features of preferred and dispreferred turn shapes. In J. M. Atkinson & J. Heritage (Eds.), *Structures of social action: Studies in conversation analysis* (pp. 57–101). Cambridge, England: Cambridge University Press.

Pomerantz, A. M. (Ed.). (1989). Special section on the Dan Rather/George Bush Episode on CBS News, in *Research on Language and Social Interaction, 22*, 213–326.

Psathas, G. (Ed.). (1979). *Everyday language: Studies in ethnomethodology*. New York: Irvington Press.

Sacks, H. (1963). Sociological description. *Berkeley Journal of Sociology, 8*, 1–16.

Sacks, H. (1974). *Public lecture*. Ann Arbor Linguistics Institute. Ann Arbor, MI.

Sacks, H. (1984a). Notes on methodology. In J. M. Atkinson & J. Heritage (Eds.), *Structures of social action: Studies in conversation analysis* (pp. 21–27). Cambridge, England: Cambridge University Press.

Sacks, H. (1984b). On doing being ordinary. In J. M. Atkinson & J. Heritage (Eds.), *Structures of social action: Studies in conversation analysis* (pp. 413–429). Cambridge, England: Cambridge University Press.

Sacks, H., Schegloff, E., & Jefferson, G. (1974). A simplest systematics for the organization of turn-taking for conversation. *Language, 50*, 696–735.

Schegloff, E. A. (1968). Sequencing in conversational openings. *American Anthropologist, 70*, 1075–1095.

Schegloff, E. A. (1986). The routine as achievement. *Human Studies, 2*, 111–151.

Schegloff, E. A. (1987). Between macro and micro: Contexts and other connections. In J. Alexander, B. Giesen, R. Munch, & N. Smelser (Eds.), *The micro-macro link* (pp. 207–234). Berkeley & Los Angeles: University of California Press.

Schegloff, E., Jefferson, G., & Sacks, H. (1977). The preference for self-correction in the organization of repair in conversation. *Language, 53*, 361–382.

Schegloff, E. A., Sacks, H. (1973). Opening up closings. *Semiotica, 7*, 289–327.

Schenkein, J. N. (Ed.). (1978). *Studies in the organization of conversational interaction*. New York: Academic Press.

Sudnow, D. (1972). *Studies in social interaction*. New York: Free Press.

Turner, R. (1970). Words, utterances, and activities. In J. Douglas (Ed.), *Understanding everyday life* (pp. 169–187). London, England: Routledge & Kegan Paul.

van Dijk, T. A. (1987). Discourse and power. Manuscript: University of Amsterdam.

van Dijk, T. A. (1989). Structures of discourse and structures of power. In J. A. Andersen (Ed.), *Communication Yearbook 12* (pp. 18–59). Newbury Park, CA: Sage.

Wieder, D. L. (1988). From resource to topic: Some aims of conversation analysis. In J. A. Andersen (Ed.), *Communication Yearbook 11* (pp. 444–454). Newbury Park, CA: Sage.

Zimmerman, D. H. (1988). On conversation: The conversation analytic perspective. In J. A. Andersen (Ed.), *Communication Yearbook 11* (pp. 406–432). Newbury Park, CA: Sage.

Zimmerman, D. H., & West, C. (Eds.). (1980). Language and social interaction. Special issue of *Sociological Inquiry, 50*, v.–425.

APPENDIX

The transcription notation system employed for data segments is an adaptation of Gail Jefferson's work (see Atkinson & Heritage, 1984, pp. ix–xvi; Beach, 1989, pp. 89–90). The symbols may be described as follows:

:	*Colon(s):*	Extended or stretched sound, syllable, or word.
_	*Underlining:*	Vocalic emphasis.
(.)	*Micropause:*	Brief pause of less than (0.2).
(1.2)	*Timed Pause:*	Intervals occur within and between same or different speaker's utterance.
(( ))	*Double Parentheses:*	Scenic details.
( )	*Single Parentheses:*	Transcriptionist doubt.
.	*Periods:*	Falling vocal pitch.
?	*Question Marks:*	Rising vocal pitch.
↑↓	*Arrows:*	Marked rising and falling shifts in intonation.
°°	*Degree Signs:*	A passage of talk noticeably softer than surrounding talk.
=	*Equal Signs:*	Latching of contiguous utterances, with no interval or overlap.
[ ]	*Brackets:*	Speech overlap.
[[	*Double Brackets:*	Simultaneous speech orientations to prior turn.
!	*Exclamation Points:*	Animated speech tone.
-	*Hyphens:*	Halting, abrupt cut off of sound or word.
> <	*Less Than/ Greater Than Signs:*	Portions of an utterance delivered at a pace noticeably quicker than surrounding talk.

Part IV

Foci of Theory Building: Individuals and Their Associations

Once again caution must be exercised in reading the following chapters. This book is not merely an arbitrary collection of essays, but rather it consists of chapters which build on one another—because their authors share significantly similar assumptions about the roles ontology, axiology, and epistemology play in constructing theories.

Many of our textbooks and academic institutions emphasize certain "areas," or subject matters, related to specific academic disciplines. As a result, the final section of this book will address concerns related to some of those areas. Again, no attempt is made to provide a comprehensive survey, rather you will find only representative illustrations. They should further our understanding of how the process of theorizing relates to the conceptual bases human beings bring to their search for understanding.

To make sure that the transition is made somewhat easier and perhaps more meaningful, in the chapter written by Stamp, Vangelisti, and Knapp, we will return to our earlier focus on individual human beings and interactions between individuals. The next chapter, by Robert Fortner, is included at that point in order to remind us of two factors: (a) even so-called "mass" communication has its beginning and end with individuals, and (b) "mass communication" often finds its meaning in the interactions between individual human beings. As we consider the contribution of Gouran, Hirokawa, McGee, and Miller, one central factor related to sociocultural settings becomes our focus. Human beings associate; they form groups, they form organizations. The very concept of culture implies sharing, and the very concept of society implies structure and organization. Such structure has as its base some mutually accepted standards and rules—in traditional societies usually those which have culturally emerged and which have been communicated over generations.

Finally, Cushman's and Kovacic's chapter is used as a kind of summary. I could easily have placed it in Section 2, due to its conceptual orientation. But I decided the points this book is trying to make would be better served if the chapter were inserted at the end. You may wonder about the detailed explanation I have provided in this instance. It serves as a reminder that all of us make choices; all of us make decisions as we face either concepts or physical entities in our lives. They do not all automatically *fit* in accordance with some inherent law or value. Many of them would fit just as well somewhere else. As long as we share the choice-maker's assumptions, or are at least made aware of them, human interaction can continue without too much friction. Otherwise, bitter disagreements or conflicts may arise. The history of our world, including the roles intellectuals and scholars have played, is full of such incidents which frequently have more to do with personal feelings and assumptions than anything that exists in some absolute universe or real world.

What I would like to accomplish by placing the rules perspective chapter at the book's end, is a renewed recognition of the fact that indeed there exist many perspectives related to the study of humans communicating. All of them may have some contribution to make, depending on our various needs and assumptions. As I indicated in the first chapter, I am grateful to Aubrey Fisher for sharing that insight and opening that conceptual door for me—and I wish he could have lived longer so that I could have walked through more such doors alongside of him. Furthermore, the relationships of theory building and research are strongly developed in this chapter. Concepts, ideas, and theories are very important—so are our attempts to ascertain whether or not they have any practical implications for human beings; whether or not the phenomena they specify can be demonstrated to exist in the actual, interactional processes of communication.

Chapter 5

Criteria for Developing
and Assessing Theories
of Interpersonal Communication

Glen H. Stamp
Ball State University

Anita L. Vangelisti
Mark L. Knapp
University of Texas at Austin

> *Metatheoretical debate is consuming so much effort that it is inhibiting
> (paralyzing would be too strong a word, but we like it) research. The business
> of rhetorical and communication theorists is to research and theorize, not
> to metatheorize. We hope that in metatheory this chapter will be literally
> the last word, at least for a few years.*
>
> —Bowers and Bradac (1984, pp. 887–888)

> *Interpersonal communication is a vague, fragmented, and loosely defined
> subject that intersects all the behavioral, social, and cultural sciences. There
> are no rigorous definitions that limit the scope of the field, no texts that
> comprehensively state its foundations, and little agreement among practi-
> tioners about which framework or methods offer the most promise for
> unifying the field.*
>
> —Bochner (1985, p. 27)

The above two quotes are taken from two of the handbooks published within
the field of communication in the mid 1980s. The Bowers and Bradac quote is
the final sentence in the *Handbook of Rhetorical and Communication Theory*;
the Bochner excerpt is the opening sentence in the *Handbook of Interpersonal
Communication*. We believe both statements still provide important perspectives
for viewing the status of theory in interpersonal communication.

The fact that there are so many theoretical options available to those interested
in interpersonal communication[1] (laypersons and academic researchers alike)

---

[1] One need only look at textbooks on theory such as Littlejohn (1989) for a sampling of the many
available theories in the social sciences generally and communication specifically.

seems to support Bochner's belief that the development of *a* theoretical point of view may not be possible or desirable. Indeed, the nonemergence of a single unifying theory may facilitate theoretical work because it encourages scholars to compare and contrast competing theoretical approaches. By weighing the strengths and weaknesses of various theoretical frameworks, we are able to further refine those theories guiding research in interpersonal communication.

Bowers and Bradac caution, however, about engaging in too much metatheoretical debate since both theoretical discussions and systematic research must take place if communication science is to advance. In recent years, there has been sufficient growth in both research and theory in interpersonal communication to warrant a reexamination of the central issues raised by Bowers and Bradac regarding communication theory. In addition to examining these fundamental issues, we review several exemplary theories of interpersonal communication in light of the issues. Finally, we provide a number of recommendations for future theorizing and research in interpersonal communication.

FUNDAMENTAL ISSUES

Berger (1991) has suggested that "there is a need to develop a relatively small set of overarching research questions with which to guide inquiry so that discourse at the level of theory will be facilitated" (p. 111). Such questions would allow researchers in disparate areas to combat the general fragmentation in the communication field and facilitate scholarly discourse pertaining to fundamental issues which most agree are important. Bowers and Bradac (1984) have identified "a number of competing axioms (which) undergird contemporary research and theory" (p. 872).[2] We believe that four of these axioms are sufficiently central that they represent the lifeblood for understanding any view of interpersonal commu-

---

[2]The seven sets of competing axioms are:

1a.
Communication is the Transmission and Reception of Meaning.
1b.
Communication is the Generation of Meaning.

2a.
Communication is Individual Behavior.
2b.
Communication is the Relationship among Behaviors of Interacting Individuals.

3a.
Human Communication is Unique.
3b.
Human Communication is a Form of Animal Communication.

nication theory and that they, therefore, may serve as a starting point for combating the "black hole" created by the absence of fundamental themes in communication theory (Berger, 1991, p. 111).[3] In addition, these axioms reflect broader epistemological, ontological, and philosophical concerns above and beyond what one might identify as the specific domain of interpersonal communication theory. These four foundational issues are: communication is the generation of *meaning*; communication is the *relationship* among behaviors of interacting individuals; communication is *processual*; and communication is *contextualized*.

Meaning

The dilemma of *meaning* is one that has long plagued social scientists and communication theorists. The positions taken include (a) meaning being "inside" the person (Ogden & Richards, 1923); (b) meaning having specific, and measurable, empirical referents (Osgood, Suci, & Tannenbaum, 1957); (c) meaning being connected with the "speech acts" used to accomplish particular aims (Searle, 1969); and (d) meaning being relativistic and dependent on cultural considerations (Sapir, 1921).

Grossberg (1982) reviewed the ways scholars represent meaning within interpersonal relations by identifying three predominant responses to this statement: "Communication is the ____ of meaning between individuals through ____" (p. 172). The three views of meaning derived from these responses are "correspondence through exchange," "sharing through emergence," and "constitution through interpretation." Meanings are, respectively, actual *entities* (units) which can be exchanged, emergent *products* shared by interlocutors, or the *environment* through which life is experienced (Grossberg, 1982). Central questions for interpersonal communication researchers concern both "what meaning means" and "where meanings lie." Simply put, we may ask whether meaning is representational (a thing is a thing), whether meaning is personalized by individual or *shared* experiences, or whether meaning actually constitutes the relationship between two individuals.

The stance taken here is a pragmatic one: An understanding of interpersonal life will be advanced with a position less concerned with the exchange of units and more oriented toward examining how meanings are shared or how meanings

---

[3]Three of Bowers and Bradac's (1984) axioms were not selected. *Axiom 3* (concerning the uniqueness of communication) was not included in the current chapter because the purpose of the chapter is to address criteria for evaluating theories of human interaction. Establishing that communication is uniquely human (rather than a form of animal communication) is not the topic of this chapter. *Axiom 6* (concerning human beings' ability to "not communicate") is subsumed by our discussion of Axiom 1 (communication is the generation of meaning). Finally, *Axiom 7* (concerning the impact/force of communication in society) is implicit in our discussion of the other axioms. If, as we suggest, communication is the generation of meaning (*Axiom 1b*), is the relationship among behaviors of interacting individuals (*Axiom 2b*), is processual (*Axiom 4a*), and is contextualized (*Axiom 5a*), it is necessarily a ubiquitous and powerful force in society.

constitute relationships. It is difficult to accept the position that meaning is exchanged because such a position implies a literal meaning for any social action—a position attacked by Menzel (1978) and Rommetveit (1980). An alternative position views meaning as a pluralistic phenomena—that is, any action is susceptible to multiple meanings. As such, the search for literal meaning is fruitless. What social actors and social scientists must accept is that whatever is meant is not necessarily what is said, that misunderstanding may be more predominant than understanding, and that social interaction is based on (indeed, that it relies on) individuals' faith in a shared social world (Rommetveit, 1980, p. 109).

Given that interpersonal meanings both construct and are constructed by social interaction, it would be ill advised to locate meaning within one, or the other, interactant. Instead, meanings are positioned in the nexus of a close relationship as negotiated phenomena and do not *belong* to either person. That which is meaningful emerges through, or is reflected in, pattern, redundancy, information, and restraint (Bateson, 1972, pp. 131–132). Meanings, therefore, are pluralistic endeavors negotiated by participants within their relationship.

Such a conceptualization also reformulates constructs such as "intentions" within a different epistemological framework. As actors in the world, each of us communicates from within the framework of our individual intentions. We formulate intentions based on our "meanings" of situations and people. In addition, we continually interpret the behaviors of others as meaningful. From the initial interactions between two people to the development of a close relationship, each person's intentions vis-à-vis the other, along with the attributions each makes about the intentions of the other are integral to the formation and maintenance of the relationship (Kelley, 1979). Interactional intentions, therefore, subsume both an encoder and a decoder perspective on intent (Stamp & Knapp, 1990). The meaning of an individual intention, from an interpersonal communication perspective, is less meaningful than the role of intentions in the ongoing negotiated process of a relationship. The tasks of interpersonal communication theorists, therefore, are: to examine *a variety of meanings* over time, relationships, and situations and to examine *how meanings are created and sustained through interaction.*

Relationship

A second fundamental issue in any communication theory focusing on interpersonal transactions is the degree to which *relationship* is a contributing factor in explaining behavior. Liberal interactional or relational approaches (Bateson, 1972; Watzlawick, Beavin, & Jackson, 1967) posit that individuals are only understood within the context of their relationships and that individual behaviors are not meaningful in and of themselves.

From a broad-based relational approach one might question not only the relevance of examining individual verbal and nonverbal behaviors exhibited by a person, but the actual existence of the *self*. From a symbolic interactionistic perspective, the *self* has no meaning without an *other*. Indeed, the very notion of the self is that of a social self arising through interactions with significant others. Self, therefore, is not internal nor do we have just one real self (Hart & Burks, 1972)—an ontological perspective that flies in the face of much of what is accepted in current American culture (Bellah, Madsen, Sullivan, Swidler, & Tipton, 1985, 1991; Lannamann, 1991; Lasch, 1979).

On the surface it would appear that a communication theory concerned only with relationships should eschew issues associated with the individual communicator (i.e., individual cognitions, attitudes, or beliefs) for issues concerned with relationships (where those cognitions, attitudes, or beliefs are jointly created, negotiated, maintained, or changed). As Bateson (1972) advises, we might be better off to "think first of the relationships and consider the relata as defined solely by their relationships" (p. 154). On a conceptual level, however, we need to acknowledge that the association between individual selves and relationships is reflexive—individual selves are part of what make up our social world. Not only do relationships define individuals, but individuals also define relationships. Furthermore, from a practical perspective, one way for researchers to explore relationships is to examine the emotions, cognitions, and behaviors of the individuals comprising those relationships.

In short, a relational approach need not preclude the study of individuals or individual perspectives. Indeed, examining the nuances of individual perspectives may be a necessary step to fully understanding relationships (Hewes & Planalp, 1987) in that individual perspectives may provide researchers with otherwise unavailable information. Rather than completely avoid the study of individual relational partners, we suggest that communication theorists interested in the development, maintenance, and dissolution of interpersonal bonds would be well advised to examine *the characteristics of individuals in relationship to others* rather than study individuals apart (isolated) from their interpersonal relationships.

Process

The concept of process is a *taken-for-granted* within the field of communication over the last 30 years. The primary influence is often traced to Berlo (1960):

> Communication theory reflects a process point of view. A communication theorist rejects the possibility that nature consists of events or ingredients that are separable from all other events. He (sic) argues that you cannot talk about the beginning or the end of communication or say that a particular idea came from one specific source, that communication occurs in only one way and so on. (p. 24)

While one would be challenged to examine an introductory communication textbook and not encounter the notion of process within the first few chapters, and while most communication theorists view communication as a process, Knapp and Miller (1985) point out that the bulk of the pre-1980 research tended to be more static than processual in nature (p. 15). Explanations for lack of process oriented research include the tendency to view *change* through the eyes of Western culture. The tendency toward linear thinking and traditional mechanistic worldviews that have predominated in this culture encourage teachings that value stability over change (Capra, 1984). For example, the literature focusing on change within organizations is often oriented toward ways to either manage change (see Smircich & Calas, 1987, for references) or resist change (see Monge & Eisenberg, 1987, for references). Change is often associated with perceptions of threat by the members of the organization even though current organizational thinking posits an emergent, ever-changing communication structure within organizations (Jablin, Putnam, Roberts, & Porter, 1988, pp. 297–298).

Similarly, work on close relationships has tended to theorize more about the constant process of change while, at the same time, studying relationships within a climate valuing stability rather than change (Duck, 1990). In practice, this orientation may manifest itself in people recalling events associated with their relationship's development as a stable, orderly progression (Huston, Surra, Fitzgerald, & Cate, 1981) when, in fact, it was highly changeable and often chaotic (Duck, 1985). The tendency to value stability may also explain why some people expect or desire consistent behavioral patterns from relationship partners and have trouble adjusting to changes even though change should be assumed within ongoing relationships (Werner & Haggard, 1985, p. 61).

Two steps must be taken before we are able to remedy the disparity between the way change is treated by interpersonal theory and the way it is typically treated in empirical research. First, we need to evaluate our interpersonal theories to see if they provide predictions and explanations for how both change and stability occur. It is one thing to state that communication is processual and that it is constantly changing. It is another to specify the mechanisms by which such changes occur. Sigman (1991) notes, for example, that partners in continuous social relationships use communication devices to deal with the changes created by physical separations. Among other things, partners may jointly establish a definition for the separation or they may define their experiences (during separation) as accountable to the relationship.[4] Such devices exemplify the ways partners jointly manage change within their relationship.

Second, researchers need to closely examine patterns of communication behavior over time. We need to emphasize sequences of behavior, cognitions, and emotions rather than individual acts. In addition, we need to study communicative acts that serve to sequence (regulate) interpersonal relationships and we need to examine those acts longitudinally.

---

[4]Knapp, Hart, Friedrich, and Shulman (1973) similarly found that people tend to mark conversational leave-taking by signaling that the relationship will continue beyond the scope of the conversation.

In the Sigman (1991) study, interpersonal communication is used by participants to deal with an impending or recent change. Other investigations may examine communication as a vehicle for change or they may focus on the impact of changes in communication on interpersonal relationships. In short, there are a variety of approaches that scholars may take in theorizing about and observing communication processes. Rather than prioritize one approach over another, we note simply that since interpersonal communication is processual, a well-founded theory of interpersonal communication should specify *how, when, and why communication behaviors change over time.*

Context

The fourth, and final, issue is context. Bateson (1978) argues that understanding context is foundational to understanding interpersonal communication since "without context, words and actions have no meaning at all" (p. 15). This foundational nature is reflected in the use of context as an organizing principle within the handbooks and textbooks in the discipline. Context has been conceptualized in several different ways: (a) as the areas which broadly define the communication discipline (interpersonal, group, organizational, mass) (Littlejohn, 1983); (b) as "distinct social and institutional settings" (Chaffee & Berger, 1987, p. 537); (c) as distinctions within a particular arena such as task/work, social, and family (Knapp & Miller, 1985); (d) as objects or characteristics that comprise an environment (Tversky & Hemenway, 1983); (e) as perceptions of role relationships in different settings (Wish, Deutsch, & Kaplan, 1976; Wish & Kaplan, 1977); (f) as message variables including language style, affect displays, and overt statements regarding intentionality; and (g) as situational variables such as participants' understanding of their social roles, recognition of others' territorial boundaries, and knowledge of special social occasions (Bowers & Bradac, 1984). Context, then, may encompass psychological, behavioral, and environmental perspectives.

Although context is often thought of as a static entity that can be easily understood, in reality, any context is an emergent process (Bateson, 1978; Branham & Pearce, 1985; Gergen, 1980). Contexts can be subdivided into *retrospective* context (all of the actions that precede a particular behavior that might help interpret that behavior) and *emergent* context (all of the events following the behavior which might help interpret the behavior) (Gergen, 1980). In addition, there is a difference between context in theory and context in experience (Branham & Pearce, 1985). In theory, we may realize that our surroundings change. In our experience, however, we rely on a shared social context to communicate with one another. Meaningful contextual information is only derived through an examination of ongoing interaction sequences between individuals and their environments (Bateson, 1978). The attempt to understand an ephemeral context, while at the same time studying a phenomenon (communication) that relies on participants' assumptions of contextual sharedness and stability, presents a challenge to communication theorists. An examination of retrospective and emergent contexts as well as current behaviors may help us understand communicative episodes in more depth. Taking into consideration additional contextual information allows for better formulated "thick descriptions" (Geertz, 1973).

Our goal here is not to define context, nor to put context at the forefront of interpersonal theory construction (Berger, 1991), but to specify the role it should play in interpersonal communication theory. In discussing the study of interpersonal messages, Bowers (1989) states that researchers should not adopt a single definition of communication messages. We believe that Bowers' words of caution apply similarly to context. Rather than prioritize a particular type of context over another, we suggest only that theories of interpersonal communication need to address the interface between communication and context. Whether the context be socially constructed by participants, internally generated by individuals, "objectively" observed by outsiders, or temporally generated, it affects and is affected by communication. Any theory of interpersonal communication, therefore, should describe *the association between communication and context*.

EXEMPLARY THEORIES

Seven theories have been selected for review as they pertain to the previous four issues. The chosen theories are dialectical theory, relational theory, uncertainty reduction theory, attribution theory, nonverbal expectancy violations theory, social exchange theory, and constructivism. Our selection was based on relevance and distinctiveness. The theories had to fall within the general parameters of a "middle range" theory, which pertained primarily to the development or maintenance of interpersonal interactions. We, therefore, sought representative theories that were not too general (such as general systems theory or symbolic interactionism), or too specific (such as information theory) (Littlejohn, 1983, p. 303), and that were perceived to be relatively distinct from one another. Although many theories that might be included were not [interdependence theory (Kelley et al., 1983; Kelley & Thibaut, 1978) coordinated management of meaning (Pearce & Cronen, 1980), social penetration theory (Altman & Taylor, 1973), action assembly theory (Greene, 1984), speech accommodation theory (Street & Giles, 1982), etc.], our assessment of those theories, as they apply to the fundamental issues, would undoubtedly address similar considerations.

The theories represented here, as well as other potentially relevant theories, account for interpersonal interactions in unique ways. At the same time, however, the theories have culturally based commonalities. Collectively, the various theories of interpersonal communication—those developed by interpersonal communication scholars as well as those originating in other disciplines—reflect a philosophical perspective. They exhibit the ontological orientation that the nature of our existence as human beings is fundamentally linked to our social relationships as well as the epistemological perspective that systematic observation and reflection will provide insight into these fundamental aspects of social life. In this chapter, we point out the distinctions between a number of interpersonal communication theories. We would be remiss, however, not to remind ourselves that none of the theories emerged from an intellectual vacuum. Rather, each shares with the others common philosophical assumptions reflecting particular cultural values.

Dialectical Theory

Dialectical theory emphasizes the study of relationship contradictions as forces that explain and predict interpersonal behavior. Contradiction is an inherent conflict between opposing factors experienced by interactants within their social relationships. A contradiction is formed whenever two tendencies or forces are interdependent (the dialectical principle of unity) yet mutually negate one another (the dialectical principle of negation) (Baxter, 1988). Unless the contradictions are interconnected in this paradoxical fashion, they do not meet the criteria of a relational dialectic. Relational theorists and researchers have uncovered such contradictions as autonomy/connection (Askham, 1976; Baxter, 1988), novelty/ predictability (Bochner & Eisenberg, 1987; Yerby, Buerkel-Rothfuss, & Bochner, 1990), openness/closedness (Altman, Vinsel, & Brown, 1981; Bochner, 1984), expressiveness/protectiveness (Rawlins, 1983a), dependance/independence (Rawlins, 1983b), judgment/acceptance (Rawlins & Holl, 1988), and marital role/parental role (Cissna, Cox, & Bochner, 1990) within various close relationships.

Meaning. Dialectical theory offers the perspective that certain contradictions are experienced and managed within close relationships. The theory does not provide an explicit statement concerning the origin or nature of relational partners' meanings. However, in a sense, what is experienced (issues of autonomy/connection, for example) might be considered as *meanings* negotiated by the participants. A particular couple may have negotiated an arrangement where both feel that a balance exists between autonomy for self and connection with the partner. This negotiation may have been explicit (partners go out once a week with their individual friends and one night is set aside to be together) or implicit (partners feel that they receive confirmation of their autonomy through their individual careers and seize the opportunities they have to be together). Influencing the meaning of any particular behavior or activity are the overall needs of each person or the needs of each person at any particular point in time. One spouse may not derive as much pleasure from going out with his/her friends and desire more connection with the spouse while the other spouse may feel the opposite. In addition, each spouse may have individualized meanings for *autonomy* and *connection*. Although spouses may assume that the connection or autonomy they seek is average or normal, in actuality, such assumptions will need to be negotiated with their relational partners.

Dialectical theory might also address meaning by focusing on the issues that relational partners see as meaningful. Meaningful issues of autonomy and connection may take many forms within relationships which necessitate negotiation. Spouses who have different *meanings* for how much time should be spent at work and at home, for holiday traditions, or for leisure activities represent a few examples that may arise in a relationship. In addition, the autonomy/connection dialectic may be activated when one party attributes intent to the actions of the other which impinge on his or her autonomy needs. Such an attribution may be relationally specific; that is, the actions of the spouse may deviate from previous actions thereby allowing a particular attribution to be made.

The benefit of dialectic theory, in terms of meanings in interpersonal relationships, is that the central dialectics in relationships (autonomy/connection, novelty/predictability, openness/closedness) provide a means for explaining relational, as opposed to individual level meanings. However, to date, the research has not explored issues of meaning from a dialectical perspective.

Relationship. Supporters of dialectical theory argue that it is a relationally based theory. Indeed, it is this aspect that close relationship theorists, dissatisfied with what they see as the individually based theories dominating the field, have cited as the major reason for their adherence to the dialectical approach (Baxter, 1988; Bochner, 1984). Baxter (1988) states "although . . . dialectical contradictions . . . are experienced and acted upon by the individual parties, they are situated in the relationship between the parties" (p. 258).

Dialectical tensions are situated within the relationship because the *relationship* cannot exist when the tensions are not managed. For example, unless each party within a relationship sacrifices some autonomy, the parties cannot be connected with one another. However, the sacrifice of too much autonomy may also threaten the relationship since excessive connection may threaten the autonomy of relational partners (Baxter, 1988).

The experience and management of dialectical tensions, therefore, are based on a relational level of analysis. The constraint of autonomy, as well as the achievement of autonomy, is experienced by an individual within the relationship. However, the strategies used to manage the tensions, to achieve more autonomy or more connection, for example, are conceptualized as a relational or situational response rather than as an individual accomplishment (Baxter, 1988; Rawlins, 1983b).

To date, most of the research on relational dialectics has been oriented toward examining the dialectical tensions presented by certain types of relationships. Less information is available concerning how individuals communicatively manage those tensions. While we know, for example, that most participants within close relationships report experiencing the autonomy/connection dialectic, the specific ways in which that tension is communicatively managed are not well understood.

Process. Process is an important dimension within the dialectical perspective. The notion of process implies that the dialectics are always present within relationships and experienced, to various degrees, by the relational partners. Change occurs when partners struggle to reconcile the contradictions, when, for whatever reason, those contradictions surface within the relationship with more immediacy than was previously experienced. Interactants respond strategically to the contradictions. Through communication (or the lack thereof), the dialectic is managed (or not managed) and the relationship is maintained, dissolved, or changed.

Unfortunately, the dynamics of process pertaining to dialectical tensions remain relatively unexplored. While theorists and researchers universally assert the processual nature of dialectical tensions, the fact remains that the research "fails to examine how these dialectical tensions play themselves out through time" (Baxter, 1988, p. 272). Typically, studies focus on the tensions at a single point in time. One longitudinal research program using a dialectical framework examined the experience and communication management of two dialectical tensions during the transition to parenthood (Stamp, 1991). The autonomy/connection dialectic was found to be particularly problematic in that spouses simultaneously experienced less connection with one another and less autonomy for themselves. They experienced more closeness to and more distance from each other after the birth of the baby. Spouses maintained both autonomy and connection through a combination of strategic openness and closedness.

Although the process dimension is acknowledged as a key feature within dialectical theory, longitudinal research is needed to explain both the changes in particular tensions (e.g., increases/decreases in the need for autonomy or connection) and the ways relational participants communicatively manage those changes.

Context. According to dialectical theory, specific tensions manifest themselves within close relationships. The context of a relationship—the relationship *type*—influences the particular dialectic which is experienced within the relationship. For example, the primary dialectic within a stepfamily is the tension between marital and parental relationships (Cissna et al., 1990), whereas the primary tensions within a parent-adolescent relationship are the dialectic of historical perspective and contemporary experience and the dialectic of judgment and acceptance (Rawlins & Holl, 1988). Relational contexts create particular dialectics which, in turn, influence communication within the relationship. Cissna et al. (1990), for example, indicate that, within stepfamilies, the emergence of a dialectic creates the need for communication reinforcing the solidarity of the marriage in the minds of the stepchildren. Dialectic theory may be useful in explaining genres of communication typical of particular types of relationships.

Although dialectical theory does not directly deal with the impact of the environment, environmental context may influence both the experience and management of a tension within specific relationships. A couple may organize either their space or their time in an attempt to manage the dialectic of autonomy and connection. Certain parts of the house (the bathroom, a workroom) may be considered off-limits to one spouse or certain times may be set aside (Sunday morning) for the couple to spend together in leisurely connection. Although one could certainly speculate that this association between specific contexts and specific communication is present due to the influence of dialectic tensions, empirical support has not appeared which helps to predict and explain such an association.

Relational Theory

The genesis of relational theory is typically credited to Bateson (1972) while the popularization of the theory belongs to what has become known as the Palo Alto Group. The core assumptions of relational theory are twofold. First, all messages have two levels: a content level (which involves the literal interpretation of discourse) and a relationship level (which provides information about how the content message should be classified) (Watzlawick et al., 1967). The second assumption posits that relationships can be categorized in two predominant ways: a symmetrical relationship characterized by similarity in message exchange (e.g., boasting followed by boasting) or a complementary relationship characterized by difference (e.g., boasting followed by acquiescence) (Bateson, 1972, pp. 68–69).

According to Millar and Rogers (1976, 1987), any message can be interpreted as asserting a definition of the relationship (a one-up movement), as requesting acceptance of the other's definition of the relationship (one-down), or as providing no relational definition at all (one-across). The next contiguous message in the sequence then defines the two-message transaction as either complementary or symmetrical. Through this message-exchange process, three relational dimensions (control, trust, intimacy) are constituted (Millar & Rogers, 1976, 1987; Rogers & Millar, 1988). Although a number of axioms and theorems have been proposed pertaining to symmetrical and complementary configurations (Millar & Rogers, 1987; Parks, 1978), the research to date has concentrated primarily on the control dimension of interpersonal relationships and the operationalization of such control dimensions as domineeringness and dominance (Courtright, Millar, & Rogers-Millar, 1979; Rogers, Courtright, & Millar, 1980).

Meaning.   Relationship theorists treat meaning in terms of message sequencing. A message is meaningful only vis-à-vis either the previous message or the subsequent message in a sequence. For example, a particular statement (W: "What did you expect of me when we got married?") merely asserts a definition of a relationship; it is only through a response (H: "Well, uh, . . . I really didn't have any expectations of you") that the transaction is meaningful. In this case, the transact is complementary since the first statement is codable as "one-down" and the second statement is codable as "one-up" (Rogers & Millar, 1988).

Meaning, therefore, is interactionally negotiated by participants through their messages. This is not to say that interactants necessarily agree on the meaning of messages. In fact, two interactants may punctuate messages quite differently. The classic example of a husband withdrawing and the wife nagging (H: "I withdraw because she nags"; W: "I nag because he withdraws") illustrates different meanings that occur due to differences in participants' perceptions of the message sequence (Christensen & Heavey, 1990). The important distinction between individual meaning and relational meaning is that the individual meaning occurs retrospectively as either spouse thinks of the event; the relational meaning, however, occurs as the messages are uttered (Millar & Rogers, 1987, p. 117). While two people may disagree on the punctuation of the content, the meaning for the relationship is constituted within the interactional sequence.

Relationship. The primacy of relationship within relational theory is derived from systems theory which posits that the whole is considered greater than the sum of its individual parts. From such a perspective, individual differences (Machiavellian, apprehensive, etc.) have little more than a "trifling influence" on long-term close relationships (Bochner, 1984, p. 584). Rather, when the emphasis is on relationship, the qualities of relational associations take precedence over the qualities of individuals. The focus of analysis, therefore, is the form of the relationship, rather than the content of individual acts (Rogers & Millar, 1988). Such an emphasis might include an examination of ongoing rituals that are established and maintained through purposeful communication or rules that govern behavior within the relationship (Bochner, 1984). Rituals and rules are created and maintained through redundant communication patterns and help constitute relationship definition.

Theory and research on relational control exemplify the perspective of relational theory. Bateson (1972) defines control as a characteristic of relationships rather than of individuals. His view is that "a human being in relation with another has very limited control over what happens in that relationship. He (sic.) is part of a two person unit, and the control which any part can have over any whole is strictly limited" (p. 267). Given this, there is no such thing as a dominant statement. Instead, a domineering statement is only meaningful when it is situated within a behavioral sequence (Courtright et al., 1979). While the control dimension has been well established through systematic research, future inquiry needs to examine other proposed relational dimensions such as intimacy and trust (Millar & Rogers, 1987).

Process. Because relational theorists are more concerned with the form of messages than the specific content, defining a relationship is an ongoing process. While any two part message exchange is potentially codable as a symmetrical or complementary exchange, at the very least, from a process point of view, the next message in the sequence (the third interact) can change the pattern of the interaction. From a global processual perspective, it is only through the ongoing exchange of redundant message forms that a relationship is defined.

Symmetry and complementarity, therefore, refer both to specific patterns of interaction as well as types of relationships (Bochner, 1984). A relationship, however, need not be defined as either symmetrical or complementary since any particular relationship may alternate between the two forms—a condition known as a "parallel relationship" (Lederer & Jackson, 1968). Although theoretical and clinical works have noted the natural fluctuations in complementarity and symmetry that occur in relationships, longitudinal empirical work has been limited primarily to clinical populations. In addition to broadening the base of its samples, research using relational theory would benefit from studies that move beyond sequences of interacts to include sequences of conversations and perhaps even sequences of relationships.

Context.   For relational theorists, the relationship itself is an overall context influencing message patterns. For a husband and wife, therefore, the "relationship is the context for the episodes they enact: it provides the 'frame' for their trips to the beach and their work" (Pearce, 1989, p. 46). Within each relationship, however, we would speculate that different arenas shape the configuration of messages between intimates in various ways. A couple with a parallel relationship may have symmetry in one area of their relationship (housework) and complementarity in other areas (child care). Messages with the same form initiated by one spouse (e.g., "Could you please do the dishes?"; "Could you please pick-up the children?") but referring to different relational contexts may be responded to differently by the other spouse. Theoretical and empirical work needs to unravel the connections between specific contexts and communication patterns within relationships.

In addition, messages themselves may change the context—a process known as "textual reconstruction" (Branham & Pearce, 1985, p. 19). For example, a couple may have special idiomatic messages that indicate the beginning or ending of certain interactional sequences (saying "I want some ice cream" to propose sexual intercourse) (Bell, Buerkel-Rothfuss, & Gore, 1987, p. 53). Although research has uncovered the existence of such ritualistic communication within close relationships, the ways in which such idioms assert relationship definitions are not known because the subsequent messages have not been examined.

Uncertainty Reduction Theory

One of the original goals of uncertainty reduction theory was to provide researchers with a model that focused directly on interpersonal communication processes by "employing communication relevant constructs which, in turn, lead to the formation of hypotheses which directly involve communication behavior" (Berger & Calabrese, 1975, p. 99). The central assumptions of the theory are: (a) that when individuals meet for the first time, their primary concern is to reduce their uncertainty about their own behavior and the behavior of others, and (b) that interactants' abilities (or inabilities) to reduce uncertainty influence the ways they communicate. Communicators are seen as "naive scientists" (Heider, 1958) who seek to make sense out of their social world. The ability to predict and explain others' behavior, therefore, is rewarding to interactants whereas remaining in a state of ambiguity would be relatively costly. In fact, uncertainty reduction theorists not only predict that high levels of uncertainty will result in increased information seeking, but also that increases in uncertainty produce decreases in liking (Berger & Calabrese, 1975). Researchers have used uncertainty reduction theory to explore such disparate topics as conversational planning (Berger, 1987a; Berger & Bell, 1988) and events that increase uncertainty in personal relationships (Planalp & Honeycutt, 1985; Planalp, Rutherford, & Honeycutt, 1988).

Meaning.   For adherents of uncertainty reduction theory, meaning is derived by individual interactants via their current (and prior) interactions with others. Communication behavior, therefore, serves at least two roles for communicators (see Berger & Calabrese, 1975, p. 101). First, communication behavior is something in the environment that interactants seek to predict and explain. By reducing their uncertainty about communication behavior, interactants are able to make sense of their social environments. Second, communication behavior is used to formulate predictions and explanations. By interacting with others, individuals are able to reduce their uncertainty about why others behave the way they do and how others will behave in the context of future interactions. It also is possible, however, that interaction will increase (rather than decrease) uncertainty. People may behave so inconsistently that others are unable to predict their behavior. The meanings assigned to such inconsistent behavior will likely differ from the meanings assigned to more consistent, predictable behavior. In short, meaning is both *assigned to* communication and *derived from* communication.

Given that communicators cannot altogether avoid perceptual biases (e.g., Kellermann, 1988; Nisbett & Ross, 1980; Ross & Sicoly, 1979), the meaning gained from any interaction may be distorted or inaccurate. Like most theorists who focus on recipients' interpretations of communication behavior, uncertainty reduction theorists readily embrace these perceptual limitations. Why? Because the biased predictions and explanations made by communicators will influence their current and future interactions with others.

To understand how interactants assign and derive meaning from interaction, uncertainty reduction theorists must examine the full range of predictions and explanations that those interactants make about others. To date, the majority of research using uncertainty reduction theory has focused on initial interactions. Planalp and her colleagues (Planalp & Honeycutt, 1985; Planalp et al., 1988), however, have suggested that uncertainty reduction may occur throughout the life-cycle of relationships. There may be some times when reducing uncertainty is a very salient, important activity for relational partners. At other times, however, individuals may choose (consciously or unconsciously) to maintain a particular level of uncertainty about their relationship or about their partner.

Regardless of the developmental stage of the relationship, uncertainty reduction theorists treat the assignment of meaning as an individual activity carried out in the context of a relationship. To move beyond the level of individual communicators to an understanding of how meanings constitute relationships, theorists must examine the way in which participants negotiate the predictions and explanations made by each individual.

Relationship. According to uncertainty reduction theory, relationships evolve as the individuals within those relationships reduce their uncertainty about each another. At the "entry phase" (Berger & Calabrese, 1975, p. 100) of an interaction when participants are unacquainted, individuals' behavior, predictions, and explanations are governed, in large part, by communication rules and norms. Because the type of information made available by rules and norms is relatively general, communicators at this phase will experience comparatively high levels of uncertainty. Efforts will then be made to reduce this uncertainty using active, passive, or interactive strategies (Berger & Bradac, 1982) to seek information about the other.

Because uncertainty reduction is rewarding, theorists suggest that relational variables such as liking, intimacy level of communication content, and nonverbal affiliative expressiveness are inversely associated with uncertainty (Berger & Calabrese, 1975). Indeed, the research has demonstrated that uncertainty in personal relationships is typically seen by relational partners as negative (Planalp & Honeycutt, 1985) and that reduced uncertainty is associated with liking (Clatterbuck, 1979; Gudykunst, Yang, & Nishida, 1985). Uncertainty reduction theorists therefore maintain that the course of relational development depends, to a great extent, on individuals' ability and willingness to reduce their uncertainty about one another.

Although this perspective offers extremely useful explanations for individual strategies of uncertainty reduction, the impact of relationships and relational qualities on uncertainty (and vice versa) is not clear. Examining how partners jointly create, negotiate, and reduce their uncertainties may be one way to address this issue.

Process. Berger (1986) notes that uncertainty is relevant to interpersonal communication processes in at least two ways. First, and most generally, uncertainty is a central concern for individuals engaging in any communication interaction. Reducing uncertainty about others' communication behavior is necessary if interactants are to coordinate their communicative activities over time. Second, uncertainty reduction allows individuals to make predictions concerning the outcome of a given interaction and/or the outcomes of a relationship. In obtaining information about their conversational partners, individuals make decisions about whether future interactions will be rewarding. The nature of both current and future interactions are affected by uncertainty reduction.

The process of reducing uncertainty is seen as an ongoing endeavor since individuals predict how their conversational partners will behave prior to any interaction. To plan and select their own communication behaviors, people must first make some predictions about how their behaviors will fit with the behavior of others. In this sense, Berger and his colleagues (Berger, 1975; Berger & Calabrese, 1975) note that interactants engage in *proactive* prediction-making— they make predictions about others' behaviors before those behaviors have been enacted. After an interaction begins, however, these proactive predictions may be modified based on the information interactants gain from the conversation. If a conversational partner behaves in a way that violates the individual's initial predictions, *retroactive* explanations will be made for the behavior. Although examining proactive and retroactive strategies may be relatively straightforward, examining the full process of uncertainty reduction will be more difficult. Predictions, for example, may be linked to retrospective explanations (and subsequent predictions) in systematic ways. Similarly, uncertainty/ambiguity in one relationship may be linked to certain behaviors (e.g., efforts to reduce uncertainty) in another relationship.

Context. Because uncertainty reduction theorists see interactants as striving to make sense of their social world, one role of context is as a source of information (Berger, 1987b). For instance, we would expect that familiar, predictable contexts would typically be associated with less uncertainty than unfamiliar, unpredictable contexts. Indeed, the ambiguity of certain contexts has been found to increase uncertainty. To reduce uncertainty, interactants placed in an ambiguous context tended to ask more questions overall, tended to ask more demographic questions (Rubin, 1977), and had significantly longer interactions (Rubin, 1979). It is important to note that these findings do not suggest that ambiguous contexts necessarily provide more or less information than unambiguous contexts. Instead, they suggest that the type of information provided by ambiguous contexts may encourage people to engage in uncertainty reduction strategies.

Given the variety of communication-relevant information available in any context, the associations between context, uncertainty reduction, and communication are still largely unexplored. We would speculate that context is used by interactants, in combination with the communication behavior of others, to reduce uncertainty. For example, if a person's communication behavior is inappropriate (e.g., too informal, too loud, too intimate) for a given context, other interactants may make retroactive explanations for that behavior that will affect subsequent interactions with the person. Similarly, if interactants know they will be meeting others in a particular environment, they will make proactive predictions about how those people will behave. At the same time, context may be seen by interactants as an object of uncertainty. Prior to the entry phase of an interaction, participants may seek information about the context (e.g., Is it formal or informal?) so that they can make normatively based predictions about others' communication behavior. When contextual information is scarce, interactants should experience more difficulty predicting and evaluating others' behavior. As a result, making choices about their own behavior should be relatively difficult. However, it is also possible that in *extremely* uncertain situations, individuals' choices about their own behaviors become very clear (e.g., interactants may decide to change the context or to remove themselves from it).

Attribution Theory

Like uncertainty reduction theory, attribution theory is based on the assumption that human beings seek to make sense of their social environment (Heider, 1958). Unlike uncertainty reduction theory, however, attribution theory emphasizes individuals' causal perceptions over their tendencies (or abilities) to predict behavior. Social behavior, in other words, is interpreted in terms of its perceived causes. When attributional processes are triggered, individuals seek out and assign a cause to the trigger behavior. Research on attribution theory has found that attributions are typically made when peoples' expectations are violated (e.g., Pyszczynski & Greenberg, 1981). Once causal explanations are made, they shape perceivers' feelings, thoughts, and subsequent actions.

Since its inception with Heider's (1958) classic work, attribution theory has taken a number of different pathways. Kelley's (1973) research on the covariation principle, for example, provides predictions concerning whether individuals will make internal or external attributions for a given behavior. Internal attributions are typically made when others act similarly to a variety of people (distinctiveness), when their behavior is consistent over time and modality (consistency), and when their behavior is similar to those performed by others (consensus) (Kelley, 1973; McArthur, 1972). In contrast, Jones and Davis (1965) emphasize participants' judgments of others' intentions as a primary force in shaping attributions. Other researchers have examined attributional biases (Ross & Sicoly, 1979; Taylor & Fiske, 1978), thereby placing limitations on the relatively orderly, sequential manner in which people were originally thought to formulate attributions (Heider, 1958). Further, Newman (1981) and Fincham (1985) have expanded the traditional internal–external dichotomy to include interpersonal attributions (e.g., "because he doesn't like me") and relational attributions (e.g., "because we are a warm, open couple"), respectively.

Meaning. Because attribution theory relies on individuals' assessments of causality as a means of interpreting behavior, meaning lies primarily with the individual making the attributions. Communication behavior is interpreted or given meaning when individual communicators assign causal attributions to it. Although these attributions may be biased or incomplete (Nisbett & Ross, 1980), attribution theorists claim that such biases are real and salient to participants. As a result, attributions (biases and all) are used by individuals to assess their own and others' interactive behavior. To date, little is known about how interactants "chunk" or punctuate one another's behavior to derive meaning from an interaction. It is possible, for example, that people who focus primarily on the behavior of others (as opposed to their own behavior) are likely to view their own communication as having little impact on others' actions. Similarly, those who see their own behavior as inextricably linked to the behavior of others might view their relationships as uncontrollable (Minuchin, Rosman, & Baker, 1978). In either case, relational partners' perceptions may have a great deal of impact on the meanings they derive from an interaction.

Traditionally, attributions have been defined as internal cognitive processes. More recently, however, the potential impact of expressing attributions in conversation has been examined (Hilton, 1990; Weber & Vangelisti, 1990). The transition from viewing attributions as internal cognitions to viewing them as interpersonal and negotiable may very well change attribution theory. Once attributions are expressed, they not only become representational of individuals' thoughts and feelings, but also presentational of individuals' social or relational image (Duck & Pond, 1989). Meaning changes from something that is derived by individuals to something that is negotiated by interactants. We would anticipate that the expressed *meaning* of an attribution, therefore, may be modified to fit a particular audience or setting. If the presented message varies substantially from the represented thoughts and feelings, others' interpretations of the expressed attribution may be based on the presentational aspects of the message more so than its representational content.

Relationship. For attribution theorists, relationships are both defined and evaluated in terms of the causes partners assign to one another's behavior. In the initial stages of a relationship, participants' attributions (e.g., "She hasn't called because she's busy" versus "She hasn't called because she's inconsiderate") may have a major impact on partners' decisions about whether to continue the relationship. Further, when examining marital relationships, researchers have found that distressed individuals tend to make internal and global attributions for their partner's negative behaviors, whereas those who are nondistressed tend to make external and specific attributions for the same behaviors (Fincham, Beach, & Baucom, 1987; Fincham & O'Leary, 1983; Holtzworth-Munroe & Jacobson, 1985).

Although the association between certain causal attributions and relational distress has been widely accepted by researchers (e.g., Fincham, 1985) and therapists (e.g., Baucom & Epstein, 1990), the causal direction of the association has not been established. It is possible, for example, that making particular causal attributions for a partner's behavior encourages relational satisfaction. In contrast, it is also possible that partners who are initially satisfied tend to make certain types of causal attributions. In all likelihood, both scenarios reflect a portion of what happens in long-term relationships. Now that a relatively strong link has been established between attributions and relational satisfaction, theory and research need to more closely examine the causal nature of this link.

Process.   The formation of attributions is an ongoing process for interactants. Participants observe one another's communication behavior, interpret it by assigning a causal attribution to the behavior, and then use the attribution to guide the selection of their own response(s). Causal inferences not only help interactants interpret communication behavior, but they also "serve as determinants of the perceiver's subsequent feelings, expectations and behaviors" (Seibold & Spitzberg, 1982, p. 93). Although the association between attributions and individuals' feelings and behaviors is well-established, the causal direction of this association and the precise ways in which each variable affects the other(s) are largely unexplored.

Further, while it is possible for interactants to formulate attributions prior to interacting with someone, the literature has, for the most part, emphasized retrospective causal explanations over proactive predictions (Berger & Calabrese, 1975). One result of this emphasis has been a tendency, on the part of attribution theorists, to strongly distinguish between attributions (explanations) and expectations (predictions) about behavior (Fincham, 1985). Another consequence is that attributions are usually treated as one-time, static events rather than as ongoing processes. Although distinctions such as these may make for more simple research designs, they place undue limitations on the usefulness of attribution theory. Research evidence suggests that people engage in attributional activity before (Berger, 1975, 1987a; Berger & Bell, 1988), during (Daly, Weber, Vangelisti, Maxwell, & Neel, 1989), and after (Sillars, 1980) conversations. Because attributional processes are both anticipatory and explanatory, they must change as people interact, obtain more (or different) information, and reassess their previous perceptions. Broadening the scope of the theory to include dynamic anticipatory and concurrent attributions would make for a more complete account of attributional processes.

Context.   Contextual information is used by individuals to formulate their attributions (Kelley, 1973; McArthur, 1972). If, for example, a person is behaving in ways that are inappropriate to the context, contextual information will be considered by others when they make attributions about the inappropriate behavior. In contrast, if an individual is behaving in ways that are appropriate to the context, attributional processes may not even be activated because the behavior does not violate observers' expectations (Pyszczynski & Greenberg, 1981).

Although most empirical research on attributions has examined participants' use of contextual information in specific contexts, it is important to note that people may not limit their observations of context to the present situation. Contextual information existing both prior to, and after an observed event may affect attributions made about that event. As noted by Fincham (1985), "attributions made for a past event may be influenced as much by the event's perceived consequences as its perceived antecedents" (p. 227). In other words, contextual information may be gleaned both from the events that followed and those that preceded an individual's behavior.

Most research on attributions attempts to generalize peoples' attributions across contexts. However, noting that distressed couples tend to make different attributions than nondistressed couples (e.g., Fincham & O'Leary, 1983; Holtzworth-Munroe & Jacobson, 1985) or that people tend to make different attributions about success versus failure (Weiner et al., 1987), does not provide us with a full picture of individuals' attributional patterns. People may make one sort of attribution in one context and a very different attribution (about the same person or event) in another context.

Further, if an attribution is expressed in conversation, context will certainly be taken into consideration by most speakers as they decide how to communicate the attribution to others. For instance, we would hypothesize that if the context is a very formal one, communicators will be somewhat circumspect in expressing their attributional thoughts. If the setting is private, attributions may be expressed in more direct, candid ways. In addition, after an attribution is verbalized, contextual information may be used by recipients to interpret (and make subsequent attributions about) the expressed attribution.

Nonverbal Expectancy Violations Theory

The notion that people have expectancies about how others communicate is reflected in a number of communication theories (e.g., Andersen, 1985; Burgoon, 1978, 1983; Burgoon & Hale, 1988; Cappella & Greene, 1982; Patterson, 1983). Of these, Burgoon's nonverbal expectancy violations theory has generated an extensive program of research.

According to Burgoon and her colleagues, expectancies are best defined as "cognitions about the anticipated communicative behavior of specific others, as embedded within and shaped by the social norms for the contemporaneous roles, relationships, and context" (Burgoon & Walther, 1990). Using Staines' and Libby's (1986) distinction between predictive and prescriptive expectations as a base, Burgoon and her colleagues focus on predictive expectations—those involving an anticipation of what *will* happen (prediction) rather than emphasizing what *should* happen (prescription) during an interaction.

Although nonverbal expectancy violations theory avoids the evaluation inherent in prescriptive expectations, individuals' tendencies to evaluate one another's communication behavior is a central component of the theory. When people's expectancies concerning another individual's nonverbal behavior are violated, evaluations are made. Whether the violation is evaluated in a positive or negative way depends on both the interpretation of the behavior and its desirability (perceived reward/cost). If a behavior is interpreted as one meant to foster immediacy (Burgoon & Hale, 1988) and it is rewarding to the recipient, a positive evaluation will be made.

Meaning. For adherents of nonverbal expectancy violations theory, the meaning of a nonverbal behavior (or sequence of behaviors) becomes particularly relevant when expectancies are violated. After a violation (e.g., a person stands too close, talks too loudly, touches others too often), participants use their knowledge of social norms to interpret the behavior. They also assess the behavior's desirability based on their own personal preferences. Meaning, therefore, is derived by individuals.

Although empirical research using nonverbal expectancy violations theory has focused primarily on individuals' interpretations of behavior, it is important to note that individual evaluations do not preclude the influence of social interaction. Nonverbal expectancy violations theory does not suggest that meaning is independent of social norms and social interaction. In fact, individual guidelines for interpreting nonverbal behavior are based, to a large extent, on people's experience in previous interactions as well as on social norms and standards.

Relationship. On a global level, nonverbal expectancy violations help individuals to judge the nature of their interpersonal relationships. Burgoon and Walther (1990) found, for example, that, in U.S. culture, with the exception of the handshake, most forms of touch are unexpected when people are forming first impressions. Among other variables, however, the status relationship between speakers affected the extent to which participants expected touch. Touch from high-status, attractive, and same gender communicators was most expected, whereas touch from low-status, unattractive, opposite gender communicators was least expected. If, in an initial encounter, a person was touched a great deal by a low-status individual, the person who was touched may reevaluate the nature of his or her relationship with the violator (e.g., "I'm not sure I like this person anymore").

The evaluation of nonverbal expectancy violations also provides a means for assessing the appropriateness of specific behaviors in a relationship. However, the impact of particular relationship qualities and idiosyncracies on nonverbal expectancies have not been thoroughly investigated. In long-term romantic relationships, partners may develop a variety of idiosyncratic expectancies for nonverbal behavior (Montgomery, 1988). If one partner violates the expectancies of the other (e.g., by displaying a great deal of affection in a public place), the other partner may use his or her knowledge of social norms (e.g., one should not display affection in public places) along with his or her own personal preferences (e.g., but I enjoy affectionate displays) to evaluate the behavior.

Although nonverbal expectancy violations give individuals a way to evaluate their relationships, the evaluation of one partner's behavior by another provides researchers and theorists with a limited view of the relationship. Even examining the expectancies and behaviors of both partners is not the same as examining the relationship that those expectancies and behaviors create. One way for researchers to address this issue would be to study the conversations of relational partners following a nonverbal expectancy violation. Data such as these would provide an initial indication of how expectancy violations impact the communicative qualities of relationships.

Process. Because expectancies may be violated at any point in an interaction, the perception and evaluation of violations may also occur at virtually any time. What may be of particular interest to communication researchers, however, is not just *when* a violation occurs, but *how* the timing of a violation impacts subsequent communication behavior. Research on nonverbal expectancy violations has yet to systematically address this issue. It is possible, for example, that violations in initial interactions are judged more harshly and therefore, have more of an effect on later interactions than violations in long-term, established relationships. Partners in long-term relationships may let a negative violation "pass" (Hopper, 1981) if they believe that their anticipations will be met over time (Thibaut & Kelley, 1959). In contrast, since those involved in initial interactions have very little history, they may have less incentive to continue interacting with a person who negatively violates their expectations.

It is also intriguing to note that the behaviors that constitute a nonverbal expectancy violation may change over time. Children have different expectancies about how people will react to their use of personal space than adults do. Newcomers to an organization may have different nonverbal expectancies than they will after having been employed for several months. People who grew up in the 1950s may have different expectancies for nonverbal behavior than those who were raised in the 1980s. In short, people's nonverbal expectancies are dynamic—and should be treated as such. The passage of time may affect the nonverbal behaviors individuals anticipate during their interactions with others.

Context. Contextual cues play a large role in people's nonverbal expectancies as well as in their evaluations of unexpected behaviors. One source of information that participants use in judging what is expected in a given interaction is the context. For example, many of the vocal cues that are expected at a football game would probably not be expected at a wedding. If, however, a person were to violate the expectancies of most people at a wedding (perhaps by letting out an enthusiastic "Whoop!"), that violation might be judged, in part, by the context (e.g., Is the wedding formal? Is it being held outdoors? Are most of the guests relatively young?).

To date, research using nonverbal expectancy violations theory has focused on expectancies that can be generalized across contexts. One important area for theorists to develop, therefore, involves interactants' use of contextual cues in forming expectancies and judging expectancy violations. Interactants may, for instance, use contextual cues as a means of learning about what comprises a nonverbal expectancy violation. Also, contextual cues may influence the nature of nonverbal expectancies. By observing the context, those who are unfamiliar with the behaviors expected in a particular situation may be able to learn what others anticipate of them. By watching the responses of others to a violation, they may be able to detect how that violation is typically evaluated.

Social Exchange Theory

Like many of the theories examined thus far, social exchange theories emphasize individuals' tendencies to observe and assess others' communication behavior. Unlike these other theories, however, social exchange theories have at their core the assumption that individuals will act to maximize their interpersonal rewards and minimize their interpersonal costs. People's satisfaction with the outcomes of an interaction—or indeed with the outcomes of a relationship—is directly linked to the rewards they receive and the costs they incur (Burgess & Huston, 1979; Thibaut & Kelley, 1959).

The way rewards and costs are assessed depends, in part, on how they measure up to two standards: people's comparison level (CL) and their comparison level for alternatives (CLalt). By observing the interpersonal behavior that surrounds them, individuals develop expectations or standards for how interactions and relationships should occur. They acquire ideas about the typical ratio of rewards to costs. These general expectations comprise their CL. At the same time, through personal experience, people develop expectations for the rewards and costs that they, themselves, are likely to receive. These more personalized expectations comprise their CLalt. An individual may have a very high CL for romantic relationships, but a very low CLalt. If this is the case, the individual will be likely to stay in a relatively dissatisfying relationship because s/he does not believe that there are any more rewarding alternatives available. In contrast, a person who has a high CLalt will be less likely to remain in a dissatisfying relationship because s/he sees numerous alternative relationships. The extent to which people are dependent on their relationships, to a great extent, is a function of their CLalt.

Meaning. Because people share many of the same experiences (e.g., physical pain, sadness when leaving a loved one, happiness when being reunited), some generalizations can be made about the types of communication behaviors that people perceive as rewarding and costly. For instance, Foa (1971) and his associates (Foa & Foa, 1972) have argued that objects of exchange (rewards and costs) fall into six categories: love, status, information, money, goods, and services.

Behavior (within any of these six categories) defined as rewarding or costly may vary from person to person. One person may define love in terms of affective behavior whereas another may define it in terms of instrumental behavior (Wills, Weiss, & Patterson, 1974). Furthermore, what is rewarding to one person (e.g., a big family reunion) may be very costly to another. Although social exchange theory allows for variations in what individuals see as rewarding and costly, it does not indicate how rewards and costs are established and renegotiated by relational partners. Because individuals' perceptions of categories such as love, status, and information are likely to vary from relationship to relationship, it would be useful to examine how the meanings associated with rewards and costs are established.

Relationship. For social exchange theorists, relationships are evaluated in terms of their perceived rewards and costs. If rewards exceed costs, the relationship is relatively satisfying. If costs outweigh rewards, the relationship is comparatively dissatisfying. Whether individuals continue a relationship, however, is not solely based on the outcomes (reward/cost ratio) they receive. To dissolve a current relationship, partners must perceive that alternatives to the relationship are both attractive and attainable. If the alternatives are less attractive or if they are unattainable, individuals may stay in a relatively unrewarding relationship.

Social exchange theory emphasizes the impact of exchange processes on relationships. We would speculate, however, that relationships also impact exchange processes. For example, the process for evaluating rewards and costs in a relationship may differ for long-term and short-term associations. Because long-term relationships have a history and an anticipated future, partners may not feel the need to reciprocate rewards (and to have rewards reciprocated) as frequently as those involved in short-term relationships do (Knapp & Vangelisti, 1992). As long as they believe that they will, on average, receive more rewards than costs, long-term relational partners will likely see their relationship as rewarding. In contrast, those involved in short-term relationships may feel the need to exchange rewards frequently in order to reinforce the perception that the relationship is a rewarding one.

Levinger, Senn, and Jorgensen (1970) further note that some rewards may be more salient when they come from intimates than when they come from acquaintances. A smile from a loved one will likely be more valued than a smile from a stranger. Similarly, harsh words from an acquaintance may be quickly disregarded, whereas the same words, spoken by a spouse may strongly impact the relationship. Levinger et al.'s observation hints at the importance of studying rewards and costs in conjunction with interpersonal relationships. Examining individuals' perceptions of rewards and costs may provide a very distorted view of how partners jointly manage resources in the relationship. In contrast, studying partners' conversations about the definition and/or distribution of rewards and costs may begin to explain how the relationship (as opposed to the individual interactant) operates.

Process. Because social exchange theorists view interactants as motivated to maximize their rewards and minimize their costs, the evaluation of rewards and costs is seen by most as a continual process. Throughout the course of an interaction or a relationship, participants assess the ratio of rewards to costs they receive. As long as rewards exceed costs and the potential rewards from alternatives are not comparatively high, individuals will tend to continue in their current situation.

Although social exchange theory depicts the evaluation of rewards and costs as an ongoing process, most research in the area assesses participants' perceptions of rewards and costs at a single point in time. In practice, rewards and costs are examined as if they are relatively static and unchanging. Furthermore, numerous theorists (e.g., Duck & Sants, 1983; Kellermann, Broetzmann, Lim, & Kitao, 1989; Lallje & Abelson, 1983; Langer, 1989; Langer & Newman, 1979; Schank & Abelson, 1977) have noted that people do not constantly evaluate their social surroundings. It is very possible, for example, that certain communication behaviors (i.e., unexpected behaviors) or certain contexts (i.e., unfamiliar contexts) stimulate evaluative processes. Some researchers have suggested that evaluative processes are especially relevant during crises or relational "turning points" (e.g., Baxter & Bullis, 1986; Lloyd & Cate, 1985). Others (Clarke & Mills, 1979) have argued that partners in particular types of relationships are more likely to evaluate one another's behavior in terms of rewards and costs. Regardless of whether evaluation is stimulated by a particular event, behavior, or relational quality, the onset, duration, and termination of evaluation merit further study.

Context. Although social exchange theory has not thoroughly addressed the influence of the environment on people's perceptions of rewards and costs, the context associated with any communication behavior may be critical in determining whether the behavior is perceived as rewarding or costly. In fact, the same behavior may be seen as a reward in one context and a cost in another. For example, intimate nicknames (e.g., pickle-face) may be very rewarding when received in private (Hopper, Knapp, & Scott, 1981), but may be embarrassing or even insulting when used in public settings. Although revealing a personal nickname in public might indicate that one partner is either malicious or naive, we might also speculate that the two partners constructed the context in different ways. To understand why such an occurrence would be rewarding or costly to the relationship, we need to examine the ways contextual information is used and perceived by participants. To date, social exchange theorists have not systematically examined such issues.

Information gleaned from the environment may also provide people with alternatives to their current situations and/or relationships. People who find themselves in an alternative-rich environment may have more stringent standards for their relationships than those who are in an alternative-poor environment. Further, if the alternatives provided by the context are unattractive or few in number, people may evaluate their current circumstances more positively than they otherwise would. For example, dissatisfied relational partners who are isolated from attractive alternatives may come to believe that the costs they are incurring from their current relationship are "normal." Because they have very few alternatives, their own relationship may be seen as less costly. Situations such as these raise interesting issues concerning the potential role of various communication media in offering relational alternatives. In a deprived environment, people may use images presented in books, on television, or in movies to create imaginary alternatives to their own relationships.

Constructivism

Constructivist theory emerged, in part, from an integration of two distinct, but compatible lines of thought (Burleson, 1987; Delia, 1977; Delia & Crockett, 1973). The first, Kelly's (1955) personal construct psychology, posits the personal construct as the basic cognitive structure that people use in assessing their social surroundings. Constructs are bipolar dimensions (e.g., happy–sad, large–small, attractive–unattractive) that serve in the organization, evaluation, interpretation, and anticipation of events.

The second theoretical base of constructivism is Werner's (1957) structural developmental theory. Werner notes that "wherever development occurs, it proceeds from a state of relative globality and lack of differentiation to states of increasing differentiation, articulation, and hierarchic integration" (p. 126). Given this view of development, constructivists predict that children's personal constructs will become more differentiated, articulated, and integrated as they reach adulthood (e.g., Clark & Delia, 1977; Delia, Kline, & Burleson, 1979). Furthermore, since individual development varies from person to person, constructivist researchers suggest that people will systematically differ in terms of the complexity of their personal construct systems.

The link between construct complexity and communication is relatively straightforward. Individuals with complex constructs tend to be better able to "represent and understand the cognitive, affective and motivational features of others' perspectives" (Burleson, 1987, pp. 310–311). Because of these well developed interpretive abilities, cognitively complex individuals are more likely to engage in person-centered communication than those who are less cognitively complex (for reviews see Burleson, 1987; O'Keefe & Sypher, 1981).

Cognitive complexity is typically measured by Crockett's (1965) Role Category Questionnaire. To complete the questionnaire, participants are required to describe a peer that they know well and like as well as a peer that they know, but dislike. They are instructed to describe both peers in as much detail as possible. The descriptions then can be coded in terms of construct differentiation (the number of different constructs used in the descriptions), abstraction (the extent to which constructs are refined and abstract), or organization (the extent to which constructs are integrated). Since differentiation scores have been demonstrated to be moderately to highly associated with abstraction and organization scores (O'Keefe & Sypher, 1981), differentiation is often used as a general measure of cognitive complexity.

Meaning. According to constructivists, social interaction is the vehicle through which conversationalists create and modify their individual interpretations of their social world. Meaning, in short, is constructed via social interaction. Interaction, however, is not equated to communication. Interaction is conceptualized as a negotiation process in which participants present their own views and coordinate their individual actions. Communication, in contrast, is seen as strategic. Delia, O'Keefe, and O'Keefe (1982) note that "We see human communication as a process of interaction in which the communicative intentions of participants are a focus for coordination" (p. 159). Communication is, therefore, a particular (strategic) type of interaction.

Two clusters of cognitive tools serve individuals in their interpretation of meaning. The first is comprised of *interpretive principles*. These principles are very general assumptions used to coordinate people's knowledge of social rules with their observations of events that are occurring in a specific interaction. Grice's (1975) maxims (e.g., "Be relevant," e.g., "Be cooperative") are one example of this sort of general principle. The second cluster of interpretive tools is more specific. *Organizing schemes* are used to make connections between particular sorts of acts. For instance, a flexible script for initial interactions (e.g., Kellermann, Broetzmann, Lim, & Kitao, 1989) would be termed as an organizing scheme. Taken together, general interpretive principles and organizing schemes allow individuals to interpret the meanings presented to them by others.

Although both interpretive principles and organizing schemes may be developed via social interaction, their association with social interaction remains largely unexplored. Constructivist research has been limited, for the most part, to studies emphasizing the relationship between cognitive complexity and the production of listener adapted messages. An important exception to this is a study by Burleson, Delia, and Applegate (1992) that found a link between maternal communication and children's cognitive and social competencies.

Relationship. For constructivists, relationships are typically seen as a source of information that can be used by participants in constructing their messages. The appropriateness of a strategic choice varies in terms of relational qualities such as intimacy, dominance or superiority, and liking. When talking to an intimate, speakers might (appropriately) select a very different strategy than when talking to a superior. Similarly, speakers' strategic choices for a well-liked superior might be very different than they would be for a superior they dislike. Regardless of speakers' relationship with their target, individuals who are cognitively complex should be more skillful in adjusting their communicative choices to the relationship than those who are less cognitively complex.

In addition to serving as a source of information, we would hypothesize that the nature of relationships is determined, in part, by the appropriateness of speakers' strategic communication choices. For example, if an attempt is made to persuade, and the speaker does not take into consideration the target's emotional state, goals, or beliefs, the target may become annoyed, hurt, or may simply ignore the persuasive strategy. If, in contrast, the target's emotional state, goals, and beliefs are considered, the association between speaker and target will likely be different. In both of these examples, the appropriateness of a speaker's choice on a specific occasion may impact the outcome of that interaction. Over time, however, we would also suspect that the repetition of appropriate (or inappropriate) choices would impact more global outcomes such as relational satisfaction, trust, respect, or even commitment.

Process. According to constructivist theory, message construction and interpretation is an ongoing process. Participants gather information before constructing their messages and watch others' responses to the message so that they can adjust subsequent utterances. At the same time, message recipients decode speakers' utterances and construct their own responses. Delia, O'Keefe, and O'Keefe (1982) note that:

> Present action permits validation or modification of interpretive schemes; future choices will reflect the success or failure of the present choice. In this way, every act collapses past, present, and future; and thus, every act emerges from a new past into a new future. (p. 156)

Because both speakers and recipients enter any communication situation with previously established interpretive schemes, their past experiences play a role in their interpretation of current messages. Constructivist researchers, however, have yet to examine the link between individuals' past experiences and their interpretations of current messages. Past experiences, for example, may encourage the development of particular interpretive schemes over others. This would likely affect individuals' interpretations of the messages they receive. Even individuals' abilities to modify their interpretive schemes may be affected by past experience. Since their interpretive schemes are more complex, individuals who are high in cognitive complexity should be better equipped to evaluate the information they gather both before and during an interaction. They should also be better able to utilize previously constructed interpretive schemes to adjust their communication to the current situation than those who are less cognitively complex.

Context. Constructivist researchers view communication as contextual. Communicators use context to evaluate the appropriateness of their own speech as well as the speech of others. In short, what is appropriate and effective in one context may be inappropriate and ineffective in another.

Although constructivist researchers note that contextual information provides conversationalists with a guide for selecting (appropriate) communication strategies, they have not examined the ways conversationalists use contextual cues. It is possible, for example that particular settings (e.g., those that are unfamiliar) encourage a focus on context. Individuals who are cognitively complex may be more skilled in selecting and/or utilizing relevant cues from their social environments than those who are less cognitively complex. Further, since speakers also evaluate the utterances of others, contextual cues may serve as a source of information as individuals assess the utterance(s) that precede and follow their own.

DISCUSSION

The seven theories reviewed here bring to light various issues pertaining to theory evaluation. Certainly, the relative strengths and weaknesses of each theory could be evaluated according to some common list of criteria. Littlejohn (1989), for example, offers the five criteria of *scope, appropriateness, heuristic value, validity,* and *parsimony* as a basis for comparing various theoretical perspectives. Although evaluating theories one against another may be a useful intellectual exercise, such evaluations offer little in terms of deciding that one theory is *better* than another. There are at least three reasons why evaluative comparisons of various theories may be problematic.

First, theories tend to focus on different phenomena. While the foregoing theories all purport to explain the development or maintenance of interpersonal interactions and all share certain philosophical assumptions, each emphasizes different components or qualities of interaction. Dialectical theory focuses on *tension, contradiction,* and *polarity* while relational theory examines *patterns, forms,* and *levels.* Uncertainty reduction theory concentrates on *ambiguity* and *sense-making*, attribution theory examines *perceptions* and *causal explanations*, and nonverbal expectancy violations theory emphasizes *predictive explanations* and *overt behavior*. Social exchange theory uses the economic metaphor of *rewards* and *costs* while constructivism concentrates on *categories*, *cognitive complexity*, and *schemas*.

Admittedly, there is much overlap among these theories. For example, uncertainty reduction may be part of a larger dialectic of stability and change governing relationship development (Baxter, 1988); attribution theory, nonverbal expectancy violations theory, and constructivism examine communicators' cognitive sense-making abilities; social exchange and relational theory each examine outcomes of communication exchanges. In spite of such overlaps, the theories do not use the same terms, examine the same things, or speak to the same issues; in short, fair comparisons are not likely to be made because the theories lack commensurability with one another. Bochner (1984) explains:

> the triumph of one theoretical perspective over others still would have to assume commensurability among competing viewpoints, and the main lesson to be learned from Kuhn is that no such common ground for theory choice has ever existed in the history of science. (p. 32)

The second reason evaluative comparisons may be problematic involves the feasibility (indeed, the validity) of offering a single explanation for social actions. Gergen (1980) asserts that any experimental finding may be used as evidence to support almost any theoretical perspective. As evidence for this assertion, he chose seven examples of experimental findings that supported seven different theories. He randomly distributed four sets of the findings and four of the theories to a dozen advanced seminar students. Each theory was randomly matched with a finding and the students were asked to explain the results using the theory. The students were able to make the connections with relative ease. While this procedure seems antithetical to the most basic truths held about scientific inquiry, the history of social science is replete with examples of experiments which attempted to arbitrate between theories and failed to do so (Bochner, 1985, Gergen, 1973, 1980).

It is easy enough to illustrate Gergen's findings using the theories discussed in this chapter and a research study cited in support of one of the theories. Pyszczynski and Greenberg (1981) examined a particular dimension of attribution theory: that "the observation of unexpected events leads to the instigation of attributional processing" (p. 31). The conditions of the study were as follows: male subjects observed the experimenter asking a female student (actually a confederate) to do either a small favor (leading to an expectancy of compliance) or a large favor (leading to an expectancy of refusal). The confederate either confirmed or disconfirmed the expectancy of the subject. The subjects then examined a copy of a blank, 20-item questionnaire the confederate had supposedly completed earlier. On the questionnaire were five "helping-relevant" questions (questions designed to explain the confederate's response to the experimenter) and five "interesting questions" (questions providing other information about the confederate). Subjects were told they could see the confederate's answers to any five questions. As predicted, subjects chose more "helping-relevant" questions when the confederate did not confirm the subjects' expectancies. The results were explained in terms of attribution theory since the subjects' information seeking preferences served as "an indicator of their tendency to engage in a causal analysis" (p. 33).

The results could also be explained in terms of dialectical theory (since the students perceive the confederate as a potential relationship partner, they seek to initially accept the other person rather than judge—thereby temporarily choosing one pole of the dialectic tension of "judgment/acceptance"—by choosing compatible information); relational theory (while asking for a large favor is a one-up move, the two messages differ greatly in intensity, therefore, creating a situation whereby the confederates' denial of a small favor creates an unexpected symmetrical exchange while the acceptance of a large favor creates an unexpected complementary exchange); uncertainty reduction theory (the student attempts to reduce the uncertainty created by the confederates' unexpected choice); nonverbal expectancy violations theory (since the student observes the confederate violating an anticipated communicative behavior, the student attempts to make a positive evaluation by examining potentially relevant information); social exchange theory (observing the confederate conforming to expectations minimizes the perceived potential for interpersonal rewards; the student seeks answers to questions which would provide other information about the confederate); and constructivism (the interpretive scheme of the student either provides easy categorization (expectation confirmed) or difficult categorization (expectation not confirmed) thereby necessitating helpful information).

While one might dispute the above interpretations, they point out the difficulty in discerning "what limits might be placed over such inter-translation of results from one domain to another" (Gergen, 1980, p. 252). Our purpose is certainly not to discredit the research used in this illustration. Indeed, with so much research that is variable-analytic in nature and so few researchers willing to place themselves at the mercy of the academic community by taking a theoretical position (Berger, 1991), this study represents a fine example of theoretically based empirical work. Our purpose is to merely illustrate the potential overlap of theoretical explanations.

The third objection to making evaluative comparisons between various theories concerns the relationship between theorists and their subjects (or data). While one would hope for a strong correspondence between the way in which theorists and actual participants view fundamental issues, in reality, the perspectives may be different depending on who is doing the analysis. Indeed, a dilemma arises when one examines most theories; the propositions of the theory are often treated as if the interactants would use the core concepts of the theory in describing their own behavior. To cite just one example from one of our chosen theories, Berger (1987b) states that "to interact in a relatively smooth, coordinated, and understandable manner, one must be able to both predict how one's interaction partner is likely to behave, and, based on these predictions, to select from one's own repertoire those responses that will optimize outcomes in the encounter" (p. 41). Such a statement implies more conscious awareness than may actually be present.[5] This is not to say that this theory itself is in error; rather, this type of inferential leap is common when one is attempting to account for the communicative behavior of interactants.

No theorist has privileged access to the true motivations of the participants nor is any theorist an impartial observer. Theoretical explanations of social behavior cannot fully distinguish indistinct perspectives. Since true objectivity is an illusion in social science theorizing, one would speculate that the very nature of formulating and testing theories might involve innocent confirmation of the positions one is advocating.[6] Evaluative comparisons of competing frameworks, therefore, may be less than useful.

Our three objections to engaging in evaluative comparisons of various theories lead to the somewhat paradoxical position that any two theories may be dissimilar in what they attempt to describe and, yet, may account for the same empirical results. Such a quandary would seem to make it difficult to arbitrate between theories. Can theories be judged? Or are all theories of equal value? Although these questions are difficult to answer, the emergent position taken within the social sciences is a pragmatic response looking more toward the interpretation of meanings than the rendering of facts (Bochner, 1985; Gergen, 1980). Because theories may provide different, but equally valid explanations for similar data, *accuracy* is not the most relevant criteria for judging a theory. Rather, a theory should be generative:

> The generative theory is one that challenges the guiding assumptions of the culture, raises fundamental questions regarding social life, fosters reconsideration of that

---

[5]Other theorists (e.g., Duck & Sants, 1983) have criticized the tendency of scholars to view interactants as constantly evaluating their own interpersonal behavior. The thesis that individuals often operate mindlessly (Langer, 1989; Langer & Newman, 1979), without conscious awareness of their own or others' behavior is widely accepted among both psychologists and communication researchers (e.g., Kellermann, Broetzmann, Lim, & Kitao, 1989; Lallje & Abelson, 1983; Schank & Abelson, 1977).

[6]In addition, theory building may inherently involve a type of paradoxical recursiveness. Indeed, Gergen (1973) has asserted that all social theories are historical products since the more potent the theory in explaining behavior the more apt that theory is to be publicly disseminated, and consequently, utilized by the public as explanatory mechanisms for their own behavior. A theory such as uncertainty reduction may be validated through dissemination as more people use the concepts as explanatory mechanisms for accounting for their own interpersonal lives. As Gergen (1973) states, "science and society constitute a feedback loop" (p. 311).

which is "taken for granted" and thereby furnishes fresh alternatives for social action. (Gergen, 1980, p. 261)

Although we have pointed out the relative strengths and weaknesses of several theories, we suggest, along with Berger (1991), that current theories in interpersonal communication would be more generative if they addressed a "small set of overarching research questions" (p. 111). Using the four foundational issues (meaning, relationship, process, and context) as a framework, we propose several such questions to guide future theory and research in interpersonal communication.

First, scholars need to examine the association between various (multiple) meanings and human interaction. *How do the development, maintenance, and use of various meanings for interpersonal communication affect communicative outcomes (and vice versa)?* Although each of the theories reviewed allows for the use and observation of multiple meanings, little is known about how and why different meanings are generated, how those meanings are sustained, and how the development and maintenance of particular meanings affect communicative outcomes.

Second, communication theorists need to examine the complex interconnections between communication and various interpersonal relationships. *How do interactants' dyadic, group, and cultural relationships affect their interpersonal communication (and vice versa)?* Hewes, Roloff, Planalp, and Seibold (1990) suggest that "Interpersonal communication must be approached from theoretical positions that integrate both the individual processes and the social forces that shape social interaction" (p. 164). While the theories reviewed in this chapter certainly have implications for the development and dissolution of relationships, many (e.g., uncertainty reduction, attribution, nonverbal expectancy violations, social exchange, and constructivism) typically approach relationships from the perspective of the individual. Those that have moved beyond the level of the individual to the level of the relationship (e.g., dialectical and relational theories) have yet to provide systematic predictions or explanations concerning the links between individuals, dyads, and larger social groups.

Third, communication scholars need to examine communication as a dynamic process that occurs over time. *How do sequences of communication behaviors affect individual, dyadic, and group outcomes over time (and vice versa)?* Despite frequent discussion concerning the importance of process, theorists and researchers often assume that research findings obtained in a single instance or episode will occur in the same manner over time and across instances. The theories reviewed in this chapter are no exception. In addition, theorists have tended to focus on single behaviors or categories of behavior at the expense of multiple behaviors and behavioral sequences (Knapp, 1985). If, as claimed by theorists, communication is processual, both theorists and researchers need to place process at the center of their work rather than relegate it to a secondary position.

Fourth, and finally, interpersonal theorists need to consider context as an integral component of any communication event. *How does context affect interpersonal communication (and vice versa)*? Although the theories reviewed provide opportunity for examining the effect of context on communication (and/or other variables), they do not specify how and why context impacts communication. In the tradition of Bateson (1972, 1978), Rawlins (1987) emphasizes the interdependent, reflexive relationship between communicators, messages, and context. He notes that people and messages both transform and are transformed by context. Since context and communication are inextricably linked, examining (and theorizing about) one to the exclusion of the other may yield research (and theory) that is invalid.

Different theories are bound to vary in the way they account for meaning, relationship, process, and context. Indeed, one of the benefits of fostering various theoretical perspectives within the field is that these perspectives will provide unique approaches to communicative phenomena. Such theoretical pluralism, however, should not come at the expense of thoroughly addressing issues that are central to understanding interpersonal communication.

Theories should "function to render experience intelligible, to 'give meaning' to such experience" (Gergen, 1980, p. 258) and to encourage theoretical discourse (Bochner, 1985). One could certainly speculate that interactants, like theorists, encounter situations that necessitate the use of more than a single theory. For example, in any situation, people might have their expectancies violated. Such violations may result in uncertainty. In the process of trying to reduce their uncertainty, interactants may begin to formulate attributions about their current situation. If their attributions are erroneous and emphasize negative qualities of their relationships with others, the interactants may experience tension between themselves and others. Because of that tension, they will likely see fewer rewards and more costs. During the ensuing exchange they may assert a relationship definition which their cognitively complex partner perceives as . . . and so on.

Similarly, we might examine one particular issue (such as meaning) in terms of the theories reviewed in this chapter and find a great deal which renders experience intelligible. If we take a single example of an interaction between spouses, we could look at the various meanings each assigns to issues of autonomy and connection, or the way each reduces uncertainty about the communication behavior of the other through the assignment of meaning to that behavior. We might further ask whether there are attributions made by each that help in the interpretation of the behavior or whether there are expectancy violations present that modify the meaning of a particular nonverbal behavior (or sequence of behaviors). We could also look for the rewards and costs that spouses perceive as salient, whether a particular message sequence leads to meaningful conclusions, or whether spouses who are high in cognitive complexity construct distinct relational messages from those who are low in cognitive complexity. Any one of these perspectives might lead us to choose a particular theory that is most helpful in explaining the phenomena under examination—not because that theory explains the facts more accurately, but because it raises more interesting questions about the way in which social life is managed through communication by the participants.

REFERENCES

Altman, I., & Taylor, D. (1973). *Social penetration: The development of interpersonal relationships.* New York: Holt, Rinehart, & Winston.

Altman, I., Vinsel, A., & Brown, B. B. (1981). Dialectical conceptions in social psychology: An application to social penetration and privacy regulation. In L. Berkowitz (Ed.), *Advances in experimental social psychology: Vol. 14* (pp. 107–160). New York: Academic Press.

Andersen, P. A. (1985). Nonverbal immediacy in interpersonal communication. In A. W. Siegman & S. Feldstein (Eds.), *Human behavior and the environment: Advances in theory and research* (Vol. 2, pp. 181–259). New York: Plenum.

Askham, J. (1976). Identity and stability within the marriage relationship. *Journal of Marriage and the Family, 38*, 535–547.

Bateson, G. (1972). *Steps to an ecology of mind.* New York: Ballantine.

Bateson, G. (1978). *Mind and nature: A necessary unity.* New York: E. P. Dutton.

Baucom, D. H., & Epstein, N. (1990). *Cognitive-behavioral marital therapy.* New York: Brunner/Mazel.

Baxter, L. A. (1988). A dialectic perspective on communication strategies in relationship development. In S. W. Duck (Ed.), *Handbook of personal relationships: Theory, research, and interventions* (pp. 257–273). Chichester: Wiley.

Baxter, L. A., & Bullis, C. (1986). Turning points in developing romantic relationships. *Human Communication Research, 12*, 469–493.

Bell, R. A., Buerkel-Rothfuss, N. L., & Gore, K. E. (1987). "Did you bring the yarmulke for the cabbage patch kid?" The idiomatic communication of young lovers. *Human Communication Research, 14*, 47–67.

Bellah, R. N., Madsen, R., Sullivan, W. M., Swidler, A., & Tipton, S. M. (1985). *Habits of the heart.* New York: Harper & Row.

Bellah, R. N., Madsen, R., Sullivan, W. M., Swidler, A., & Tipton, S. M. (1991). *The good society.* New York: Harper & Row.

Berger, C. R. (1975). Proactive and retroactive attribution processes in interpersonal communication. *Human Communication Research, 2*, 33–50.

Berger, C. R. (1986). Uncertain outcome values in predicted relationships: Uncertainty reduction theory then and now. *Human Communication Research, 13*, 34–38.

Berger, C. R. (1987a). Planning and scheming: Strategies for initiating relationships. In R. Burnett, P. McGhee, & D. Clarke (Eds.), *Accounting for relationships: Social representations of interpersonal links* (pp. 158–174). London: Methuen.

Berger, C. R. (1987b). Communicating under uncertainty. In M. E. Roloff & G. R. Miller (Eds.), *Interpersonal processes: New directions in communication research* (pp. 39–62). Newbury Park, CA: Sage.

Berger, C. (1991). Why are there so few communication theories: Communication theories and other curios. *Communication Monographs, 58*, 1, 101–113.

Berger, C. R., & Bell, R. A. (1988). Plans and the initiation of social relationships. *Human Communication Research, 15*, 217–235.

Berger, C. R., & Bradac, J. J. (1982). *Language and social knowledge: Uncertainty in interpersonal relations.* London: E. E. Arnold.

Berger, C. R., & Calabrese, R. J. (1975). Some explorations in initial interaction and beyond: Toward a developmental theory of interpersonal communication. *Human Communication Research, 1*, 99–112.

Berlo, D. K. (1960). *The process of communication.* New York: Holt.

Bochner, A. P. (1984). The functions of human communication in interpersonal bonding. In C. C. Arnold & J. W. Bowers (Eds.), *Handbook of rhetorical and communication theory* (pp. 544–621). Boston: Allyn and Bacon.

Bochner, A. (1985). Perspectives on inquiry: Representation, conversation, and reflection. In M. L. Knapp & G. R. Miller (Eds.), *Handbook of interpersonal communication* (pp. 27–58). Newbury Park, CA: Sage.

Bochner, A. P., & Eisenberg, E. M. (1987). Family process: Systems perspectives. In C. R. Berger & S. H. Chaffee (Eds.), *Handbook of communication science* (pp. 540–563). Newbury Park, CA: Sage.

Bowers, J. (1989). Introduction. In J. Bradac (Ed.), *Message effects in communication science* (pp. 10–23). Newbury Park, CA: Sage.

Bowers, J., & Bradac, J. (1984). Contemporary problems in human communication theory. In C. C. Arnold & J. W. Bowers (Eds.), *Handbook of rhetorical and communication theory* (pp. 871–893). Boston: Allyn and Bacon.

Branham, R. J., & Pearce, W. B. (1985). Between text and context: Toward a rhetoric of textual reconstruction. *Quarterly Journal of Speech, 71*, 19–36.

Burgess, R. L., & Huston, T. L. (Eds.). (1979). *Social exchange in developing relationships.* New York: Academic Press.

Burgoon, J. K. (1978). A communication model of personal space violations: Explication and an initial test. *Human Communication Research, 41*, 129–142.

Burgoon, J. K. (1983). Nonverbal violations of expectations. In J. M. Wiemann & R. P. Harrison (Eds.), *Nonverbal interaction* (pp. 77–111). Newbury Park, CA: Sage.

Burgoon, J. K., & Hale, J. L. (1988). Nonverbal expectancy violations theory: Model elaboration and application to immediacy behaviors. *Communication Monographs, 55*, 58–79.

Burgoon, J. K., & Walther, J. B. (1990). Nonverbal expectancies and the evaluative consequences of violations. *Human Communication Research, 17*, 232–265.

Burleson, B. R. (1987). Cognitive complexity. In J. C. McCroskey & J. A. Daly (Eds.), *Personality and interpersonal communication* (pp. 305–349). Newbury Park, CA: Sage.

Burleson, B. R., Delia, J. G., & Applegate, J. L. (1992). Effects of maternal communication and children's social-cognitive and communication skills on children's acceptance by the peer group. *Family relations, 41*, 264–272.

Cappella, J. N., & Greene, J. O. (1982). A discrepancy-arousal explanation of mutual influence in expressive behavior for adult-adult and infant-adult interaction. *Communication Monographs, 49*, 89–114.

Capra, F. (1984). *The tao of physics.* New York: Bantam Books.

Chaffee, S. H., & Berger, C. R. (1987). What communication scientists do. In S. H. Chaffee & C. R. Berger (Eds.), *Handbook of communication science* (pp. 99–122). Newbury Park, CA: Sage.

Christensen, A., & Heavey, C. L. (1990). Gender and social structure in the demand/withdrawal pattern of marital conflict. *Journal of Personality and Social Psychology, 59*, 73–81.

Cissna, K. N., Cox, D. E., & Bochner, A. P. (1990). The dialectic of marital and parental relationships within the family. *Communication Monographs, 57*, 44–61.

Clark, M. S., & Mills, J. (1979). Interpersonal attraction in exchange and communal relationships. *Journal of Personality and Social Psychology, 37*, 12–24.

Clark, R. A., & Delia, J. G. (1977). Cognitive complexity, social perspective-taking, and functional persuasive skills in second- to ninth-grade children. *Human Communication Research, 3*, 128–134.

Clatterbuck, G. W. (1979). Attributional confidence and uncertainty in initial interaction. *Human Communication Research, 5*, 147–157.

Courtright, J. A., Millar, F. E., & Rogers, L. E. (1979). Domineeringness and dominance: Replication and expansion. *Communication Monographs, 46*, 179–192.

Crockett, W. H. (1965). Cognitive complexity and impression formation. In B. A. Maher (Ed.), *Progress in experimental personality research* (Vol. 2, pp. 47–90). New York: Academic Press.

Daly, J. A., Weber, D. J., Vangelisti, A. L., Maxwell, M., & Neel, H. (1989). Concurrent cognitions during conversations: Protocol analysis as a means of exploring conversations. *Discourse Processes, 12*, 227–244.

Delia, J. G. (1977). Constructivism and the study of human communication. *Quarterly Journal of Speech, 63*, 66–83.

Delia, J. G., & Crockett, W. H. (1973). Social schemas, cognitive complexity, and the learning of social structures. *Journal of Personality, 41*, 413–429.

Delia, J. G., Kline, S. L., & Burleson, B. R. (1979). The development of persuasive communication strategies in kindergartners through twelfth-graders. *Communication Monographs, 46*, 241–256.

Delia, J. G., O'Keefe, B. J., & O'Keefe, D. J. (1982). The constructivist approach to communication. In F. E. X. Dance (Ed.), *Human communication theory* (pp. 147–191). New York: Harper & Row.

Duck, S. (1985). Social and personal relationships. In M. L. Knapp & G. R. Miller (Eds.), *Handbook of interpersonal communication*. Newbury Park, CA: Sage.

Duck, S. W. (1990). Relationships as unfinished businesses: Out of the frying pan and into the 1990s. *Journal of Social and Personal Relationships, 7*, 5–28.

Duck, S. W., & Pond, K. (1989). Friends, romans, countrymen, lend me your retrospective data: Rhetoric and reality in personal relationships. In C. Hendrick (Ed.), *Review of Personality and Social Psychology, Vol. 10: Close Relationships* (pp. 17–38). Newbury Park, CA: Sage.

Duck, S. W., & Sants, H. K. A. (1983). On the origins of the specious: Are interpersonal relationships really interpersonal states? *Journal of Social and Clinical Psychology, 1*, 27–41.

Fincham, F. D. (1985). Attributions in close relationships. In J. Harvey & G. Weary (Eds.), *Attribution: Basic issues and applications* (pp. 203–234). New York: Academic Press.

Fincham, F. D., Beach, S. R. H., & Baucom, D. H. (1987). Attribution processes in distressed and nondistressed couples: 4 Self-partner attribution differences. *Journal of Personality and Social Psychology, 52*, 739–748.

Fincham, F. D., & O'Leary, K. D. (1983). Causal inferences for spouse behavior in maritally distressed and nondistressed couples. *Journal of Social and Clinical Psychology, 1*, 42–57.

Foa, U. G. (1971). Interpersonal economic resources. *Science, 171*, 345–351.

Foa, U. G., & Foa, E. B. (1972). Resource exchange: Toward a structural theory of interpersonal communication. In A. W. Siegman & B. Pope (Eds.), *Studies in dyadic communications* (pp. 291–325). New York: Pergamon.

Geertz, C. (1973). *The interpretation of cultures*. New York: Basic Books.

Gergen, K. (1973). Social psychology as history. *Journal of Personality and Social Psychology, 26*, 309–320.

Gergen, K. (1980). Toward intellectual audacity in the social sciences. In R. Gimour & S. W. Duck (Eds.), *The development of social psychology* (pp. 239–270). New York: Academic Press.

Greene, J. O. (1984). A cognitive approach to human communication: An action assembly theory. *Communication Monographs, 51*, 289–306.

Grice, H. P. (1975). Logic and conversation. In P. Cole & J. L. Morgan (Eds.), *Syntax and semantics, Vol. 3: Speech acts* (pp. 41–58). New York: Academic Press.

Grossberg, L. (1982). Does communication theory need intersubjectivity? Toward an immanent philosophy of interpersonal relations. M. Burgoon (Ed.), *Communication yearbook 6* (pp. 171–205). Newbury Park, CA: Sage.

Gudykunst, W. B., Yang, S. M., & Nishida, T. (1985). A cross-cultural test of uncertainty reduction theory: Comparisons of acquaintances, friends, and dating relationships in Japan, Korea, and the United States. *Human Communication Research, 11*, 407–454.

Hart, R. P., & Burks, D. M. (1972). Rhetorical sensitivity and social interaction. *Speech Monographs, 39*, 75–91.

Heider, F. (1958). *The psychology of interpersonal relations.* New York: Harcourt, Brace & World.

Hewes, D. E., & Planalp, S. (1987). The individuals' place in communication science. In C. R. Berger & S. H. Chaffee (Eds.), *The handbook of communication science* (pp. 146–183). Newbury Park, CA: Sage.

Hewes, D. E., Roloff, M. E., Planalp, S., & Seibold, D. R. (1990). Interpersonal communication research: What should we know? In G. M. Phillips & J. T. Wood (Eds.), *Speech communication: Essays to commemorate the 75th anniversary of the Speech Communication Association* (pp. 130–180). Carbondale, IL: Southern Illinois University Press.

Hilton, D. J. (1990). Conversational processes and causal explanation. *Psychological Bulletin, 107*, 65–81.

Holtzworth-Munroe, A., & Jacobson, N. S. (1985). Causal attributions of married couples: When do they search for causes? What do they conclude when they do? *Journal of Personality and Social Psychology, 48*, 1398–1412.

Hopper, R. (1981). The taken-for-granted. *Human Communication Research, 7*, 195–211.

Hopper, R., Knapp, M. L., & Scott, L. (1981). Couples' personal idioms: Exploring intimate talk. *Journal of Communication, 31*, 23–33.

Huston, T., Surra, C., Fitzgerald, N., & Cate, R. (1981). From courtship to marriage: Mate selection as an interpersonal process. In S. W. Duck & R. Gilmour (Eds.), *Personal relationships 2: Developing personal relationships* (pp. 53–88). London: Academic Press.

Jablin, F. M., Putnam, L., Roberts, K. H., & Porter, L. W. (Eds.). (1988). *Handbook of organizational communication: An interdisciplinary perspective.* Newbury Park, CA: Sage.

Jones, E. E., & Davis, K. (1965). From acts to dispositions. *American Psychologist, 34*, 107–117.

Kellermann, K. (1988). The negativity effect in interaction: It's all in your point of view. *Human Communication Research, 16*, 147–183.

Kellermann, K., Broetzmann, S., Lim, T., & Kitao, K. (1989). The conversational MOP: Scenes in the stream of discourse. *Discourse Processes, 12*, 27–62.

Kelley, H. H. (1973). The process of causal attribution. *American Psychologist, 28*, 107–128.

Kelley, H. H. (1979). *Personal relationships: Their structure and process.* Hillsdale, NJ: Lawrence Erlbaum Associates.

Kelley, H., Berscheid, E., Christensen, A., Harvey, J., Huston, T., Levinger, G., McClintock, E., Peplau, E., & Peterson, D. (1983). Analyzing close relationships. In H. Kelley, E. Berscheid, A. Christensen, J. Harvey, T. Huston, G. Levinger, E. McClintock, L. Peplau, & D. Peterson (Eds.), *Close relationships* (pp. 20–67). New York: W. H. Freeman.

Kelley, H. H., & Thibaut, J. W. (1978). *Interpersonal relations: A theory of interdependence.* New York: Wiley.

Kelly, G. A. (1955). *The psychology of personal constructs.* New York: W. W. Norton.

Knapp, M. L., & Vangelisti, A. L. (1992). *Interpersonal communication and human relationships* (2nd ed.). Boston: Allyn & Bacon.

Knapp, M. L. (1985). The study of physical appearance and cosmetics in western culture. In J. A. Graham & A. M. Klingman (Eds.), *The psychology of cosmetic treatments* (pp. 45–76). New York: Praeger.

Knapp, M. L., Hart, R. P., Friedrich, G. W., & Shulman, G. M. (1973). The rhetoric of goodbye: Verbal and nonverbal correlates of human leave-taking. *Speech Monographs, 40*, 182–198.

Knapp, M. L., & Miller, G. R. (1985). Introduction: Background and current trends in the study of interpersonal communication. In M. L. Knapp & G. R. Miller (Eds.), *Handbook of interpersonal communication* (pp. 7–24). Newbury Park, CA: Sage.

Lallje, M., & Abelson, R. P. (1983). The organization of explanations. In M. Hewstone (Ed.), *Attribution theory: Social and functional extensions* (pp. 65–80). Oxford: Blackwell.

Langer, E. J. (1989). *Mindfulness.* Reading, MA: Addison-Wesley.

Langer, E. J., & Newman, H. M. (1979). The role of mindlessness in a typical social psychological experiment. *Personality and Social Psychology Bulletin, 5*, 295–298.

Lannamann, J. W. (1991). Interpersonal communication research as ideological practice. *Communication Theory, 1*, 179–203.

Lasch, C. (1979). *The culture of narcissism.* New York: W. W. Norton.

Lederer, W. J., & Jackson, D. D. (1968). *The mirages of marriage.* New York: W. W. Norton.

Levinger, G., Senn, D. J., & Jorgensen, P. W. (1970). Progress toward permanence in courtship: A test of Kerckhoff-Davis hypotheses. *Sociometry, 33*, 427–443.

Littlejohn, S. (1983). *Theories of human communication* (2nd ed.). Belmont, CA: Wadsworth.

Littlejohn, S. (1989). *Theories of human communication* (3rd ed.). Belmont, CA: Wadsworth.

Lloyd, S. A., & Cate, R. M. (1985). Attributions associated with significant turning points in premarital relationship development and dissolution. *Journal of Social and Personal Relationships, 2*, 419–436.

McArthur, L. A. (1972). The how and what of why: Some determinants and consequences of causal attribution. *Journal of Personality and Social Psychology, 22*, 171–193.

Menzel, H. (1978). Meaning—Who needs it: In M. Brenner, P. Marsh, & M. Brenner (Eds.), *The social contexts of method* (pp. 140–171). New York: St. Martin's Press.

Millar, F. E., & Rogers, L. E. (1976). A relational approach to interpersonal communication. In G. R. Millar (Ed.), *Explorations in interpersonal communication* (pp. 87–103). Newbury Park, CA: Sage.

Millar, F., & Rogers, E. (1987). Relational dimensions of interpersonal dynamics. In M. Roloff & G. Miller (Ed.), *Interpersonal processes: New directions in communication research* (pp. 117–139). Newbury Park, CA: Sage.

Minuchin, S., Rosman, B. L., & Baker, L. (1978). *Psychosomatic families.* Cambridge, MA: Harvard University Press.

Monge, P. R., & Eisenberg, E. M. (1987). Emergent communication networks. In F. M. Jablin, L. Putnam, K. H. Roberts, & L. W. Porter (Eds.), *Handbook of organizational communication: An interdisciplinary perspective* (pp. 304–342). Newbury Park, CA: Sage.

Montgomery, B. M. (1988). Quality communication in personal relationships. In S. W. Duck (Ed.), *Handbook of personal relationships: Theory, research, and interventions* (pp. 343–359). Chichester: Wiley.

Newman, H. (1981). Communication within ongoing intimate relationships: An attributional perspective. *Personality and Social Psychology Bulletin, 7*, 59–70.

Nisbett, R., & Ross, L. (1980). *Human inference: Strategies and shortcomings of social judgment.* Engelwood Cliffs, NJ: Prentice-Hall.

O'Keefe, D. J., & Sypher, H. E. (1981). Cognitive complexity measures and the relationship of cognitive complexity to communication: A critical review. *Human Communication Research, 8*, 72–92.

Ogden, C. K., & Richards, I. A. (1923). *The meaning of meaning.* London: Kegan, Paul, Trench, and Tubner.

Osgood, C., Suci, G., & Tannenbaum, P. (1957). *The measurement of meaning.* Urbana: University of Illinois Press.

Parks, M. R. (1978). Relational communication: Theory and research. *Human Communication Research, 4*, 179–191.

Patterson, M. L. (1983). *Nonverbal behavior: A functional perspective.* New York: Springer-Verlag.

Pearce, W. B. (1989). *Communication and the human condition.* Carbondale, IL: Southern Illinois University Press.

Pearce, W. B., & Cronen, V. E. (1980). *Communication, action, and meaning: The creation of social realities.* New York: Praeger.

Planalp, S., & Honeycutt, J. M. (1985). Events that increase uncertainty in personal relationships. *Human Communication Research, 11*, 593–604.

Planalp, S., Rutherford, D. K., & Honeycutt, J. M. (1988). Events that increase uncertainty in personal relationships II: Replication and extension. *Human Communication Research, 14*, 516–547.

Pyszczynski, T. A., & Greenberg, J. (1981). Role of disconfirmed expectancies in the instigation of attributional processing. *Journal of Personality and Social Psychology, 40*, 31–38.

Rawlins, W. K. (1983a). Openness as problematic in ongoing friendships: Two conversational dilemmas. *Communication Monographs, 50*, 1–13.

Rawlins, W. K. (1983b). Negotiating close friendship: The dialectic of conjunctive freedoms. *Human Communication Research, 9*, 255–266.

Rawlins, W. K. (1987). Gregory Bateson and the composition of human communication. *Research in Language and Social Interaction, 20*, 53–77.

Rawlins, W. K., & Holl, M. (1988). The communicative achievement of friendship during adolescence: Predicaments of trust and violation. *Western Journal of Speech Communication, 51*, 345–363.

Rogers, L. E., Courtright, J. A., & Millar, F. E. (1980). Message control intensity: Rationale and preliminary findings. *Communication Monographs, 47*, 201–219.

Rogers, L. E., & Millar, F. E. (1988). Relational communication. In S. Duck (Ed.), *Handbook of personal relationships: Theory, research, and interventions* (pp. 289–306). Chichester: Wiley.

Rommetveit, R. (1980). On 'meanings' of acts and what is meant and made known by what is said in a pluralistic social world. In M. Brenner (Ed.), *The structure of action* (pp. 108–149). New York: St. Martin's Press.

Ross, M., & Sicoly, F. (1979). Egocentric biases in availability and attribution. *Journal of Personality and Social Psychology, 37*, 322–336.

Rubin, R. B. (1977). The role of context in information seeking and impression formation. *Communication Monographs, 44*, 81–90.

Rubin, R. B. (1979). The effect of context on information seeking across the span of initial interactions. *Communication Quarterly, 27*, 13–20.

Sapir, E. (1921). *Language: An introduction to the study of speech.* New York: Harcourt, Brace, & World.

Schank, R., & Abelson, R. (1977). *Scripts, plans, goals, and understanding.* Hillsdale, NJ: Lawrence Erlbaum Associates.

Searle, J. (1969). *Speech acts: An essay in the philosophy of language.* Cambridge, England: Cambridge University Press.

Seibold, D. R., & Spitzberg, B. H. (1982). Attribution theory and research: Review and implications for communication. In B. J. Dervin & M. J. Voight (Eds.), *Progress in communication sciences III* (pp. 85–125). Norwood, NJ: Ablex.

Sigman, S. J. (1991). Handling the discontinuous aspects of continuous social relationships: Toward research on the persistence of social forms. *Communication Theory, 1*, 106–127.

Sillars, A. L. (1980). Attributions and communication in roommate conflicts. *Communication Monographs, 47*, 180–200.

Smircich, L., & Calas, M. (1987). Organizational culture: A critical assessment. In F. M. Jablin, L. Putnam, K. H. Roberts, & L. W. Porter (Eds.), *Handbook of organizational communication: An interdisciplinary perspective* (pp. 228–263). Newbury Park, CA: Sage.

Staines, G. L., & Libby, P. L. (1986). Men and women in role relationships. In R. D. Ashmore & F. K. DelBoca (Eds.), *The social psychology of female-male relations* (pp. 211–258). New York: Academic Press.

Stamp, G. H. (1991). *The transition to parenthood through communication: An interpretation of spousal accounts.* Unpublished doctoral dissertation, Department of Speech Communication, University of Texas at Austin.

Stamp, G. H., & Knapp, M. L. (1990). The construct of intent in interpersonal communication. *Quarterly Journal of Speech, 76*, 282–299.

Street, R. L., & Giles, H. (1982). Speech accommodation theory: A social cognitive approach to language and speech behavior. In M. Roloff & C. Berger (Eds.), *Social cognition and communication* (pp. 193–226). Newbury Park, CA: Sage.

Taylor, S. E., & Fiske, S. T. (1978). Salience, attention, and attribution: Top of the head phenomena. *Advances in experimental social psychology, 2*, 249–288.

Thibaut, J. W., & Kelley, H. H. (1959). *The social psychology of groups*. New York: Wiley.

Tversky, B., & Hemenway, K. (1983). Categories of environmental scenes. *Cognitive Psychology, 15*, 121–149.

Watzlawick, P., Beavin, J. H., & Jackson, D. D. (1967). *The Pragmatics of Human Communication*. New York: Norton.

Weber, D. J., & Vangelisti, A. L. (1990). "Because I love you ...": The tactic use of attributional expressions in conversation. *Human Communication Research, 17*, 606–624.

Weiner, B., Frieze, I., Kukla, A., Reed, L., Rest, S., & Rosenbaum, R. M. (1987). Perceiving the causes of success and failure. In E. E. Jones, D. E. Kanouse, H. H. Kelley, R. E. Nisbett, S. Valins, & V. Weiner (Eds.), *Attribution: Perceiving the causes of behavior* (pp. 95–120). Hillsdale, NJ: Lawrence Erlbaum Associates.

Werner, H. (1957). The concept of development from a comparative and organismic point of view. In D. B. Harris (Ed.), *The concept of development* (pp. 125–146). Minneapolis: University of Minnesota Press.

Werner, C., & Haggard, L. (1985). Temporal qualities of interpersonal relationships. In M. Knapp & G. Miller (Eds.), *Handbook of interpersonal communication* (pp. 59–99). Newbury Park, CA: Sage.

Wills, T. A., Weiss, R. L., & Patterson, G. R. (1974). A behavioral analysis of the determinants of marital satisfaction. *Journal of Consulting and Clinical Psychology, 42*, 802–811.

Wish, M., Deutsch, M., & Kaplan, S. (1976). Perceived dimensions of interpersonal relations. *Journal of Personality and Social Psychology, 33*, 409–420.

Wish, M., & Kaplan, S. (1977). Toward an implicit theory of interpersonal communication. *Sociometry, 40*, 234–246.

Yerby, J., Buerkel-Rothfuss, N., & Bochner, A. P. (1990). *Understanding family communication*. Scottsdale, AZ: Gorsuch Scarisbick.

Chapter 6

Mediated Communication Theory

Robert S. Fortner
Calvin College

> *My own view is that we have been wrong in taking communication as*
> *secondary. Many people seem to assume as a matter of course that there*
> *is, first, reality, and then, second, communication about it. . . . What we call*
> *society is not only a network of political and economic arrangements, but*
> *also a process of learning and communication.*
>
> —Williams (1976, p. 11)

"Of all things," John Dewey once wrote, "communication is the most wonderful."
Perhaps this helps explain another comment, made years later by Marshall
McLuhan. McLuhan suggested that the reason that communication was difficult
to study was because it is to human beings what water is to a fish—the very
environment. How, then, do we go about understanding the wonder of the
environment that we inhabit, particularly in an age when the means of
communication have become so complex, so ubiquitous, and so numerous?
Where, indeed, do we begin? That, of course, is the problem of theory.

There is no single theory of communication that encompasses all human
dialogue, information transfer, or media activity. There are, in fact, multiple
theories that attempt to explain different aspects of the complex interactions
which comprise communication. Some people argue, too, that what occurs
through the medium of the press, or television, is not actually communication.
Since communication is an interactive (or transactive) process, and the
information transferred via mechanical or electronic media flows in only one
direction that reaction seems warranted. After all, there is little opportunity for
audiences to respond or provide meaningful feedback as part of the activity

initiated by journalists, advertising copywriters, television scriptwriters, radio disc jockeys, and so forth.

Even deciding what to call communication occurring via mechanical or electronic devices (e.g., radio, television, computers) is a problem. *Mass communication* elicits images of *mass society*, a passive, easily manipulated audience that many communication scholars reject. For others, the term *mass media* is too technology-oriented, concentrating on the *means* of communication, rather than the *process*. *Broadcast communication* and *electronic media* are both too specific, eliminating communication occurring via books, magazines, newspapers, films, even videotapes that no longer have to be broadcast over the airwaves to be viewed. *Mediated communication*, too, is objectionable because of what it implies—that public speaking, for instance, uses no medium for its transfer from speaker to listener—which is technically untrue, since the air (a medium) carries the sound wave created by the speaker's voice to the eardrums of the hearers. Sometimes it must seem that we really haven't moved very far from Lasswell's famous dictum that what we are concerned with is *"Who says what* in which *channel* to *whom* with what *effect?"* (Laswell, 1948). We have yet to deal with the technical considerations in our mass media theory.

Nevertheless, we must use some convention. To that end, this chapter is concerned with *mass communication theory,* resulting in attention to both technology and audience size. This term emphasizes communication theory that reaches large, unrelated and separated audiences, such as movies, radio and television, and newspapers. This term also implies attention to mass audiences that confront mechanically mediated forms of communication (newspapers, magazines, books, and films) and electronically mediated forms (radio, television, and audiovisual tapes). The chapter will not focus on other electronic forms (the telegraph, telephone, coaxial cable, or microwave, including satellite communication).

The concern of the chapter, too, is communication *theory*—or explanation— and its social, political, economic, and intellectual roots. It is not a history of communication media, although clearly history itself is significant—because it is in history that the roots of communication theory are to be found.

Outlining mass communication theory is difficult because of the problem of determining which of the many "subphenomena" of communication (itself the phenomenon to be explained by theory) to include. Take the case of television. There are a number of subphenomena to explain. There are theories about how the technology works: how it transfers information from transmitter to receiver, how the camera or microphone affect the original content, how editing enhances, detracts from, or alters the original image and sound patterns captured by the camera and microphone, and so on. Related to this is the issue of how best to employ the technological capabilities of the recording and editing system—how does one judge the goodness or beauty of the final product? All of these issues are *aesthetic, engineering* and *ethical* questions, requiring, in turn, aesthetic, information, and moral theories. How people make judgments concerning what material to tape, or where to place the final product (in time), on what sort of distribution system and appealing to what audiences are issues requiring us to employ *economic* theory. What impacts these products have on members of the audience, in turn, require some combination of *political*, *sociological*, and *psychological* theory.

It is the combination of these concerns which constitutes communication theory as applied to media, or mass communication, theory. This is what gives mass communication theory its richness, and what makes it so difficult to explain, this is its *wonder* (or confusion and complexity) and the dimensions of the *environment* it seeks to explain.

THE ENVIRONMENT OF MASS COMMUNICATION THEORY

Theory does not develop in a vacuum, but responds to specific environments. We tend to think that the most germane environment for theory construction is its intellectual one—this volume is, in fact, premised on that assumption. Obviously this is an important consideration. For mass communication theory, however, this intellectual environment was not primary. Technological possibility was the first order environment for theory-building.

Communication technologies seemingly offered solutions to long-standing problems between peoples. Many theories developed based on the assumed opportunities offered by technology. Technology had a "messianic property" (see Carey & Quirk, 1970a, 1970b; Fortner, 1978; Schultze, 1987). As R. N. Vyvyan, the engineer in charge of constructing Marconi's first wireless stations in North America put it,

> The invention and perfection of broadcasting has given to humanity a new method of conveying understanding, an opportunity of breaking down distrust between nations, of appreciating the music, the culture, the moral and intellectual development of other nations. . . . From a social and educational point of view the value of broadcasting is immeasurable. It has raised the standard of education, musical appreciation, and entertainment, to a new level, and has conveyed the words of the greatest spiritual and moral teachers of the period to the smallest and remotest cottages. May it not be hoped that with wise guidance its use will exert a great pacific influence on international relations and that it may be of some assistance in producing a helpful spirit between nations of mutual cooperation in the advancement of civilization? (Vyvyan, 1974, pp. 217–218)

Many people saw this messianic potential as inherent in communications technology. It would supposedly eliminate distance, involve scattered citizens in a common democratic experience, create the mass marketplace that would make the American dream a reality. In short, communication would be a power for good, overcoming political weakness or cultural inferiority. According to this understanding, communication would bring big-city culture to every small town across America. Communication would provide an electronic Chautauqua, a means to educate and elevate the ill-educated masses comprising the American people.

Such technological optimism was not confined to North America. The great European empires expected communications technologies to tie their scattered lands together, extending their political and economic control over vast regions of the earth. They used submarine cables, for instance, to centralize imperial authority in Paris, London, or Berlin. Such cables reduced the authority of the "man on the spot"—the colonial governor in far-flung regions. By the beginning of World War II, 350,000 miles of submarine cables had been laid, over 155,000 by Great Britain alone. At the beginning of both world wars, the warring powers immediately set out to cut the cables that connected the imperial European capitals with their colonies to reduce the resources available to the adversary. Britain cut German cables within hours of the beginning of World War I, while her own remained intact. At the start of World War II, Britain again cut the German cables, while Italy cut Britain's major cables in the Mediterranean.

People saw that radio had the same messianic potential. People searched with their radios for long-distance signals. In the United States many communities pressured local broadcasters to institute a "silent night" to allow people the opportunity to search for distant stations free from interference. They heard lectures, symphony concerts, and famous entertainers from afar. They crossed the barriers of space and time with small radio sets.

The Dutch were the first to establish wireless radio contact with their colonies, beginning a service in 1919 to the Dutch East Indies (now Indonesia). The British created an Imperial wireless network which was fully functioning—after fits and starts—by 1932. The Germans operated two wireless stations in the United States to provide secure communication across the Atlantic, not wanting to be dependent on the British. The United States government eventually took control of these stations—which had come under the control of the Nazi government in 1933—in the days leading up to World War II, again leaving Germany without independent access to U.S. newspapers or the American public.

These worldwide events nurtured mass communication theory. The supposed power of technology to bind people together and elevate culture, however, also had a dark side. The understanding that technology had direct, immediate effects also led to fear. While communication had the potential to bind people together, it could also be put to evil purposes. People recognized that the new means of communication, particularly radio in the 1930s and 1940s, would be used to stir up mass hysteria, undermining rational public discourse and democratic life. Such fears could be summed up in one "devil term": propaganda.

World War I saw the first uses of wireless for propaganda. The widespread use of propaganda through news control, cartooning, and editorial opinion in the press, and through public lecture tours, posters, billboards, and graphic photographic portrayals of atrocities seemed to demonstrate the potential of propaganda. Hitler even credited the British propaganda effort of World War I as being a major contribution to the German defeat in his manifesto, *Mein Kampf.*

The 1930s saw the emergence of both communist and fascist newspapers and magazines in the Western world. Millions of Americans reportedly considered voting for candidates such as the "radio priest," Father Charles Coughlin, Senator Huey Long of Louisiana (soon to be assassinated), and Frances Townsend in the 1936 U.S. presidential election. Although these fears were greatly overstated, the adroit use of media, and the publication of weekly newspapers and magazines by such ideologues, heightened fears that the American public might be led to fascism or communism. NBC eventually removed Coughlin's weekly radio program from the air, ostensibly for his anti-Semitic remarks. It seemed to the public, political leaders and scholars alike that the mass media were potentially powerful purveyors of evil, even as they were potential preservers of good.

In 1938 Orson Welles' famous "War of the Worlds" radio program, a dramatization of a Martian invasion of the United States, and broadcast as news reports, reportedly sent panic through as many as a million listeners. Hitler and the Italian dictator, Mussolini, were apparently using radio and film successfully to consolidate their power and convince their respective populations to support aggression in Europe and North Africa. The age of the demagogue and the dictator—with influence heightened by the dramatic potential of radio—seemed to have arrived.

This context contributed much to the early theorizing about the significance of mass communication. Some German researchers, having seen Hitler rise to power and enforce his will prior to the war, emigrated to the United States. The U.S. military, responding to the fears generated by propaganda in World War I and the political context of Europe viewed from afar, engaged American researchers to conduct experiments with American soldiers to determine the potential impact that propaganda might have on them (see Hovland, Lumsdaine, & Sheffield, 1949).

This context led American mass communication theory to an early preoccupation with its direct effects. This early research was not so concerned with the differences between media, but—like much persuasion research—with the differences in content which might lead to different results. Because the early researchers were not trained in communication research methods, but in political science, sociology, or psychology, they borrowed freely from the assumptions and methodologies of these social scientific disciplines. The researchers used both experimental and survey methods, searching for a way to explain the *assumed* effects of the use of mass media. In turn, they assumed that a study of effects would eventually make it possible for them to *predict* the impact of different messages, thereby thwarting evil uses of the media, and assisting "good" ones. For example, the right messages could "inoculate" soldiers and citizens against the effects of propaganda. Media effects would thus be controllable, because they were predictable.

In this early theorizing, mass communication was a "magic bullet," similar in effect to the wonder drugs of medical science. Mass communication was a mystic route to a better society when used by good people seeking good ends. With such ends clearly identified, the "communalism" which the media seemed to offer to all citizens might also be realized. The messianic promise could become reality.

The American preoccupation with the effects of mass communication has continued. Manufacturers have insisted that they should know how to increase their market shares, assure the success of new products, and choose among the media for their advertising campaigns. Advertisers have demanded to know the value of their investments in the media (the U.S. advertising industry spends nearly half of all *global* expenditures on advertising), and how to increase the effectiveness of their "propaganda." Politicians, political parties, and political action groups (PACs) have desired to know how to present candidates—or manipulate the media—to gain election victories, or sway public opinion. Television companies have demanded to know how to increase their ratings—so as to increase their profits. All such activities imply that the media can have direct and often immediate effects on people's attitudes, beliefs, and behaviors.

Periodic public expressions of concern about the role of the media in American society, particularly in the post-World War II period, have also prompted waves of government-funded research on media effects. The best known instance of federal involvement was the massive Surgeon General's report on televised violence. This six volume report was published in 1972 after long wrangling between the television industry, the National Institute of Mental Health, and the academic community (see Rowland, 1983, for a critical history of the Surgeon General's report). The report helped legitimize the subsequent development of communication theory on the effects of television (Surgeon General's Scientific Advisory Committee, 1972). The practical effect of government involvement was to encourage the development of direct effects theory, partly because this approach generated funds for research.

The environment for the development of mass communication theory, then, has resulted in two different theoretical dimensions. One is based on "messianic promise," and the distortion of that promise. The other dimension we may call "reactive theory." In this environment, the rapid development and application of communications technology, the changing public response to this development (including the fears and expectations of the technology), and the demands of various U.S. industries and the federal government for ways to exploit the technology (e.g., to increase profits or make better soldiers) or prevent damage to the social fabric (e.g., from violence or the election of the "wrong" candidate) created an impetus for theory to react to events and expectations.

Such an environment has not encouraged dispassionate theory building. Neither has such theory building seemed "useful" or "relevant" to the public debate about the value or damage of the mass media. Unfortunately, too, reactive theory has often had apparently shallow intellectual roots, or these roots have been lost because of the pressures of the moment. As a result, tracing these roots is a difficult enterprise.

THE EUROPEAN ROOTS OF MASS COMMUNICATION THEORY

The European intellectual influence on mass communication theory is both significant and complex. Ironically, however, its significance can be missed if too much attention is paid to the methodological aspects of theory building and testing (which is principally an American contribution). Its very complexity, too, may make its contribution seem muddled—or contradictory.

Europe contributed a variety of perspectives on the problems of communication in society. Since most European countries variously struggled with the problem of integrating the people within their borders into cohesive national populations, particularly after the French Revolution in 1789, many European social theorists concerned themselves with issues of nationalism, language fragmentation, class separation, and national and provincial animosities. One principal question was how people could develop common cause, how they could develop connection when so much seemed to divide them.

The French sociologist Emile Durkheim argued that in the modern era *organic* solidarity had replaced *mechanical* solidarity as the basis for bridging the divisions in society. Mechanical solidarity—as a theoretical construct—brought about social cohesion among people who were alike, who shared a common life and thus developed a set of common beliefs, customs, and values. People living together in a village, sharing religious rituals, rites of passage, a common history, had such solidarity. Organic solidarity, the basis of social cohesion among heterogeneous people who had to search for commonness (in class, union, business, religious, or professional interests), was more fragile. It operated in societies where individuals were differentiated and social differences overshadowed similarities. It functioned where the identified common interests of people could change, thus shifting the basis of social differentiation. These two concepts, Durkheim suggested, were the result of differing divisions of labor in society (Durkheim, 1964).

The German sociologist Ferdinand Tönnies saw that the *Gemeinschaft*-dominated (loosely translated as *community*) associations of preindustrial Europe were replaced by the *Gessellschaft*-dominated (*society*-dominated) structures of modernity—particularly those of commerce. *Gemeinschaft*, Tönnies argued, was "a lasting and genuine form of living together," while *Gessellschaft* was "transitory and superficial." Like Durkheim, Tönnies saw the older form of association as "a living organism," the new "as a mechanical aggregate and artifact (Tönnies, 1955, pp. 38–39)." (Tönnies' terms, however, were opposite in their meaning to Durkheim's.)

Another German sociologist, Max Weber, was also concerned about the new mechanisms that were developing as means to control society. He examined the relationship between religion and capitalism in *The Protestant Ethic and the Spirit of Capitalism* and the development of bureaucracy in *The Theory of Social and Economic Organization* (Weber, 1947).

Karl Marx and Friedrich Engels also tackled the problem of solidarity among people in modern societies. They shared the questions of other theorists about "what made society possible," but concentrated on the development of "class consciousness" within different groups of the society as the means to achieve solidarity. They did not recognize such solidarity as being contained within given societies, but saw the interests of classes extending across frontiers. They argued that modern society had simplified class antagonisms, splitting people "into two great hostile camps, into two great classes directly facing each other: bourgeoisie and proletariat" (Marx & Engels, 1848).

There is not space here to detail the thinking of any of these theorists. It must suffice to say that their common concern with the means by which people in modern societies would relate to one another, how their governments would exercise power, how their institutions and classes would struggle or achieve common purpose, set out a framework within which communication theory would develop. From the European perspective communication theory must be seen as part of *social theory* (a useful survey of many of these ideas can be found in DeFleur & Ball-Rokeach, 1989, Chapter 6). Such theories (both social theory generally and communication theory more specifically) aimed to explain not just media effects, but the *means of connection* between people. In the European tradition, theorists believed that the press, for instance, had an integral role in making such connections (see Hardt, 1979).

Theory thus explained the media's role both in encouraging social cohesion and social conflict. This theory, in turn, was rooted in Europe's press "reality," which was fragmented into elite and "common" newspapers. There were many papers that were fiercely partisan and ideological in their defense of the interests of their constituency (particularly following the Russian Revolution in 1917 and the subsequent anti-Bolshevist movements which resulted in Italian fascism and German Nazism). There were papers that reflected the nationalist sentiments of Europe's minority ethnic communities. In short, the European media landscape was one where opinion, class and ethnic interests, and ideology mattered more than events. Interpretation and perspective were more valuable than raw news.

This landscape also contained another important feature: the assumption that people were psychologically uniform, that human nature was consistent across all people (see DeFleur & Ball-Rokeach, 1989, pp. 164–165). This meant that powerful messages could lead to massive effects: The magic bullet could affect people consistently and forcefully. The experience of countries during World

War I (including the United States) seemed to confirm this assumption. British propaganda was credited, for instance, with influencing Americans to enter the war on her side, rather than the other. British propaganda was replete with images of Germans as murderous Huns committing atrocities against innocents (especially women and children) and torpedoing passenger liners. Such images were included in posters, photographs (some faked), cartoons, news stories (in the British press and distributed through the British press agency, Reuters), books, and speeches (see Fortner, 1993).

In the highly charged ideological environment of European communication through the war (including the 1917 revolution in Russia that led to the Soviet state), the recriminations that followed the armistice through the 1920s, and the propaganda war that erupted in the early 1930s with the rise of Nazism, communication was clearly important. Throughout this period concern about the disruption of social harmony (which Durkheim labeled *anomie*), the rise of "mass society states" based in propaganda (such as Germany, Italy and Japan), and the loss of natural solidarity all contributed to the assumption that media were powerful determiners of human destiny and the exercise of political power.

Many of those now considered the early "communication theorists," or who influenced future theorists, came from this background. Paul Lazarsfeld, for instance, emigrated to the United States from Austria in the early 1930s after establishing a research institute at Vienna University. This institute was the first basing its work on empirical research methods. After coming to the United States, Lazarsfeld taught at Columbia University and began the Bureau of Applied Social Research, working in marketing and audience research. Lazarsfeld felt the differences in approach to media theory once in the United States, and eventually contrasted the two perspectives as *administrative* and *critical* research (Lazarsfeld, 1941).

Other important figures in the development of a European perspective are often grouped together as the Frankfurt School of critical theory (those Lazarsfeld had contrasted with administrative researchers). Significant critical scholars from this tradition include Theodor Adorno, Max Horkheimer, Walter Benjamin, and Herbert Marcuse (see Arato & Gebhardt, 1982; Held, 1980). All four of these theorists fled from Germany when the Nazis took power. Benjamin committed suicide on the Spanish border with France after the fall of Paris, rather than be arrested by the Nazis. Adorno, Horkheimer, and Marcuse all came to the United States, but only Marcuse became an American citizen (1940). Horkheimer returned to Germany in 1950, and Adorno in 1960.

Marxism was a significant influence on the Frankfurt School, but its representatives added analytic dimensions to Marxism that had not been explored (although perhaps anticipated) by Marx. Like other Europeans, the Frankfurt School theorists were concerned with how individuals and groups gain political and economic power over others in society. In their own ways, members of the Frankfurt School each saw the media, from musical recordings to radio and print media, as mechanisms for domination and hegemony. (Marcuse's work [1964] is probably the best known work emerging from the Frankfurt School. Other significant works include Benjamin [1968], and Horkheimer [1972]).

The second generation Frankfurt School theorists (i.e., post World War II) were led by Jürgen Habermas, perhaps the most influential European theorist and social critic of the 1970s and 1980s. Habermas' work is premised on an anti-positivist critique (thereby denying much of the intellectual undergirding of "effects theory") that denies that knowledge is "value-free" (see Habermas, 1984, 1987).[1] Habermas' goal was both to expose the inherently ideological character of all scholarship and to offer his own *ideal* of society where truly democratic communication would be encouraged. His "ideal speech community" would include all members of society in a rational dialogue about matters of mutual interest. Such ideas were also developed in the work of the Chicago School of sociology (discussed later in this essay) and by other scholars, notably Paulo Freire (see Freire, 1970, 1973).

THE NORTH AMERICAN ROOTS OF MASS COMMUNICATION THEORY

The environment in North America for understanding communication was fundamentally different than that of Europe. Although propaganda could work on this large continent (an opinion seemingly confirmed by the popular press accounts of mass panic in response to Orson Welles' adaptation of *War of the Worlds* in 1938 and the rise of both ideology and demagogues in that decade) North America did not have the cultural, language, or ethnic homogeneity of European countries. Despite a century of the melting pot in the United States, large ethnic communities still existed across the country, the foreign-language press was vibrant in many large cities, and obvious differences existed in the cultural values of differing regions (New England, the midwest, the South, etc.), residence (urban and rural), religion (Catholics and Protestants), race (Whites and Blacks), and so on. Yet the democratic experience was alive. Certainly abuses and tensions existed, evils were perpetrated, violence and witch hunts often erupted. The United States was no Eden. Its diversity, however, called into

---

[1]Positivism had been introduced into social science, including communication study, by American researchers, anxious to use it as a means of attaining the legitimacy for their work that was accorded to researchers in the physical sciences. The approach has become known as the American tradition. It was the distinction between "value-free" and "value-latent" research that led Lazarsfeld, familiar with both strains of communication research, to write his essay contrasting the two forms in 1941. He credited Horkheimer with the idea of critical research, and distinguished it from administrative research "in two respects: it develops a theory of the prevailing social trends of our times, general trends which yet require consideration in any concrete research problem; and it seems to imply ideas of basic human values according to which all actual or desired effects should be appraised" (Lazarsfeld, 1941, p. 9).

question many of the assumptions of Europe. In Canada, too, the multiculturalism ethic (as opposed to the melting pot) meant that differences would exist, but these differences were assumed to be less important than other factors: climate, topography, size, national identity, or economic domination—first by Great Britain and then the United States. The Canadian experience was also fundamentally different from that of Europe.

As already suggested, the focus of mass communication theory in North America was on its *effects*. Mass communication had developed within America's pragmatic tradition (i.e., identify a problem and then discover practical solutions for it). This tradition suggested to advertisers, for instance, that they should assure that they were spending their money wisely. It suggested to newspapers, and later radio and television stations, that they should demonstrate their superiority in attracting large audiences, and in creating memorable advertisements. In such an environment it was nearly inevitable that researchers would be attracted to commercially defined (and pragmatic) problems.

There was the additional issue of making democracy work in a pluralistic society, and resulting interest in noncommercial (but still pragmatic) applications of media power—especially the development of public opinion. This issue created problems for theorists. The first was defining an appropriate role for the press, or media, since people assumed that the media would influence public opinion and voter behavior. But the press saw itself as an adversary of government, and perpetuated such myths as the public's right to know, and objectivity. It defined its own role as watchdog of government, leading inevitably to the issue of media bias.

This was, of course, a practical issue that could be construed easily to have theoretic implications both for a theory of mass communication and political theory more generally. Therefore, many political scientists, such as C. Wright Mills, Harold Laski, and Harold Lasswell, examined what we would now call political communication problems. Lasswell's behavioral orientation led him to be particularly interested in the role of the press in political campaigns (see Lasswell, 1936).

Such concerns were part of the ongoing public dialogue that attempted to deal with politics pragmatically. It was rooted in a long tradition. At least since the time of Alexis de Tocqueville's (1830) remarks in *Democracy in America* on the developing relationship between the people and their government, Americans had assumed a central position and value for public opinion percolating from the grass roots to influence public policy. The federal government, too, had undertaken projects, including the creation of toll roads, the mail service (including free carriage of newspapers from one paper to another), the franking system for members of Congress (which allowed them to mail information to their constituencies free of charge), the Pony Express, rural free delivery, and so on, to encourage constituency-and-Congressional communication.

The most significant political commentator who influenced thinking about public opinion was Walter Lippmann. Lippmann's influence was greatest during the period when the United States was groping its way forward out of its historic isolation, particularly following World War I (Steele, 1980). Lippmann published *Public Opinion* in 1922, in which he argued that "experts" had natural advantages in the "manufacture" of consent. "Every leader," he wrote,

> is in some degree a propagandist. Strategically placed, and compelled often to choose even at the best between equally cogent though conflicting ideals of safety for his institution, and candor to his public, the official finds himself deciding more and more consciously what facts, in what setting, in what guise he shall permit the public to know.... The manufacture of consent is capable of great refinements no one, I think, denies.... [A]s a result of psychological research, coupled with the modern means of communication, the practice of democracy has turned a corner. ... Within the life of the generation now in control of affairs, persuasion has become a self-conscious art and a regular organ of popular government. (p. 158)

The other problem concerned the role of mass communication in a pluralistic, culturally differentiated, society. This problem itself had two aspects. One concerned *meaning*. How did people make sense out of the various messages composed by a commercial press? How did that commercially driven press determine the nature of news that would appeal to culturally polyglot urban communities? The second concerned technology. What was the role of the changing technologies in enabling societies to establish a common order? How could cultural differences, geographic separation, and the dilution of political power which accompanied such realities be bridged?

In the United States the important theorists concerned with answering the first of these two aspects were sociologists working together at the University of Chicago, in one of this country's most diverse ethnic and cultural centers. The perspective that emerged from their collective work eventually became known as the Chicago School of sociology. Significant contributors to this school of thought were George Herbert Mead, who theorized about *meaning*, John Dewey, concerned with the creation and maintenance of publics, and Robert Park, who focused on the role of news. The Chicago School pioneered in the application of ethnographic methods, borrowed from anthropological work undertaken in primitive tribal societies, to urban settings. It shared in the pragmatism that was considered a hallmark of American culture, and was less concerned with *effects* than with the maintenance of society. It was, in effect, the American equivalent of the Frankfurt School. One member's (Mead's) work became the root of the intellectual tradition known as symbolic interactionism (see Blumer, 1969). The Chicago School also influenced the perspective (along with that of Kenneth Burke) of Hugh Dalziel Duncan, a later sociologist who applied the ideas more specifically in a communication context (see Duncan, 1968, 1969).

On the second front, concerned with technology, the work of Lewis Mumford (an American) and Harold A. Innis (a Canadian) are crucial. Mumford, who wrote some 30 books over his career, explained the role of technology in history, and particularly the development of cities through the application of technologies. In a series of works beginning with *Technics and Civilization* in 1934, he began to characterize historical periods "in terms of their dominant inventions and sources of power or energy" (Carey, 1979, p. 21). Innis, who initiated his theoretical work by examining the role of the fur trade and the Canadian Pacific Railway in Canadian history, eventually extended the perspective developed there (the "staple theory") more generally to the relationship between communications technology and the extension and maintenance of empire. Innis, whose field was actually economics, studied at the University of Chicago with members of the Chicago School, and was the mentor of Marshall McLuhan, probably the most popular media theorist of the 1960s. Innis' perspective was that communications technologies most strongly influenced the nature of social organization and the distribution and maintenance of political and economic power, while McLuhan was concerned more with the organization of sensory experience that resulted from the application of communications.

Theorists in both Europe and North America obviously confronted a variety of issues, as these brief explanations should indicate. Both traditions emerged from the peculiar historical circumstances with which the theorists grappled. Part of the reason that the perspectives seem so different is that European and North American history has differed. The problems to be explained, and the resultant theories that attempted to do so differed as well.

Europeans inhabited a linguistically fragmented landscape that had reconstituted itself after centuries of feudalism. Many of the feudal inequalities remained, however, even after the introduction of capitalism and the rise of mercantilism. Karl Marx, Friedrich Engels, and Vladimir Lenin offered explanations for such inequalities, and for the role of communication in perpetuating them. The final break-up of the European empires in the aftermath of World War I, the resultant struggles between political parties within countries to cope with economic hardship, the failure of the organized church to explain adequately the carnage of the war and appropriate responses to it, the resurgence of nationalism and the rapid spread of propaganda as a tool for heightening national consciousness, all contributed to a volatile context for the development of mass communication theory in the 1920s and 1930s.

In North America the imperatives differed. Both Canada and the United States covered large land masses, and were populated by emigrants often eager to leave behind the squabbles of Europe. The taming of the continent was still underway as mass communication systems began, and the messianic promise of the telegraph, telephone, wireless, and radio impressed itself on the rhetoric both of politicians eager to encourage geographic expansion and increasing population, or to exploit populism, and of businessmen and entrepreneurs eager to sell increasing quantities of goods for profit. Even the obvious differences that split peoples into separate groups (such as race) were often subsumed under the messianic expectations of these technologies. Many of the squabbles that erupted in the communications arena concerned the usurpation of these expectations by greed, monopoly, and frivolity. There was always room, however, to worry about the results of taking entertainment media into the home—with the consequent emphasis on behavioral effects—and to look at the potential of communications to help forge a common identity from disparate ethnic elements in these societies.

REPRESENTATIVE THEORETICAL CONSTRUCTS
FOR MASS COMMUNICATION

This rather lengthy (although cursory) introduction to the problem of mass communication theory is meant to indicate the complexity of issues that theorists have attempted to explain. The remainder of this chapter concentrates on representative constructs, and particularly on their ontological and epistemological roots. This will allow the major disputes in the intellectual tradition of mass communication theory to emerge in the discussion.

A useful starting point for considering theoretical constructs is to admit that each of the various theories that people have suggested as means to organize knowledge about mass communication constitute ways of knowing communication itself. That is, each theory suggests a path we may follow to understand mass communication. Each path will follow a different route—provide a different map of the reality of mass communication—but each claims to end in the same place: explanation of this phenomenon. The maps, however, do not actually lead to the same destination, despite their claims. The reason for this is that the *maze* they attempt to solve begins with differing assumptions about the essential nature of human beings, of the universe, and of the ultimate (see Chapter 1).

European and North American maps for theorizing about mass communication vary. We have already seen some of the reasons for the differences. There is, however, a final element that helps explain them. That is the nature of *legitimacy* accorded to theories developed within the intellectual environment of the two continents. In Europe mass communication theory must achieve legitimacy within an intellectual environment that has itself been defined by traditions of skepticism, conflicting political ideologies, and idealism. Theories developed within a humanistic framework encompassed by these traditions have achieved prominence. In North America mass communication theory must achieve legitimacy within an intellectual environment defined by traditions of capitalist accommodation, political triumphalism, and behaviorism. A scientific framework responsive to its three traditions has prevailed.

Attributes of the European tradition in mass communication theory include such elements as:

- power relations among the various constituent classes that make up society (social theory);

- the production and legitimation of "texts" by mass media industries, and the role of such texts in perpetuating social inequalities, establishing commonalities, and maintaining traditional methods of discourse within societies (cultural theory); and

- the process of gaining and maintaining political power, propping up the authority of the state, and providing the basis for manipulating people for economic or political ends (critical theory). These are generalizations, of course. They are indicative, however, of the principal issues European mass communication theorists have faced. They reflect, too, the realities of the European situation discussed earlier, and the dynamics of legitimation within these realities.

On the North American side of the Atlantic, the realities were different, and consequently so was the basis of legitimation. Mass communication theory in the United States and Canada largely sought its legitimacy within a social science framework. Some general results for theory-building included:

- an emphasis on psychological responses to mass communication, and consequent attention to individuals in relation to this communication;

- social theory driven by the necessity of aggregating individual responses to mass communication in heterogenous societies, and consequent attention to public opinion formation and maintenance by democratically elected assemblies;

- the development of "ritual theory" applied to mass communication, based in the greater legitimacy accorded to religious experience.

- attention to the systemic development of mass communication, with consequent emphasis on socialization, legitimation, and control through such systems. Again, however, these are generalizations.

Examination of the theoretical perspectives developed on both sides of the Atlantic indicates, too, that cross-fertilization frequently occurred. Cultural and critical theory from Europe has affected theory-building in the United States and Canada; anthropological and ritual theory from North America has also found its way into perspectives in Europe. Theorists use catch-words, such as *global village, culture industry*, or pro social effects on both sides of the Atlantic.

EUROPEAN MAPS FOR MASS COMMUNICATION THEORY

Let us return to the metaphor: theory-building as map-making, and take up the construction of maps by European theorists. We begin with the Frankfurt School. Specifically our questions here (as in all theories to follow) are: (a) what are human beings like in communication, and (b) how do we know that our answer to this question is correct? This first question concerns ontology, the second, epistemology.

CRITICAL THEORY

European theorists have maintained what we may call a paradigm of consciousness. They have argued that in communication human beings have developed and maintained a collective consciousness that is perpetuated in and through social interaction. We will use Jürgen Habermas as the example of this theoretical approach (see Habermas, 1973, 1975). Habermas (1984) wrote on this issue:

> If we assume that the human species maintains itself through the socially coordinated activities of its members and that this coordination has to be established through communication—and in certain central spheres through communication aimed at reaching agreement—then the reproduction of the species *also* requires satisfying the conditions of a rationality that is inherent in communicative action. These conditions have become perceptible in the modern period with the decentration of our understanding of the world and the differentiation of various universal validity claims. (p. 397)

Habermas thus emphasizes that (a) human beings maintain themselves by social coordination (b) achieved through communication (c) that is fundamentally rational (i.e., based in the human being's acquisition and use of knowledge), and (d) differentiated (i.e., human beings acquire and use knowledge differently; thus knowledge cannot have universal validity).

As Thomas McCarthy explains,

> Taking Durkheim's analysis of the shift from mechanical to organic solidarity as his point of departure, Habermas examines the process whereby social functions originally fulfilled by ritual practice and religious symbolism gradually shift to the domain of communicative action. This disenchantment means a growing sublimation of the spellbinding and terrifying power of the sacred into the rationally binding/bonding force of criticizable claims to validity. In virtue of this "communicative liquification" of the basic religious consensus, the structures of action oriented to reaching understanding become more and more effective in cultural reproduction, social integration, and personality formation. (Translator's Introduction, Habermas, 1984, p. xxii)

We can see in this explanation the skepticism of the European tradition (here applied to religion), and attention to differentiated social groups and the means of cultural reproduction. Habermas went on to argue that reason, which had originally been a tool of emancipation (since the Enlightenment), had become a tool of oppression and authority as a result of the expansion of bureaucracies (and bureaucratic thinking) and increasingly technological societies (Habermas, 1987, pp. 306–312).

So far as his intellectual roots were concerned, Habermas acknowledged that they extended to Kant and Marx (who, he said, provided philosophical intentions that could be made "scientifically fruitful"). He also noted (referring to both

American and European sociologists) that his work took seriously the perspectives of Weber, Mead, Durkheim, and Talcott Parsons (Habermas, 1984, p. xi).

The epistemological *proof* of Habermas' assertions can be seen in the nature of Europe's fragmentation itself. Europe was, in fact, an archetype of differentiated social organizations, nationally-based monopoly cultural industries, and co-opted religious institutions. It had also been a continent beset with alternative politically-inspired discursive constructs (communism, socialism, fascism and nazism being the most prominent), each of which claimed knowledge that would serve as the basis for a new translational solidarity. Such discursive constructs also seemed to certify the epistemological accuracy of the emphasis on bureaucratization. Each developing construct sought legitimacy through bureaucratic means: establishing political parties, controlling the means of communication, adopting cultural expressions that claimed historical roots, and denying the validity of alternative constructs.

CULTURAL THEORY

A second European theoretical tradition emerged from Great Britain and can be seen in the work of scholars such as Richard Hoggart, Stuart Hall, and Raymond Williams, who will serve as the exemplar. This tradition, which we call the *cultural studies perspective*, shares some elements with the Frankfurt School. These elements would include the emphasis on socially differentiated knowledge (particularly class-based knowledge), and skepticism about the *power of the sacred*. The British cultural studies perspective is differentiated, however, by its attention to the production and consumption of texts, particularly printed texts—novels, essays, and newspapers, and the impacts on production by the industrial revolution, and on consumption by the development of transnational production styles (Hoggart, 1986). Stuart Hall, working out of the Birmingham Centre for Contemporary Cultural Studies, contributed to this perspective, too, emphasizing an "encoding/decoding" model for audience/mass communication interaction. This model acknowledged that mass communication is a structured activity, and involves active viewers (see Morley, 1989, p. 17).

Raymond Williams was concerned about the significance of the development of differing styles of writing and their portrayals of "reality," but also about the cultural changes wrought by new means of communication. One specific issue he addressed provides the basis for establishing the ontological perspective employed. Williams, discussing the idea of mass communication—particularly the idea of *masses* itself—suggests that we could view the masses (aggregated audiences) as rational beings speaking our language, or interested beings sharing our common experience. Too often, Williams says, we use the approach suggesting that the mass is a "mob: gullible, fickle, herdlike, low in taste and habit." The difference in approach, he continues, is the result of our intention in communicating. "If our purpose is art, education, the giving of information or opinion, our interpretation will be in terms of the rational and interested being. If, on the other hand, our purpose is manipulation—the persuasion of a large number of people to act, feel, think, know, in certain ways—the convenient formula will be that of the masses" (Williams, 1987, p. 303).

Williams wonders why people accept roles as agents for producing such "mass" communication, separating themselves from the convictions of the source, and making the audience an object for manipulation. The problem with such roles, he says, is that, "Any practical denial of the relation between conviction and communication, between experience and expression, is morally damaging alike to the individual and to the common language" (Williams, 1987, p. 304). The operations of such "agents," he says, suggests that society itself has "ratified . . . a conception of society which relegates the majority of its members to mob-status" (Williams, 1987, p. 304).

Williams (1987) thus critiques what we may call the ontology of mass society, and the mass communication that functions within it. His own ontological view, however, is to deny legitimacy to such a society or its communication. He argues that "any real theory of communication is a theory of community." The techniques of the mass society and its communication, he says, are irrelevant to a "genuine" theory of communication (p. 313). This genuine communication, functioning in the interests of community creation and maintenance, provides the basis for a common experience, a shared community culture (p. 317).

Williams recognizes the inequalities that exist in society that make communication difficult, and shares some of the perspective of British cultural critics who preceded him, such as Mathew Arnold, John Ruskin, William Morris, and T. S. Eliot. These critics were concerned with preserving the best intellectual and imaginative work as the basis of culture. Williams (1987) also embraces a more anthropological understanding of culture, however, defining a culture not only in terms of its intellectual and imaginative work, but also as a whole way of life. This second conception, he says, is the crucial one in understanding differing class cultures (p. 325).

Like Habermas, Williams emphasizes the role of human beings in maintaining society through coordination, although he emphasizes the cultural dimensions of this coordination rather than its social. Williams is also less interested in the institution building process based in bureaucratization emphasized by Habermas, but is concerned with institutionalization of cultural forms and the assumptions about cultural consumption that inform the production of such forms. He argues for a position of centrality for communication as the means by which cultures are produced and maintained, but regards the moral dimensions of the communication/culture relationship as crucial, rather than their rational (or knowledge-based) dimensions. He, too, denies the universal validity of knowledge (or cultural forms), but emphasizes the role of differentiated communities in interpreting and using knowledge created by others.

The validity of this approach to communication rests on two foundations: texts and classes. Analysis of texts had a long history in Britain. By the 1950s so much analysis had been performed that their "meaning" was well known. Their significance was such that, even when an entirely new form of communication—radio—was introduced, the struggle that ensued over control of its texts was fought on old battlegrounds (see LeMahieu, 1988, and Shiach, 1989). The existence of class interests in Britain is also an unquestioned assumption. Basing analysis of culture in class terms, then, is, if not unassailable, at least a formidable design.

SEMIOTIC THEORY

French theorists provided a third important theoretical European perspective on mass communication. Like the British cultural studies tradition, the semiotic approach concerned itself with texts. Like Williams, semioticians concerned themselves with intention in communication. The differences, however, were more important than the similarities.

Semiotic theorists largely confined themselves to considering the production of texts (common language used in conversation, films, etc.), believing that their symbolic structure, based in the intentions of the producer, would be read by audiences as the author(s) intended. The audience was thus relegated to a subsidiary and largely passive role in communication. Meaning was found in the texts themselves, the intentions of the author(s) deduced from universal signs discovered in textual analysis, and the response of the audience assumed to follow from the included signs.

The father of semiotics was Ferdinand de Saussure, the Swiss linguist who taught both in Paris and Geneva. It was not his scholarship that attracted the interest of mass communication theorists, but a reconstruction of his theory as taught in three courses in Geneva from students' notes and his own fragmentary notes. The work that resulted, *Course in General Linguistics*, influenced theorists, particularly French theorists at first (since it was published in French), concerned with film *texts*. What emerged from the application of Saussure's theory to such texts was a *grammar* of film.

This grammar of film was based in Saussure's notion of a law of signs. Signs, Saussure said, were the unions of "signifiers," or sound images (a form that signifies), and what is "signified," that is, concepts (or ideas) (See Culler, 1986, p. 28). Signs, he argued, were arbitrary, "that . . . is unmotivated, i.e. arbitrary in that it actually has no natural connection with the signified" (i.e., words have no obvious, logical or necessary relationship to what they signify) (Saussure, 1959, p. 69).

Saussure's based his theory in the comparative study of languages. By age fifteen he knew French, German, English, Latin, and Greek, studied Indo-European languages, and taught Sanskrit in Paris. His attention to linguistic laws fit within the French intellectual tradition of codifying language begun by Diderot with the creation of the *Grande Encyclopedia* in the 18th century.

Two important aspects of Saussure's theory concern us here. First, it was based in recognition that people within societies (those "linked together by speech") would "reproduce—not exactly of course, but approximately—the same signs united with the same concepts" (Saussure, 1959, p. 13). In other words, the end-units of a language, its signs, were based in societies of sign-using people who would come to use them to express common (or shared) concepts. Second, the signifiers of a language were fixed within the linguistic community. As Saussure (1959) put it,

> The masses have no voice in the matter, and the signifier chosen by language could be replaced by no other. . . . No individual, even if he willed it, could modify in any way at all the choice that has been made; and what is more, the community itself cannot control so much as a single word; it is bound to the existing language (p. 71)

Saussure pursued this lack of voice in another respect, too. He explained that "syntagmatic solidarities" operated, that is, "almost all units of language depend on what surrounds them in the spoken chain or on their successive parts" (p. 127). Signs, then, function within contexts; words function within sentences with their legitimate syntax. From Saussure's perspective, this context is social, fixed, and syntagmatic.

This linguistic theory was extended to film by both French and Italian theorists. Principal among them were Roland Barthes and Christian Metz. Other theorists include Umberto Eco and Pier Paolo Pasolini (see Wollen, 1969, Chapter 3). Like language, scholars have seen film as composed of signs whose relationships are fixed, both by the social context within which the film was produced, and by the syntactic context, or succession of signs, included within the film. This approach concentrates on the text, assuming meaning is lodged within it, even while suggesting that this meaning is grounded in the social (or human) context of the film's birth. This grounding, however, is made tenuous from an ontological perspective by the insistence of near-inevitability in the signifier-signified relationship expressed by the signs used (trivializing the audience's decoding activity). The epistemological grounding of this perspective is also grounded in the text, which sometimes seems to leave the *human* components of the theory in a peripheral position.

This was not, however, what semioticians intended. Despite the attention to the structures inhibiting individual interpretation, semioticians have also attempted to emphasize the creation of meaning by both coders (text creators) and decoders (text readers). The creation of meaning is thus to be seen as a process of negotiation between coder and decoder through the medium of the text (Fiske, 1982, p. 49).

On this side of the Atlantic Charles Sanders Peirce has been the principal scholar of semiotics, but his influence has been far more limited, largely because his work, which was contemporary with Saussure's, remained largely unpublished for 20 or more years after his death in 1914. Peirce's approach to semiotics was more comprehensive than Saussure's, but it still remains largely unexploited.

NORTH AMERICAN MAPS FOR MASS COMMUNICATION THEORY

If the contribution of European theorists can be distilled to a concern with contexts of various kinds (e.g., social, cultural, structural), that of North American theorists should be seen largely as concerned with individual behavior or with communication systems. We find the psychological foundations of the first "map" in behaviorism, particularly the work of B. F. Skinner. We find the foundations of the second in the social theories of the Chicago School of sociology, and in anthropology, especially in ritual theory. Each of the approaches, like those of the European perspectives, has a peculiar ontological perspective, and epistemological justification.

BEHAVIORAL THEORY

The most peculiar identifying characteristic of behaviorism is its insistence that it is actions—what people do—that is crucial to understanding individuals. Behaviorists are not concerned with what is often referred to as the "black box" of the human mind, the disaggregation of motives, beliefs, values, and opinions, but with behavior itself. They thus claim to practice a "value-free" social science on the model of the physical sciences.

Skinner (1974) explained the essence of what he called "radical behaviorism" as follows:

> What is felt or introspectively observed is not some nonphysical world of consciousness, mind, or mental life but the observer's own body. This does not mean ... that introspection is a kind of physiological research, nor does it mean (and this is the heart of the argument) that what are felt or introspectively observed are the causes of behavior. An organism behaves as it does because of its current structure, but most of this is out of reach of introspection. At the moment we must content ourselves, as the methodological behaviorist insists, with a person's genetic and environmental histories. What are introspectively observed are certain collateral products of those histories. (p. 15)

Skinner did not deny the existence of internal processes (e.g., thinking, feeling, valuing), but argued that such internal processes could not be observed (except introspectively). Therefore, the psychologist had to "content" himself with studying people's "genetic and environmental histories."

This perspective resulted in the creation of what we call the stimulus-response theory of communication. Under this perspective, the products of mass communication (e.g., radio and television programs, films, comic books, etc.) are stimuli of behavior. The nature or quality of the stimuli can be manipulated to determine the effects on various populations. The internal processing and intellectual or emotional response to the stimuli are unobservable and must be ignored.

The ontological assumptions of behaviorism (or stimulus-response based communication theory) suggest that we can understand human beings by observing externals—what they do in response to various environmental stimuli. People may thus be more passive than active in achieving their destiny; they are manipulable animals responsive to constructed media stimuli. Behaviorism, too, focuses on the actions of individuals, and suggests that social organization or behavior is the aggregation of the behaviors of individuals responding to environmental stimuli. Changing the stimuli will alter individual behavior, and ultimately, through reward and punishment of individual behavior, the aggregate—social behavior.

This perspective has influenced an immense amount of mass communication research, particularly in the United States. Even that research that has not been ostensibly shaped by this perspective has been influenced by it, partially as a result of the commercial orientation of U.S. media and the demands of both advertising and media communities.

Another influence has been the nature of the U.S. political system. Here the influence has been two-fold. First, and most apparent, has been the question of effectiveness in reaching and influencing the U.S. electorate. Politicians obviously are interested in (re)election. Second, and somewhat less evident, has been the necessity of creating defensible public policy in response to citizen concerns about the influence of the media. These concerns has been varied. They have ranged from anxieties about advertising for dangerous products (cigarettes being the plainest example), to those about political exploitation (negative political advertising), children's behavior (particularly aggression and violence as a function of watching television), urban riots (especially after the 1966–1967 conflagrations in Newark and Detroit) and treatment of women, African Americans, homosexuals and other groups as a consequence of their portrayals by the media.[2]

Such concerns have also spurred a large number of other research studies. They have focused on, among other things, the role of the media in influencing voters'

---

[2]The number of government-funded studies on such issues is enormous. Examples include the National Advisory Commission on Civil Disorder (1967–1968), the National Commission on the Causes and Prevention of Violence (1968–1969), the Surgeon General's Scientific Advisory Committee on Television and Social Behavior (1969–1972), and the Attorney General's Commission on Pornography (1988). See Rowland (1983).

decisions, the bias of the press in political campaign coverage, the influence of political advertising, the importance of the media in setting the agenda for public policy deliberation or political decision-making (illustrative examples of this enormous body of work would include Lazarsfeld, Berelson & Gaudet, 1948; Katz & Lazarsfeld, 1955; Klapper, 1960; Schramm, 1960; McGinnis, 1969; Schramm & Roberts, 1971; Patterson, 1980; Iyengar & Kinder, 1987.)

Such studies are not single-minded in their approach to these topics. They do actually demonstrate a broad diversity in their specific theoretical perspective. Some demonstrate the classic stimulus-response approach; others have developed various strains in this empirically based theory: massive effects, limited effects, one-step, two-step, and multistep flow models, agenda-setting, uses and gratifications. All, however, have their starting point in the behavioral perspective, even when criticizing its ontological basis.

We find the epistemological focus of such theories of mediated communication in their efforts to construct laws of human behavior. The value of such laws would be in their ability to predict behavior based on study of specific content (say, political information during a campaign) and to inform clients (political candidates or advertisers) concerning the most powerful types of information to use, salient themes or issues to stress, or media mix to employ to achieve the desired results (votes or sales).

RITUAL THEORY

Just as behaviorally based theories of mediated communication have emphasized reactive response to media stimuli, ritually based theories have emphasized the process by which people in social groups construct meaning using the content of media. Such theorists have emphasized the affirmation of values and opinions that people achieve by using the media. People do not read the newspaper, as Carey (1989) has argued, primarily to gain information, but to attend a "mass: a situation in which nothing new is learned but in which a view of the world is portrayed and confirmed" (p. 20).

This approach, based in religion, borrows concepts from the Chicago School of sociology, Emile Durkheim (especially *The Elementary Forms of Religious Life*), and anthropology (particularly Clifford Geertz) (see Carey, 1989, pp. 19–23 for other significant influences on this approach). The definition of communication Carey provides perhaps best summarizes the theory and provides the basis of discussing its ontology. "Communication is a symbolic process whereby reality is produced, maintained, repaired and transformed" (Carey, 1989, p. 23).

The notion of communication as a symbolic process implies that what happens in the mind's "black box" is important. That is where we make the connections between "names" and what is "named." Second, Carey's statement also implies a continual and social process, sometimes progressing, sometimes regressing, as reality is formed and shaped among and by members of a society, group, or public. This suggests, of course, active participatory human beings, not targets for messages.

As with other theories already discussed, the epistemological "proof" for this theoretical perspective can be found in the nature of the society wherein it arose. Clearly the "reality" experienced by different groups of Americans (e.g., African Americans, American Indians, Irish or Polish immigrants, and so on) has differed. Their levels of group solidarity have differed, as have their success in being assimilated into the wider society, their self-images, their degrees of co-optation by the society. Yet they have been largely subjected to the same media content. To what, then, should we attribute their differences?

The answer to this question is complex—and beyond the scope of this chapter. This theory suggests, however, that an important aspect of the answer is that people do not approach media content as individuals, but as people tied into a symbolic universe that organizes their daily lives and makes sense of their experience. Epistemologically, the validity of the theory is confirmed by the differences in the society, rather than its similarities.

SYSTEMS THEORY

There are a number of theoretical approaches to communication employing what we may call *systems* theory. They would include such approaches as mathematical theory, cybernetic theory, or even engineering-based systems theory (see, for instance, Shannon & Weaver, 1949; Cherry, 1966; Nevitt, 1982, especially Chapter 3; or Dizard, 1985). The systems theory we shall examine here, however, developed within the work of the Canadian economist, Harold A. Innis, and his student, Marshall McLuhan (see Creighton, 1978, concerning Innis).

Innis' consciousness about communication issues was influenced both by his work at the University of Chicago, and by his own study of the development of Canada. (Influences on Innis can be seen in Innis, 1956.) Innis gradually moved from study of economic subjects—the fur and lumber trade in Canada, and the Canadian Pacific Railway—to the study of empires, and the bias of communication (see Innis, 1951, 1971, 1972).

One of Innis' principal concerns was the development of dependency. His study of Canada led him to see his country's early economic dependency on Great Britain replaced by dependency on the United States. He also saw Canada struggling to remain culturally independent, even as it seemed unable to achieve economic independence. Innis (1952) wrote:

> We are indeed fighting for our lives. The pernicious influence of American advertising reflected especially in the periodical press and the powerful persistent impact of commercialism have been evident in all the ramifications of Canadian

life. The jackals of communications systems are constantly on alert to destroy every vestige of sentiment toward Great Britain holding it of no advantage if it threatens the omnipotence of American commercialism. This is to strike at the heart of cultural life in Canada. (pp. 19–20)

Innis' (1972) study of empires led him to the conclusion that every medium of communication tended "to create monopolies of knowledge to the point that the human spirit breaks through at new levels of society and on the outer fringes. . . ." (p. 117). These monopolies, he wrote, "tended to alternate as they emphasized religion, decentralization, and time, and force, centralization, and space" (Innis, 1972, p. 166). Media of communication were thus space biased (leading to political organization), or time biased (leading to religious organization) (see Innis, 1951, Chapter 2). To Innis, then, the means of communication had significant social consequences. Those that were more permanent (such as stone) tended to favor ecclesiastical systems, with priests in positions of authority. This had been the case, he said, in Egypt. More transportable media (such as parchment, or later, newspapers and radio) were space biased, leading to political and legal organization and, eventually, imperialism—the extension of political authority over space.

What caused the failure of authority, however, was the development of new means of communication. New methods allowed for different monopolies of knowledge to develop; they allowed people to resist authority—particularly if they were far removed from the centers of power. New means of communication allowed the human spirit to break out along the outer fringes of authority.

Innis' systems theory was technology-based. It would be unfair, however, to label him a *technological determinist*, with its ontological implications. Innis believed in the creative human spirit, but also in the limitations that could be imposed on that spirit by technology exercised by authority. He demanded that we recognize that technology was not benign—that its bias led to its use for particular ends. However, he did not despair at the determinism that seemed to result from the analysis, because he saw many examples of the ability of people to break the centralized monopolies' control. He even made a plea for time-biased media in *The Bias of Communication*. Ontologically, then, Innis recognized the tension between technology and its application in society (leading to control), and the human spirit that sought to reach its full and unfettered potential.

Innis' method of analysis was fundamentally comparative. The societies he examined spanned the centuries, from the ancient kingdoms of Babylon and Egypt, through Germany's Third Reich. He also examined multiple technologies, from parchment and stone tablets, to the newspaper, telegraph, and radio. The epistemological basis of his method was thus comparison and the search for patterns, and the willingness to examine any society to determine the validity of this method.

Marshall McLuhan, who studied under Innis, developed an alternative systems theory. While his basic perspective was Innis inspired (McLuhan said his own book, *The Gutenberg Galaxy*, was a "footnote to the observations of Innis on the subject of psychic and social consequences"), McLuhan also brought a perspective as a literary critic to bear on his systemic analysis (see McLuhan's "Introduction" cited in Innis, 1951, p. ix). This perspective had two implications for his analysis. First, part of his writing itself took the form of poetry, using anecdote or aphorism to *prove* his point. His method was as much literary as *scientific*. Second, his textual orientation led him to a greater concern with the relationship between human beings and technology that mirrored the relationship between people and texts.

McLuhan's (1964) conclusion about humanity and technology was that,

> we have extended our central nervous system itself in a global embrace, abolishing both space and time as far as our planet is concerned. Rapidly, we approach the final phase of the extensions of man—the technological simulation of consciousness, when the creative process of knowing will be collectively and corporately extended to the whole of human society, much as we have already extended our senses and our nerves by the various media. (pp. 3–4)

Clearly Innis and McLuhan differed ontologically. While Innis concerned himself with the tension between technological extensions (and their consequent monopolies of knowledge, bias, and preference for particular forms of social/political organization), McLuhan made what we may call anthropomorphic claims, attaching human characteristics to technology (technologies, he said, extended human capability: the wheel extended the leg, television the eye, and so on). There was no tension, there was co-optation, or synthesis. Ontologically this statement implied a superior position for media or technology to humankind. This position, too, implied a tension, although one quite different than what Innis suggested. The ontological tension in McLuhan's claim was that, while human capability was the basis for its own extension through technology, this capability was surpassed: technology was meta-human. This was, in fact, technological determinism.

Beyond this, too, was McLuhan's (1964) famous assertion that, "the medium is the message" (p. 7). What he meant by that statement was that "the personal and social consequences of any medium—that is, of any extension of ourselves—result from the new scale that is introduced into our affairs by each extension of ourselves, or by any new technology" (p. 7; see also p. 21). The ontological implications of this remark concerned the relative importance of textual creators vis-à-vis the medium. Clearly the creators did not matter. As Ben Lieberman put it, McLuhan rejected completely "any role for the content of communication," discarding "the power of ideas, of values, of emotions, of cumulative wisdom—to say nothing of the hard facts of geography, economics, politics, and the human glory and tragedy of life and death" (cited in Stearn, 1967, pp. 223–224). In other words, technology's power surpassed that of human creation itself.

The most problematic element of McLuhan's assertions is the issue of epistemology. How do we know that what we think we know is true—from McLuhan's theoretical position? That is precisely where criticism of McLuhan begins. Yet there is no happy answer. Nevertheless, this has not caused rejection of McLuhan's claims. He continues to have both detractors and disciples. He remains one of the most influential, and most villified, of all media theorists.

SYNTHESIS IN MEDIA THEORY

The theories discussed here do not begin to exhaust the possibilities suggested for understanding media. We have but touched on the work of the Chicago School, and have left untouched the symbolic perspective represented by Ernst Cassirer and Susan Langer, the structuralism of Roland Barthes or Michael Foucault, Herbert Blumer's symbolic interactionism, Aflred Schutz's phenomenology, dramatism and social symbolization in the work of Kenneth Burke and Hugh Dalziel Duncan, psychoanalytic or feminist perspectives, Walter Ong's concern with "orality and literacy," or even the semiotic position of Charles Peirce. We could double this chapter and still not do justice to mediated theory. Those discussed, however, are representative of the breadth of perspective brought to bear on this ubiquitous form of communication in the effort to make sense of it.

There are two last perspectives, however, that provide useful closure to this abbreviated survey of mediated theory, and particularly to our emphasis on ontological and epistemological roots. Each represents a revision, or synthesis, of perspectives. Neither theory, however, is the last word in mediated theory; there are still many contradictions in both assumption and method to reconcile before some magical last word will emerge.

The first synthesis telescopes semiotic, audience, and social structural perspectives into a common effort to determine "how groups of people generate and reproduce cultural meaning" (Borchers, 1989, p. x). This synthesis is still in its formative stages, but offers possibly rich means of explaining at least some aspects of the mediated communication experience. Perhaps the best articulation of this developing perspective is included in an essay by David Morley. Morley is concerned about the use of texts within the "discursive formation of specific societies," within their symbolic universes. It is at the intersection of text and such discursive formations (universes of discourse) that "interpellation" occurs. Using Stuart Hall's work, Morley (1989) then suggests that recognizing the role of these universes of discourse to interpellate texts moves:

> away from the assumption that every specific reading [of a text] is already determined by the primary structure of subject positions and to insist that these interpellations are not given and absolute, but rather, are conditional and provisional, in so far as the struggle in ideology takes place through the articulation/disarticulation of interpellations. This is to lay stress on the possibility of contradictory

interpellations and to emphasize the unstable, provisional, and dynamic properties of subject positioning. It is also to recognize that subjects have histories and that past interpellations affect present ones, rather than to "deduce" subjects from the subject positions offered by the text and to argue that readers are not merely bearers or puppets of their unconscious positions. It is to insist . . . on the "mulitaccentuality of the sign" which makes it possible for discourse to become an arena of struggle. (p. 20)

This rather abstruse prose is rooted in Saussure's semiotic theory, but recognizes an active interpreting audience functioning within a specific social context. Text producers, signs in the text, audiences functioning within universes of discourse, and socio-cultural and historical structures all have roles to play in negotiating the meaning that will eventually emerge within a given context. Ontologically this approach is richer than any of these single perspectives alone, and the theory moves us one step forward. Other authors represented in *Remote Control* take different positions, and adopt a variety of methodologies to study mediated texts—principally television soap operas. We would have to judge epistemological certainty on a case by case basis. Morley's essay, for instance, depends on logical and ideological constructs to provide its epistemological foundation.

The second synthesis combines perspectives gained from Erving Goffman and Marshall McLuhan. It suggests "that the mechanism through which electronic media affect social behavior is not a mystical sensory balance, but a very discernible rearrangement of the social stages on which we play our roles and a resulting change in our sense of 'appropriate behavior' " (Meyrowitz, 1985, p. 4). Meyrowitz says that he had been influenced by Goffman's insistence that social life was a "kind of multistaged drama in which we each perform different roles in different social arenas, depending on the nature of the situation, our particular role in it, and the makeup of the audience" (p. 2). What he picked up from McLuhan, he remarks, was the idea that media extend the senses, and that the introduction of a new medium of communication into a culture would change its "sensory balance," thus altering people's consciousness. "But McLuhan," Meyrowitz says, "offers few specific clues as to why people with different sensory balances behave differently" (p. 3). Meyrowitz uses Goffman to illuminate McLuhan, and McLuhan to extend Goffman (for instance, see Goffman, 1967, 1969).

What Meyrowitz (1985) is concerned with is thus "situational geography," and the practices that occur within places/situations. The title of his book, *No Sense of Place*, implies his conclusion: that electronic media have "undermined the traditional relationship between physical setting and social situation" (p. 7).

Meyrowitz both defends and criticizes McLuhan. He admits that McLuhan lacks "a clear set of propositions to explain the means through which media reshape specific behaviors," and says that what is missing "is any real attempt to link an analysis of media characteristics with an analysis of the structure and dynamics of everyday social interaction" (pp. 22–23). Goffman's work serves as the basis for establishing this link.

In Meyrowitz's analysis, however, Goffman needs McLuhan, too. The situation model, Meyrowitz says, is static and descriptive, and needs to be variable and predictive. Media, he continues, have changed the nature of the boundary line that separates one situation from another. Instead of static physical boundaries, media have created fluid and dynamic ones. Media create new events and new behaviors as a consequence (see Meyrowitz, 1985, pp. 42–43).

Meyrowitz uses Goffman's notion of "frontstage" and "backstage" behavior to argue for a new situational definition. Frontstage behavior is that, Goffman says, that occurs for public consumption; backstage is what occurs before a more limited audience, or in private. What media create, Meyrowitz says, is "middle region" behavior, a merging of these separate concepts. Media reveal backstage behavior to those for whom it was not intended: the behavior of parents to children, of men to women, of political "heroes" to citizens. The boundaries between adulthood and childhood, masculinity and femininity, high and low status, are blurred. Media destroy unique places that contained specific behaviors; they create the basis for new group identities. Television "reveals the simple humanity, the ordinariness of almost everyone it 'exposes' to an audience" (Meyrowitz, 1985, p. 155). What happens is that "Electronic media ... bypass the isolating characteristics of place and thereby blur the differences between people at different stages of socialization and between people in different socialization processes" (p. 157).

Meyrowitz's perspective takes seriously the role of electronic media, but also the nature of texts. It highlights the struggles of people coping with media, too, but takes their struggles seriously, and does not suggest that they are powerless. Rather the implication is that as people come to understand the nature of the new boundary lines drawn by the media between social situations, they will alter their behaviors. People are neither totally in control, nor totally at the mercy of either media or messages.

The ontological value of Meyrowitz's argument is that several significant aspects of media experience are accorded value. He neither belittles humankind nor makes technology out to be an irresistible behemoth. His focus is on the conduct of everyday life, and the difficulties raised by technology for such conduct. Although Meyrowitz provides several case studies to demonstrate the workings of his theory, the epistemological validity of his assertions is still open to question. It, like its contemporary synthesis, still requires additional demonstration and testing.

CONCLUSIONS

There is no single map to understanding mediated communication. Several significant realities have influenced the construction of a variety of available maps. These include both physical and mental realities, ranging from geography to ideology, with particular emphasis on national identities and intellectual traditions. It is the variety of media experiences, too, that have influenced the construction of theory, since the control and use of media in both Europe and North America varies nearly as much as the linguistic or national landscape.

An important obstacle to achieving any unified theory to explain mediated communication is the differing assumptions about the nature of man, of knowledge, of appropriate methods to study this phenomenon, of validity in applying these methods. It is unlikely that we shall achieve a single understanding of the working of mediated communication, since it is unlikely that we will ever agree to common assumptions on these important issues.

REFERENCES

Arato, A., & Gebhardt, E. (Eds.). (1982). *The essential Frankfurt school reader.* New York: Continuum.

Benjamin, W. (1968). The work of art in the age of mechanical reproduction. *Illuminations.* New York: Harcourt, Brace and World.

Blumer, H. (1969). *Symbolic interactionism: Perspective and Method.* Englewood Cliffs, NJ: Prentice-Hall.

Borchers, H. (1989). Preface. *Remote control: Television, audiences and cultural power.* In E. Seiter, H. Borchers, G. Kreutzner, & E. Warth (Eds.). London: Routledge.

Carey, J. (1979). *The roots of modern media analysis: Lewis Mumford and Marshall McLuhan.* Paper presented at the annual conference, Association for Education in Journalism, Houston, TX.

Carey, J. (1989). *Communication as culture: Essay on media and society.* Boston, MA: Unwin Hyman.

Carey, J., & Quirk, J. (1970a). The mythos of the electronic revolution. *The American Scholar, 39,* 219–241.

Carey, J., & Quirk, J. (1970b). The mythos of the electronic revolution. *The American Scholar, 39,* 395–424.

Cherry, C. (1966). *On human communication: A review, a survey and a criticism* (2nd ed.). Cambridge, MA: MIT Press.

Creighton, D. (1978). *Harold Adams Innis: Portrait of a scholar.* Toronto, Canada: University of Toronto Press.

Culler, J. (1986). *Ferdinand de Saussure* (Rev. ed.). Ithaca, NY: Cornell University Press.

DeFleur, M., & Ball-Rokeach, S. (1989). *Theories of mass communication* (5th ed.). New York: Longman.

Dizard, W. (1985). *The coming information age: An overview of technology, economics and politics* (2nd ed.). New York: Longman.

Duncan, H. (1968). *Symbols in society.* New York: Oxford University Press.

Duncan, H. (1969). *Symbols and social theory.* New York: Oxford University Press.

Durkheim, E. (1964). *The division of labor in society.* G. Simpson (Trans.). New York: Free Press.

Fiske, J. (1982). *Introduction to communication studies.* London, England: Methuen.

Fortner, R. (1978). *Messiahs and monopolists: A cultural history of Canadian communication development 1846–1914.* Unpublished doctoral dissertation, Urbana, IL.

Fortner, R. S. (1993). *International communication: History, conflict and control of the global metropolis.* Belmont, CA: Wadsworth.

Freire, P. (1970). *Pedagogy of the oppressed.* New York: Seabury Press.

Freire, P. (1973). *Education for critical consciousness.* New York: Seabury Press.

Goffman, E. (1967). *Interaction ritual: Essay on face-to-face behavior.* Garden City, New York: Anchor Books.

Goffman, E. (1969). *Strategic interaction.* Philadelphia, PA: University of Pennsylvania Press.

Habermas, J. (1973). *Theory and practice.* Boston, MA: Beacon Press.

Habermas, J. (1975). *Legitimation crisis.* Boston, MA: Beacon Press.

Habermas, J. (1984). *The theory of communicative action (Vol. 1.): Reasons and the rationalization of society* (Thomas McCarthy, Trans.). Boston, MA: Beacon Press.

Habermas, J. (1987). *The theory of communicative action (Vol. 2.): The critique of functionalist reason* (Thomas McCarthy, Trans.). Boston, MA: Beacon Press.

Hardt, H. (1979). *Social theories of the press: Early German and American perspectives.* Newbury Park, CA: Sage.

Held, D. (1980). *Introduction to critical theory: Horkheimer to Habermas.* Berkeley, CA: University of California Press.

Hoggart, R. (1986). *The uses of literacy: Aspects of working class life with special reference to publications and entertainments.* Cambridge, MA: Polity Press.

Horkheimer, M. (1972). *Critical theory.* M. J. O'Connell (Trans.). New York: Herder and Herder.

Hovland, C., Lumsdaine, A., & Sheffield, F. (1949). *Experiments in mass communication.* Princeton, NJ: Princeton University Press.

Innis, H. (1951). *The bias of Communication.* Toronto, Canada: University of Toronto Press.

Innis, H. (1952). *The strategy of culture.* Toronto, Canada: University of Toronto Press.

Innis, H. (1956). *Essay in Canadian economic history.* Edited by Mary Q. Innis. Toronto, Canada: University of Toronto Press.

Innis, H. (1971). *A history of the Canadian Pacific Railway.* Toronto, Canada: University of Toronto Press. (First published in 1923)

Innis, H. (1972). *Empire and communications.* Revised by Mary Q. Innis. Toronto, Canada: University of Toronto Press.

Iyengar, S., & Kinder, D. (1987). *News that matters: Television and American opinion.* Chicago, IL: University of Chicago Press.

Katz, E., & Lazarsfeld, P. (1955). *Personal influence: The part played by people in the flow of mass communication.* Glencoe, IL: The Free Press.

Klapper, J. (1960). *The effects of the mass media.* Glencoe, IL: The Free Press.

Lasswell, H. (1936). *Politics: Who gets what, when, how.* Cleveland, OH: World.

Lasswell, H. (1948). The structure and function of communication in society. In L. D. Bryson (Ed.), *The communication of ideas.* New York: Harper.

Lazarsfeld, P. (1941). Remarks on administrative and critical communications research. *Studies in philosophy and social science: Problems of modern mass communication, 9,* 2–16.

Lazarsfeld, P., Berelson, B., & Gaudet, H. (1948). *The people's choice.* New York: Columbia University Press.

LeMahieu, D. (1988). *A culture of democracy: Mass communication and the cultivated mind in Britain between the wars.* Oxford, England: Clarendon Press.

Lippmann, W. (1922). *Public opinion.* New York: The Free Press.

Marcuse, H. (1964). *One dimensional man.* London, England: Sphere Books.

Marx, K., & Engels, F. (1967). *The communist manifesto* (Samuel Moore, Trans.). London: Penguin Books. (This translation first published in 1888.)

McGinnis, J. (1969). *The selling of the President 1968.* New York: Trident Press.

McLuhan, M. (1964). *Understanding media: The extensions of man.* New York: McGraw-Hill.

Meyrowitz, J. (1985). *No sense of place: The impact of electronic media on social behavior.* New York: Oxford University Press.

Morley, D. (1989). Changing paradigms in audience studies. In E. Seiter, H. Borcher, G. Kreutaner, and E. Worth (Eds.), *Remote control: Television, audiences, and cultural power.* London, England: Routledge.

Nevitt, B. (1982). *The communication ecology: Re-presentation versus replica.* Toronto, Canada: Butterworths.

Patterson, T. (1980). *The mass media election: How Americans choose their president.* New York: Praeger.

Rowland, W. (1983). *The politics of TV violence: Policy uses of communication research.* Newbury Park, CA: Sage Publication.

Saussure, F. (1959). *Course in general linguistics.* C. Bally & A. Sechehaye (Eds.), Wade Baskin (Trans.). New York: McGraw-Hill.

Schramm, W. (Ed.). (1960). *Mass communications* (2nd ed.). Urbana, IL: University of Illinois Press.

Schramm, W., & Roberts, D. (Eds.). (1971). *The process and effects of mass communication* (Rev. ed.), Urbana, IL: University of Illinois Press.

Schultze, Q. (1987). The mythos of the electronic church. *Critical Studies in Mass Communication, 4,* 245–261.

Shannon, C., & Weaver, W. (1949). *The mathematical theory of communication.* Urbana, IL: University of Illinois Press.

Shiach, M. (1989). *Discourse on popular culture.* Cambridge, MA: Polity Press.

Skinner, B. (1974). *About behaviorism.* New York: Alfred A. Knoph.

Stearn, G. (Ed.). (1967). *McLuhan: Hot and cool.* New York: Signet.

Steele, R. (1980). *Walter Lippmann and American century.* New York: Random House.

Surgeon General's Scientific Advisory Committee. (1972). *Television and growing up: The impact of televised violence.* Washington, DC: USGPO.

Tocqueville, A. D. (1969). *Democracy in America* (George Lawrence, Trans., J. P. Mayer, Ed.). Garden City, NY: Anchor Books. (Originally published in 1830)

Tönnies, F. (1955). *Community and association.* London, England: Routledge and Kegan Paul. (Originally published in 1887)

Vyvyan, R. (1974). *Marconi and wireless.* Yorkshire, England: EP Publishing Limited. (Originally published in 1933)

Weber, M. (1947). *The Protestant ethic and the spirit of capitalism: The theory of social and economic organization.* A. M. Henderson & Talcott Parsons (Eds.), London, England: Oxford University Press.

Williams, R. (1987). *Culture and society: Coleridge to Orwell.* London, England: The Hogarth Press.

Wollen, P. (1969). *Sign and meaning in the cinema.* Bloomington, IN: Indiana University Press.

Chapter 7

Communication in Groups: Research Trends and Theoretical Perspectives

Dennis S. Gouran
Penn State University

Randy Y. Hirokawa
Michael Calvin McGee
Laurie L. Miller
University of Iowa

> *Research on small groups has gotten out of hand! The rate of production of small group studies has increased tremendously in recent decades. At the same time, the rate at which empirical results have been adequately digested and integrated into theoretical formulations has not kept pace. If we continue to generate studies at even the present rate, without a major "leap forward" in terms of integrative theory, we shall drown in our own data.*
> —McGrath and Altman (1966, p. 9)

In 1970, Ernest Bormann published his frequently cited critique of small group research questioning the value of the knowledge being reported and the appropriateness of the methods by which it was being generated. In many respects, he echoed the observations of McGrath and Altman in the foregoing quotation. Although less dramatic in tone than McGrath and Altman, Bormann was nevertheless concerned with what he regarded to be the barrenness of much of the research and an excessive emphasis on statistically sophisticated research designs to explore seemingly trivial questions. Although Bormann appeared, in fact, to be indicting a research tradition that was not unique to small group research, his essay led to a great deal of discussion, further critiques, and efforts to bring sharper focus, as well as clearer direction, to this area of study (e.g., Gouran, 1970, 1973; Larson, 1971; Mortensen, 1970).

Particularly disturbing to these other critics were the lack of attention to discussion content and, perhaps more importantly, the absence of solid theoretical foundations for the sorts of questions being asked and the occasional hypotheses being tested.[1] In the more than 20 years that have passed since Bormann aired his criticisms, research on communication in groups has changed in many ways. In other respects, it has remained subject to some of the original indictments. For the most part, however, developments in the conduct of inquiry that occurred during the 1980s have produced a reasonably coherent and well-founded body of knowledge concerning the functions and evolution of communication in groups. To appreciate the progress that has occurred, one must first understand something of the character of the scholarship that preceded Bormann's critique and the subsequent evolutionary paths it followed through the 1970s and 1980s when clear theoretical perspectives began to emerge.

EARLY DEVELOPMENTS

That observations such as those Bormann and others were making in the early 1970s should arise was almost inevitable in light of two factors. First, prior to 1965, a limited amount of the scholarship about groups produced in communication would qualify as research (Gouran, 1985, pp. 90–92). Most of those writing about group process did so from a pedagogical perspective. Hence, there was not much information to synthesize or to integrate within any theoretical framework. Second, the few scholars actually doing research more often than not modeled their inquiries on work in social psychology and sociology (e.g., Crowell, Katcher, & Myamoto, 1955; Harnack, 1951, 1955; Johnson, 1943; Pyron, 1964; Pyron & Sharp, 1963; Sharp & Milliken, 1964).

Personal, structural, and contextual variables were the foci of these studies. Even with the important work of Robert F. Bales (1950) on interaction analysis, specific characteristics of discussion content were typically of limited interest. Ongoing work in these fields reflected an empiricist bias and was often descriptive in nature. The thinking underlying much of the research was that we could learn about group process by quantifying particular classes of variables and then either examining their intercorrelations or assessing variance attributable to differences in the conditions under which groups performed particular types of tasks. Hence, one finds studies focusing on such relationships as cohesiveness and group productivity (e.g., Schacter, Ellertson, McBride, & Gregory, 1951), leadership style and group member satisfaction (e.g., Lewin, Lippitt, & White, 1939), and size of majority and conformity (e.g., Asch, 1956) dominant in research on groups throughout the period.

Although some of the research on groups in sociology and social psychology was theoretically grounded and relied on experiments to test specific hypotheses,

---

[1] Concern about the absence of theory was by no means restricted to communication studies of group process but encompassed work on groups in such cognate disciplines as social psychology and sociology as well (e.g., McGrath & Altman, 1966, pp. 67–77; Shaw, 1970, pp. 356–364).

a good deal was not. The studies mentioned earlier were either outgrowths of field theory, Kurt Lewin's attempt to apply the thinking and some of the language of physics to the social realm, or principles of general psychology. But even in cases such as these, the underlying theoretical considerations were not about groups or group process as such. They had much more to do with individual behavior that happened to be manifest in group settings.

In choosing work in social psychology and sociology as the model, communication scholars exhibited little inclination to deal with issues central to understanding the role of communication in the types of groups they studied. A notable exception was Edwin Black (1955), who examined interaction sequences in decision-making discussions from a rhetorical perspective to determine the causes of breakdown. Otherwise, as previously mentioned, investigations up to the mid-1960s dealt primarily with personal, structural, and contextual variables, and the interrelationships among them. Studies were largely derivative rather than originative. In addition, the influence of other fields was felt primarily in terms of research design and the selection of variables for study rather than in a reliance on such theories as existed. That influence was not to be felt until sometime later. Perhaps because of the focus on the individual, communication scholars did not see theoretical connections to their own work.

The year 1964 marked the beginning of a new emphasis on the characteristics of communicative exchanges in decision-making and problem-solving groups with the publication of a landmark study of idea development by Scheidel and Crowell (1964). This was followed by research examining sequences of feedback (Scheidel & Crowell, 1966) as well as studies by Geier (1967) on the communicative traits of leaders in task-oriented groups and Berg (1967) on the thematic development of discussion content.

The emphasis on communication evident in this small body of emergent scholarship was reinforced by participants at the Speech Association of America Conference on defining the field held in New Orleans (see Kibler & Barker, 1969). Conferees took the position that the Speech Communication should consider its legitimate domain "the ways in which messages link participants during interactions" (p. 33). The move toward aspects of communicative behavior as a focus of inquiry continued with the publication of articles by Gouran (1969) and Fisher (1970a), both of whom examined the communication/consensus relationship in decision-making groups—albeit from quite different perspectives. Whereas Fisher sought to determine how consensus is reached, Gouran attempted to distinguish groups achieving consensus from those failing to do so in terms of specific communication variables. At the same time, Leathers (1969, 1970) was doing work on the ways in which particular types of utterances affect subsequent patterns of interaction.

By the time most of the previously mentioned critiques appeared, then, the concern about more intensive investigation of communicative behavior had already been addressed in limited ways by several different scholars. In addition, a focus on the context of decision making and problem solving was beginning to emerge. The paucity of theoretically grounded inquiry was to remain a problem for some time to come, however, as empiricist thinking and correlational approaches continued to prevail. Although research was revealing some interesting connections among isolated variables, the logical bases for these relationships were rarely apparent.

THEORETICAL PRECURSORS FROM COGNATE DISCIPLINES

It is difficult to ascertain precisely when the systematic study of group communication began. What appears certain, however, is the fact that the initial impetus *did not* come from communication scholars, per se. Rather, initial theoretical and research interest in group communication originated largely in the fields of social psychology and sociology (Gouran, 1985). Although their influence was general and not to be felt until the late 1970s and early 1980s, three landmark bodies of theory in social psychology and sociology were to help establish and provide the foundation for communication study of group processes: (a) field theory, (b) social exchange theory, and (c) social systems theory. For this reason, we examine each in some detail.

Field Theory

Kurt Lewin is regarded by many as one of the most prominent social psychologists in this century. An emigrant from Nazi Germany in the 1930s, his special interest in the study of individual behavior in group settings led to the development of a theoretical orientation called "field theory," which profoundly influenced the manner in which social scientists studied group processes (Ridgeway, 1985, p. 37).

Lewin's theoretical orientation has its roots in the "Gestalt" school of psychology that emerged in Germany between World War I and II (Deutsch & Krauss, 1965). A defining notion of Gestalt psychology is the belief that people do not experience the world in terms of isolated pieces of information; rather, they organize their environment in terms of systems or "fields" of perceptions and experience (Koffka, 1935).

Lewin (1939, 1947, 1951) applied the concept of field to groups as a whole, and proposed the existence of "psychological fields." The psychological field of a group consists of the objects and persons in the immediate environment that have positive or negative emotional importance (or "valence") to the members of the group. Lewin proposed that groups, and the individuals who comprise them, naturally move toward positively valenced objects in their psychological field, while simultaneously moving away from negatively valenced ones. This movement is not haphazard, but rather reflects attempts to reach desired positions or locations between positively and negatively valenced objects in the group's psychological field. These desired positions represent the goals of the group.

Lewin argued that the goals of a group have a dynamic quality to them. That is, they are constantly changing as group members seek to reach different optimal positions among the positively and negatively valenced objects in their psychological field. Moreover, the goals of a group activate psychological forces that either push group members toward, or away from, particular objects and people in the group's psychological field. These forces cause group members to "locomote" or move around within the group field. The general direction of this locomotion or movement ("vector"), according to Lewin, is the net result of the attraction and repulsion forces in the group field acting on an individual at that time.

Lewin's field theory represented an attempt to apply principles and concepts of physics to the explanation of group behavior, but from a clearly phenomenological perspective. In Lewin's view, behavior always must be interpreted from the perspective of the actor rather than the observer. Despite his insistence that behavior must be understood as it is subjectively experienced, Lewin's epistemology was nevertheless consistent with objectivist thinking and in the tradition of the then prevalent belief in the natural sciences that reality is independent of the observer and ultimately discoverable.

Although some have criticized the abstract and mechanical nature of the theory,[2] it remains clear that many of the underlying assumptions of field theory have exerted a strong influence on the study of particular aspects of group process—most notably, the study of group cohesiveness (Shepherd, 1964). More importantly, however, field theory prompted group researchers to consider group process as the operation of complex sets of interrelated variables. From the Lewinian perspective, no one aspect of group process, for instance, behavior, can be examined and understood apart from its relation to other aspects of the group, such as norms, leadership, task, and so forth (Ridgeway, 1985, p. 39). Insofar as the study of groups in the field of communication is concerned, the principal contribution of Lewin's work was to emphasize the importance of contextual influences on interaction.

Social Exchange Theory

Social exchange theory is widely regarded as one of the more historically significant theoretical approaches to the study of small groups. This body of theory attempted to account for group behavior in a very different manner from field theory. Whereas field theory treated the group as a holistic entity, social exchange theory attempted to account for individual acts in terms of general

---

[2]As a result, the specific details of Lewin's theoretical framework—namely, valence, vector, and locomotion—have not been widely applied in the study of group processes.

principles of reinforcement and elementary economics. From this more atomistic perspective, members of groups emit behaviors that maximize rewards and minimize costs. Behavior also serves as reinforcing stimuli. In short, how a member of a group behaves can be rewarding or costly to one or more other group members. In principle, all directly observable behavior of group members can be accounted for in terms of approach and avoidance tendencies related to one's history of reinforcement in particular interactional environments.

In the language of social exchange theory, a *reward* is an outcome or experience that one finds enjoyable or pleasurable, while a *cost* is an outcome or experience that one finds painful or undesirable. The theory assumes that group members are *profit-seekers* and over time engage in behaviors that produce comparatively more rewards than costs (Homans, 1961). Furthermore, social exchange theory maintains that individuals compare the rewards and costs (profit rate) against those profit rates they could be receiving in order to decide whether or not to alter their behavior or their relationships. According to Thibaut and Kelley (1959), if one's comparison level (the expected level of satisfaction one can derive in a relationship) falls below the comparison level for alternatives, he or she may terminate the existing relationship. This can occur either literally (as when one drops out of a group) or symbolically (as when one refrains from active involvement).

Social exchange theory was very influential in psychological studies of such aspects of group process as leadership emergence, member satisfaction, and social influence (Ridgeway, 1985). It was an outgrowth of the general principles of learning theory as they developed under behaviorism, with its emphasis on the so-called laws of effect and exercise. Behaviorists early on took as their model the Newtonian description of celestial mechanics. Although this body of theory, like field theory before it, has also been criticized on several fronts,[3] the social exchange theory perspective has persisted in psychological explanations of individual behavior in social entities such as the small group (Ridgeway, 1985, p. 42).

Despite its concern with interaction, however, the line of thinking exerted little direct influence on communication research on groups. Its principal contribution would appear to lie in its recognition that interaction in groups is sequential and that any given act, in part, is shaped by what has preceded and also has conse-

---

[3]First, critics argue that social exchange theory miscasts people as rational economic beings guided solely by the desire to seek and maintain profits in interaction. They suggest that people may have other motivations besides profit-seeking (e.g., altruism or obligation). Second, social exchange theory has been criticized for its explicitly reductionistic perspective. That is, it reduces the causes of group behavior to simple individual motivations of profit-seeking, while ignoring a whole host of social, structural, and environmental causes of behavior. Third, it is nonfalsifiable. In particular, critics have suggested that the basic concepts of the theory—rewards, costs, and profit—are so vague that they can easily be interpreted to fit the available data (Turner, 1974). That is to say, any outcome of group interaction can be interpreted as rewarding or cost-provoking depending on the perspective of the investigator. Thus, there is no easy way to test the basic propositions and predictions of the theory.

quences, or implications, for the acts that follow. It further underscored the importance of communication as a source of influence on developments in the relational domain. This gave added credibility to the notion of communication in groups as a continuously evolving process that was to become an object of sustained interest in the 1980s. Finally, it reinforced the view that human behavior is law-governed and no different in that sense from the behavior of other animate and inanimate objects.

Social Systems Theory

Social systems theory, as is similarly true of social exchange theory, cannot be easily attributed to a single originator. However, many have suggested that most of the major insights for this theoretical orientation come from the sociological theories of Talcott Parsons (Ridgeway, 1985). Parsons was interested primarily in societies, but his thinking nevertheless influenced later views of group process (Nixon, 1979, pp. 40–42).

Like field theory, this perspective grew out of the notion that groups are holistic systems characterized by interdependence among their subparts in direct interaction with their social environment. As a social system, the theory maintains that a group must satisfy certain basic *functional prerequisites* (fundamental conditions or requirements) if the system is to remain operational. According to Parsons (see Parsons, Bales, & Shils, 1953), the structure and communicative interaction of a group arises from its continual efforts to satisfy the following needs:

1. *Pattern maintenance:* The establishment and maintenance of a set of attitudes, values, beliefs, and behavioral practices that give a group its distinctive character or identity, and facilitate the group's efforts to meet its goals and objectives.
2. *Adaptation:* The successful removal or management of environmental and situational threats and barriers to effective goal attainment, as well as the effective accumulation of environmental resources needed for goal attainment.
3. *Integration:* The development of rules and procedures for coordinating activities of group members and for achieving a sense of cohesiveness and unity.
4. *Goal attainment:* The development of sufficient organization and control of group behaviors and resources to meet task demands and expectations minimally.

Interestingly, Parsons' thoughts concerning functional prerequisites were applied to the study of group interaction in two different (though not necessarily incompatible) ways. The first approach was taken by Robert Freed Bales (1950, 1953), and the second by George Casper Homans (1950, 1961).

Bales' Approach. Bales simplified Parsons' original view of functional pre-requisites in applying them directly to task-oriented small groups. According to Bales, task groups alternate between (a) *task demands*, which pertain to issues associated with the group's efforts to accomplish its task, and (b) *socioemotional demands*, or a group's efforts to establish effective working relationships among its members. Within his framework, task demands relate to the reduction and satisfaction of needs for adaptation and goal attainment, whereas socioemotional demands lead to the enactment of behaviors aimed at pattern maintenance and integration needs. Bales maintains that there is an inherent tension between the task and socioemotional needs of a group; what groups must do to accomplish their task often works against what the members need to do to maintain positive interpersonal relationships. This creates a situation in which participants experience tensions that necessarily arise in response to conflicting needs. These tensions, in turn, are a source of motivation and prompt acts that aim toward restoration of a balanced state within the system, or what biologists often referred to as homeostasis.

Despite the fact that the task and socioemotional demands of a group are often at odds, Bales argued that a group must minimally satisfy both sets of problems to be effective. Thus, he maintained that successful groups develop a *dynamic equilibrium* in which their attention to task and socioemotional problems alternates on a continual, and often rapid, basis. To achieve the sense of stability such dynamic equilibrium provides, members develop specialized roles that focus on the accomplishment of particular aspects of the task or socioemotional needs of the group. For instance, a group member may assume the role of the group's task leader, while another adopts the role of its social leader. According to Bales, these various roles, and the attention to particular classes of problems, result in the formation of the group's social structure and the development of its patterns of interaction.

This type of mechanistic thinking reflects the same sort of influence that the dominant 19th-century view of lawfulness in the physical sciences had exerted on field theory and social exchange theory. It was not until the impact of work in quantum mechanics was felt that theorists would begin to see such phenomena in a probabilistic light and to turn their attention to the development of stochastic models.

Homans' Approach. Homans agreed with Bales that groups should be analyzed as social systems characterized by interdependent subparts. However, he rejected the view that a group's social structure and interaction patterns are the result of its efforts to satisfy particular prerequisites. Instead, he argued that structure and interaction patterns are a consequence of its efforts to deal with the pressures exerted on the group by its environment. His essential difference with Bales, then, was not ontological or epistemological, but rather the variables that are most critical to understanding what governs the operations of social systems.

Homans maintained that certain conditions a group confronts account for three important categories of characteristics. These include: (a) *activities*, things (other than interaction) people do as part of the group; (b) *sentiments*, feelings and beliefs held by group members; and (c) *interaction*, reciprocal behavior among people in the group. Some of these relate to the group's *external system* and others to its *internal system*.

Homans believed that the elements of a group's internal system are produced by its members' reactions to the elements of its external system. He uses the example of a work-group to illustrate this interrelationship between external and internal systems. The demands of the organization (environment) produce certain external system sentiments within group members, such as the desire to earn a lot of money. These sentiments lead group members to engage in various job-related activities that, in turn, require them to interact with one another to perform those activities. As a result, members develop characteristics that define and influence the internal system, for instance, feelings of liking and camaraderie. These sentiments lead to further interactions among those individuals, as well as participation in nontask-related activities, such as parties or get-togethers. Ultimately, these internal system sentiments, activities, and interactions affect how group members feel about their jobs, how they perform job-related activities, and how they deal with others in the group.

Of the three theoretical orientations discussed, social systems theory has probably had the most direct impact on the study of group communication processes. While social systems theory is not without its problems and critics,[4] its basic assumptions were important to the thinking that contributed to the emergence of the two dominant perspectives discussed later. The two key ideas are (a) that communication is addressed to particular needs or exigencies and, therefore, has functional significance; and (b) communication evolves in ways that contribute to the emergence of stable states in the life of a group.

THE TRANSITIONAL PERIOD IN COMMUNICATION STUDIES OF GROUPS

Between 1970 and 1978, according to Cragan and Wright (1980), 114 studies dealing with groups were published in communication journals. Although a majority of these dealt with task-oriented groups, a substantial number did not. Cragan and Wright found a basis for classifying the studies in their sample in terms

---

[4]The most noteworthy criticism of this theoretical orientation is that it is inherently teleological (Ridgeway, 1985, p. 46). In assuming that a group must meet basic functional prerequisites to be effective, it also implies that whatever effective groups do must necessarily serve essential functions. Critics of functional theory take exception to this teleological assumption because it rules out the possibility of non-functional behaviors and patterns of behaviors. All communication, of course, serves some function. The question of interest is what types of acts best serve the function of satisfying requisites that are essential to the successful performance of a task.

of whether they continued traditional lines of research or introduced new ones. Within the category of "traditional lines," they saw three groups: "leadership, discussion methods, and pedagogy" (p. 200). The so-called "new lines" were designated as "communication variables affecting group outcomes, process of communication in groups, and communication variables studied in groups" (pp. 200–201). The last category consisted of investigations involving factors, some of which are themselves communication variables, that affect the content of group participants' utterances.

Sixty-four of the previously mentioned 114 published studies examined by Cragan and Wright represented *new lines*, and all of these reflected attention to communicative behavior. The percentage of published reports having this emphasis seemed clearly to establish the trend initiated by Scheidel and Crowell (1964) and revealed that critics' voices had not fallen on deaf ears. Neither had the criticisms concerning the lack of theoretical grounding gone unheeded. However, in the latter regard, progress was neither rapid nor significant. At best, it could be considered only modest.

Fisher and Hawes (1971) took a grounded-theory perspective in the development of their "Interact System Model" and argued essentially that theory should derive from empirical observations of communication in groups and be constructed on the basis of the patterns and consistencies that occur. This view was consistent with the general empiricist rejection of causality (see Bunge, 1979, pp. xv–xix) in its emphasis on the discovery of statistical regularities, as opposed to the confirmation of presumed antecedent/consequent relationships. It also emphasized the stochastic, as opposed to lawful nature, of group interaction. The model and its authors' injunctions about theory development spawned several studies (e.g., Ellis, 1979; Ellis & Fisher, 1975; Fisher, 1970b; Mabry, 1975; Stech, 1975). In spite of the amount of research activity generated, theory development was slow, as scholars working in this area appeared to be more concerned—indeed preoccupied—with identifying the best category system and examining the assumptions underlying different methods of statistical analysis.

Gouran (1973) urged small group scholars to think in terms of a structure consisting of contexts, communication variables, and outcomes, within which to locate particular sets of observed and hypothetical relationships. This structure presumably would enable researchers to begin conceiving propositions that constitute the sorts of clusters entering into formal theories. The proposal had little immediate or direct impact on the generation of theory but may have had some utility as an organizational and metatheoretical framework for identifying the range of research questions that are possible. It also encouraged wider adoption of the hypothetico-deductive model that was exerting substantial influence in social psychology and beginning to find its way into social scientific inquiry in other areas of communication. From this perspective, which is decidedly rationalistic, social phenomena are presumed to have causal antecedents that can be identified and framed within a propositional structure that permits the deduction and testing of specific hypotheses. Confirmation of predictions is taken as support of both the existence and direction of causality (Kaplan, 1964, pp. 9–11). This view, ontologically speaking, was at odds with that of Fisher and Hawes, who saw interaction as contingent rather than lawful.

Hampering the development of theory perhaps was the absence of consensus about the questions and contexts to which such formulations should apply. This lack of agreement is evidenced by the wide array of variables investigated by researchers throughout the 1970s and well into the 1980s. Among the many concerns represented in scholarly literature during this period were: reactions to deviant behavior (e.g., Alderton, 1980; Bradley, 1980; Valentine & Fisher, 1974); reticence and communication apprehension (e.g., Burgoon, 1976; Lustig & Grove, 1975; Sorenson & McCroskey, 1977); conflict and conflict management (e.g., Schultz & Anderson, 1984; Wall & Galanes, 1986; Wall, Galanes, & Love, 1987; Wall & Nolan, 1987); consciousness-raising (e.g., Chesebro, Cragan, & McCullough, 1974); risk-taking/choice shift/polarization (e.g., Alderton, 1982; Cline & Cline, 1980; Kellermann & Jarboe, 1987; Meyers, 1989a, 1989b; Meyers & Seibold, 1989, 1990); personality characteristics of group members (e.g., Bochner & Bochner, 1972; Rosenfeld & Plax, 1975); communicative characteristics of different types of group participants (e.g., Cegala, Wall, & Rippey, 1987; Lumsden, Brown, Lumsden, & Hill, 1974; Sargent & Miller, 1971; Schultz, 1982); attitudinal characteristics of group members (Putnam, 1979); creative problem solving (e.g., Jablin, 1981; Jablin, Seibold, & Sorenson, 1977; Philipsen, Mulac, & Dietrich, 1979); and gender/communication relationships (e.g., Alderton & Jurma, 1980; Bormann, Pratt, & Putnam, 1978; Bunyi & Andrews, 1985; Mabry, 1985; Spillman, Spillman, & Reinking, 1984).

Despite the fragmentation of interests this brief overview illustrates, by the close of the 1970s, research on communication in groups was concentrating increasingly on decision making and problem solving. Even when the focus was not on decisional or problem-solving processes, in most instances, inquiries such as those referred to above were conducted within the context of the decision-making or problem-solving group. In addition, these studies often have had direct or indirect implications for understanding the ways in which communication functions in decision-making groups. (For a more comprehensive review, see Cragan & Wright, 1990.)

By 1970, research involving communication in groups also began to show two general thrusts. Most studies within these domains exhibited concern either with the relationship of communication to decisional outcomes and responses to those outcomes or with communication as a process in which decisions and solutions to problems develop.

Those manifesting the first orientation saw decisions as final choices among sets of alternatives made by group members (e.g., Bell, 1974; Kline, 1972; Knutson & Kowitz, 1977). These choices could differ in respect to such variables as the amount of agreement they elicit (Hill, 1976), satisfaction of group members (Jurma, 1978), and perceived quality (Gouran, Brown, & Henry, 1978). Variance in outcomes, these scholars assumed, was directly attributable to the presence or absence of communicative acts having specifiable properties, such as orientation, informativeness, and objectivity. Outcomes, then, were seen as amenable to inclusion in mathematical functions. Hypotheses often were expressed verbally as functions, but few, if any, studies in this tradition described them in precise mathematical terms.

Scholars reflecting the second orientation saw decisions as ideas (proposals) undergoing continuous modification, accommodation, and development (e.g., Ellis & Fisher, 1975; Fisher, 1979; Fisher, Drecksel, & Werbel, 1978). Identifying the probable occurrence of certain categories of communicative behavior rather than precise causal linkages was the principal concern of these investigators.

To the first group, decisions have properties and can be viewed as good or bad, correct or incorrect, of high quality or low quality, workable or unworkable, and the like. Their thinking reflects a clearly deductive emphasis, in that there is presumably a set of underlying factors that would account for variation in any or all of these properties and that can be derived from other known or assumed relationships. To the latter group, decisions are mutually negotiated agreements that fluctuate in their level of acceptability throughout the process in which they are created and as such are lacking in objective properties. The logical orientation of these scholars exhibits a strong inductive character. Outcome-oriented scholars were concerned with how communication facilitates or interferes with a group's ability to satisfy the requisites of informed choice, whereas their process-oriented counterparts wanted to discover how decisions are reached, independently of their particular merits. This also represents a rather clear difference in the axiology of these two groups of scholars. The first group's values emphasize uses of research to improve the process. The second group's are more centrally focused on understanding how the process works.

EMERGENCE OF DOMINANT PERSPECTIVES

As scholarship dealing with communication in decision-making groups moved into the 1980s, both groups of researchers mentioned above began to find better theoretical grounding for their inquiries. The impetus came largely from developments in other disciplines, however. In the first case, influence was traceable to developments in social and cognitive psychology. In the latter instance, sociology—particularly the work of Anthony Giddens (1976, 1977)—was a major source of influence.

The Functional Perspective

In 1972, Irving Janis published his influential book *Victims of Groupthink*. This work proved to be the forerunner of a more systematic and theoretically oriented examination of decision making that he subsequently co-authored with Leon Mann (see Janis & Mann, 1977) and of his more recent work on how to improve policy making (see Janis, 1989). Janis was concerned with the sources of effective and ineffective decision making in groups and did much to reinstate the notion that the manner in which both groups and individuals examine information in relation to choices available to them appreciably affects their ability to solve problems and to avoid potentially adverse consequences.

Although Janis and Mann (1977, p. 10) denied that one can know at the moment of choice whether the *best* decision has been reached, they nevertheless maintained that the likelihood that it has is directly related to conformity with specifiable procedures and decision-making practices. Considerable weight was later given to this supposition in a study by Herek, Janis, and Huth (1987), in which the characteristics of vigilance were shown to be strongly related to independent expert assessments of the quality of a substantial number of foreign policy decisions involving international crises.

The perspective espoused by Janis (1972, 1982) and Janis and Mann (1977) was strongly reminiscent of the adaptations teachers of discussion had made in John Dewey's (1910) description of the reflective thinking process (e.g., Baird, 1927; Ewbank & Auer, 1941; McBurney & Hance, 1939). Although there has been disagreement concerning how direct Dewey's influence was (see Borchers, 1968; Harnack, 1968), it is difficult to deny the strong resemblance between his conception of reflective thinking and a variety of rational models that describe informed choice.[5] Janis and Mann's identification of *vigilance* and the set of procedures it suggests as the key to effective decision making is also quite similar to the conception of the "standard agenda," about which Phillips (1966) had written several years earlier.

Despite their popularity, the pedagogical uses of rational models in speech communication had generated little research. The primary evidence consisted of studies by Brilhart and Jochem (1964), Bayless (1967), and Larson (1969), in which the outcomes of discussions adhering to agendas based on the reflective thinking model were compared to those of discussions in which competing agendas were employed. At best, these inquiries provided limited support for the reflective thinking perspective; however, the investigators failed to control input or to assure that it conformed to the requirements of the agendas investigated. Somewhat ironically, then, it was not until psychologists began examining rational models for their theoretical value that they influenced communication research on groups in any significant way.

That rational models of decision making were gaining currency in the conduct of inquiry was apparent in the number of investigations beginning to reflect such a perspective in the mid and late 1970s (e.g., Courtright, 1978; Marr, 1974) and

[5]We note here that the notion of a rational model and rationalist thought should not be confused. As applied to decisional and problem-solving processes, "rational" refers to making choices that have the best prospect of meeting a group's objectives. We use the term "rationalist thought" to refer to a particular epistemological view (rationalism) that holds that truth becomes knowable through the process we ordinarily think of as deductive reasoning.

well into the 1980s. Hirokawa (1982) attempted to determine the relationship of vigilance to consensus, decision quality, and participant satisfaction in decision-making groups. Vigilance represented a cluster of behaviors that were, for the most part, polar opposites of Janis' (1972) "symptoms of groupthink" and, in many respects, the behavioral instantiation of the steps in the Dewey (1910) reflective thinking sequence. In a similar inquiry, Hirokawa (1983) identified five functions derived from the characteristics of vigilance and sought to determine their correlation with expert ratings of solutions to a traffic problem.

Undertaking a descriptive analysis of communicative behavior, Hirokawa and Pace (1983) presented several reasons for differences in the effectiveness of groups whose decisions were independently evaluated by an expert in the subject matter on which participants' discussions had focused. Findings were generally supportive of the implications of Janis and Mann's notions concerning the role of vigilance in decision making. Recent research by Hirokawa (1988) and Hirokawa, Gouran, and Martz (1988) has provided additional evidence for the functional perspective.

From the functional perspective, the central role of communication in problem-solving and decision-making discussions, in principle, is to assure that the requirements of the task are satisfied (Gouran & Hirokawa, 1983). To the extent that they are, better decisions and more effective solutions to problems are likely. The functional perspective reflects a rationalist epistemology and an ontological view that is consistent with objectivist thought on the nature of reality, especially in respect to causality (see Popper, 1965, pp. 215–247).

Not all post 1970s research concerned with the effectiveness or quality of decisions reveals the influence of rational models such as that developed by Janis and Mann (e.g., Burleson, Levine, & Samter, 1984; Hirokawa, Ice, & Cook, 1988; Jarboe, 1988), nor have all studies conducted from a rationalistic perspective shown as strong an influence of the particular views of Janis and Janis and Mann as those above (e.g., Gouran, 1984; Gouran, Hirokawa, & Martz, 1986). In addition, not all outcome-oriented scholars have been especially interested in the quality or effectiveness of decisions. Some of the outcomes of interest have included the acceptability of a solution by an external audience (Harper & Askling, 1980), the severity of punishment recommended for socially proscribed behavior (Gouran & Andrews, 1984; Gouran, Ketrow, Spear, & Metzger, 1984), consensus (DeStephen, 1983; DeStephen & Hirokawa, 1988; Pace, 1988), ideational output (Jablin, 1981), and choice shift (Cline & Cline, 1980; Mayer, 1985; Meyers, 1989a, 1989b).

The fact that studies focusing on outcomes other than the effectiveness or quality of decisions have not reflected a concern with rational models of choice should not be construed as meaning they are without theoretical grounding. Such studies have drawn on a variety of perspectives, such as attribution theory (e.g., Alderton, 1980), consistency theory (e.g., Gouran, Ketrow, Spear, & Metzger, 1984), and social comparison theory (e.g., Mayer, 1985). Moreover, some inquiries involving the effectiveness or quality of decisions reached by groups have shown a hybrid influence. Gouran, Hirokawa, and Martz (1986), for instance, found some utility in decision theory as articulated by Janis and Mann (1977), but also drew heavily on various aspects of theories of social cognition synthesized by Nisbett and Ross (1980).

What studies such as those mentioned earlier have in common with ones more directly concerned with rational approaches to problem-solving and decision-making discussion is the notion that the characteristics of members' communicative behavior affect (are causally related to) the outcomes groups achieve. In this sense, they clearly reflect the view that communication serves particular functions and that the manner in which it does contributes directly to the end states in which groups find themselves. The epistemological perspective is unquestionably rationalistic and has a strong objectivist flavor. This is not to suggest that every study reflecting the functional perspective has been conducted in accordance with the hypothetico-deductive model. This model, however, has been more frequently in evidence than not and has been influential in the thinking of scholars interested in the functions of communication even when their investigations have been merely descriptive.

Tests of the implications of functional theory have not been consistently supportive of the view that how well communication functions to assure that task requirements are satisfied contributes directly to the quality of outcomes groups achieve. Part of the difficulty is that attention to a task requirement alone has been all too often taken as evidence of sufficiency. Other factors, however, need to be considered. Particularly important appears to be the appropriateness of the inferences that group members make when they are attempting to satisfy task requirements.

In an effort to bring clearer focus to the study of communication in problem-solving and decision-making groups for those interested in the effectiveness of solutions and quality of decisional outcomes, Gouran (1986) adapted several features of Wyer and Carlston's (1979) model of person perception and pointed out several ways in which communication can function to shape erroneous collective inferences. The basic notion is that the choices made by groups are no better than the inferences on which they are based. To the extent that communication contributes to erroneous, questionable, or otherwise indefensible inferences about matters under consideration, the members of a group are predisposed to make inappropriate choices.

The relationship Gouran hypothesized has been partially supported in studies by Mason (1984) and Martz (1986) with laboratory groups in which the appropriateness of decisions for a case study was independently determined. Gouran (1984, 1990b) and Gouran, Hirokawa, and Martz (1986) also found evidence of communication's contributing to erroneous collective inferences in case studies of the Watergate conspiracy, the Challenger disaster, and the Meese Commission.

Although no one in communication has as yet constructed a formal theory of the communication/inference/choice relationship, studies grounded in cognitive perspectives on inferential judgment are beginning to cohere within a common theoretical frame of reference and have provided a clear basis for understanding differences in the outcomes achieved by effective and ineffective decision-making groups. Other variables that promise to expand our understanding of sufficiency are bias and clarity of evaluation (see Hirokawa, Oetzel, Aleman, & Elston, 1991). Hewes (1986), however, has reminded us that many of the causal claims being advanced have yet to be established in rigorous mathematical ways and has raised some serious questions about how strong the communication/choice relationship may be.

The Developmental Perspective

Among scholars concerned with decision development, research since 1980 has revealed a more direct influence of theory on inquiry and a greater effort to refine and modify theory than has been true among outcome-oriented investigators, despite such recent efforts as the one by Gouran, Hirokawa, Julian, and Leatham (1993). The latter group has tended to draw on theory selectively and primarily for its explanatory value. The difference, in part, may be attributable to the fact that those attempting to understand the development of decisions in groups are asking a more limited set of questions. More likely, however, is that they appear to agree on a set of assumptions about the generative mechanisms that give rise to interaction and what properties of utterances constrain the manner in which it unfolds.

Work on decision development had its origins in the previously mentioned study by Scheidel and Crowell (1964); however, prior to 1980, virtually no theory—no social theory, that is—existed to account for the patterning and relative predictability of interaction sequences being reported in published research. Studies, such as those by Bales and Strodtbeck (1951), Bennis and Shepherd (1956), and Tuckman (1965), had revealed considerable evidence of patterning in interaction, but these investigations were largely descriptive. Scheidel and Crowell (1964) used information theory statistics to determine the amount of redundancy in interaction sequences; however, this application had little to do with social determinants of the characteristics of the interaction process. In addition, inconsistencies across studies either generated little comment or were accounted for in terms of differences in the methodological approaches taken in individual investigations. With a rather devastating critique of this body of scholarship by Hewes (1979), research on decision development in groups began to take on a markedly theoretical character.

Theoretically grounded research on decision development was given impetus in a study by Poole (1981) and two subsequent essays (Poole, 1983a, 1983b) in which he formulated the propositional structure from which one can derive particular expectations about the process by which members of groups arrive at given decisional states. Since the publication of Poole's original study, a number of others emanating from the structurational perspective have appeared (for example, McPhee & Seibold, 1981; Poole, McPhee, & Seibold, 1982; Poole & Roth, 1989a, 1989b; Poole, Seibold, & McPhee, 1985; Seibold, McPhee, Poole, Tanita, & Canary, 1981).

Common to research in the structurational mold is the notion that rules and resources (structures) that guide action are at the base of overt behavior, or social practices. Social practices and structures exert reciprocal influence; hence, as the rules and resources group member possess give rise to individual activity, that behavior, in turn, may lead to alterations in rules and resources. Structuration, then, is a process in which rules and resources are continuously produced and reproduced in conjunction with the practices to which they lead. Social practices, of necessity, are further constrained by environmental influences, which can also trigger alterations in the rules and resources that give rise to the actions of groups.

The structurational perspective has led to some significant contributions in our understanding of various aspects of decision making in groups, including differences in decision paths (Poole, 1981), interaction sequences (Poole & Doelger, 1986), the development and functions of argument (Seibold, McPhee, Poole, Tanita, & Canary, 1981), communicative influence and argument (Seibold & Meyers, 1986), and the probability of selecting particular decision alternatives (Poole, McPhee, & Seibold, 1982; Poole, Seibold, & McPhee, 1985).

In light of the number of different facets of the surface-level behavior of decision-making groups the structurational perspective appears to accommodate, scholars subscribing to it have taken strides toward an integrative theory, or at least toward a limited number of potentially integrative theories. What the perspective has not yet stimulated is research accounting for differences in outcomes along dimensions in which many people are interested, that is, the quality, effectiveness, correctness, and utility of decisions. Whether it will evolve to that level of sophistication remains to be determined.

Although the developmental perspective has retained much of the empiricist influence evident in the earlier mentioned research of the late 1960s and 1970s, more recent inquiry is beginning to exhibit the intrusion of rationalist thinking. Developmental scholars continue to view outcomes as merely stages in a group's interaction, but some have begun to generate sets of propositions that lead to specific predictions about the conditions under which particular choices are likely to be made (e.g., Gouran, 1990a; Meyers & Seibold, 1990). The structuration perspective itself, as applied to group interaction, moreover, suggest a kind of reciprocal causality in which rules and resources of groups affect the characteristics of interaction and vice versa. This view of causality lends itself to the formation of specifically testable hypotheses although it is not yet clear what types, or classes, of rules and resources or social practices, in principle, are likely to have causal force as opposed to merely coincidental significance by virtue of their relationship to some other unobserved or unrecognizable causal influence.

DIRECTIONS

Despite the limitations of research on communication in groups identified in this review, impressive progress in that portion dealing with decision-making and related problem-solving processes has been made in the past 25 years, and especially since 1980. Inquiry has moved out of the more or less exploratory, atheoretical, unfocused mode and now exhibits the influence of two reasonably clear, well-developed, and theoretically grounded orientations, with communication as the central concern of each. The characterization of small group research by McGrath and Altman (1966) at the beginning of this chapter has lost much of its force. Researchers investigating the communication/outcome relationship have found a basis for attributing the quality or effectiveness of decisions to the ways in which information is processed and the role communication plays in a group's ability to make informed choices. Scholars interested in how decisions develop are currently being guided by a set of theoretical principles that appear to have utility for understanding many different aspects of communicative activity.

Research emanating from the functional perspective is heavily grounded in rationalist assumptions concerning the nature of causality, discovery of the principles that account for human behavior (in this case choices), and the means of confirmation. Inquiry, in most instances, has been in the hypothetico-deductive tradition. Scholarship deriving from the developmental perspective has exhibited a much greater influence of empiricist thought. More recently, however, theoretical developments have led to formulations about the relationships among communicative events that are more nearly consistent with rationalist views of knowing and causality. Finally, research within the two lines of inquiry seems to reflect a different set of values. Outcome-oriented researchers tend to undertake inquiry in the interest of making groups more effective, whereas their process-oriented counterparts appear to be more concerned with knowledge for its own sake.

These two perspectives and the differences they reflect in their underlying epistemological, ontological, and axiological assumptions thus far have not led to any significant conflicts. The absence of such paradigmatic clash, however, is largely attributable to the fact that the scholars involved have been concerned with different phenomena. How long such compatibility may persist is difficult to gauge, especially if there is greater convergence on those aspects of group process and aims with which each perspective has been more or less independently and uniquely concerned.

As to what the future holds, one can only guess. And to attempt to dictate how it should unfold would undoubtedly be audacious. Even to describe one's premonitions carries the risk of being seriously in error. As Gerald Miller (1984) has so aptly observed, the directions research takes in a field of inquiry are determined at any given point by those doing it and the sorts of issues to which they are attracted, not by stipulations, predictions, or even the merits of arguments for the previously identified, and competing, philosophical perspectives on the proper conduct of inquiry. Given the possibilities for a convergence of scholarship within the two orientations described and the demonstrated utility of the theoretical principles accompanying them, however, one has good reason for encouraging continuation along the lines that have evolved. Neither body of inquiry appears close to the exhaustion of its potential, nor has either led to many direct tests of the propositions and assumptions in the theories and theoretical premises on which it has drawn.

Sustained work within the two orientations that emerged in the past decade may eventually lead to further integration and ultimately a single, unified perspective in which the relationship between the process of decision development and the characteristics of decisions can be more systematically explored and understood. Gouran (1988) has made an initial attempt to link the study of decision development and decision outcomes in an essay in which he discusses the concept of "appropriateness" of decisions as one to which other indices of effectiveness seem to be necessarily subordinate.

An appropriate decision or problem solution is one the members of a group are obliged to make in light of their specific purposes, the inherent logical requirements of the task, and what the analysis of relevant information according to commonly agreed upon rules of evidence establishes. Within this definitional framework, one cannot examine decisions apart from the process in which they arise. Research emphasizing the role of single variables or even sets of variables (for example, the communicative behavior contributing to erroneous inferences) is probably inadequate to account for the variation in the appropriateness of the choices groups reach. Consequently, an examination of the process by which the rules and resources (structures) underlying the communication (social practices) leading to particular choices are produced and reproduced may ultimately hold the key to understanding fully phenomena we can now only partially explain.

Whether or not future scholarship on communication in groups moves in the direction of a unified perspective or amalgam of the two that are presently evident, researchers in the area are perhaps well advised to focus more of their inquiries on the behavior of extant groups. Too few of the group studies generated in the field of communication have been conducted in settings in which tasks have been consequential, either for the participants or external publics. The ecological validity of much of the research is therefore suspect.

If the group situations we study do not matter, then one cannot have a great deal of confidence that the communicative behavior of those who participate in them closely resembles that occurring in situations in which the tasks performed are of importance. Putnam and Stohl (1990) make this point most effectively in their plea for the study of *bona fide* groups, as did Becker (1980) before them. In the case of decision-making groups, history has provided many artifacts of significance and often records of the interactions involved in their production

(Neustadt & May, 1986). Researchers might profit and contribute more reliable knowledge about the communicative behavior of groups by taking greater advantage of these resources.

One also hopes that research in the future will not ignore or neglect the personal, social, and environmental variables conceivably having a bearing on the interaction of the members of groups. Reading more recently published work contributes to the perception that, in trying to distinguish communication research from that in other disciplines, some scholars may have discounted factors that can and do influence communicative behavior and, thereby, the way in which groups perform their tasks. To this end the work of Bormann (1986) on symbolic convergence is instructive. The search for uniform patterns of interaction to account for the outcomes groups achieve is probably a futile one since the development of communicative behavior is so inextricably tied to the paths along which given sets of circumstances may take a group and its members. Knowledge will progress more rapidly if scholars exert greater effort to explain differences in outcomes by including non-communicative influences than is likely if they choose to dismiss or minimize their importance.

Finally, we should not overlook the need to determine how interaction in groups is affected by the intervention of communication technology, and of microcomputers in particular. Some work has already been done in this area (e.g., Beauclair, 1987; Hiltz, Johnson, & Turoff, 1986). Most work to date, however, consists of descriptions of the potential uses of computer technology (e.g., DeSanctis & Gallupe, 1984; Huber, 1984). As more groups begin to engage in the sort of asynchronous communication that computer-mediated activity often creates, we need to begin determining what other consequences follow. In this respect, work reported by Jessup and Valachic (1993) is promising.

Of particular interest in this area is the use of so called "expert systems" and "group decision support systems." Indeed these systems represent the fastest growing computer-mediated technology being employed to assist groups in overcoming fallacies of human judgment and other problems inherent in social decision making. Researchers thus need to begin examining the role and impact of these systems on the nature and quality of the interaction processes followed by groups in arriving at a decision, as well as the overall quality of the decisions or solutions they produce. Given the apparent strengths and weaknesses of expert and GDSS systems (Bobrow, Mittal, & Stefik, 1986; Duda & Shortliffe, 1983), researchers also need to begin addressing the question of when expert systems are most useful for facilitating group decision making and problem solving.

A DASH OF INSPIRATION

In 1974, Ivan Steiner published an article entitled, "Whatever Happened to the Group in Social Psychology?" The essay seemed to herald the end of the so-called Golden Age of small group research and portended that as an area of inquiry it would not be resurrected. His pessimism may have reflected the earlier expressed concerns of McGrath and Altman (1966). Scholars in communication, however, were at that very time establishing that the study of groups is viable and that many interesting avenues remain to be explored. Especially in the areas of decision making and problem solving does this appear to have been true. Not only has the amount of activity been generous (Cragan & Wright, 1990), but in studies undertaken by representatives of the profession, as this review demonstrates, the advancement of knowledge has been increasingly systematic. As James Davis (1986) observed in his preface to *Communication and Group Decision-Making*, such work as the volume illustrates gives clear "cause for optimism" (p. 12).

Whatever happened to the group in social psychology? For us, the question does not really matter, since the group has remained the object of sustained scholarly interest in the communication discipline for over 25 years, particularly among those seeking to bring clarity to the communicative process by which humans functioning in groups arrive at consequential choices. They have done so through continuing refinements of the lenses that their differing philosophical (ontological, epistemological, and axiological) perspectives have provided and, thereby, have created a more nearly complete image of decisional and problem-solving processes. Such insights into the future as we have, therefore, are for a bright rather than dismal one and a period in which our knowledge of communication in groups increases not only in volume, but in its coherence, reliability, and utility as well. Differences in the philosophical perspectives from which research has been conducted notwithstanding, we have a much better understanding of communication in groups than ever before. One could even argue that it has been this very diversity in point of view that is responsible for achievements to date as well as the continued promise the area of study holds.

REFERENCES

Alderton, S. M. (1980). Attributions of responsibility for socially deviant behavior in decision-making discussions as a function of situation and locus of control of attributer. *Central States Speech Journal, 31,* 117–127.

Alderton, S. (1982). Locus of control-based argumentation as a predictor of group polarization. *Communication Quarterly, 30,* 381–387.

Alderton, S. M., & Jurma, W. E. (1980). Genderless/gender related task, leader communication, and group satisfaction. *Southern Speech Communication Journal, 46,* 48–60.

Asch, S. E. (1956). Studies of independence and a minority of one against a unanimous majority. *Psychological Monographs, 70*(9) (Whole No. 416).

Baird, A. C. (1927). *Public discussion and debate.* Boston, MA: Ginn.

Bales, R. F. (1950). *Interaction profile analysis.* Reading, MA: Addison-Wesley.

Bales, R. F. (1953). The equilibrium problem in small groups. In T. Parsons, R. F. Bales, & E. Shils (Eds.), *Working papers in the theory of action* (pp. 111–161). Glencoe, IL: Free Press.

Bales, R. F., & Strodtbeck, F. L. (1951). Phases in group problem-solving. *Journal of Abnormal and Social Psychology, 46,* 485–495.

Bayless, O. L. (1967). An alternate pattern for problem-solving discussion. *Journal Communication, 17*, 188–198.

Beauclair, R. A. (1987). *An experimental study of the effects of group decision support system process support applications on small group decision making.* Unpublished doctoral dissertation, Indiana University, Bloomington, Indiana.

Becker, S. L. (1980). Directions of small group research for the 1980's. *Central States Speech Journal, 31*, 221–224.

Bell, M. A. (1974). The effects of substantive and affective conflict in problem-solving groups. *Speech Monographs, 41*, 19–23.

Bennis, W. G., & Shepherd, H. A. (1956). A theory of group development. *Human Relations, 9*, 415–437.

Berg, D. M. (1967). A descriptive analysis of the distribution and duration of themes discussed by small task-oriented groups. *Speech Monographs, 34*, 172–175.

Black, E. B. (1955). Consideration of the rhetorical causes of breakdown in discussion. *Speech Monographs, 22*, 15–19.

Bobrow, D., Mittal, S., & Stefik, M. (1986). Expert systems: Perils and promise. *Communications of the ACM, 29*, 880–894.

Bochner, A. P., & Bochner, B. (1972). A multivariate investigation of Machiavellianism in four-man groups. *Speech Monographs, 39*, 227–285.

Borchers, G. L. (1968). John Dewey and speech education. *Western Speech, 32*, 127–137.

Bormann, E. G. (1970). The paradox and promise of small group research. *Speech Monographs, 37*, 211–217.

Bormann, E. G. (1986). Symbolic convergence theory and communication in group decision-making. In R. Y. Hirokawa & M. S. Poole (Eds.), *Communication and group decision-making* (pp. 219–236). Newbury Park, CA: Sage.

Bormann, E. G., Pratt, J., & Putnam, L. L. (1978). Power, authority, and sex: Male response to female leadership. *Communication Monographs, 45*, 119–155.

Bradley, P. H. (1980). Sex, competence, and opinion deviation: An expectation states approach. *Communication Monographs, 47*, 101–110.

Brilhart, J. K., & Jochem, L. M. (1964). Effects of different patterns on outcomes of problem-solving discussion. *Journal of Applied Psychology, 48*, 175–179.

Bunge, M. (1979). *Causality and modern science* (3rd ed.). New York: Dover.

Bunyi, J. M., & Andrews, P. H. (1985). Gender and leadership emergence: An experimental study. *Southern Speech Communication Journal, 50*, 246–260.

Burgoon, J. K. (1976). The unwillingness to communicate scale: Development and validation. *Communication Monographs, 43*, 60–69.

Burleson, B. R., Levine, B. J., & Samter, W. (1984). Decision-making procedure and decision quality. *Human Communication Research, 10*, 557–574.

Cegala, D. J., Wall, R. D., & Rippey, G. (1987). An investigation of interaction involvement and the dimensions of SYMLOG: Perceived communication behaviors of persons in task-oriented groups. *Central States Speech Journal, 38*, 81–93.

Chesebro, J. W., Cragan, J. F., & McCullough, P. (1974). The small group technique of the radical revolutionary: A synthetic study of consciousness raising. *Speech Monographs, 41*, 136–146.

Cline, R. J., & Cline, T. R. (1980, Fall). A structural analysis of risky shift discussions. *Communication Quarterly, 28*, 26–36.

Courtright, J. A. (1978). A laboratory investigation of groupthink. *Communication Monographs, 45*, 229–246.

Cragan, J. F., & Wright, D. W. (1980). Small group research of the 1970's: A synthesis and critique. *Central States Speech Journal, 31*, 197–213.

Cragan, J. F., & Wright, D. W. (1990). Small group communication research of the 1980s: A synthesis and critique. *Communication Studies, 41*, 212–236.

Crowell, L., Katcher, A., & Myamoto, S. F. (1955). Self-concepts of communication skill and performance in small group discussion. *Speech Monographs, 22,* 20–27.

Davis, J. H. (1986). Foreword. In R. Y. Hirokawa & M. S. Poole (Eds.), *Communication and group decision-making* (pp. 7–12). Newbury Park, CA: Sage.

DeSanctis, G., & Gallupe, B. (1984). *Group decision support systems: A new frontier.* Unpublished manuscript, University of Minnesota, Department of Management Sciences, Minneapolis, Minnesota.

DeStephen, R. S. (1983). High and low consensus groups: A content and relational interaction analysis. *Small Group Behavior, 14,* 143–162.

DeStephen, R. S., & Hirokawa, R. Y. (1988). Small group consensus: Stability of group support of the decision, task process, and group relationships. *Small Group Behavior, 19,* 227–239.

Deutsch, M., & Krauss, H. B. (1965). *Theories in social psychology.* New York: Basic Books.

Dewey, J. (1910). *How we think.* Boston, MA: Heath.

Duda, R., & Shortliffe, E. (1983, April). Expert systems research. *Science,* 261–268.

Ellis, D. G. (1979). Relational control in two group systems. *Communication Monographs, 46,* 153–166.

Ellis, D. G., & Fisher, B. A. (1975). Phases of conflict in small group development: A Markov analysis. *Human Communication Research, 1,* 195–212.

Ewbank, H. L., & Auer, J. J. (1941). *Discussion and debate: Tools of a democratic society.* New York: Appleton-Century.

Fisher, B. A. (1970a). Decision emergence: Phases in group decision-making. *Speech Monographs, 37,* 53–66.

Fisher, B. A. (1970b). The process of decision modification in small discussion groups. *Journal of Communication, 20,* 51–64.

Fisher, B. A. (1979, Fall). Content and relationship dimensions of communication in decision-making groups. *Communication Quarterly, 27,* 3–11.

Fisher, B. A., Drecksel, G. L., & Werbel, W. (1978). Social information processing analysis (SIPA): Coding ongoing human communication. *Small Group Behavior, 10,* 3–21.

Fisher, B. A., & Hawes, L. C. (1971). An interact system model: Generating a grounded theory of small groups. *Quarterly Journal of Group Behavior, 57,* 444–452.

Geier, J. G. (1967). A trait approach to the study of leadership in small groups. *Journal of Communication, 17,* 316–323.

Giddens, A. (1976). *New rules of sociological method.* New York: Basic Books.

Giddens, A. (1977). *Studies in social and political theory.* New York: Basic Books.

Gouran, D. S. (1969). Variables related to consensus in group discussions of questions of policy. *Speech Monographs, 36,* 387–391.

Gouran, D. S. (1970). A response to "The paradox and promise of small group research." *Speech Monographs, 37,* 218–219.

Gouran, D. S. (1973). Group communication: Perspectives and priorities for future research. *Quarterly Journal of Speech, 59,* 22–29.

Gouran, D. S. (1984). Communicative influences related to the Watergate coverup: The failure of collective judgment. *Central States Speech Journal, 35,* 260–268.

Gouran, D. S. (1985). The paradigm of unfulfilled promise: A critical examination of the history of research on small groups in speech communication. In T. W. Benson (Ed.), *Speech communication in the twentieth century* (pp. 90–108, 386–392). Carbondale, IL: Southern Illinois University Press.

Gouran, D. S. (1986). Inferential errors, interaction, and group decision-making. In R. Y. Hirokawa & M. S. Poole (Eds.), *Communication and group decision-making* (pp. 93–112). Newbury Park, CA: Sage.

Gouran, D. S. (1988). Group decision making: An approach to integrative research. In C. H. Tardy (Ed.), *A handbook for the study of human communication* (pp. 247–268). Norwood, NJ: Ablex.

Gouran, D. S. (1990a). Exploiting the predictive potential of structuration theory. In J. A. Anderson (Ed.), *Communication yearbook 13* (pp. 313–322). Newbury Park, CA: Sage.

Gouran, D. S. (1990b). Factors affecting the decision-making process in the Attorney General's Commission on Pornography: A case study of unwarranted collective judgment. In R. S. Rodgers (Ed.), *Free speech yearbook 28* (pp. 104–119). Carbondale, IL: Southern Illinois University Press.

Gouran, D. S., & Andrews, P. H. (1984). Determinants of punitive responses to socially proscribed behavior: Seriousness, attribution of responsibility, and status of offender. *Small Group Behavior, 15*, 524–544.

Gouran, D. S., Brown, C. R., & Henry, D. R. (1978). Behavioral correlates of perceptions of quality in decision-making discussions. *Communication Monographs, 45*, 51–63.

Gouran, D. S., & Hirokawa, R. Y. (1983). The role of communication in decision-making groups: A functional perspective. In M. S. Mander (Ed.), *Communications in transition* (pp. 168–185). New York: Praeger.

Gouran, D. S., Hirokawa, R. Y., Julian, K. M., & Leatham, G. B. (1993). The evolution and current status of the functional perspective on communication in decision-making and problem-solving groups. In S. A. Dietz (Ed.), *Communication yearbook 16* (pp. 573–600). Newbury Park, CA: Sage.

Gouran, D. S., Hirokawa, R. Y., & Martz, A. E. (1986). A critical analysis of factors related to decisional processes involved in the Challenger disaster. *Central States Speech Journal, 37*, 119–135.

Gouran, D. S., Ketrow, S. M., Spear, S., & Metzger, J. (1984). Social deviance and occupational status: Group assessment of penalties. *Small Group Behavior, 15*, 63–86.

Harnack, R. V. (1951). Competition and cooperation. *Central States Speech Journal, 3*, 15–20.

Harnack, R. V. (1955). An experimental study of the effects of training in the recognition and formulation of goals upon intra-group cooperation. *Speech Monographs, 22*, 31–38.

Harnack, R. V. (1968). John Dewey and discussion. *Western Speech, 32*, 137–149.

Harper, N. L., & Askling, L. R. (1980). Group communication quality of task solution in a media production organization. *Communication Monographs, 47*, 77–100.

Herek, G., Janis, I. L., & Huth, P. (1987). Decision making during international crises: Is quality of process related to outcome? *Journal of Conflict Resolution, 31*, 203–226.

Hewes, D. E. (1979). The sequential analysis of social interaction. *Quarterly Journal of Speech, 65*, 56–73.

Hewes, D. E. (1986). A socio-egocentric model of group decision-making. In R. Y. Hirokawa & M. S. Poole (Eds.), *Communication and group decision-making* (pp. 265–292). Newbury Park, CA: Sage.

Hill, T. A. (1976). An experimental study of the relationship between opinionated leadership and small group consensus. *Communication Monographs, 43*, 246–257.

Hiltz, S. R., Johnson, K., & Turoff, M. (1986). Experiments in group decision making: Communication process and outcome in face-to-face versus computerized conferences. *Human Communication Research, 13*, 225–252.

Hirokawa, R. Y. (1982). Consensus group decision-making, quality of decision, and group satisfaction: An attempt to sort "fact" from "fiction." *Central States Speech Journal, 33*, 407–415.

Hirokawa, R. Y. (1983). Group communication and problem-solving effectiveness II: An exploratory investigation of procedural functions. *Western Journal of Speech Communication, 47*, 59–74.

Hirokawa, R. Y. (1988). Group communication and decision-making performance: A continued test of the functional perspective. *Human Communication Research, 14*, 487–515.

Hirokawa, R. Y., Gouran, D. S., & Martz, A. E. (1988). Understanding the sources of faulty group decision-making: A lesson from the Challenger disaster. *Small Group Behavior, 19*, 411–433.

Hirokawa, R. Y., Ice, R., & Cook, J. (1988). Preference for procedural order, discussion structure and group decision performance. *Communication Quarterly, 36*, 217–226.

Hirokawa, R. Y., Oetzel, J., Aleman, C., & Elston, S. (1991). *The effects of evaluation clarity and bias on the relationship between vigilant interaction and group decision-making efficacy.*

Unpublished manuscript, University of Iowa, Department of Communication Studies, Iowa City, Iowa.

Hirokawa, R. Y., & Pace, R. C. (1983). A descriptive investigation of the possible communication-based reasons for effective and ineffective group decision making. *Communication Monographs, 50*, 363–379.

Homans, G. C. (1950). *The human group.* New York: Harcourt Brace Jovanovich.

Homans, G. C. (1961). *Social behavior: Its elementary forms.* New York: Harcourt Brace Jovanovich.

Huber, G. P. (1984). Issues in the design of group decision support systems. *MIS Quarterly, 8*, 195–204.

Jablin, F. M. (1981). Cultivating imagination: Factors that enhance and inhibit creativity in brainstorming groups. *Human Communication Research, 7*, 245–258.

Jablin, F. M., Seibold, D. R., & Sorenson, R. L. (1977). Potential inhibitory effects of group participation on brainstorming performance. *Central States Speech Journal, 28*, 113–121.

Janis, I. L. (1972). *Victims of groupthink.* Boston, MA: Houghton Mifflin.

Janis, I. L. (1982). *Groupthink* (2nd ed.). Boston, MA: Houghton Mifflin.

Janis, I. L. (1989). *Crucial decisions: Leadership in policy making and crisis management.* New York: Free Press.

Janis, I. L., & Mann, L. (1977). *Decision making.* New York: Free Press.

Jarboe, S. (1988). A comparison of input-output, process-output, and input-process-output models of small group problem-solving effectiveness. *Communication Monographs, 55*, 122–142.

Jessup, L. M., & Valachic, J. S. (Eds.). (1993). *Group support systems: New perspectives.* New York: Macmillan.

Johnson, A. (1943). An experimental study of the analysis and measurement of reflective thinking. *Speech Monographs, 10*, 83–98.

Jurma, W. E. (1978). An experimental study of the relationship of leader-structuring style and task ambiguity to the resulting satisfaction of group members. *Small Group Behavior, 9*, 124–134.

Kaplan, A. (1964). *The conduct of inquiry.* San Francisco, CA: Chandler.

Kellermann, K., & Jarboe, S. (1987). Conservatism in judgment: Is the risky shift-ee really risky, really? In M. L. McLaughlin (Ed.), *Communication yearbook 10* (pp. 259–282). Newbury Park, CA: Sage.

Kibler, R. J., & Barker, L. L. (Eds.). (1969). *Conceptual frontiers in speech-communication.* New York: Speech Association of America.

Kline, J. A. (1972). Orientation and group consensus. *Central States Speech Journal, 23*, 44–47.

Koffka, K. (1935). *Principles of gestalt psychology.* New York: Harcourt Brace Jovanovich.

Knutson, T. J., & Kowitz, A. C. (1977). Effects of information types and level of orientation on consensus-achievement in substantive and affective small-group conflict. *Central States Speech Journal, 28*, 54–63.

Larson, C. E. (1969). Forms of analysis and small group problem-solving. *Speech Monographs, 36*, 452–455.

Larson, C. E. (1971). Speech communication research on small groups. *Speech Teacher, 20*, 89–107.

Leathers, D. G. (1969). Process disruption and measurement in small groups communication. *Quarterly Journal of Speech, 55*, 287–300.

Leathers, D. G. (1970). The effects of trust destroying behavior in the small group. *Speech Monographs, 37*, 180–187.

Lewin, K. (1939). Field theory and experiment in social psychology: Concepts and methods. *American Journal of Sociology, 44*, 868–896.

Lewin, K. (1947). Frontiers in group dynamics. *Human Relations, 1*, 5–41.

Lewin, K. (1951). *Field theory in social science.* New York: Harper & Row.

Lewin, K., Lippitt, R., & White, R. K. (1939). Patterns of aggressive behavior in experimentally created "social climates." *Journal of Social Psychology, 10*, 271–299.

Lumsden, G., Brown, D. R., Lumsden, D., & Hill, T. A. (1974, Fall). An investigation of differences in verbal behavior between black and white informal peer group discussions. *Today's Speech, 22*, 31–36.

Lustig, M. W., & Grove, T. G. (1975). Interactional analysis of small problem-solving groups containing reticent and non-reticent members. *Western Speech Communication, 39*, 155–164.

Mabry, E. A. (1975). Exploratory analysis of a developmental model for task-oriented groups. *Human Communication Research, 2*, 66–74.

Mabry, E. A. (1985). The effects of gender composition and task structure on small group interaction. *Small Group Behavior, 16*, 75–96.

Marr, T. J. (1974). Conciliation and verbal responses as a function of orientation and threat in group interaction. *Speech Monographs, 41*, 6–18.

Martz, A. E. (1986). *An investigation of the functions of communication in the production and acceptance of unwarranted inferences by members of decision-making groups.* Unpublished master's thesis, The Pennsylvania State University, University Park, Pennsylvania.

Mason, G. E. (1984). *An empirical investigation of inferential and related communication processes distinguishing between effective and ineffective decision-making groups.* Unpublished doctoral dissertation, Indiana University, Bloomington, Indiana.

Mayer, M. E. (1985). Explaining choice shift: An effects coded model. *Communication Monographs, 21*, 92–101.

McBurney, J. H., & Hance, K. G. (1939). *Discussion in human affairs.* New York: Harper & Brothers.

McGrath, J. E., & Altman, I. (1966). *Small group research: A synthesis and critique of the field.* New York: Holt.

McPhee, R. D., & Seibold, D. R. (1981). The valence model unveiled: A critique and alternative formulation. In M. Burgoon (Ed.), *Communication yearbook 5* (pp. 259–278). New Brunswick, NJ: ICA Transaction Press.

Meyers, R. A. (1989a). Persuasive arguments theory: A test of assumptions. *Human Communication Research, 15*, 357–381.

Meyers, R. A. (1989b). Testing persuasive arguments theory's predictor model: Alternative interactional accounts of group argument and influence. *Communication Monographs, 56*, 112–132.

Meyers, R. A., & Seibold, D. R. (1989). Assessing number of cognitive arguments as a predictor of group shifts: A test and alternative interactional explanation. In B. E. Gronbeck (Ed.), *Spheres of Argument: Proceedings of the sixth SCA/AFA conference on argument* (pp. 576–583). Annandale, VA: Speech Communication Association.

Meyers, R. A., & Seibold, D. R. (1990). Perspectives on group argument: A critical review of persuasive arguments theory and an alternative structurational view. In J. A. Anderson (Ed.), *Communication yearbook 13* (pp. 268–302). Newbury Park, CA: Sage.

Miller, G. R. (1984). Where to next? Some thoughts on future research in small group communication. In R. S. Cathcart & L. A. Samovar (Eds.), *Small group communication: A reader* (4th ed., pp. 494–503). Dubuque, IA: William C. Brown.

Mortensen, C. D. (1970). The status of small group research. *Quarterly Journal of Speech, 56*, 304–309.

Neustadt, R. E., & May, E. R. (1986). *Thinking in time: The uses of history for decision makers.* New York: Free Press.

Nisbett, R. E., & Ross, L. (1980). *Human inference: Strategies and shortcomings of social judgment.* Englewood Cliffs, NJ: Prentice-Hall.

Nixon, H. L., II. (1979). *The small group.* Englewood Cliffs, NJ: Prentice-Hall.

Pace, R. C. (1988). Communication patterns in high and low consensus discussions: A descriptive analysis. *Southern Speech Communication Journal, 53*, 184–202.

Parsons, T., Bales, R. F., & Shils, E. (1953). *Working papers in the theory of action.* Glencoe, IL: Free Press.

Philipsen, G., Mulac, A., & Dietrich, D. (1979). The effects of social interaction on group generation of ideas. *Communication Monographs, 46,* 119–125.

Phillips, G. M. (1966). *Communication and the small group.* Indianapolis, IN: Bobbs-Merrill.

Poole, M. S. (1981). Decision development in small groups I: A comparison of two modes. *Communication Monographs, 48,* 1–24.

Poole, M. S. (1983a). Decision development in small groups II: A study of multiple sequences in decision-making. *Communication Monographs, 50,* 206–232.

Poole, M. S. (1983b). Decision development in small groups III: A multiple sequence model of group decision-making. *Communication Monographs, 50,* 321–341.

Poole, M. S., & Doelger, J. A. (1986). Developmental processes in group decision making. In R. Y. Hirokawa & M. S. Poole (Eds.), *Communication and group decision-making* (pp. 35–62). Newbury Park, CA: Sage.

Poole, M. S., McPhee, R. D., & Seibold, D. R. (1982). A comparison of normative and interactional explanations of group decision-making. *Communication Monographs, 49,* 1–19.

Poole, M. S., & Roth, J. (1989a). Decision development in small groups IV: A typology of group decision paths. *Human Communication Research, 15,* 323–356.

Poole, M. S., & Roth, J. (1989b). Decision development in small groups V: Test of a contingency model. *Human Communication Research, 15,* 549–589.

Poole, M. S., Seibold, D. R., & McPhee, R. D. (1985). Group decision-making as a structurational process. *Quarterly Journal of Speech, 71,* 74–102.

Popper, K. R. (1965). *Conjectures and refutations: The growth of scientific knowledge.* New York: Harper Torchbooks.

Putnam, L. L. (1979). Preference for procedural order in task-oriented small groups. *Communication Monographs, 46,* 193–218.

Putnam, L. L., & Stohl, C. (1990). Bona fide groups: A reconceptualization of groups in context. *Communication Studies, 41,* 248–265.

Pyron, H. C. (1964). An experimental study of the role of reflective thinking in business and professional conferences and discussions. *Speech Monographs, 31,* 157–161.

Pyron, H. C., & Sharp, H., Jr. (1963). A quantitative study of reflective thinking and performance in problem-solving discussion. *Journal of Communication, 21,* 46–53.

Ridgeway, C. L. (1985). *The dynamics of small groups.* New York: St. Martin's Press.

Rosenfeld, L. B., & Plax, T. G. (1975). Personality determinants of autocratic and democratic leadership. *Speech Monographs, 42,* 203–208.

Sargent, J. F., & Miller, G. R. (1971). Some differences in certain communication behaviors of autocratic and democratic leaders. *Journal of Communication, 21,* 233–252.

Schacter, S., Ellertson, N., McBride, D., & Gregory, D. (1951). An experimental study of cohesiveness and productivity. *Human Relations, 4,* 229–238.

Scheidel, T. M., & Crowell, L. (1964). Idea development in small groups. *Quarterly Journal of Speech, 50,* 140–145.

Scheidel, T. M., & Crowell, L. (1966). Feedback in group communication. *Quarterly Journal of Speech, 52,* 273–278.

Schultz, B. (1982). Argumentativeness: Its effect in group decision-making and its role in leadership perception. *Communication Quarterly, 30,* 368–375.

Schultz, B., & Anderson, J. (1984). Training in the management of conflict: A communication theory perspective. *Small Group Behavior, 15,* 333–348.

Seibold, D. R., McPhee, R. D., Poole, M. S., Tanita, N. E., & Canary, D. J. (1981). Argument, group influence, and decision outcomes. In G. Ziegelmueller & J. Rhodes (Eds.), *Dimensions of argument: Proceedings of the second summer conference on argumentation* (pp. 663–692). Annandale, VA: Speech Communication Association.

Seibold, D. R., & Meyers, R. A. (1986). Communication and influence in group decision-making. In R. Y. Hirokawa & M. S. Poole (Eds.), *Communication and group decision-making* (pp. 133–156). Newbury Park, CA: Sage.

Sharp, H., Jr., & Milliken, J. (1964). The reflective thinking ability and the product of problem-solving discussion. *Speech Monographs, 31,* 124–127.

Shaw, M. E. (1970). *Group dynamics: The psychology of small group behavior.* New York: McGraw-Hill.

Shepherd, C. R. (1964). *Small groups: Some sociological perspectives.* San Francisco, CA: Chandler.

Sorenson, G., & McCroskey, J. C. (1977). The prediction of interaction behavior in small groups: Zero history versus intact groups. *Communication Monographs, 44,* 73–80.

Spillman, B., Spillman, R., & Reinking, K. (1984). Leadership emergence: Dynamic analysis of the effects of sex and androgyny. *Small Group Behavior, 12,* 139–158.

Stech, E. (1975). Sequential structure in human social communication. *Human Communication Research, 1,* 168–179.

Steiner, I. D. (1974). Whatever happened to the group in social psychology? *Journal of Experimental Social Psychology, 10,* 94–108.

Thibaut, J. W., & Kelley, H. H. (1959). *The social psychology of groups.* New York: Wiley.

Tuckman, B. W. (1965). Developmental sequences in small groups. *Psychological Bulletin, 63,* 384–399.

Turner, J. H. (1974). *The structure of sociological theory.* Homewood, IL: Dorsey.

Valentine, K., & Fisher, B. A. (1974). An interaction analysis of innovative deviance in small groups. *Speech Monographs, 41,* 413–420.

Wall, V. D., & Galanes, G. J. (1986). The SYMLOG dimensions and small group conflict. *Central States Speech Journal, 37,* 61–78.

Wall, V. D., Galanes, J. J., & Love, S. B. (1987). Small task-oriented groups: Conflict, conflict management, satisfaction, and decision quality. *Small Group Behavior, 18,* 31–55.

Wall, V. D., & Nolan, L. L. (1987). Small group conflict: A look at equity, satisfaction, and styles of conflict management. *Small Group Behavior, 18,* 188–211.

Wyer, R. S., & Carlston, D. (1979). *Social cognition, inference, and attribution.* Hillsdale, NJ: Lawrence Erlbaum Associates.

Chapter 8

Human Communication: A Rules Perspective

Donald P. Cushman
SUNY-Albany

Branislav Kovacic
University of Hartford

> *The primary function of communication is to establish relations among human beings and to provide a means for monitoring and maintaining or terminating such relationships.... The primary tool of communication is the symbol ... The primary effect of communication is interpreted in terms of the self-concepts involved. The primary power of communication lies in its capacity to develop consensus that coordinate and guide human behavior.*
> —King (1989, pp. 2–3)

Human communication processes have been examined productively from a variety of scientific theoretical perspectives. Three theoretical orientations of proven utility are the positivistic, systems and rules perspectives. Each of these orientations is useful because it provides scientists with a model for developing warranted expectations regarding the patterns of regularity present in human communication processes, a model of research procedures for verification of the presence or absence of such patterns in human interaction, and paradigmatic exemplars of theories which shed differential light on human communication processes.

This essay is aimed at explicating the unique (a) philosophic assumptions, (b) theoretic claims, and (c) paradigmatic exemplars of various rules theoretic approaches for scientifically exploring the human communication process.

All theorists operate out of an assumed or stated philosophic perspective which limits the focus of their inquiry and the range of phenomena to which their theory applies. Rules theoretic philosophic assumptions as explored below limit the domain of inquiry to individual or cultural choice situations in which communication with another is required for coordinating two people's behavior in achieving some goal.

All theorists must within their theoretic philosophic perspective posit some generative processes or mechanism which creates communication regularities which are trackable. Coordination rules theorists normally explore self concept, organizational tasks and culture as three generative processes for yielding regular communication behavior.

All theorists must within their philosophic and theoretic perspective offer evidence capable of publicity tracking and specifying the reoccurent communication patterns present in interaction. These patterns represent the practical level of their construction. The remainder of this chapter attempts to demonstrate how three theorists performed these necessary theoretic operations in constructing communication theory.

The unique insights that a rules perspective can provide into human communication processes were first articulated for our discipline by Cushman and Whiting in 1972, when they argued

> Communication is an activity which gains meaning and significance from consensually shared rules. What is transmitted in communication is structure or information, but not all experiences from which we extract information are communication experiences. Communication requires in addition that at least two individuals attempt to take one another into account by developing and utilizing communication rules to guide and constitute the significance of their communicative acts ... As a discipline, communication should make the explication of such rules a central concern, for they provide communication with its defining characteristic. ... (pp. 217–218)

Since 1972, several diverse research programs aimed at clarifying and redeeming these claims have emerged within our discipline. This essay is thus a review of the cumulative efforts of rules theoretic scientific inquiry into the human communication process.

RULES—THEORETIC PHILOSOPHIC ASSUMPTIONS

> *There is at the center of all inquiries a core set of beliefs which illuminate particular perspectives and points of view on life. The articulation and apprehension of those beliefs is critical to an understanding of an actor's perspective on life. Nowhere is an understanding of one's viewpoint more important than in communication.*
>
> —King (1989, pp. 1–2)

It is an ancient view that successful human interactions are restricted by the available means which exist for securing a preferred, intended outcome. This view has been the basis for numerous accounts of individual conduct and social organization, and it is at the heart of the opposition of pragmatism to idealism. It is unequivocally the first principle of rhetorical and communication theory from the time of Aristotle to the present. The most visible, modern expression of the intentionalist position and related issues is action theory. The action theory tradition centers on a conception of humans as creatures of freedom and choice, who are typically engaged in intentional, goal-directed behavior and are capable of acting rather than merely being acted upon. The viability of a rules theory of human communication rooted in action theory depends upon a series of assumptions.

The Action Assumption

First, action theorists investigate intentional and choice-oriented activities governed by practical necessity. These behaviors are evaluative and are termed *actions*. Action theorists restrict their domain of inquiry to those realms of human behavior in which persons have some degree of choice among alternatives, are able to critique their performance, and can respond to practical forces confronting the successful achievement of the preferred alternative. Fay and Moon (1977) summarize as follows:

> According to this distinction, actions differ from mere movements in that they are performed in order to achieve a particular purpose, and in conformity to some rules. These purposes and rules constitute what we shall call the "semantic dimension" of human behavior—its symbolic or expressive aspect. An action, then, is not simply a physical occurrence, but has a certain intentional content which specifies what sort of an action it is, and which can be grasped only in terms of the system of meanings in which the action is performed. A given movement counts as a vote, a signal, a salute or an attempt to reach something, only against the background of a set of applicable rules and conventions and the purposes of the actors involved. (p. 209)

A consensus seems to exist among action theorists that to attribute or ascribe the quality of action to a human behavior is to claim that some agent is the author or cause of the behavior which was brought about. Several important implications regarding the nature of scientific inquiry from within an action-theoretic perspective follow from this first assumption. These implications center on the nature, structure, and verification of action-theoretic explanations.

Action theory requires an explanation of human behavior in terms of the intentional link between an agent's perceptions, thoughts, and behavior so that the agent's perceptions and thoughts explain why the behaviors occurred. Charles Taylor (1970) elaborates:

> Explanation in terms of purpose therefore involved taking into account the conceptual forms through which agents understand and come to grips with their world. That people think of their environment in certain concepts, that is, use

certain modes of classification is an element in accounting for what they do. Indeed, it can be said to define what they do. For if we think of actions as defined by the purposes or intentions which inform them, then we cannot understand man's action without knowing the concepts in which they form their intentions. (p. 60)

In order to see an event as a human action, it is necessary to interpret the empirically observable behaviors in terms of the mental categories of the actors involved, to assure the appropriate interpretation and/or motivations for the behavior. One must demonstrate what meanings are present in the actions.

The Social Coordination Assumption

Second, action theory reflects upon human actions in which an agent's choice among alternative courses of action and efforts to achieve a goal do require the cooperation of others, in which case communication becomes a necessary stage in goal attainment. These are termed *coordination situations* and necessarily employ communication to regulate consensus among agents with regard to the cooperative achievement of a goal. Action theorists with a communication orientation restrict their domain of scientific inquiry to coordination situations. Why? Because it is only within the domain of coordination situations that human action requires the transfer of symbolic information or communication to facilitate goal-directed behavior. Cushman and Pearce (1977) summarize as follows:

> ... (1) there exists a class of human action which involves conjoint, combined, and associated behavior; (2) that the transfer of symbolic information facilitates such behavior; (3) that the transfer of symbolic information requires the interaction of sources, messages, and receivers guided and governed by communication rules; and (4) that the communication rules form general and specific patterns which provide the basis for explanation, prediction, and control of communication behavior. (p. 178)

Actions are social insofar as, by virtue of the interpretations or meanings attached to an action by an agent, that meaning includes and takes into account the interpretations or meanings attached to the same action by the other agents involved. It follows that in order to call an action social, in addition to the observable behavior involved such as making an utterance, one must examine the mental categories or interpretations of meaning involved in one actor taking other actors' mental categories and interpretations into consideration. A researcher must show what interpretations and meanings are present in the observable interaction and whether they are shared or not. Several important implications regarding the nature of scientific inquiry into human communication processes from within an action theoretic perspective follow from this second assumption. These implications involve a conceptualization of the function, structure, and processes of human communication in coordination situations.

One instance of a coordination task that requires the cooperation of others for goal attainment—and is thus governed and guided by communication rules—is the traditional marriage ceremony. The goal of such a ceremony is to unite a couple in matrimony. In order to attain such a goal, each participant must engage in various sequences of verbal behavior, which, according to the rules, constitute a verbal commitment. When these verbal episodes are sequenced in a certain way in the appropriate situation, they count as a marriage contract. The function of human communication in such a context is to regulate the consensus needed to coordinate behavior. The structure of human communication is the content and procedural rules involved in regulating consensus. The process of human communication entails the adaptation of the rules involved in regulating consensus to the task at hand.

The Creative Emergence—Standardized Usage
Interpretative Meaning Assumption

Third, it is assumed that there are two classes of coordination situations: those in which the interactants attempt through negotiation to generate the rules that will form the basis of communication sequences in coordinated goal attainment, and those in which some social institution already exists which has provided such rules. The former are termed creative emergent situations; the latter are termed standardized situations. Several important implications regarding the nature of scientific inquiry within an action-theoretic perspective follow from this third assumption. These implications indicate how one constructs and verifies a rules theory that aspires to explanation, and understanding while employing traditional empirical research methodology.

The first problem created by the attempt to verify a rules theory is how one can empirically separate rule-governed from non rule-governed patterns of behavior. When human communication patterns constitute a rule, they do so because such behaviors are consciously coordinated through mutual dependence between interactants. A rule exists when—and only when—two (or more) people employ similar meanings under certain conditions because both expect each other to employ those shared meanings, and each is aware of the other's expectation. Thus, a pattern of behavior becomes empirically verifiable as rule-governed when mutual expectation of what constitutes appropriate communication behavior serves as a standard to judge and evaluate conduct, which one now has the right to expect. This becomes obvious when some interactants violate these expectations. Habits are descriptive of human behavior; rules are evaluative of such behaviors and are thus monitored by those employing the rule.

The second problem created by an attempt to verify a rules theory of human communication is what does one measure. Three types of observations are normally the basis for scientific facts regarding human interaction. *First*, we can measure empirical patterns of individual or group interpretation of symbols. *Second*, we can measure individual or group patterns of interaction (discourse patterns). *Third*, we can measure individual or group patterns of behavior which follow from symbolic interaction. A rules theoretic perspective argues that any complete test of an action theoretic claim must invoke the use of all three types of observations. Interpretative patterns are necessary to understand the rules of interactive or social meanings, discourse patterns are necessary to understand the discourse rules governing and guiding the interaction, and behavioral patterns are necessary for providing feedback on rule following and rule violating behaviors.

Having examined in some detail the assumptions that underlie the rules-theoretic approach to scientifically exploring human interaction, we are now in a position to explore the theoretic claims of various rules researchers.

THEORETIC CLAIMS OF VARIOUS RULES THEORISTS

> *A scientific theory is the basic principles whose repeated application yield an explanation and understanding of the complex reality we see.*
> —Cushman (1990, p. 3)

The idea that human communication processes are in some sense "governed" by rules is an intuitively appealing one. It underpins the popular belief that there are socially correct and appropriate norms and conventions which govern and guide various (a) cultures and their communication patterns, (b) language—their meaning and grammatical systems, and (c) types of interpersonal relationships and the kind of interaction appropriate in each. This intuition motivates our frequent appeals to cultural values, dictionary meanings and the rules of grammar, and the rules of etiquette in correcting others and defending our own communicative actions. Despite our intuitive belief in rule governed and guided behavior, we are in need of a working definition of communication rules.

In a formal sense, communication rules may be viewed as prescriptions as to appropriate communication behaviors which have social force. Rules, as such, have no truth value. A rule is prescriptive in that it provides a basis for evaluating the appropriateness or inappropriateness of some behavior. The force of a rule derives from its relationship to some system of human activity. Rules are distinguishable from causal regularities in that the former are prescriptive and condition human behavior while the latter are descriptive and constant in human behavior. Rules prescribe what is socially appropriate behavior, and condition its social interpretation (appropriate or inappropriate) when it should occur (in order to meet the expectations of others). Causal regularities are descriptive of behavior, and report the constant conjunction between two events (an antecedent and consequent). Rules, as such, are thus social conventions that can be violated by individuals or changed by groups, whereas causal relationships—constant conjunctions—respect no such individual or collective conditionality.

A rules theory of human communication processes refers to the set of action theoretic principles, arguments and empirical observations which are linked in such a manner as to provide a warrant for the explanation and understanding of human interaction patterns when judged by the research community. Four such rules theoretic approaches to explanation and understanding of human communication patterns are present in the communication research literature. These may be characterized as structural, functional, strategic, and critical rules perspectives.

Structural Rules Perspectives

Communication is explored *structurally* by investigating the theoretic principles which govern and guide the coherance of recurring patterns of interaction sequences such as conflict sequences. The normative structure of interaction sequences is explained and understood by appealing to the theoretic principles governing their emergent meanings, or standardized social, organizational and interpersonal interpretive systems of meanings. These structural rules are thus viewed as "out of time" and "impersonal rules" which constrain and enable human interaction (Manicas, 1980).

Communication takes place within emergent or preexisting social structures. Because individual communicators are located in such emergent or social structures, we can say that their communicative activities do not create or produce the structures or interaction system, but rather they reproduce and transform them. Social structure, as such, exists "out of time" and is "impersonal" and separate from any single manifestation of it. Social structure, in the form of a language and interactional system, enables interactants to say and do some things, and constrains them from saying and doing other things. The fact that social structures emerge or preexist for interactants explains their constraining power over individual communicators (Sanders & Cushman, 1984).

Functional Rules Perspective

Communication is explored *functionally* by investigating the theoretic principles which prescribe the content and sequence of interactions necessary for obtaining a given goal such as making marriage vows. The normative content and structure of recurring patterns of interaction are explained and understood as necessary to achieve some goal such as establishing a relationship of friend, doing a peer review in an organization, or getting married in our culture. These are coordination tasks with emergent and standardized meaning systems located in the dyad, the organization and the culture. In each of these instances, conventional or standard, symbolic patterns develop which facilitate the completion of these non-linguistic tasks. Agents, as part of their socialization process, participate in a variety of coordination tasks and, as such, learn a variety of standard symbolic patterns for coordinating behaviors.

Although some interactions draw upon a variety of these conventional patterns, and permit choice by the interactants as to which specific patterns will be employed and how they will be constructed, others may be situated to involve a single pattern of conventions which are well monitored and enforced by all involved in a given task. We term the latter pattern a standardized usage, and the nonlinguistic task which generates the appropriate communication rules for fulfilling the task as a generative mechanism. The importance of achieving the goal involved in the coordination task to the agents involved will exert practical force on the agent to follow the rules. In such instances, an agent is expected to employ the standardized usage and, if he or she fails to do so, he or she and the other agents involved attempt to enforce a return to the appropriate conventions. The decision to take a coordination task as the basic unit for analysis in exploring patterns of functional communication rules requires that we

1. determine the recurrent tasks within a given society which require coordination,
2. describe the episodic communication sequences which constitute the standardized usage, and
3. locate the initial conditions which provoke communicators to employ the standardized usage.

On this view, coordination tasks generate functional rules which determine the content and sequential unfolding of the goal directed communication behavior required to coordinate nonlinguistic behaviors, in regard to some task. Such functional rules are both general and necessary in regard to that coordination task and can thus be employed to develop theories (Cushman, King, & Smith, 1988).

Strategic Perspectives

Communication may be explored strategically as a system of normative rules which govern and guide the use of communication moves aimed at following some interaction strategy. For example, one may employ leading questions and/or confrontational statements of facts (communication moves) to prove someone is lying (communication strategy). Similar patterns of communication moves and strategies are present in the conflict resolution, compliance gaining and political communication literatures.

On this view, communication strategies aimed at integration, coordination, and control of interaction contain a range of communicative moves capable of fulfilling that strategy and which moves are employed depend upon the response of other to one's use of one or more of these moves. The general strategy employed by the interactant and the response of the other determines which one of the array of communication moves is most appropriate in pursuing the strategy.

The strategic objectives may be task specific as in conflict resolution, response specific as in attempting to neutralize another's argument or interactional and social system specific as in making a case for promotion in an organization.

Critical Perspectives

Communication may be explored critically as a system of normative rules which limit or constrain access to and the functioning of effective communication. These limitations and constraints may systematically distort understandings, the truth content, the sincerity, and the appropriateness of communication (Habermas, 1970a). The critical theoretic rules perspective has as its goal the attempt to explain and understand how power or these systematic distortions work, their effects upon interaction and their potential for correction.

Investigations in critical theory seek to locate the principles of distortion or power as manifest in the unfolding of interaction (communication structures), the goals of interactive systems (communication functions) and the strategies being employed by various interactants (communication strategies). The implications of such systematic distortions are drawn out to those involved in the interaction and potential solutions to the problem explored (Huspek, 1989, 1990).

In the final analysis a given researcher may use structural, functional, strategic and critical perspectives alone or in combination to locate theoretic rules principles which explain and create an understanding of the communicative interaction of agents within their normative rules systems.

What then has our rather brief inquiry into the philosophic and theoretic underpinnings of rules theory revealed? We have argued at a philosophic level that communication rules theorists make several rather specific assumptions. *First*, they limit their interest to reflexive behaviors and *human actions* that are intentional and choice oriented and thus involve explanations based on an actor's perceptions on a situation and intentions in undertaking a behavior. *Second*, rules theorists examine human actions that are intentional and entail *coordination activities* or interaction with others. Rules theorists with a communication focus are particularly interested in this latter category of behaviors. Actions that are interactive require that individuals share meanings and this in turn entails the use of common rules of reference or communication rules. *Third*, it is assumed that human actions aimed at coordinating interaction can employ two types of rules of reference; those in which the interactants *negotiate emergent meanings* or rules and those in which the rules of references have been *previously established or standardized* in order to obtain a recurrent goal such as taking marriage vows.

Communication theorists who employ a rules perspective thus focus upon the intentional meanings communicators can present and sustain in interaction with others in order to coordinate their activities with others. When such meanings are sustained in interaction or gain the assent and cooperation of others, they then form the basis for after-the-fact explanations in the case of negotiated or emergent meanings and before-the-fact explanations in the case of standardized meanings of human interaction. However, such explanations are valid only so long as the interactive meanings upon which they are based are sustained within the coordination process. Thus the principles of explanation upon which a rules theory rests are not universal nor invariant. Rather, they are interaction system specific, socially achieved and interactionally maintained regularities which may change over time. Such communication rules may last a long time such as in the case of a cultural ritual like a marriage ceremony or may be momentary as in the case of an argument or misunderstanding. When such an interactively achieved consensus takes place and can be sustained in interaction, then we have argued that at a theoretic level a rules theorist can employ one or more of four types of explanatory principles: structural, functional, strategic and/or critical to provide an understanding of this socially achieved coordination of human behavior. *Structural explanations* seek to explain the shared meanings and coherence of human communication processes in terms of the sequencing of individual contributions to the interaction. *Functional explanations* seek to understand the shared meaning and coherence of human communication in terms of the standardized interaction patterns that are required for obtaining some reoccurring goal. *Strategic explanations* seek to understand the shared meaning and coherence of human communication processes in terms of the most effective strategies contingent upon the previous moves of other interactants. *Critical explanations* seek to understand the shared meaning and coherence of human communication processes in terms of the limits or constraints imposed on interaction by normative and empirical systems of power. Most rules researchers employ these explanatory principles in combination to generate their theoretic claims.

We are now in a position to explore the actual use of these rules specific philosophic assumptions and theoretic principles of explanation in paradigmatic exemplars.

PARADIGMATIC EXEMPLARS OF RULES THEORIES

> *The latter half of the twentieth century has witnessed another revolution in communication which has restructured the character of society and its educational institutions. This communication revolution has introduced into the academic arena a marketplace of the practical and technological world with the premise that that which is most valuable is that which can be applied. The emphasis is on the adaptation of a specific set of skills and knowledge to specific areas. It is not the importance of the skills or knowledge in and of themselves but the adaptation of them to the marketplace that is important.*
>
> —King (1989, p. 7)

Scholars with major research programs positioned within a rules theoretic perspective are large in number, varied in interests, and span a significant period of time. These include several programs begun in the early 1980s and continuing to date such as Cushman and associates' work on the interpersonal relationship processes (Cushman & Cahn, 1985), Pearce and associates' work on the coordinated management of meaning (Pearce & Cronen, 1980), Sanders and associates' work on strategic interaction (Sanders, 1987), Philipsen and associates' work on the ethnography of communication (Philipsen, 1992), and Donohue and associates' work on negotiation and conflict resolution (Donahue, Cushman, & Nofsinger, 1980). No less than 100 research monographs have been published within our field since 1980 by these scholars and many others, which seek to contribute to the development of the rules theoretic tradition. It is impossible in the space allocated here to summarize all or even the most significant contributions to this scholarly tradition. Rather, we have selected portions of the work of three theorists as exemplars which illustrate the development of communication theory within this perspective.

More specifically, we shall explore portions of the works of (a) Michael Huspek and his associates aimed at developing a critical hermeneutic within a rules perspective, (b) Gerry Philipsen and his associates aimed at exploring communication as a cultural resource, and (c) Donald Cushman and his associates aimed at exploring the role of communication in establishing, maintaining, and terminating mate relationships. Examining such research exemplars allow the authors to reveal the flesh, bone, and excitement that comes with the development of practical theories within this research tradition.

MICHAEL HUSPEK AND ASSOCIATES' WORK ON A CRITICAL HERMENEUTIC

Critical theory attempts to explore the role of power in distorting human interaction and to locate communication competencies which show promise of emancipating interactants from the consequences of such distortions. As Huspek (1991) argues, "theory must be critical if we are not to remain trapped within a hermeneutic circle where dominant ideologies or oppressive cultural practices go unrecognized or are reproduced under the guise of scientific objectivity" (p. 225). Huspek (1991) goes on to argue that, "If our theories are to be critical and emancipatory in ways that are responsive to speakers' practical needs, they require development through means of a critical hermeneutic inquiry" (p. 225).

Although theory must be critical if it is to be humane, not all critical theorists position themselves within a rules theoretic tradition. Some, such as Habermas (1970a, 1970b) turn to such transcendental ("out" of space and time) criteria as truth, freedom, and justice for evaluating human interaction; others such as some feminists evolved an ideological conception of desired equality while still others such as some Black and Hispanic American minorities developed leverage from a legal conception of equal opportunity. It is in exploring the ideological and cultural oppression found in concrete, empirical human interaction from a critical hermeneutic that Huspek positions himself within a communication rules theoretic tradition. A critical hermeneutic stance explores the consensus achieved and maintained in interaction by tacking back and forth between the individual intentions and meanings of the interactants and the operative consensus in order to reveal the distortions a given consensus forces upon the individual meanings and behaviors of those involved. A critical hermeneutics according to Huspek (1991), "proves itself critical and emancipatory by grounding itself in the realm of practice, tapping into the life world meanings that inform speakers' everyday discursive struggles and then going on to search out within the horizons of the life world meanings fully actualized or implicit instances of ideological critique and emergent communicative competencies" (p. 225).

One instance of such a critical hermeneutic at work is to be found in Huspek and Kendall's (1991) study "On Withholding Political Voice" among White lower class American workers. This study focuses on "the reasons behind unskilled workers withholding their voice from the political arena, ". . . on how the ideology of a dominant political culture fails to penetrate the workers life world and how the workers develop an oppositional set of meanings that, ironically, discourage workers from publicly voicing political dissent" (Huspek & Kendall, 1991, p. 17). This analysis opens by noting the fundamental role citizens have in America in voicing their political opinions and interests to the press and their political representatives. Huspek and Kendall (1991) conclude that "inextricably bound up with this view is the belief that both democracy and freedom may be diminished, when citizens withhold their voice from the political arena" (p. 1). Next they note the limited participation of many Americans in the political process both in terms of the percent who vote and those who are active in political campaigns and interest groups. In an effort to locate the locus of this problem they turn to an ethnographic analysis of power and powerless talk about the political process by workers in a lumberyard. Such talk is termed "Shit Talk" and "Crybaby Talk."

Political talk from the workers' point of view is characterized by "corruption, greed, backstabbing" and can be traced to the need for self aggrandizement by powerholders. *Shit talk* is, according to the workers, the discourse employed by powerholders to minimize the input and significance of the powerless. This basic approach to the powerless discourages the powerless from becoming active in the interaction process. The constant rationale provided by the powerless, on the other hand, for nonparticipation in the interaction process is that their opinions and interests will be viewed as *Crybaby talk*; they will be seen as "cryin" and "bitchin." Thus, they withhold their input into the political process further diminishing their communicative power.

In providing their critical hermeneutic analysis of workers' political talk, Huspek and Kendall (1991) examine the structure, function and strategies employed by workers and powerholders in order to provide an explanation of how and why discourse has the effect it has upon the interactants. They contrast the individual intentions and meanings of the workers and the powerholders with the interactively established consensus of *Shit talk* and *Crybaby talk* in order to explain the power and powerlessness of interaction.

Huspek and Kendall (1991) conclude:

> First, if the alternative political vocabulary provides the workers with a morally based social identity, as Nietzsche averred, (1967) a morality that celebrates powerlessness as a virtue may be steeped in resentment. Second, and perhaps more important here, if an alternative vocabulary legitimizes political inaction in ways that protect speakers from undue political recriminations, it may simultaneously discourage speakers from seizing opportunities to gain freedoms that are gained only in and through the public contestation of values, policies, and norms. (p. 15)

Another instance of a critical hermeneutic at work is to be found in Huspek's (1989) study "Linguistic Variability and Power" on the use of a "You Know" verbal qualifier among workers in an industrial lumberyard. Socially disadvantaged speakers—White lower class American workers in the study—use the "You Know" verbal qualifier very frequently in contrast to another verbal qualifier—"I Think"—employed mostly by powerful speakers. Huspek argues that these two linguistic variants, verbal qualifiers, do not simply mark off a powerful speech community from a disadvantaged and powerless one. Rather, he insists, one should examine the relative effectiveness of the use of the "You Know" variant.

Huspek's critical hermeneutic analysis revealed that lumberjacks use the *You Know* verbal qualifier for different purposes, and achieve different goals across a range of social and communicative contexts. In some situations these disadvantaged speakers are able to use the *You Know* sequence to assert power, to express solidarity, and to critically think. These are instances in which they are able to overcome linguistic and symbolic inequalities created and protected by powerholders. In other contexts, however, they fail to escape their socially and symbolically inferior position.

In both studies, communication rules assumptions and rules theoretic explanatory principles such as the structure, function, and strategies of interactants are employed to develop theories of and insights into a critical communication rules perspective.

GERRY PHILIPSEN AND ASSOCIATES' WORK ON COMMUNICATION AS A CULTURAL RESOURCE

Over the past 15 years, Gerry Philipsen and his associates have attempted to develop a unique theoretic program within the traditionally nontheoretic ethnography of speaking research methodology. Philipsen (1987) begins his analysis by suggesting that every society must deal with "the inevitable tension between the impulse of individuals to be free and the constraints of communial life" (p. 246). Society is thus viewed as the generative mechanism for cultural communication patterns aimed at resolving this tension. Communication is a cultural resource which society employs to integrate individuals into a community, while maintaining their individual identity. Philipsen and his associates then go on to provide a rules theoretic analysis of how communication as a cultural resource is employed to resolve this problem.

Every society, if it is to establish a sense of community or shared identity, must resolve three communication problems. *First*, the need to coordinate diverse lines of action, or the problem of *alignment*. *Second*, the need to define oneself and the relationship of self to society, or the problem of *meaning*. *Third*, the need for standards which permit and distribute discourse or the problem of *form*. Problems of alignment, meaning, and form are resolved by cultural communication aimed at establishing rituals, myths, and social dramas which integrate individuals into the culture.

The manner in which a community's consensus is tested is through three social acts: (a) *ritual*, which functions to "maintain the consensus necessary for social equilibrium order, especially the non-rational consensus"; (b) *myth*, which "posits a super-sensable world of meaning and values from which the least member of a tribe can borrow something to dignify and give coherence to life"; and (c) *social drama*, which "serves to define boundaries of a group and to reintegrate those members whose acts have tested its boundaries" (Philipsen, 1987). These necessary cultural forms or recurrent interaction patterns facilitate cultural coordination and thus invite explication through an ethnography of speaking. Such an explication will generate rules theories of these cultural communication processes.

The basic tenants of Philipsen and Associates' methodology is then articulated by providing a description of an ethnographer's general task ". . . to grasp the native's point of view, his relation to life, and to realize his world vision" (Malinowski, 1922). The ethnography of speaking will then attempt to explicate the common cultural knowledge or communication rules, which one must share in order to use language appropriately within society.

A precise application of Philipsen and Associates' theoretic and research perspective can be found in their analysis of communication as a cultural resource in various subcultures of American society. In "Teamsterville," Philipsen explores the cultural communication rules for presenting and defending one's male role within a community of truckers residing on the edge of Chicago. In Teamsterville on a summer evening, the appropriate place for talk is on a street corner or in a bar. Next, Philipsen (1975) addresses the communication rules involved in "the appropriateness of speaking versus other actional strategies (such as silence, violence, or nonverbal threats) in male role enactment or self-presentation" (p. 14). Two structural sequences or rituals are located for fulfilling the task of bringing about a recognition of one's manliness in Teamsterville. They are:

1. "When the social identity relationship of the participants in a situation is symmetrical, the situation can appropriately realize a great amount of talk by a Teamsterville man" (Philipsen, 1975, p. 15). (Symmetrical social identity relationships are operationalized as individuals matched by age, sex, ethnicity, occupational status, and residents who are longtime friends. The two principal situations where such interactions occur are the street corner for boys, and the corner bar for men).

2. A high quantity of speaking is considered inappropriate in situations where the participants' identity relationships are asymmetrical (Philipsen, 1975, p. 15). (Asymmetrical relationships are operationalized as those involving a wife, child, boss, or outsider. Speaking through intermediaries is appropriate for these situations in which a Teamsterville resident must impress or influence status superiors or outsiders. Pride is taken in having "connections," like the ward committeeman, who will intercede in one's behalf. The use of talk is inappropriate in situations when a man has been insulted, and he seeks to influence the behavior of a status inferior. Physical action is obligatory in such situations for the successful performance of a masculine role.)

A particularly insightful procedure was employed by Philipsen (1976) for assessing the commonality of expectations in regard to the rules cited above as well as the consequences which ensue from failing to follow the rules. Each violation of the foregoing communication rules resulted in an attempt by all the males present to force the violator to conform to the appropriate episodic sequence by citing the rules. When the cited rule failed to elicit the appropriate behavioral response, all males present broke off interaction with the violator, viewing him as an "outsider" who was unable to discern a threat to the credibility of his male role.

Philipsen developed a general theoretical claim that "the ends and means of speaking are culturally contingent." Ethnographic research has provided ample evidence that social groups defined as speech communities possess different conceptions of persons, social relations, and communicative practices that link members in a relation of shared social identity. These components of culture are revealed in the interlocutors' talk. Philipsen (1992) argues that the most appropriate ethnography of speaking is culturally contexted conversation analysis. One can understand communicative practices only in particular contexts by capturing the meanings the participants create, exchange, and sustain in the real structure of social interaction—"real-life" sequences of conversation.

Two of Philipsen's ethnographic studies illustrate and justify his general theoretical claim that communicative practices are culture-specific and culture-rich. In the first study, "Deep Perplexity, Cultures and Ethnography," Philipsen (1984) examines a concrete political event involving speakers who use different cultures while trying to settle accounts in public. The event that triggered personal and political conflict occurred in July of 1971, when the late Richard J. Daley, then Mayor of Chicago, gave high City office to a son of his friend and political ally. To his surprise, the Mayor was publicly accused by a university professor, a new member of the City Council, of nepotism and of using "connections" to secure political office and power to appoint his friends. While the Mayor accused the professor for "undermining society" and the Mayor's legitimacy, the professor (and the mass media) claimed that the Mayor was immoral. Philipsen argues that these accusations make sense only if we understand that parties to a conflict drew on two opposite, even exclusive, social and moral codes. The Mayor used the arguments rooted in the *code of honor* that not only justified but demanded that powerholders appoint their friends, and members of local ethnic community. The professor (and the mass media), on the other hand, drew on the *code of dignity* that demanded equality of opportunity, and merit regardless of ethnic background as criteria for fair political appointments. *Since these codes contained irreconcilable values, the speakers were not able to compromise. The stronger speaker, the Mayor, won.*

In the second study, "A Chinese-American Way of Speaking: The Conative Function," Philipsen and Fong (1991) examine the ways in which immigrant Chinese parents try to persuade their adult children, first generation Chinese Americans, to get married. They found that the Chinese parents use four persuasive strategies. First, they employ *indirect linguistic strategies*, which do not directly express their goals. They assume and expect that children would get the message. Second, the parents rely on *communication through intermediaries*. In this case, relatives, siblings, or close friends act as messengers who convey parental wishes and desires to the adult child. Third, the parents frequently employ *unspoken action strategy* when they rely on particular nonverbal acts rather than talk to express demands or requests. Finally, *if the three strategies fail and do not produce desired consequences*, the parents use *direct communication strategy*. As a last resort, the parents use direct statements to unequivocally express their wishes.

Americans, on the other hand, use communication differently. In "What We Need is Communication": "Communication" As a Cultural Category, Katriel and Philipsen (1981) explore the communication rules Americans employ in separating two types of interaction: communication and mere talk. The need for communication as opposed to mere talk arises when a cultural member's preferred relationship to others is called into question by events or others. Under such circumstances, the offended individual seeks out a cultural member and attempts to initiate the "communication ritual." The purpose of this ritual is to resolve the sense of problematic identity that a cultural member is experiencing by engaging in intimate interaction. The structure of this episodic sequence (Katriel & Philipsen, 1981) is prescribed.

  (a) *Initiation*, a communication is initiated by a member of an intimate pair through announcing a problem;

(b) *Acknowledgement*, the addressee shows his/her willingness to enact the sequence by acknowledging the legitimacy of the other's intimate problem;

(c) *Negotiation*, the initiator discloses the problem, discussing its ingredients and implications—the addressee merely empathizes;

(d) *Reaffirmation*, discrepant positions, needs and interpretations between committed individuals are brought into relief (p. 315).

Katriel and Philipsen (1981) view communication as a process of social interaction in which the participants negotiate definitions of self and others, that is, as a culturally distinctive solution to the universal problem of fusing the personal with the communal. In the ideology in which *communication* is a pivotal term, affirming oneself in and through a process of social interaction is the highest good.

Philipsen and his associates employ communication rules assumptions and rules theoretic principles of explanation by exploring the functions, structures and strategies involved in explicating communication as a cultural resource. In so doing, they develop communication rules theories which govern and guide cultural interaction in America.

CUSHMAN AND ASSOCIATES' WORK ON
COMMUNICATION IN MATE RELATIONSHIPS

Cushman and associates have attempted over the past 15 years to explore in some detail the role communication plays in establishing, maintaining, and terminating various types of interpersonal relationships. Central to their inquiry has been the acceptance of communication rules assumptions.

In order to develop a verifiable construct for locating communication rules from an actor's point of view, attention has been directed to conceptualizing and measuring individual self concepts. Their rationale is as follows:

The self-concept traditionally has been viewed as the information individuals have regarding the relationship of objects or groups of objects to themselves (Mead, 1934, p. 243). Individuals moving in their environments are confronted by persons, places, things, or concepts. If they are to commit themselves to any actions toward those objects, individuals must perform two tasks. First, they must determine what the objects of their experiences are by associating them with and differentiating them from other objects they have experienced. Second, they must determine the relationship of the objects or groups of objects to themselves in terms of appropriate actions in appropriate circumstances. Their knowledge of what objects are and how they should act toward them are products of information based on past experiences. (Cushman, 1989, pp. 91–92)

The self-concept is thus conceptualized and measured as the information an individual has regarding his or her relationship to objects be they persons, places, or things. The internal organization of this self-concept information may remain stable or be modified through perception and/or the interaction with others. Cushman (1989) then explores the relationship of self-concept to the role of communication in establishing, maintaining, and terminating various types of interpersonal relationships

> Then in communication, individuals describe, assert, and propose their preferred relationship to others: "I love you," "I hate you," "I want to be your friend," "I can persuade you to go to the movies," "I hope they let me go swimming with them." These descriptions, assertions, and proposals are then accepted, questioned, or denied by others in communication. In this manner, individuals learn who they are and what they can and cannot do. Only then can an individual develop intentions and means for fulfilling those intentions. (p. 93)

In interpersonal interaction, individuals communicate their preferred type of relationship to others, that is, friends, lovers, mates. These proposals may then be accepted, negotiated or rejected by others. For example, La Gaipa (1977) reports that 55% of friend and Booth (1972) reports that 80% of mate relationship attempts are rejected by others. Through such interpersonal communication processes, one learns what one can and cannot do and how and who one can establish interpersonal relationships with. Further Cushman and Associates have demonstrated that *different types of interpersonal relationships such as friend and mate are rooted in different types of self-concept support* (Cushman, Valentinsen, & Dietrich, 1982). In addition, they have also established that *differing degrees of relational intimacy such as casual friend, good friend, and best friend involve differing amounts of self-concept support* (Cushman, 1989; Bahk, 1993).

Inasmuch as the self-concept consists of an individual's perceptions regarding his or her relationship to others, and *differing types and degrees of self-concept support* by others, lead to differing types of interpersonal relationships and levels of intimacy, then a communication rules theory could be developed by locating and measuring these types and levels of perceived self-concept support conveyed through interaction. While Cushman and associates have investigated such interpersonal relationships as friend, lover, and mate, their most extensive efforts have been in how one establishes, maintains and terminates mate relationships. Let us explore the results of that effort.

Cushman and associates employ the term *mate* to denote any opposite sex other for which one clears the field of competitors. Such relationships normally involve a major proportion of individuals who are going steady, engaged, married, or cohabitating.

Establishing a Mate Relationship. Mate selection is explored by Cushman and associates through a three-stage communication filtering process which involves (1) a field of availables, (2) a field of approachables, and (3) a field of reciprocals.

Field of Availables. People with whom one interacts but whom one does not find desirable and does not approach to initiate a mate relationship with constitute one's *field of availables* (see also Berger and Calabreze, 1975; and Duck, 1976).

Field of Approachables. Within one's field of availables, there exists a subset of individuals whom one finds desirable and whom one can approach in order to initiate a mate relationship. Cushman and associates have explored the communication rules governing what one must convey to another for the other to recognize that one wants to establish a mate relationship in six cultures around the world. *Table 8.1 lists what this entry level self-concept support must communicate.*

In America, one must communicate to the other that he or she is intelligent, physically attractive, and sexually appealing. Cushman, Valentinsen, and Dietrich (1982) found these qualities to be matching variables, meaning that one prefers as a mate another who has about the same amount of intelligence, physical attraction, and sex appeal as one thinks he or she has. Americans appear to worry if the other is not about the same as they are in this regard and if not would refuse to clear the field.

Field of Reciprocals. Within one's field of approachables exists a subset of individuals who will reciprocate when attempts are made to establish a mate relationship. That is, they will not only communicate to the person who initiates the relationship that they view them also as intelligent, physically attractive, and sexually appealing, but they will over time attempt to deepen the intimacy of the relationship. *Table 8.1 lists what types of intensity self-concept support must be communicated for the intimacy of mateship to increase in six cultures throughout the world.*

In America, Cushman, Valentinsen, and Dietrich (1982) found that the more each person involved in a mate relationship communicated respect, affection, and psychological support, the more rapidly a mate relationship increased its levels of intimacy from a casual date, to a steady date, to fiance, to mate. Note that entry level variables must be present to begin the relationship but do not deepen the relationship through frequent communication. However, the intensity variables when reciprocated do increase the depth of intimacy the more often they are communicated. One can communicate perceived self-concept support of the types listed above either *directly* or *indirectly*. For example, I can tell you I respect you directly or communicate the same thing indirectly when we talk about the things you are interested in. Cushman and associates have developed an interpersonal topic penetration profile for tracking what topics are most discussed between mates in each culture and how the topic penetration influences indirect self-concept support (Nicotera, Cushman, & Lin, 1991).

While space does not allow a full discussion of all the cultures listed in Table 8.1, the entry and intensity variables work in a similar manner as in America. Note how the differences in these entry level and intensity level self-concept

TABLE 8.1
Mate Selection Process

	United States	Yugoslavia	Bolivia	China	Korea	Japan
Entry Rules						
Field of Approachables	Intelligent Physically attractive	Intelligent Attractive Sexually appealing	Intelligent Passionate Good looking	High moral standards Common interest Family finances	Intelligent Sound health Handles money well Value similarity	Competent Value similarity Sound health Handles money well
Initiation	Sexually appealing					
Intensity Rules						
Field of Reciprocals	Respect Affection Psychological support	Likable Tolerant Right interests Sense of humor Trustful	Understanding Responsible Trustworthy Respectful Loving	Workability Emotionally compatible Loving	Easy to talk to Assertive Understanding Value similarity	Easy to talk to Affectionate Honest
Deepening the Intimacy						
Research Citation	Cushman, Valentinsen, and Dietrich (1982); Cushman, Schroder, and Brenner (1983); Cushman and Cahn (1993)	Foldy, Danielson, and Cushman (1988)	Cushman and King (1991)	Ju (1993)	Nicotera, Cushman, and Lin (1992)	Cushman and Nashida (1985)

support variables across cultures complicate the problems involved in providing the correct kind of self-concept support to establish and deepen mixed culture mate relationships.

Maintaining Mate Relationships. Both common sense and research indicate that maintaining a mate relationship may be even more difficult than establishing one. Common sense tells us that once a mate relationship is established, it may be difficult to wake up each morning and have to communicate to another that one is intelligent, physically attractive, and sexually appealing, and then to successfully deal with the broad range of issues and problems that emerge each day while constantly communicating respect, affection, and support for the other. In addition, researchers tell us that between 45% and 55% of all mate relationships will be terminated and that 55% of those individuals will form new mate relationships 60% of which will terminate again (Glick, 1987). Of those who terminate mate relationships, 46% of the impetus to terminate is explained by the quality of the mate relationships, 33% by the availability of an alternative quality relationship, and 9% by external pressure from friends and family (Green & Sporakowski, 1983). Thus, a key element in the maintenance of a mate relationship is the task of maintaining the quality of that relationship.

A quality mate relationship according to Argyle and Furnham (1983) and Cushman (1989) comes from the reciprocal communication of psychological support, affection and respect. The lack of a quality relationship is, according to those same researchers, engendered by the reciprocal communication of negative affect, competition and criticism. *High quality communication patterns unfortunately were found in only 20 percent of a sample of mate relationships examined while low quality communication patterns were found in 75% of that sample* (Copland, Bugaighis, & Schumm, 1983).

A variety of researchers point to the manner in which mates handle conflict as a controlling factor in maintaining a high quality mate relationship (Argyle & Furnham, 1983; Cole, 1985; Cushman, 1989). Cushman and associates locates two patterns of conflict resolution in mate relationships. The first, which manifests high quality relationships and communicates psychological support, affection and respect thus deepens the intimacy of the relationship. The second pattern, which generates low quality relationships contains negative affect, competition, and criticism. Because most couples according to Copland, Bugaighis, & Schumm (1983) employ the low quality communication pattern, learning and employing the high quality pattern is an important tool for maintaining a high quality mate relationship. Table 8.2 contains an outline of both communication sequences.

In *high quality* communication relationships, mates begin a conflict by introducing a focused issue/problem with neutral affect. For example, while I love your mother, her house, and hospitality, her cooking is a problem to me and I need to talk with you about it. In a *low quality* communication relationship, mates begin a conflict sequence by lodging a complaint with negative affect. For example, you

TABLE 8.2
High and Low Quality Conflict Patterns

---

1.   High mateship quality is achieved by employing the following communication sequences
     in dealing with relational conflict:

     a.   introduce a focused issue
     b.   obtain agreement on a preportionalized issue with neutral affect
     c.   draw out implications of issue to relationship
     d.   explore suggested solutions
     e.   establish a consensus on a solution and implement it.

When such a sequence of conflict resolution is employed, it will be viewed as demonstrating
support, affection, and respect thus giving rise to increased intimacy and high relational quality.

2.   Low mateship quality is obtained by employing the following communication sequences in
     resolving relational conflict:

     a.   introduce a complaint about the other with negative affect
     b.   mate responds by confronting, defending, and cross complaining
     c.   communication of neutral or negative affect
     d.   reciprocation of negative affect
     e.   withdrawal or escalation.

When such a pattern of conflict resolution is employed, it demonstrates competition and criticism
for the other, thus giving rise to decreased intimacy and low relational quality.

From Cushman (1989, p. 101).

know how I hate your mother's cooking. Next, in a *high quality* relationship, the
respondent obtains agreement on a preportionalized issue with neutral affect. For
example, I remember you did like my mother's salads and you loved her desserts,
but I do remember that you were not that happy with her stew. In *low quality*
relationships, the respondents employ confrontation, defending and cross complaining. For example, you always complain about my mother's cooking, your
mother isn't exactly a gourmet cook. Next, in *high quality* relationships, the couple
explores potential solutions and establishes a consensus on a solution and imple-
ments it. In *low quality* relationships, cross complaining is followed by neutral or
negative affect, followed by reciprocated negative affect leading to escalation or
withdrawal.

The effect of conflict resolution in the high quality communication relationship
is to demonstrate psychological support, affection, and respect, deepening intimacy
and providing confidence in their ability to deal with future problematic issues. The
effect of conflict resolution in low quality relationship is to undermine psychological support, affection, and respect, destroying intimacy and limiting the number of
topics the couple can talk about constructively in the future. Repeated use of the
low quality pattern leads to a decline in intimacy and to conflict over the
relationship. The couples stop communicating with each other on either level.

Terminating Mate Relationship

In most people's lives, mate relationships really matter. Most Americans report
that nothing contributes more to their sense of well being than the quality of
their mate relationships (Booth, 1972). Therefore, when a mate relationship

terminates, it frequently has an overwhelming effect upon one or more of the persons involved. In the case of a family with children, such a breakup is particularly devastating. Cushman and Cahn (1986) explored just such a situation when they interviewed 15 divorced couples and their 62 children in order to locate the communication rules which governed and guided their interaction during and immediately following such a breakup.

Following Stokes and Hewitt, Cushman and Cahn begin their analysis by treating mateship termination from a communication rules perspective as an alignment problem.

> Aligning actions ... are forms of conduct, mainly verbal, in which individuals effect alignment in ... two senses ... they sustain the flow of joint actions by bringing individual acts into line with one another in problematic circumstances, and they sustain a relationship between ongoing conduct and culture in the face of recognized failure of conduct to live up to cultural definitions and requirements. (Stokes & Hewitt, 1976, p. 844)

There are a variety of communication strategies for dealing with alignment problems. Cushman and Cahn focus on the interactants' use of *accounts* in explaining the relational breakup to their children. The giving of accounts as a particular means of aligning actions is defined as making statements to explain bad, wrong, inept, or in other ways, untoward behavior in order to bridge the gap between the unwanted actions and others' expectations. The classification of types of accounts helps us to understand how they are used to align actions through communication. Cushman and Cahn employ Schonback (1980) typology of accounts into excuses, justifications, concessions and refusals. Excuses, justifications, concessions and refusals are examples of accounts which may be used to neutralize an untoward act or its consequences when one or both are called into question. Table 8.3 contains a summary of the interactants' perceptions of the account-giving process.

Fifty-six percent of the parents and 40% of the children reported that parents gave *excuses*; that is, an account in which one admits that the act in question, the divorce, is bad, but deny full responsibility for it. Twenty-two percent of the parents and 34% of the children recall parents using *justifications*; that is, an account in which one accepts responsibility for the act of divorce, but denies the pejorative qualities associated with it. Ten percent of the parents and 18% of the children reported the use of *concessions*; that is, accounts in which one parent admits responsibility for the divorce and offers restitution. Finally, 12% of the parents and 8% of the children recall the use of *refusal*; that is, a refusal provides no acknowledgement of responsibility and denies the pejorative effects of divorce.

Divorce tears apart the web of family interactions and communication. Children are particularly hurt by the sudden break-up of stable, predictable, and supportive family communication system.

TABLE 8.3
Summary of Parents' Divorce Accounts as Perceived by Parents and Their Children

Type of Account	Frequency of Accounts as Perceived by Parents (n = 30)	Frequency of Accounts as Perceived by Children (n = 62)
Excuses	56%	40%
Justifications	22%	34%
Concessions	10%	18%
Refusals	12%	8%
Total	100%	100%

From Cushman and Cahn (1986, p. 82).

Seventy percent of the children reported first hearing of the termination from their mother. One hundred percent of the children reported being emotionally upset, confused, and disoriented by the termination and account. Following the mateship termination announcement and accounting process, the children reported it was *2 months* before they could resume normal interaction with their mother and *2 years* before normal interaction occurred with their father.

Cushman and associates employed communication rules assumptions and structural, functional, strategic and critical rules theoretic principles to construct a rules theory of how one establishes, maintains, and terminates a mate relationship.

SUMMARY

Our long journey is over. We have examined in some detail the work of numerous scholars in articulating how human communication theory functions from a system and rules perspective. We have examined three rules theoretic philosophic assumptions; *the motion-action* assumption, *the information processing-social coordination* assumption and the *creative-standardized usage* assumption.

We have examined the types of theoretic claims made by rules theorists and the four explanatory principles employed in warranting those claims; the *structural, functional, strategic,* and *critical explanatory* perspectives.

Finally, we have examined three paradigmatic exemplars of various rules theoretic approaches; *Michael Huspek and associates'* work aimed at developing a critical hermeneutic within a rules perspective, *Gerry Philipsen and associates'* work aimed at exploring communication as a cultural resource, and *Donald Cushman and associates'* work aimed at exploring the role communication plays in establishing, maintaining, and terminating mate relationships.

CONCLUSION

Communication rules theoretic assumptions and theories view humankind as intentional actors who seek to pursue individual and societal interests by refining their knowledge and skills through the use of human communication in the world. As Ann Marion so aptly put it, "We want to fashion puppets that pull their own strings" (Brand, 1987, p. 95).

REFERENCES

Argyle, M., & Furnham, A. (1983). Sources of satisfaction and conflict in long-term relationships. *Journal of Marriage and the Family, 45,* 481–493.

Bahk, C. (1993). Perceptions of same-sex and opposite-sex friendships in the United States and Korea. In A. M. Nicotera & Associates, *Interpersonal communication in friend and mate relationships* (pp. 79–106). Albany, NY: SUNY Press.

Berger, C., & Calabrese, R. (1975). Some explorations in initial interaction and beyond: Towards a developmental theory of interpersonal communication. *Human Communication Research, 1,* 99–112.

Booth, A. (1972). Sex and social participation. *American Sociological Review, 37,* 183–192.

Brand, S. (1987). *The media lab: Inventing the future at MIT.* New York: Viking.

Cole, C. (1985). Relationship quality in long-term marriages: A comparison of high and low quality marriages. *Life Styles: A Journal of Changing Patterns, 11,* 248–257.

Copland, J., Bugaighis, M., & Schumm, W. (1983). Relationship characteristics of couples married thirty years or more: A four sample replication. *Life Styles: A Journal of Changing Patterns, 11,* 248–257.

Cushman, D. (1989). Communication in establishing, maintaining, and terminating interpersonal relationships: A study of mateship. In S. S. King (Ed.), *Human communication as a field of study: Selected contemporary views* (pp. 87–104). Albany, NY: SUNY Press.

Cushman, D. (1990). A rules approach to communication theory. In A. Tsujimura & L. Kincaid (Eds.), *Communication theory from an eastern and western perspective* (pp. 87–104). Japan: Nippon, LTD.

Cushman, D., & Cahn, D. (1985). *Communication in interpersonal relationships.* Albany, NY: SUNY Press.

Cushman, D., & Cahn, D. (1986). A study of communicative realignment between parents and children following the parents' decision to seek divorce. *Communication Research Reports, 3,* 80–85.

Cushman, D., & Cahn, D. (1993). Mate relationship entry, intensity, and communication variables: A preliminary study. In A. M. Nicotera & Associates, *Interpersonal communication in friend and mate relationships* (pp. 139–146). Albany, NY: SUNY Press.

Cushman, D., & King, S. (1991). *The mate selection process in Bolivia.* Unpublished manuscript, State University of New York at Albany.

Cushman, D., King, S., & Smith, T. (1988). The rules perspective on organizational communication. In G. Goldhaber & G. Barnett (Eds.), *Handbook of organizational communication* (pp. 53–97). Norwood, NJ: Ablex.

Cushman, D., & Nashida, T. (1985). In D. Cushman & D. Cahn, *Communication in interpersonal relationships* (p. 140). Albany, NY: SUNY Press.

Cushman, D., & Pearce, W. B. (1977). Generality and necessity in three types of human communication theory: Special attention to rules theory. In D. Rubin, *Communication Yearbook 1* (pp. 175–183). New Brunswick, NJ: Transaction Press.

Cushman, D., Schroeder, K., & Brenner, D. (1983). *Rules in mate relationships*: An empirical study. Unpublished paper presented at the SCA Convention.

Cushman, D., Valentinsen, G., & Dietrich, D. (1982). A rules theory of interpersonal relationships. In F. Dance, *Human communication theory* (pp. 90–119). New York: Harper & Row.

Cushman, D., & Whiting, G. (1972). An approach to communication theory: Towards consensus on rules. *Journal of Communication, 22*, 217–232.

Donohue, W., Cushman, D., & Nofsinger, R. (1980). Creating and confronting social order: A comparison of rules perspectives. *The Western Journal of Speech Communication, 44*, 5–19.

Duck, S. (1976). Interpersonal communication in developing acquaintance. In G. Miller (Ed.), *Explorations in interpersonal communication* (pp. 127–147). Beverly Hills, CA: Sage.

Fay, B., & Moon, D. (1977). What would an adequate philosophy of social science look like? *Philosophy of Social Science, 7*, 209–221.

Foldy, J., Danielson, S., & Cushman, D. (1988). The characteristics of mates and the communication patterns involved in initiating mate relationships in American culture as compared to Yugoslavian culture. *Informatologia Yugoslavica, 20*, 147–157.

Glick, P. (1987). Marriage, divorce and living arrangements. *Journal of Personality and Social Psychology, 49*, 1216–1266.

Green, R., & Sporakowski, M. (1983). The dynamics of divorce: Marital quality, alternative attraction and external pressure. *Journal of Divorce, 7*, 77–88.

Habermas, J. (1970a). On systematically distorted communication. *Inquiry, 13*, 205–218.

Habermas, J. (1970b). Towards a theory of communicative competence. *Inquiry, 13*, 360–373.

Huspek, M. (1989). Linguistic variability and power. *Journal of Pragmatics, 13*, 661–683.

Huspek, M. (1989–1990). The idea of ethnography and its relation to cultural critique. *Research on Language and Social Interaction, 23*, 293–313.

Huspek, M. (1991). Taking aim on Habermas' critical theory: On the road toward a critical hermeneutics. *Communication Monographs, 58*, 225–233.

Huspek, M., & Kendall, K. (1991). On withholding political voice: An analysis of the political vocabulary of a nonpolitical speech community. *The Quarterly Journal of Speech, 77*, 1–19.

Ju, Y. (1993). Mate selection as Cultural Choice: Reflections on findings in China, Japan, and Korea. In A. M. Nicotera & Associates, *Interpersonal communication in friend and mate relationships* (pp. 201–218). Albany, NY: SUNY Press.

Katriel, T., & Philipsen, G. (1981). "What we need is communication": "Communication" as a cultural category in some American speech. *Communication Monographs, 48*, 301–317.

King, S. S. (1989). Communication: Roots, visions, and prospects. In S. S. King (Ed.), *Human communication as a field of study: Selected contemporary views* (pp. 1–11). Albany, NY: SUNY Press.

La Gaipa, J. (1977). Testing a multi-dimensional approach to friendship. In S. Duck (Ed.), *Theory and practice of interpersonal attraction* (pp. 249–271). London: Academic Press.

Malinowski, B. (1922). *Argonauts of the western pacific*. London, England: George Routledge & Son.

Manicas, P. (1980). The concept of social structure. *Journal of Theory of Social Behavior, 10*, 65–82.

Mead, G. (1934). *Mind, self, society*. Chicago, IL: University of Chicago Press.

Nicotera, A., Cushman, D., & Lin, T. (1992). Development of mate relationships in two cultures: Theoretical universals in the United States and Korea. Paper presented at ASA, Chicago. Parts of the paper are published in Nicotera, A. M. (1993). Development of the mate relationship in two cultures: Theoretical universals in the United States and Korea. In A. M. Nicotera and Associates, *Interpersonal communication in friend and mate relationships* (pp. 147–167). Albany, NY: SUNY Press.

Pearce, W. B., & Cronen, V. (1980). *Communication, action and meaning*. New York: Praeger.

Philipsen, G. (1975). Speaking "like a man" in Teamsterville: Culture patterns of role enactment in an urban neighborhood. *Quarterly Journal of Speech, 61,* 13–22.

Philipsen, G. (1976). Places for speaking in Teamsterville. *Quarterly Journal of Speech, 62,* 15–25.

Philipsen, G. (1987). The prospect for cultural communication. In D. L. Kincaid (Ed.), *Communication theory from eastern and western perspectives* (pp. 245–254). New York: Academic Press.

Philipsen, G. (1984). *Deep perplexity, cultures and ethnography.* Unpublished manuscript.

Philipsen, G. (1992). *Speaking culturally: Explorations in social communication.* Albany, NY: SUNY Press.

Philipsen, G., & Fong, M. (1991). *A Chinese-American way of speaking: The conativite function.* Unpublished paper.

Sanders, R. E. (1987). *Cognitive foundations of calculated speech: Controlling understandings in conversation and persuasion.* Albany, NY: SUNY Press.

Sanders, R., & Cushman, D. P. (1984). Rules, constraints, and strategies in human communication. In C. Arnold & J. Bowers (Eds.), *Handbook of rhetoric and communication* (pp. 230–269). Rockleigh, NJ: Allen Bacon.

Schonback, P. (1980). A category system for account phases. *European Journal of Social Psychology, 10,* 195–200.

Stokes, R., & Hewitt, J. (1976). Aligning actions. *American Sociological Review, 41,* 838–849.

Taylor, C. (1970). The explanation of purporsive behavior. In R. Borger & F. Cioffi (Eds.), *Explanation in the Behavioral Sciences* (pp. 57–97). Cambridge, England: Cambridge University Press.

Conclusions

Fred L. Casmir
Pepperdine University

At this point, it is a great temptation to do two things (in addition to wondering if anyone ever reads conclusions). First, I could assume that you have not read the book carefully nor used its content for interactions with your instructor and your peers. Thus, here it would behoove me to try and summarize several hundred hundred pages of text—something which goes against my entire concept of what education is all about. A number of our best scholars have shared valuable insights with you, and they have done so lucidly and meaningfully. Getting in touch with the original text, with the original ideas as expressed by any author can never be supplanted by any second-hand summary of explanation. Thus I will not summarize the content of this book.

The second temptation is to, in effect, rewrite what others have supplied in order to make it fit my own perspective more completely, or simply because the authors included here were unable to state their own ideas clearly and effectively. Of course, that latter assumption would result in another dilemma—if they could not do an adequate job of writing their chapters, why in the world would I have asked them to make a contribution to the book?

These considerations cause me to avoid writing a conclusion, at least not one that follows traditional models. If you will permit me, however, I would like to express my hope that the chapters in this book have served their purpose *for you*. If there is any purpose that *I* had in mind when first planning this book, it centered on the hope that you would become an active participant in the human search for understanding—one who would do more than merely describe what she or he has observed—one who would wonder about and seek answers to vital how, what, *and why* questions. After all, your answers may significantly influence the next steps we take as human beings in our never-ending quest for knowledge and understanding.

At the risk of stating the obvious, I would like to make one final point, however. This volume itself is based on, or driven by a theory, that is by a systematic attempt to explain how at least one of our human efforts functions. The components of that theoretical foundation are the acceptance of the fact that theories are products of human efforts, and that the human beings who build them are, at the very least, strongly influenced by their sociocultural environment.

As a result, critically evaluating the development of any theory as a building process in a given sociocultural setting requires understanding and identification of the ontological, epistemological, and axiomatic foundations. That effort must precede any attempt to deal with the final product or theory. It must be the basis of our criticism, not merely an afterthought.

If you add to this my insistence that this volume should not be seen as an attempt to survey the field or area of communication, you should be able to understand the authors' desire to provide not only information in the preceding pages, but also vital process insights that go beyond describing what exists.

Author Index

Weiss, R. L., 191, 208
Weizsacker, C., 12, 41
Wengle, J., 96, 112, 129
Werbel, W., 252, 263
Werner, C., 172, 208
Werner, H., 193, 208
West, C., 137, 162
White, L. A., 87, 129
White, R. K., 242, 265
Whiting, G., 270, 294
Whitten, K. W., 19, 41
Whorf, B., 20, 41
Wieder, D. L., 158, 162
Williams, R., 209, 226, 240
Wills, T. A., 191, 208
Wish, M., 173, 208
Wittgenstein, L., 16, 34, 41, 55, 85
Woelfel, J., 25, 41
Wollen, P., 228, 240
Wood, G., 63, 85
Wood, N., 23, 41
Wrage, E., 55, 84
Wright, D. W., 249, 251, 261, 262
Wyer, R. S., 255, 268

Y

Yang, S. M., 182, 204
Yerby, J., 175, 208

Z

Zimmerman, D. H., 134, 136, 137, 154, 157, 160, 161, 162

Subject Index

radical, 229
behaviorists,
  and Newtonian model, 246
"black box", 231
"black hole", 169

C

categories, creation of, 141
change,
  and empirical research, 172
  and controversy, 24
  and Western culture, 172
  as reformulation, 94
  in "appropriate behavior", 236
  managing, 172
  resisting, 172
Chicago School of Sociology, 218, 231
choice, and alternatives, 271
classes, 227
coding,
  and glossing, 139
  and underlying patterns, 139
  as an achievement, 139
  departure point for understanding,
    140
  game, 140
  inevitable, for researchers, 138
  reflexivity of, 139
  research grounded in, 138
  rules of, 140
  the process of, 139
  understanding of, 140
cognitive complexity, 194
complementarity, 180
complementary exchange, 180
communication,
  administrative, utilitarian, 50
  American, 50
  and consensus, 243
  and construct complexity, 193
  and emergent and social structures,
    275
  and mere talk, 284

and normative rules, 276, 277
and social interaction, 285
and theory, 23, 133, 134
administrative, utilitarian, 50
argument in, 89
as bricolage, 55
as cultural resource, 282
as dynamic process, 200
as environment, 209
as object, 21
as process in groups, 247
European, 50
interactive (transactive), 209
interpersonal, 167
patterns of, over time, 172
practical, essentially, 56
problems, three resolutions to, 282
reciprocal, 289
relationships and, 289, 290
science, 51
science and humanism, 55
subphenomena of, 210
system in itself, 55
tasks, 135
technologies, 211, 220, 221
the phenomenon of, 134
three resolutions to problems, 282
communication rules,
  and causal regularities, 274
  as prescriptions, 274
  violations, 274, 283
communication theory,
  and combination of consensus, 211
  and its roots, 211
communicating,
  humans, 24
  versus communication, 1
composition, problems of, 120
concepts, single set of, 21
conflicts,
  between humanists and scientists, 4,
    48, 50
conformity, and groups, 242
connection, 175
consensus, and adaptation of rules, 272